SPORTS *and* CLASSIC CARS

PORTS

and CLASSIC CARS

Griffith Borgeson & Eugene Jaderquist

BONANZA BOOKS · NEW YORK

Dedicated to

Lillian Borgeson

and

Peggy Jaderquist

ACKNOWLEDGMENTS

No book is a solitary project. In the preparation of this manuscript we have drawn heavily on the knowledge and abilities of numerous individuals and organizations. In particular we would like to cite:

John Bond, editor of *Road and Track* — one of the outstanding
   U.S. automotive magazines;
Jack and Gloria Campbell;
James Earp;
James Talmadge;

Charles Barnard, editor of *True's Automobile Yearbook*, a good
friend and the source of many of the color photos in this
volume;

Wayne Thoms.

The organizations:

The Autocar. This esteemed British journal went far out of
its way to assist us in gathering both material and photo-
graphs for this volume;

The Commercial Motor Index (British), Fletcher and Son, Ltd.,
Norwich, England.

The Motor.

The Vintage and Thoroughbred Car.

Then there are the automotive authorities, many of them, to
whom we are indebted. All the names cannot be listed here, but
some of those whose research and talents have contributed to
this serious undertaking are:

W. Boddy, W. F. Bradley, S. C. H. Davis, Gregor Grant, George
Monkhouse, St. John C. Nixon, Harold Nockolds, Laurence
Pomeroy, Ken W. Purdy, Ralph Stein, John Bentley, Russ Catlin,
Kent Karslake, J. L. Elbert, Tom McCahill, W. L. Powlison, Frank
Kurtis, Floyd Clymer, P. S. deBeaumont, W. H. Aldington, Count
Johnny Lurani, Piero Taruffi, Juan M. Fangio, Bindo Maserati,
Gianni Lancia, Wilfred C. Leland, Abner Doble, Capt. G. E. T.
Eyston, Lt. Col. A. T. Goldie-Gardner, Donald and Geoff Healey;
Timothy Rootes; Carl Breer; James C. Zeder; Ralph Roberts
(LeBaron); Howard (Dutch) Darrin; Harley J. Earl; Charles
Chayne; Prince Metternich; Giovanni Canestrini; Gunther Molter;
Louis Chiron; H. U. Wieselmann; Phil Wright; Gordon Buehrig;
August Duesenberg; Alfred Neubauer; Enzo Ferrari; C. Catoire;
Ab Jenkins.

TABLE OF CONTENTS

INTRODUCTION

Wᴇ ʟɪᴠᴇ ɪɴ ᴀ ᴡᴏʀʟᴅ ʀɪᴄʜ ᴡɪᴛʜ ᴛᴇᴄʜɴᴏʟᴏɢɪᴄᴀʟ ᴡᴏɴᴅᴇʀꜱ, ᴏꜰ which none has seduced and enslaved us so completely as the automobile. It has revolutionized our economy, our *mores* and our once serene, static and isolated way of life. Its effects have altered the face of the planet.

But the automobile also occupies a unique status in our lives not wholly accounted for by its incomparable utility. Some Americans slave for their cars, take near parental pride in those cars, get cars before they beget families or buy homes, support a thriving industry that provides baubles and gimcrackery for their cars, collect cars, read millions of car magazines each year and form car clubs of every conceivable variety.

A few individuals live for their cars, and some even die for them. There has never been a shortage of men willing to risk and lose their lives racing cars; the potential deadliness of the automobile does not detract from its fascination and probably adds to it. Few situations can provide a more satisfactory feeling of power than being on the right side of a deadly weapon, and — like the Frontier Colt— a big, powerful, obedient car is sometimes considered an equalizer of men. It is, undeniably, also a mobile and handy means for what Veblen called "conspicuous consumption." If clothes and jewelry make the woman, cars make the man, and many a man's bank balance is estimated by the car he drives.

These are some of the reasons for the importance automobiles have assumed in our lives, and the great cars of the world have achieved recognition partly because they possess the attributes of power and prestige in larger measure than less-distinguished makes. No other cars, certainly, could match the luxury and Jeevesian obedience of the great classics of the pre-war era. And the arrogant performance of a nimble little sports car "blowing off" a chromebearer twice its size has enabled many of us to substitute conspicuous contempt for crass ostentation.

But the great cars have been more than just strong medicine for the ego. In an industry famous for its adeptness at compromise, the most memorable makes have refused to sacrifice their ideals of quality or performance even if it meant bankruptcy, as it frequently did. Some of these stubborn, dedicated ones were lucky; the principles they set out to express have had lasting appeal for a narrow, discriminating segment of the public and have survived. Others, inspired as well as dedicated, convinced the public to accept newer and better ways and thus blazed a trail that the entire industry followed.

The common denominator of the great makes has been integrity. At times their unwillingness to compromise has led them to excesses and absurdities, but more often it has produced automobiles that give a new dimension to being alive.

Take, for example, the great luxury cars of the Twenties and Thirties. They were built to impossibly demanding and costly standards of perfection and consequently were failures on the market. But if you have never driven one you have missed one of the great experiences of motoring. The classic car makes you a man of distinction even before you start it on its majestic journey.

Anyone with his foot resting possessively on its running board is the psychological equal of a millionaire.

Why? The car is massive, beautifully made and faultlessly finished, its exterior glowing with the depth of 20 or 30 coats of hand-rubbed lacquer. You open the heavy door with a light touch, and the latch slides as easily as a knife through butter. The interior is a tiny palace with furnishings of fine fabric or leather and beautifully grained, perfectly finished woods. You slip behind the big steering wheel and with another light touch close the door with a crisp, solid thud. Before you stretches the long, gleaming hood, its lines converging on a time-honored symbol —a bird, a woman, a star, a greyhound. When you turn on the ignition switch and press the starter the huge engine springs to life and like a perfectly disciplined servant quietly awaits your command. If you've never driven the car before you may have to look at the gauges to assure yourself that the power plant is really running; its smoothness is almost unbelievable. You release the big chrome-plated hand-brake lever and drop the shift lever into the starting gear of your choice; with this engine's torque top gear will do nicely. The shifting operation is smooth, positive and silent. Then you touch the throttle and at least two tons of mechanical perfection is yours to command.

You guide the great machine easily through the thickest traffic and out onto the open road. With unperturbed smoothness and dignity it accelerates up to its flying top speed. In the corners it does not roll and its tires do not squeal. When you slam on the brakes they take hold with immediate reflex and you brace yourself, but you are not hurled forward. Braking, steering, speeding, cornering — all leave you serene, relaxed and at peace with the world. Tension and apprehension were designed out of this car.

This is luxury transportation. As a concept it reached its peak in the Thirties and only a few expressions of it survive in postwar times. Sports transportation, however, is far from extinct and has a way of staging a comeback anywhere, anytime. If you care enough about cars to be reading this book you owe it to yourself to drive a *real* sports car — one that's all bone, sinew and guts, one that carries nothing it doesn't need to do the job.

Here you'll find power, but rather than the power of sheer mass, power based on ultra-efficient engineering and frequently wrested from an incredibly small engine. You'll find beauty, too — the stark, pure, unadorned beauty of perfect functional design in the body and frequently in the engine. You will probably be physically uncomfortable. Your knees will be up somewhere near your chest, your eyes will stream tears in the wind, you'll be crowded, cramped and cold. But you won't mind. The car will purr its eagerness to go the minute you touch the starter, it will steer with the kind of responsiveness that some people call psychic and it will have that exciting vitality that impels enchanted owners to talk of the "sentient" quality of their cars.

Cars can be all things to all men, and they have been built by men with widely varying talents and goals. The great cars have frequently been the creations of men who were conscious of being artists, some in that unrecognized branch of architecture called coachwork, others in the subtle and esoteric art form that mechanical engineering can sometimes be. The cars built for transportation alone have pursued their prosaic, industrious course and in so doing have contributed as much to the science of the automobile as all the radical innovators. But the automobile, as far as this book is concerned, is more than a utilitarian device. In its greatest forms it has been a vehicle designed not just for transportation but also for modern man's purest expression of technological art.

So much for the emotional and esthetic aspects of the automobile. How do you write about it? How do you cover its development in something less than a six-foot shelf? How do you select the subject matter?

In *Sports Cars and Classic Cars* we have departed from the usual methods of handling automotive material.

A cursory examination of the book will show that a considerable number of pages are devoted to tables detailing the specifications of each of the automobiles discussed individually. This is only a part of the hard core of fact around which the book is built.

The general arrangement of the material is chronological, since the development of the automobile can be divided into three consecutive and distinct periods. The first period covers the years between 1885 and 1920, and is marked by the early struggles of an infant industry and the key technical inventions that transformed a toy into a useful high-performance machine. This part of the story might be titled a prologue to the Birth of the Modern Sports Car, an event which occurred after World War I. Essentially it is of more interest to historians and engineers than to the present-day automobile fan. Where necessary, in the discussion of individual marques, this growth period has been covered.

It was omitted from the book as a separate section because of space limitations.

The first section of this book covers the between-wars sports cars, the Golden Age of this type of machinery. The second section is devoted to classic cars, which were roughly contemporaneous with the legendary sports cars. The final, Third Section, describes the post-World War II sports cars and also includes the few modern classics.

We were obliged to make a rather arbitrary decision in the process of organizing this book. The year 1925 was chosen as the beginning of the classic period, thus relegating such historic and magnificent carriages as Locomobile and Crane-Simplex to the background.

Our reason for this decision is quite simple; there is not enough space in the pages of a single section to consider all the luxury machines built since the invention of the automobile. Since we were forced to choose between the old and the new, we chose the new.

Necessarily, any automobile book which is composed chiefly of a make-by-make study of important cars will suffer from a lack of continuity of thought and will tend to be repetitive. We have tried to minimize these faults by prefacing each section with a general chapter tracing the developments during the period. These survey chapters also include the important points common to all or most of the makes described individually. Thus, the general trend in sports car design after World War I is examined in the chapter *Sports Cars Between the Wars*.

Some makes are listed two or three times. Two examples will illustrate the reasoning behind this arrangement. Bentley began as an all-out-competition sports car in 1919, changed abruptly to a classic when Rolls-Royce acquired the firm, and since World War II has returned as a classic. Mercedes underwent a slightly different evolution: immediately after World War I it was a sports car; during most of the 1930's it was a classic; and since World War II the Mercedes 300 SL has won an enviable reputation as a sports car. Thus the early Bentley and Mercedes sports cars are listed in the First Section; the classic Bentley and Mercedes are listed in the Second (Classics) Section; while the postwar versions of both cars are found in the Third Section. This method of classification is less confusing than attempting to squeeze all models of the same make into a single chapter.

Occasionally during the writing of this book we have sacrificed romance to make room for facts. Our primary aim was to produce a book that would not only tell the story of sports and classic cars but also be of value as a standard reference work. To the best of our knowledge this is the most complete book on sports and classic cars ever published.

Griffith Borgeson
Eugene Jaderquist

PART ONE

Sports Cars
Between the Wars

Top	Jaguar Roadster
Center Left	Lincoln Continental
Center Right	Carstens' Allard
Center Bottom	Type 35C Grand Pr
	Bugatti
Bottom	1927 Stutz Speedste

Top   1929 Belgian Minerva
Center Top   Ford Thunderbird
Center Left   1949 Talbot Lago
Center Right 1929 Model P1 Rolls-
               Royce
Bottom   2.9 Liter Alfa Romeo

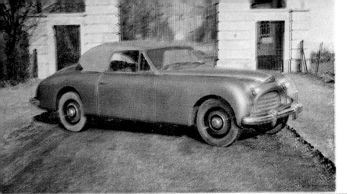

Top   Jensen Interceptor
Center Left   1940 Packard
               Convertible
Center Right   1931 Pierce Arrow
               Phaeton
Bottom   Buick Wildcat III

THE NECESSARY EXPERIMENTAL MACHINES OF EARLY AUTOMOBILE history soon became resolved into fairly standardized designs. It became increasingly apparent that they fell into four main categories — touring (including passenger and utility), sports, racing and record machines.

The sports car occupied the gap between touring and racing cars and was obviously related to both, but not in the manner usually imagined. It was chanted for decades that today's racing car was tomorrow's sports car and that the sports car was tomorrow's touring car. This neat formula was grossly misleading and far from true.

Nothing remotely resembling Offenhausers or P3 Alfas ever

came off the production lines. Defenders of automobile racing, not content to let it be simply a great popular sport, reached far for examples of its contributions to the industry. An achievement often pointed to was the adoption of the rear-view mirror by production machines after its use by Ray Harroun in the 1911 Indianapolis 500-mile race. It does not take great discernment to recognize the poverty of this "contribution." Actually any important race served the interest of the industry but seldom in the direction of setting the design of future sports cars. Racing truly improved the breed, but usually in subtle ways. Makers of lubricants, fuels, tires, bearings, alloys, piston rings, gears, spark plugs and many other components used racing machines as testing devices, transferring experience thus gained to volume production.

But the typical sports car between the wars was a production car and, rather than being derived from the racing machine, was most often based on the versatile, homely touring car. The reason is not hard to find. All cars presented different challenges to the designer but none demanded a more complex variety of virtues than the conventional machine. It had to be reliable, flexible, free from noise and vibration and easy to control. It had to perform well at low, middle and high speeds. It had to be cheap to maintain and reasonably economical to operate. It had to perform without temperament under the broadest possible conditions. The process of achieving this staggering versatility provided the most fertile field for engineering discovery.

Compare, for example, the problems of outright racing-car design. Here the engineer had tremendous freedom and just one goal — to build a car with the single function of winning a certain kind of race. He was not hindered by the million small but vital considerations that inhibit the production-car designer. Noise was not a factor; cost, reliability, flexibility — all could be ignored. The racing car could be built by hand out of the most costly materials available, it could run on outlandish fuels, it could be so temperamental that it would submit only to highly trained *virtuosi*. The car could disintegate as it crossed the finish line and if it crossed first it would have achieved its purpose. The designer of racing cars was permitted and frequently encouraged to try his wildest schemes at least once. He often made great, leaping, sudden strides in the art of coaxing high performance from recalcitrant metal, but what he learned was — more often than not — impossible to adapt to passenger or even sports machinery.

The world's-record machine was even more specialized. In

recent decades all the successful land-speed contenders have been monsters. As Captain George Eyston said with succinct accuracy: "big speed: big car." Big power plants naturally follow and the best record machines so far have borrowed their engines from aircraft. Although even these freaks among automobiles, through their probing of unknown velocities, have made important contributions to the designer's notebook, they probably had the least to offer of any variety.

Bugatti, Alfa, B.M.W., Lancia, Mercedes-Benz, Mercer, Delage, Delahaye, Stutz, Riley — all developed their sports models from touring models. In some cases — like Alfa and Bugatti — even full Grand Prix racing cars were eventually evolved from the touring chassis. Cars like the Mille Miglia Maseratis were pure *competition* sports cars and examples of the rare types of sports machine that are actually detuned outright racing models.

The sports car's umbilical attachment to the touring car resulted from the fact that, like its conventional parent, it had to be useful for everyday transportation as well as for an occasional Sunday race or hillclimb. It required reliability, the ability to function on regularly available fuel and reasonable flexibility throughout its speed range; and it had to be produced in series if it were to carry a price tag that a healthy number of consumers could afford. These consumers were aggressively aware of their specialized tastes and willing to put up with the imperfections, from the touring car standpoint, that gave the sports car its performance and *élan*. They expected and accepted a firmer ride, more noise, less payload space, a more skill-demanding gear-change mechanism; and they were even willing to learn to administer to their cars' distempers with wrench and thickness gauge. The typical sports car was a high-performance, better functioning refinement of many production-car features with occasional, infrequent inspiration from the racing-car field.

Sports cars were the last category to become firm as a breed distinct from any other, but before World War I all the categories were less clear-cut. Early first-class racing cars were often specially prepared production models, and many of the big manufacturers participated eagerly in competition. It was still possible for the potential buyer to identify the on-the-market machine with the racing version of the same make, and manufacturers could use racing victories as potent sales arguments. But the straightforward "stock" approach to competition was short-lived. Cars that raced in the Big Time soon became radically specialized, and before long they bore no resemblance to the over-the-counter models. The sheer cash cost of producing and racing machines that had no equivalent in series production was now a dubious gamble against sales, and after World War I most manufacturers took the stand that participation was no longer meaningful. Other important developments took place during the same period.

The early Twenties saw the birth of ever-increasing numbers of relatively inexpensive makes of very nimble touring cars. At the same time a set of rules governing competition events evolved that established numerous categories based on engine displacement, in the interest of providing equal opportunity and incentive for all sizes of cars. More important, the rules provided separate and distinct qualifications for "touring" and "Grand Prix" events, and now anyone with a fast little production car could compete with some hope of success. Gentlemen sportsmen recognized in this relatively amateur form of racing a new area for chivalrous living and lent it the prestige of their active participation, and the public supported the sport enthusiastically. Manufacturers began producing and marketing cars specifically designed to run in such races as the 24 Hours of Le Mans, but still retaining the wider functions of the touring concept. The sports car was born.

The sports car developed according to the demands that ordinary use, competition, and the *aficionados* made upon it. Bodies generally first were taken directly from touring models or were modified versions built to weigh less, and look lower and racier. Many small French cars of the pre- and immediately post-World War I period were extremely agile and as a class had more *chic* and frequently more zest than the cars of any other country. They created a brisk demand at home and in nearby countries, particularly in England. Domestic equivalents of the small French cars began to corner this market in the British Isles, a blow to the French manufacturers. Simultaneously the Italians were busy developing sports cars too. In the late Twenties, the angular, strictly sports-type open body began to establish its independence from the touring type of body, becoming easily recognizable by its folding windshield, removable fenders, quick-action filler caps, cut-down doors and, occasionally, such airy touches as external exhaust pipes, stone-screens for lights and radiator, and strapped-down hoods. Real streamlining was introduced on closed touring chassis, like the Mercedes-Benz *Autobahnkourier* of 1932, the Pierce-Arrow Silver Arrow and the Chrysler Airflow.

Designers and purchasers of sports cars, frequently more dedicated to the appearance than the performance of their machines, left the development of low wind-drag shapes up to the designers of both touring and G.P. cars and stood staunchly by the classic two- and four-seater open sports coachwork. In the last half of the Thirties, the tried and true yielded to progress and a few firms like Bugatti, Aston-Martin, B.M.W., and Alfa Romeo began to take real advantage of what aerodynamically correct closed as well as open bodies could do for improved speeds, fuel economy, and racing results. But up until the time that production was stopped by World War II the true sports-car body was accepted to be an open model with many appendages hanging out in the wind. Bodywise, sports cars tended to lag behind the more advanced touring cars.

Frame design had become thoroughly standardized by the end of World War I. It was almost uniformly primitive among all types of cars, consisting of channel-section side members held together by ladder-rung or X-shaped cross members. The battle for rigid frame design had been pretty generally lost although some builders went so far as to stiffen frames with truss rods. With the notable exceptions of Lancia and Morgan, most cars used solid front axles suspended from half-elliptic springs. Chain drive was retained only by Frazer-Nash, and solid rear axles were suspended from leaf springs, mostly half-elliptics. Wheel shimmy and tramp, temperamental steering geometries, and a tendency to involuntary steering effects at both front and rear ends were all nightmares for the chassis designer. The best way out seemed to be to hold axle movement to an absolute minimum by means of stiff springs and shock absorbers. Total vertical spring travel at the front was frequently less than one inch up or down with the rear suspension slightly softer, so that most of these cars shared a tendency to oversteer — for the rear wheels to break loose in a turn before the front wheels did. Although the flexibility of the standard frame was exploited to some extent and made to serve as a sort of spring, the ride was relatively uncomfortable and cornering speeds were restricted by latent steering-geometry errors which would easily place most of these cars out of control. Opinion was about equally divided in the early Twenties between torque-tube and open-shaft drive, with a steady tendency toward eliminating the torque-tube in the interest of weight saving and, among the better sports cars, use of reaction arms to relieve the springs of the axle-twisting torque of acceleration and braking. Passenger-car development made great strides in transforming rear-axle design from a "cut-and-try" art to a science. Metallurgical and machining processes progressed with design techniques until gears with an accurately predictable life could be successfully and cheaply made. Before that time, when gears failed, they and the parts around them were simply made heavier.

The hypoid-bevel final drive which was introduced by Packard in the middle Twenties had the advantage of bringing the drive-shaft closer to the ground, thereby making possible lower bodies without increasing the height of the shaft tunnel. Comfort and roominess were not such critical factors in sports-car design as efficient and reliable power transmission. For this reason high-friction hypoid-bevel gears were of little interest to builders of sports cars.

It was not until the middle Thirties that the traditional sports-car chassis began to undergo significant change, led by such examples as the early Lago Talbot, the Type 135 Delahaye, and the Type 328 B.M.W. Independent front suspension — known for more than a decade on touring cars and recently adopted by G. P. cars—was finally accepted in the sports-car field as having reached a sufficient degree of development.

Many *aficionados* regarded independent front suspension as a mark of effete degeneracy because it gave a softer, more comfortable ride. It was actually a great step forward. It improved adhesion, cornering power, and stability by keeping the tires in more constant contact with the road surface. The softer ride demanded stiffer frames as well as greatly improved steering and suspension geometry, but all these problems had been dealt with satisfactorily at last by makers of mass-production touring cars. There were numerous positive results. The greater vertical wheel travel now available not only offered a better ride, but a better balanced chassis as well. Front and rear spring rates could be made more nearly identical and accurate high-speed cornering became a simpler technique to master and a safer one to practice.

During the early Twenties most sports cars had already adopted four-wheel brakes operated either by cables or by rods, using the very popular ball-and-socket brake-actuating mechanism patented by Henri Perrot. Servo mechanisms were imperfectly understood by the industry in general and contracting bands were generally used. Progress in brake design was fairly continuous. There was a fast conversion to internal-expanding brakes, and drum sizes and lining areas shrank steadily, efficiency increasing as the industry — mainly through passenger-car development — perfected matters to the point where brakes with 10- and 12-inch drums were doing more efficient jobs than old, 18-inch assemblies. The Perrot system was eventually replaced by hydraulic actuation, at which point the hand brake, usually acting on the transmission, was promptly changed to act on the rear-wheel brake drums.

On the whole, sports-car engines were tuned versions of touring-car power units. In some cases an increase in compression ratio was enough. In others porting, valve timing, carburetion, ignition, bearings, even the metal used for block castings were altered or a redesigned cylinder head used. Some specialist manufacturers did indeed design high-output engines from scratch, like Aston-Martin and Bentley. But the Mercedes, B.M.W., Alfa Romeo and Stutz engines, for example, all started out in life in touring cars, while the Delahaye actually started in a truck. Some machines, like the Maserati and many Bugattis and later Alfa Romeo sports cars, were simply Grand Prix chassis with sports coachwork. This clouded the issue, but the point was clear that normal sports cars — as opposed to outright competition models — had to be practical as well as exciting to drive. Therefore far more were evolved out of mass-production engines than from outright racing engines.

Clutches and transmissions followed touring-car practice. Practically all clutches in the early Twenties were of the multiple-disc type, this being the only method then available for achieving smooth starts and adequate torque capacity. Clutch throw-out bearings tended to burn up when loaded at high r.p.m. and racing drivers learned to shift without declutching — a subtle art. However, the passenger-car industry learned to build single-plate clutches adequate to all reasonable loads, and these, plus relatively indestructible throw-out bearings, were both universally adopted by sports-car builders.

Transmissions were uniformly of the selective sliding type with three or four speeds forward. The first Riley Nine, a passenger car, pioneered constant-mesh gears that required only engagement of a dog clutch to change ratios. This innovation, years ahead of its time, was eventually picked up by practically the entire industry, including the sports-car field. The advent of the dog-clutch mechanism made possible the use of synchronizers and, again, legitimate industry was the innovator with synchromesh, the cam type perfected by General Motors being widely considered the most foolproof system.

In the middle Thirties unorthodox but successful transmissions began to appear, notably Wilson in England and Cotal in France. These used planetary gears controlled by bands and made possible ultra-fast shifts since only a band had to be applied and synchronization of rotating gears was no problem. The Wilson gearbox was adopted by Riley, M.G. and English and French Talbots.

During the period when stiff suspension particularly at the front end was the rule, nonreversible steering gears, through which movement could be transmitted in one direction only, were widely used out of sheer necessity. The best steering of this type used worm-and-wheel or worm-and-sector gears, the sector being simply a segment of a wheel. The worm was actually a screw and its threads meshed in the peripheral teeth of the gearwheel or sector. Turning the screw caused the wheel to rotate, but attempting to rotate the wheel produced no motion in the screw. This sort of steering prevented feed-back of road shocks to the steering wheel and had the added advantage of zero backlash, eminently desirable in the generally oversteering cars of the period. Equally important at the time was high-geared steering, which usually demanded a strong-armed driver but did make possible the almost instantaneous corrections needed to keep the old-style chassis, skittish at high speeds, on the course.

These conditions were all relaxed when the late-Thirties advent of stiffer frames and better front ends on various sports cars made it logical also to adopt current passenger-car steering. It was not as precise but the need for ultimate precision had passed, and the new steering gear, usually of the cam or worm-and-roller type, made the car far easier to direct under most conditions. Rack-and-pinion steering, used in rare instances, was more accurate but had the disadvantage of being fully reversible. All these varieties of steering gear were to be found on passenger cars before they appeared on sports cars.

By tracing its evolutionary development briefly, the somewhat widespread conception of the normal between-wars sports car as a detuned racing machine falls to pieces. What emerges instead is a type of vehicle which combined and refined the best performance-influencing features of standard production cars. The experimental period which began timidly but showed great promise in the late Thirties was interrupted by World War II and really hit its stride in postwar times.

T HE LONGEST, HARDEST ROAD FOR CARS IN ENGLAND
was the one to public acceptance. For years they
were resented, despised and legislated against
with bitter vehemence. It took demonstrated
dependability, dramatic achievement and — no

less important — a size and price that made ownership possible
for the middle class before bare tolerance of cars became acceptance and finally affection.

   The A.C. was prominent among the cars instrumental in help-
ing this transition to occur, and today few makes have a more
doggedly loyal following. It was one of the first cars made in
England for the middle-income market that offered lively perform-

ance as well as a low price. And in 1922 A.C. became the first car of less than 1,500 c.c. (91 cu. in.) displacement to top the magic 100-mile-an-hour mark for a full hour. This was a milestone in light-car performance and reliability; it created a new place of respect and a new demand for the small-displacement sports car.

A.C.'s designer, John Weller, had no thought of building small automobiles when his career began. He was a slender, worried-looking youth in his early twenties and already had the reputation of being an eccentric genius when in 1900 he met his patron. This man was John Portwine, the wealthy owner of a chain of butcher shops in South London. Each of this unlikely pair was enormously impressed by the other's gifts of energy and vision, and Portwine agreed to finance Weller's automotive ideas. More than 50 years later their first impression had not changed. Each reaffirmed his deep conviction of the other's greatness.

The first fruit of their union was a costly four-cylinder tourer showing strong early-Mercedes influence. It had the virtue of excellent design, but Portwine, perhaps because of an instructive experience with breast of pheasant, was convinced that the best odds for survival were on the side of low-cost products. He proposed the construction of a cheap commercial vehicle that could be sold in fleet lots, and in 1904 Weller designed the Autocarrier, from which the initials A.C. were finally derived.

This three-wheel delivery wagon was as brilliant a piece of engineering in its day as the Italian Lambretta motor scooter was in the post-World War II period. Its beautifully symmetrical little one-cylinder air-cooled engine was a feast for the initiated eye. It used a T-head valve layout enveloped in a deeply finned block-head assembly; the crankcase was of aluminum and there was a light flywheel on each side. All the weight was in the rims of the flywheels. Their spokes were shaped like turbine blades and they drove cooling air against the engine. Two auxiliary fans were friction-driven by the flywheel rims to cool the upper portion of the block. There was a chain drive to the single rear wheel, the compact hub of which contained a multiple-disc clutch and epicyclic two-speed transmission.

These light, powerful, fast little machines scored a major success both in the market for which they were intended and with the 'teen-age boys generally hired to drive them. These lads had small regard for life and limb and seized every opportunity to race their Autocarriers wildly through the crowded London streets. The fact that the little machines stood up beautifully to this treat-

ment was one indication of their potentialities, and the commercial
model soon evolved into the A.C. Tricar, a personal-transport
version which began building the make's reputation among
private-car owners. Just before World War I Weller firmed up
his design for a new, light, four-wheel passenger car. A prototype
was built then, but the first A.C. four-wheelers went into production in 1919. The earliest cars used Fivet side-valve four-cylinder
engines imported from France; later the entire output of the
Anzani plant in England went to power A.C.'s. Sales of the
stylish, snappy little cars were very brisk and the company soon
found it desirable to manufacture its own complete engines.

At this time the smoothest, finest engines in the world were
sixes. But they were all big engines installed in luxury cars. For
years Weller had been brooding about the creation of a small
lightweight six. In his spare time during the war years he had
worked out and perfected his concept of the small six-cylinder
power plant and in 1920 cars equipped with these 2-liter (122 cu.
in.) units went into production. They were wonderful engines
and deserved the slogan that was later coined for them: "The
First Light Six — And Still The Best." As recently as 1954 A.C.
engines were just much-refined versions of the original Weller
six. And they were still years ahead of most of their competitors.

Outwardly the six reflected Weller's concern with immaculate
appearance. Except for manifolds and distributor, there were no
projections from the smooth, continuous sides of the aluminum
crankcase-block casting, into which the head and cam cover were
blended. The overhead camshaft drove two inclined valves per
cylinder and had the then-unusual feature of being chain-driven.
The chain was necessarily a long one, and observers, sure that
excessive "whip" would cause quick failure, smiled at Weller's
unorthodox notions. He thoroughly outsmarted them by promptly
inventing and patenting a simple leaf-spring tensioner which controlled chain slack so perfectly that it was sold widely to other
manufacturers and made Weller lots of money, in addition to
solving the problem in the six. Another controversial detail of
the engine was the use of wet cylinder liners, which Weller
pioneered in the light-car field at the same time that they were
introduced in such a kingly make as Hispano-Suiza.

Emphasis on advanced design was an important factor in the
success of "The First Light Six," and it was further blessed by fate
in the person of a new governing director for the firm. He was
S. F. Edge — a handsome, quick-witted Australian — and no

man appreciated the new A.C.'s virtues more fully than he or knew how to exploit them more completely. One of Britain's first motorists, Edge had devoted his life to cars since 1895, and was the only Englishman ever to win the internationally coveted Gordon Bennett Trophy of racing's earliest years. He had been a pioneer of the six-cylinder principle when it was still regarded as an absurd notion; finally was vindicated and won fame as a Napier engineer. While he was working for the Ministry of Munitions during the war he met John Weller and found in him a kindred soul. Edge bought into A.C. just as the six was going into production.

Up to this point A.C. had led a busy but far-too-anonymous racing career in minor trials. Edge had a keen sense of public relations and a superb understanding of the conduct and exploitation of successful racing activities. He lost no time in putting his knowledge to work. He found that the A.C. staff was creative, cooperative and had a zealous spirit of loyalty. During his directorship from '21 to '29, Edge channelled these forces into a series of racing successes that impressed the A.C. initials indelibly upon British memory.

The situation when Edge entered the picture was ripe for a dramatic coup. A 1,500-c.c. competition class had been created by the F.I.A. shortly after the Armistice and the first hour record was set by a Hillman at 78.73 m.p.h. In 1921 a Lagonda pushed the figure to 79.17, and H. Kensington-Moir promptly improved it in an Aston-Martin at 86.20. Then H. O. D. Segrave set a new record of 88.67 in a 1½-liter Talbot-Darracq and Kaye Don, driving a special overhead-cam four-cylinder A.C., moved it up to 94.77. The magic 100 was very close, and Edge knew that records could come and go, but the first light car to sustain 100 m.p.h. for one hour would be the one the world would remember.

A desperate engineering race began between Talbot-Darracq and the Edge-sparked A.C. organization to build a car that could achieve this distinction. A.C. won, and in the course of setting the new hour record comfortably beyond 100 m.p.h. broke *all* existing light-car records. J. A. Joyce was the driver and his average speed was 101.39 m.p.h. for 60 minutes, with a fastest lap around Brooklands of 104.85 and a top straightaway speed of 108.4.

This feat was tremendously impressive to the British public, which became newly aware of A.C. as the car to buy. The chassis of the little record machine was almost identical to A.C. production models, a fact which helped sales no end. Quarter-elliptic springs were used at front and rear (not reversed for greater stability as in Bugatti practice, but with their small ends mounted on the axles and their butts bolted to the frame). The object was to save weight, and this method of suspension made possible a chassis frame which extended scarcely beyond the spring supports and was much shorter than the car's wheelbase. The A.C. axle was sometimes described as an outrigger, being perched far aft of the frame and anchored to the chassis only by the tips of the springs and by two slender radius rods. The transmission was an integral part of the rear-axle housing, most of which was made of aluminum.

The 91-inch, four-cylinder engine which powered the record machine was, in basic concept and general layout, a light, racing version of Weller's six. It had a single overhead camshaft, chain-driven as in the six, and actuating four valves per cylinder by means of rocker arms. The block and crankcase were a single cast-aluminum unit fitted with cast-iron cylinder liners and two side-draft carburetors. It developed 60 b.hp. per cubic inch, and was one of the most advanced engines of its time.

The A.C.'s kept proving their worth in racing. In 1921, building up to the classic 100 m.p.h. record, A.C. broke 57 track records and held a total of more than 100 Brooklands records — four times more than any other car in its class. In 1922, in addition to the one-hour, the marque set new records for six, 12 and 24 hours. In 1923 and 1924 A.C. took 77 awards. In 1925 at Montlhery, an A.C. averaged 82.58 m.p.h. for 24 hours, a new world's record, and in 1927 returned to set new records for 4,000, 5,000, 10,000 and 15,000 miles and for 10,000, 15,000 and 20,000 kilometers.

Under the canny Edge regime these speed exploits were made well known to the public. In other areas of competition A.C. performed equally well and was equally well publicized. An A.C. in 1925 was the first British car to compete in the Monte Carlo Rally; the next year it won both the Rally and the Mont-des-Mules hillclimb which follows it. In 1927 a doughty woman driver finished sixth, won the hillclimb and the *Coupes des Dames* in her A.C.

But the end of the decade brought many changes to A.C. The world depression caught up with the company, Edge retired, and the Hurlock brothers took over. From that time A.C. took a passive attitude toward racing, and began to compete instead for the customer's satisfaction in matters of styling, strictly stock performance and — above all — rock-bottom price.

The first Hurlock-produced A.C., which appeared in 1930, had the same six-cylinder engine powering the same lean, thorough-bred little chassis. Hydraulic brakes were introduced and the quarter-elliptic springs were replaced by semi-elliptics. Rakish new bodies were fitted and the cars had prompt and positive public response. In 1932 the transmission was made a unit with the engine and newer, even sportier coachwork was introduced, but prices were held to appealing lows of around $1,850.

Throughout the Thirties important modifications continued to be made. In 1935 a silent eccentric-base camshaft and three carburetors became standard equipment and a synchromesh four-speed gearbox was made optionally available. In 1936 the short sports chassis was put into production which, with a graceful two-seater body, gave 85 m.p.h. top speed and accelerated from zero to 50 m.p.h. in just 12 seconds. The excellent Wilson pre-selector gearbox became optional in the same year, and in 1937 automatic chassis lubrication was introduced. The standard 6.5-to-1, 70 b.hp. engine was available both in 7-to-1, 80-b.hp. form and with Arnott supercharger, which gave a top of 90 b.hp. and extremely rapid acceleration.

These were cars that buyers could drive with pride and plea-sure, and its makers were well content. A.C. was not the only mar-que that rose to prominence by racing in the Twenties and reaped the benefits of its efforts in the Thirties. A.C. could well afford to rest on its laurels. It had played its competition role handsomely, and its good name was permanently written in automotive history.

ALFA ROMEO

In a world of Germans and Englishmen whose friendliest attitude was tinged with condescension, Italian pride grew fierce. In the barely disguised warfare that was international racing, Alfa Romeo defended and embodied the national honor, and Italy brandished Alfa across Europe like a scathing weapon.

Alfa's drivers were the most gifted and the most intensely in-spired that the world has seen — Tazio Nuvolari, Achille Varzi, Antonio Ascari, Count Trossi, Count Brilli-Peri, Pintacuda, Gius-

eppe Farina, Luigi Fagioli were just a few. It can be argued with
reason that these men made Italy's greatest marque the greatest
racing car of them all. In the major international races from 1894
to 1949 Alfa won more races than any other make, Bugatti and
Mercedes included. The statistics, compiled by George Monkhouse in his *Grand Prix Racing Facts & Figures,* read like this:

	First	*Second*	*Third*	*Total*
Alfa Romeo	216	192	152	560
Bugatti	170	142	154	466
Mercedes	117	47	38	202

An excellent English authority prudently did not compare this
record to his country's best when he criticized the Alfa engines as
expressing "the Latin passion for superficial logic and neatness of
form." To most engineers the logic and symmetry of Alfa's power
plants seemed much more than superficial. Even in blueprint
form they had an almost unique visual appeal, a result of the
harmony of each detail with every other one, and the grace and
balance of the whole.

Some of these virtues resulted from engineering necessity.
Others were due to the remarkable attitude of the men who made
the decisions at Alfa Romeo. They unhesitatingly spent great
sums of money on finish alone because they wanted their machines
to be a credit not only to Italian industry but to Italian culture
as well. Their devotion was rewarded by the world's respect.
Even Henry Ford, a man not given to gratuitous flattery, said,
"I take off my hat when I see an Alfa Romeo go by."

Zagato-bodied Alfa Romeo
2.3-liter two-seater
of early Thirties.

Autocar

Oddly enough, Alfa's earliest origins were French. The same Milan factory that later produced cars that were so fervently Italian was built in 1906 as an assembly plant for Darracq cars, in the name of the "Societá Italiana Automobili Darracq." This alien intrusion was short-lived; in 1909 native capital took over, and the company became the "Anonima Lombarda Fabbriche Automobili," which translates roughly as the Lombardy Automobile Works, Inc. A new chassis was designed and christened the Alfa Type 1910, its name being derived from the firm's initials. The company struggled, worked up to a production of 350 cars in one year, and finally went into bankruptcy. In 1914 it was bought by a celebrated railway engineer, Nicola Romeo, and in 1918 the firm name Alfa Romeo was born.

The first postwar Alfas were pushrod-overhead-valve 4½-liter sixes and hotted versions of these began the marque's racing career in 1921, when they performed tolerably well in a number of races, including the Targa Florio. In 1922 the 3-liter pushrod RL type was put on the market as a touring automobile and, in 1923, Sivocci won the Targa Florio in a 4½-liter, followed by Ascari in second place in an RL. This event was the real beginning of the Alfa success story.

The RL and its variants, RLT and RLSS super sports, continued to be manufactured through 1929. They were notable for big, noisy piston clearances and even noisier cast-iron brake linings and exhaust. The RLSS was a short chassis version more highly tuned than the touring models and equipped with dual carburetors. One of these cars was clocked at Brooklands at the very respectable average top speed of 94 m.p.h. But Alfa's design department was just beginning to feel its way.

In 1923, the year after the RL was introduced, a new racing model was tried out in practice for the Italian Grand Prix at Monza. It was called the Type P1 and the great driver Ugo Sivocci lost his life proving the chassis unstable. The other cars of this type were withdrawn before the race and not heard of again.

At this point the name of engineer Vittorio Jano became associated with Alfa history. Jano, one of the great automotive designers of four decades, was handed the job of creating a car that could win in the *grandes épreuves*. The result was the P2 Alfa. It was an entirely new chassis, its most notable component being the 2-liter (122 cu. in.), roller-bearing, six-cylinder engine. It was the first Alfa to use overhead camshafts — two of them —

and it followed the Mercedes and Fiat innovation of a Roots supercharger, in Alfa's case coupled to the nose of the crankshaft. Power output was 160 hp. at 5,500 r.p.m., road-holding and braking qualities were outstanding and the new challenger was immediately successful. The 1924 season was the first for the P2's and that year they won at Cremona, in the European G.P. at Lyons, and filled the first four places in the Italian G.P. at Monza, where they were far faster than any of the other contenders. In 1925 the P2's took the World's Championship, but in 1926, when the FIA Formula I displacement limit was set at 1½ liters, Alfa withdrew temporarily from Grand Prix racing. The P2 cars were entered only in sports-car events until the more-or-less free-formula period of 1928 to 1930 when some of them, a bit tired by this time, succeeded in winning a few major events.

In the meantime, when the 1½-liter G.P. Formula went into force Alfa Romeo brought out a new touring and sports car, the 1½-liter six-cylinder single-overhead-cam model. The engine used five main bearings and cam drive was by vertical shaft and bevel gears at the rear of the engine. The cams acted on the valve stems through inverted cylindrical cups which were made in two threaded-together pieces, tappet clearance being adjusted by means of a wrench which meshed with teeth on the rims of the cups — the same system of adjustment which Alfa has used ever since. Suspension was by half-elliptics all around, the front springs passing through a tubular axle, *à la* Bugatti. These cars had the controversial feather-light steering which was to be a characteristic of the marque up to the beginning of World War II.

This engine was very quickly supplemented by a double-overhead-cam version and, in 1928, a Roots-blown model which, among a great many other victories, won the Mille Miglia that year. The unblown cars were good for about 75 m.p.h., but the supercharged double-overhead-cam models — which were almost always fitted with light two-seater bodies — could do 90 and better. This was the first of the great line of supercharged Alfa sports cars that was sold straight across the counter to the public, a policy which further enhanced the make's growing reputation.

Then, in 1929, the 1,750-c.c. model burst onto the competition scene in truly triumphant fashion. This tiny masterpiece demonstrated Jano's genius by winning every race in which it was entered that year, including the Grands Prix of Belgium, Ireland, Spain, Tunis, Rome, and Monza, and the Brooklands 24 Hours, the Ulster T.T., and the Mille Miglia.

The 1,750-c.c. — also called the Two Liter — came in a single overhead camshaft Turismo model, but it was the Grand Turismo-17/95-type that made history. The engine in this version was mounted 15 inches farther back in the frame to make room for a Roots supercharger which was driven off the front of the crankshaft. With its 100-m.p.h. top speed and flashing acceleration, it was one of the fastest production automobiles of its time and naturally became an outstanding contender in sports car races.

These cars firmly established Alfa's name in the English sportsman's vocabulary. A team of 17/95's was sent to England for the 1930 Tourist Trophy race and won brilliantly in pouring rain, Nuvolari first, Campari and Varzi second and third. Well-heeled young Britons became Alfa converts in significant numbers and vintage Alfas, almost unknown in Italy, still abound in England, where the cult of machinery collectors and restorers flourishes best. Naturally, it took more than speed to fascinate the connoisseur, and whatever it took the little Alfa had.

It was gaunt and graceful as a greyhound. Zagato coachwork gained near-immortality by means of the spare and rakish bodies with which the chassis were usually fitted. The Alfa rode as firm as a racing car without the kidney-jarring harshness. Its full-ball-bearing worm-and-wheel steering was as light to the touch as a fencing foil and the self-righting action of the front wheels was unusually effective — facts which lead to endless witticisms about psychic steering which sensed turns in advance and negotiated them as if it had a life of its own. The entire car did in fact have a quality of aliveness that was matched by few other examples of production machinery.

Its double-overhead-cam, six-cylinder, 1,750-c.c. engine was the treasure of Alfa's first decade of postwar production. The cam drive was by means of vertical shaft and bevel gears and the two valves per cylinder were opposed at a 100-degree angle in hemispherical combustion chambers. The light alloy crankcase carried a five-bearing counterbalanced crankshaft and a light metal sump heavily ribbed for cooling. On the blown model, the Roots supercharger was bolted to the front of the crankcase. The blower drew from a two-throat Mimini carburetor and pumped mixture through a handsomely contoured ribbed pipe with relief valve at each end, to a similarly ribbed and really beautiful six-branch manifold.

This was a legitimate racing engine, but its use of a perfectly standard lubrication system, plain bearings, and a detachable head made it an ideal sports-car powerplant. The fact that it required

10-minutes' warmup at 1,000 r.p.m. before full liberties could be taken with the throttle did not set the Alfa apart from other machines of its spirited class. The suspension was by half-elliptic springs; the front springs passed through openings in the tubular front axle in Bugatti style. A torque tube extended from the rear axle to the four-speed gearbox, which was famous for its neat little visible gate and the positiveness with which the shift lever could be sliced from gear to gear.

In addition to having all these virtues of design and handling, the double-overhead-cam, 1,750-c.c. was notably reliable and frugal with its fuel, and it was small wonder that the car was a smashing success, and consequently became the basis for Ing. Jano's next great production.

This was the 2.3 model, also known as the 20/220, the 21/220 and the Monza. Its creation was sparked by the increasing obsolescence of the P2 G.P. machine, which had been developed over a seven-year period to yield 140 m.p.h., the limit for both its engine and chassis. Like the 1,750-c.c., it was a multiple-personality car intended to cope equally well with fast touring, sports competition, and Grand Prix racing.

The bore and stroke of the 1,750-c.c. were retained but two cylinders were added in the new Monza, giving a displacement of 2,336 c.c. (142.5 cu. in.) and an output of around 160 b.hp. The valve gear remained essentially unchanged, except for the camshaft drive, which was unique, and has been a feature of each of Alfa's finest engines since that time. The eight cylinders were divided into two blocks of four cylinders each and mounted on a common crankcase. The 10-bearing crankshaft consisted of two halves, joined at the center to a gear which also did duty as a light flywheel. This central gear drove a complex train of other gears which drove both the single Roots blower mounted at the side of the crankcase, and the two overhead camshafts. A single, detachable cylinder head served both blocks; it was made of light alloy and used phosphor-bronze valve seats. No notable changes were made in the chassis.

Two 20/220's were entered in the 1931 Mille Miglia, but tire failure and road accidents kept them from scoring. A month later, Nuvolari won the Targa Florio at the wheel of one of these new straight eights, and Lord Howe and Tim Birkin promptly carried through by winning at Le Mans. From then on the Monza's success story in sports-car racing was almost as consistent as that of the 1,750-c.c. Alfa.

Its performance and adaptability were striking. With displacement increased to 2.6 liters (158.5 cu. in.) in 1932 the Monza could accelerate from zero to 60 m.p.h. in 6.9 seconds, from zero to 100 in 24.8 seconds, and it idled along through traffic at 700 r.p.m. While the 2.3 version was good for an easy 110 m.p.h., the 2.6 was clocked at 130 m.p.h. Brian Twist, writing in *The Autocar*, was amazed to find that even a Grand Prix Monza handled like a dream in the thickest city traffic.

"Too much praise," he said, "'cannot be bestowed upon a supercharged Grand Prix racing car which, coupled with a performance like a shot out of a gun, could tick over at 700 r.p.m., pick up straightaway without any spitting back or hesitations, show no signs of pinking or overheating, and which never oiled a plug through all the London traffic. And yet people question the old adage whether racing improves the breed! With a little more attention to the silence problem, this 140-m.p.h. pure-bred racing car would be a delightful, gentlemanly touring machine."

Not everyone agreed with Mr. Twist about the silence problem; many enthusiasts found the Monza's sound to be not the least of its enchantments. The whistling scream produced by the spur-cut supercharger and cam-drive gears was electrifying. Few engines could raise gooseflesh as efficiently as the central-gear-train Alfas did, even at idle.

Nevertheless, the Monza, as distinguished as it was in sports-car competition, could not cope with Bugatti and Maserati in Grand Prix racing, and Jano went to work on a new car. The result was one of the classic Grand Prix machines of all time, the P3 Monoposto. Monoposto means single-seater, and the P3 was the first European car of this kind, inspired, probably, by the American Miller car which Leon Duray had raced at Monza. The lean beauty of the Monoposto and the delicate workmanship in its every visible detail made it one of the handsomest racing cars ever made.

Its engine, a slightly enlarged version of the Monza, had a displacement of 2.65 liters (162 cu. in.) and an output of 190 b.hp. at 5,400 r.p.m. Instead of having one blower to feed all eight cylinders, it used two smaller blowers, each supplying four cylinders and drawing through its own Weber carburetor. The crankcase, crankshaft, central gear train and valve train were almost identical to Monza design. The most important new feature of the P3 was the use of a light-alloy cylinder block with integral head and steel cylinder liners.

The Monoposto dominated Grand Prix racing from its appearance in 1932 through 1934, and Italy's pride was never more thoroughly vindicated. Then came 1935, and the German steamroller in the form of Mercedes and Auto-Union took over. The P3 became obsolete for Grand Prix competition almost overnight.

This was a blow for Italy and for the marque, but it was not an unrelievedly tragic one. In the early Thirties hard times had hurt sales of the costly Monza sports cars so badly that Alfa had been forced to bring out a medium-quality sports model that was at best a compromise between Alfa's lofty standards and the requirements of low-cost manufacture. This car — variously called the 19/68, the 19/76, and the 6C-2300-B — and its super sports version, the Pescara, reverted to six-cylinder engine layout, and used chain drive to the camshafts for the first time in Alfa history. This was the cheaper, less reliable method, and even though the chassis was the last word in torsion-bar independent four-wheel suspension, lovers of the "pure" marque were sadly certain that Alfa's days of glory were over. And they might have been, if the P3's had not been forced to abdicate Grand Prix supremacy.

Alfa, like Maserati and Bugatti, had been in the habit of making replicas of their successful Grand Prix machines for sale to private owners and fairly large stores of spare parts and complete engines were kept on hand to accommodate them. When the blow fell Alfa was caught with 36 fabulously expensive P3 power plants on the factory floor and a conspicuous lack of demand for them. It was Ing. Jano's idea to use these Grand Prix engines in a new line of sports cars. Thus was born the 2.9-liter Alfa.

The P3 racing engines were all bored out to give a displacement of 2.9 liters or 177 cubic inches. They were slightly detuned by reducing compression and regrinding new cam contours which limited top r.p.m. to 5,000, at which 180 b.hp. was developed. Then, complete with Grand Prix gearbox, these magnificent power units were installed in chassis having independent front suspension and — the first time for the marque — hydraulic brakes.

Northern Italy's finest coachbuilders lavished the best of their skill and imagination upon this really incomparable chassis. When the 2.9 was first shown at the salons of Milan, Paris, and Berlin connoisseurs and engineers were stunned. King Michael of Rumania bought a 2.9 on sight and so did Bernhard of the Netherlands. These regal machines were considered the handsomest, the safest, and the fastest of their time. The factory catalog listed their top speed as 133 m.p.h., in short-chassis form with light touring body. Like the earlier high-performance Alfas, they were comfortable, reliable, flexible, and docile — a joy to drive even at low speed. The 2.9's were the most splendid sports models ever produced by Alfa Romeo and were an appropriate climax to nearly two decades of interwoven sports-Grand-Prix experience.

ALVIS

THE RED TRIANGLE OF ALVIS WON THE ETERNAL respect of Britons in a struggle that for sheer melodrama can hardly be matched by Hollywood at its blood-and-thunder best.

It happened in 1923. Alvis had been organized in 1919 by T. G. John, a civil engineer and naval architect, and in 1921 the first car was produced, a four-cylinder side-valve of 1460 c.c. (89 cu. in.) displacement. It was a good machine of its kind and won many bush-league hill climbs and speed trials, but John, who had a proud and fervent belief in the "specials" approach to manufacture, wanted a car that would give the Alvis name a glory somewhat less insular. In 1922 he hired Captain G. T. Smith-Clarke as chief engineer and manager of his Coventry works, and then the fun began.

John and Smith-Clarke put all their eggs in one basket — the design of a new overhead-valve Alvis, the classic 1,496-c.c. (91 cu. in.) "special" 12/50. This engine had a particularly unique feature, the planetary valve-spring clusters. Each valve stem was surrounded not by one, but by a cluster of nine tiny coil springs made of 16-gauge piano wire, five wound to the right and four to the left and mounted vertically in a circle between two disc-shaped retainers. The object of this arrangement was to eliminate spring surge, and it was a clever design, but when the big moment came the springs, and the 12/50 as a whole, were untested.

That moment was the 1923 Brooklands 1½-liter 200-mile race. It was in itself an important event, and confidence in the poorly financed British specials was so low that even many of the English drivers had entered foreign cars. But for the Alvis organization the race had an even more acutely significant object than maintaining British prestige. All of John's resources had been poured into the 12/50 project, and the firm was faced with liquidation. Only a performance that would entice consumer interest would keep Alvis from the bankruptcy courts.

Three 12/50's were prepared for the race, but with their usual abandon Smith-Clarke and John had funneled all their money and energy into one car, which was to be driven by Major C. M. Harvey. The Harvey 12/50 was equipped with a racing chassis and body and a special high-compression engine and sent off to Brooklands, with Alvis' future riding on it. Then, just five days before the race, it was gutted by fire. Frantically it was rushed back to Coventry for reconstruction, worked on night and day by teams of mechanics and Harvey himself, and returned to the track barely in time to start.

Patched together, scarcely driven in practice, the 12/50 faced a field of Bugattis and fast blown Fiats. The race began in a thunder of exhausts, the Fiats for 12 laps setting a blistering pace that only the best-prepared cars could match — and the unbowed Alvis was somehow among them. Car after car fell out, and even the Fiats found their own pace too hot. But the 12/50, weird valve-springs and all, ticked over without a hitch. At the 39th lap Harvey took the lead and held it to the finish. The car averaged a lusty 93.29 m.p.h. for the race and had not one trace of mechanical trouble throughout. "The old homestead" was saved.

The 12/50's performance had the desired effect of booming sales, and many 12/50's reached the hands of now-eager enthusiasts. In touring version the 12/50 had the slightly larger displacement of 1,645 c.c. (100 cu. in.) and had excellent top-gear performance and fuel economy. Furthermore, it was capable of a good 80 m.p.h., and its handling qualities were superb. The next year enthusiasts who had hastily bought the 12/50 on the basis of the spectacular Brooklands performance could point out with some smugness that their judgment had been sound. The special version that John and Smith-Clarke built for 1924 was low, short and starkly streamlined, and it succeeded in setting 39 new Class A records at Brooklands in one day.

The 12/50, now firmly established, continued to provide bread and butter for the Alvis organization for many years. It also provided enough extra capital for John and Smith-Clarke to continue their experimentation with special racing cars. For some time both men had been fascinated by the possibilities of a front-wheel-drive competition car, and now they decided to build one, primarily for use in hill climbs and sprints. It appeared in 1925, almost at the same time as the remarkably similar American Miller, made an impressive debut at Shelsley Walsh, and soon after set new Class F standing-kilometer and standing-mile records at Brooklands.

The drive layout in this car was carried out with an ingenious simplicity that gave little outward evidence of the labor and research that had been invested in it. The engine was the standard 12/50, but it was placed in the frame the wrong way around, flywheel-end forward. Between the frame rails at the front of the car a unit transmission-and-differential assembly was fitted. The front brake drums were mounted inboard against the differential housing. Each front half-axle carried two universal joints, one at the brake drum and one at the wheel. This De Dion layout was much like the Miller and Cord front ends, but differed from them in using longitudinal instead of traverse quarter-elliptic springs. The Alvis' rear axle was a simple beam, the frame was of dura-luminum, and the engine was equipped with a Roots-type super-charger.

1935 Alvis Speed Twenty,
covertible coupe body
by Van Vooren.

Autocar

The next year Alvis put in general production a car with the same drive layout and engine but with a steel frame and leaf-spring independent suspension fore and aft. At the same time a 1,491-c.c. (91 cu. in.), straight-eight, twin-overhead-camshaft-engine car with front-wheel drive was built to represent the Coventry hotrodders in competition, and from that time until World War II Alvis marketed and raced a bewildering assortment of front-wheel-drive and conventional-drive cars in a variety of sizes.

In 1927 the company introduced a 1,870-c.c. (114 cu. in.), six-cylinder car which continued in production for many years and after many refinements and with increased displacement eventually became the basis of the "Eagle" series. It did not appear as a racing special, but the first car in stock form had an engine that revved up to 6,000 r.p.m. in the lower gear ratios. In 1928 the doughty old 12/50, which had won a six-hour endurance test at Brooklands as late as 1926, began finally to fade from production, and Alvis began to concentrate on front-wheel-drive cars with a vengeance.

First a four-cylinder sports car with this layout was added to the catalogue, this time with an overhead-camshaft engine and newly designed independent suspension. It was offered in blown and unblown form, the first developing 50 b.hp., the latter 75 b.hp. Two modified versions of this model finished first and second in the 1½-liter class that year in the Le Mans 24 Hour Race. The same year the same car, blown, and fitted with a light body, finished second in the Ulster Tourist Trophy race after an exciting and classic duel with the winning Lea-Francis.

In 1929 the 1926 racing straight-eight, front-wheel-drive car was marketed in sports-car form. Its features included twin over-head camshafts, dual magnetos, and a multiplate clutch. In 1930 a team of four of these cars was given the usual all-out, "damn-the-cost" Alvis racing preparation, and entered in the Ulster T.T. They won in the 1½-liter class, but lost the overall victory on handicap to Alfa Romeo. This was a bitter blow for John and Smith-Clarke, and it turned out to be the antidote for their long-nourished racing bug. Shortly after the race they announced that the factory would no longer officially sponsor racing cars. In another important way 1930 was a year of decision for Alvis. The front-wheel-drive cars had become almost prohibitively expensive to produce, and their sales did not justify the investment. The front-wheel-drive concept was abandoned.

By 1931 Alvis had made the changeover to rear-drive cars, and the staple sporting products of the line became the beetle-backed 1,645-c.c. four-cylinder 12/60 and, in 1932, the Firefly, another four-cylinder car with an overhead-valve, 1,496-c.c. engine and fine all-around performance qualities. The same year a new high-performance car joined the Silver Eagle in the six-cylinder branch of the Alvis line. This was the dashing Speed Twenty, a 2,511-c.c. (153 cu. in.) overhead-valve model — later increased to 2,762 c.c. (169 cu. in.) and capable of a top speed of 90 m.p.h. and an effortless crusing speed of 75 m.p.h. The Speed Twenty became one of the first Alvis cars to be equipped with a gear box with syncromesh for all four forward speeds. The design for this box was developed by Alvis under license from General Motors, and was used by no other British make.

Three more major model changes took place before the war. In 1935 the 12/60 and the Firefly were supplanted by the four-cylinder Firebird series, which had 1,842-c.c. (112 cu. in.) engines, and in 1936 the Speed Twenty evolved to the 3,571-c.c. (218 cu. in.) Speed Twenty-Five. In 1936 an entirely new 4.3-liter (267.7 cu. in.) car was put into production, tested by *The Motor*, and found to be capable of 105 m.p.h. over the flying-quarter-mile.

The 4.3 might have been the most resoundingly successful of all the Alvis cars, but World War II came before the company's "specialist" method of manufacture had produced more than a few. Alvis quickly converted from automotive to aircraft production, and made a major contribution to Britain's air war.

AMILCAR

THE AMILCAR WAS A DARLING OF THE TWENTIES. As spirited as a thoroughbred horse and with almost as animate a personality, the little French car thoroughly captivated that segment of the public that wanted vivid performance in a small package and at small cost.

Most of all, the Amilcar was mysterious. The first model — the Type C4 produced in 1921 — was scarely more than a motorcycle fitted with a rudimentary little sports body. Yet it had marvelously snappy performance that was hardly warranted by its uncompli-cated 933-c.c. (57 cu. in.), four-cylinder, side-valve engine. In its first competition appearance it won the Bol d'Or, a 24-hour test of endurance and speed held on a three-mile circuit in the Forest of St. Germain. The race was hotly contested by the here-tofore unbeatable Salmsons, and was the beginning of a Salmson-Amilcar rivalry for 1,100-c.c.-class superiority that lasted for many years.

This auspicious debut whetted the interest of enthusiasts on both sides of the Channel, and the C4 soon evolved into the two-seater Type C "Grand Sport" Amilcar, also known as the "Surbaisse," which had the same inexplicably powerful engine increased to 1078 c.c. (66.4 cu. in.) displacement. The little chassis had half-elliptic springs outboard of the frame in front, a stiff axle sprung on quarter elliptics in the rear, and ribbed four-wheel brakes. It was given a Gallically rakish doorless body with boat-tail rear and skimpy cycle fenders. In this form, the Amilcar — with its 91-inch wheelbase and 43-inch track — was like a tiny scale model of the mammoth road-eaters of its time. Its performance was startling: 70 to 75 m.p.h. top speed, better than 40 miles per gallon, excellent braking, and superb road-holding and handling qualities — all at a cost well under $1,500.

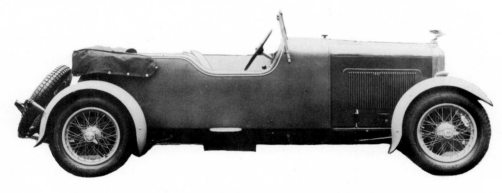

Autocar

Amilcar straight-eight four-seater of 1930. Note light-weight fabric body, cycle fenders, lack of door, running boards.

This car won many adherents for the marque, and in 1926, a sensational small six-cylinder car was added to the line. Although it was called a sports car it was a true Grand Prix racing car in exquisite miniature which could be fitted with fenders and lights for sports-car competition. The beautifully finished 1094-c.c. (66.8 cu. in.) engine had double overhead camshafts running in both plain bearings and ballraces, and power was augmented by a Roots supercharger. The wheelbase was a mere 74 inches; otherwise the chassis was similar to that of the Type C. With a racing two-seater body, the car achieved 105 m.p.h. in absolutely stock form, and at $3,300 it was a bargain that no connoisseur could ignore.

Britons as well as Frenchmen were enchanted by the new Amilcar, and the sixes began to compete with great success in

English sport. In 1926, 1927 and 1928 they dominated their displacement class in the great Brooklands J.C.C. 200-Mile race, and in 1927 also placed second regardless of size, a remarkable feat in a field which included 1.5-liter Bugattis. In 1933 a slightly modified six roared around the Montlhery oval for an hour to set a new Class G record at 115.54 m.p.h.

In 1930 Amilcar discarded the sports concept in favor of larger tourers, and the final model of the marque was a 2-liter straight-eight.

ASTON MARTIN

WHEN, IN THE EARLY FIFTIES, BRITISH SCHOOL children were called upon to donate their pennies to the cause of the B.R.M. racing car, no eyebrow was raised. Why shouldn't the kiddies do their bit in the national emergency which found Britain without a challenger for the *grandes épreuves?* It was, after all, a matter of international prestige.

A similar emergency had come about after the mastodonic Bentleys had steam-rollered their last Le Mans victory in 1930, and England was left without a champion to carry the racing green abroad. Then, in 1931, a tiny Aston Martin finished fifth in the great 24-hour race against a field packed with Mercedes, Alfas, Bugattis and Talbots. Under the complex Le Mans rules the British car qualified to compete for the next year's Biennial Cup, a prize as hotly coveted as the Grand Prix d'Endurance, which was always won by one of the larger cars.

The eyes of most of England were on A. C. Bertelli when he took his Aston Martin back to Le Mans in 1932. Businessmen were watching the effort as closely as were sportsmen; a victory by a lone British car would be interpreted by the world as a victory by the British automotive industry. It was a tensely important race for the British, for Bertelli, and for the marque; and, as it turned out, it was one of the most violent Le Mans races of them all.

The race was in the sixth lap, scarcely under way, when Dreyfus' Alfa went out of control in a turn, crashed into the bank, and rolled over. Then Marinoni stove his Alfa into a sandbank. But

these isolated incidents only set the scene for the wholesale car-
nage that followed. At White House Corner Trevoux went into
the bend much too fast, rolled over, and demolished his supercharged Bentley. Minoia's Alfa, leading Brisson's Stutz, went
boiling around the blind corner. Minoia saw with horror the
Bentley's wreckage blocking half the road, hit his brakes, spun
like a dervish, and crashed. Brisson came around the bend to
discover the spinning red Alfa a few yards away. He tried to steer
clear of the wreckage and the Stutz came to rest on its side, Brisson
thrown clear.

While cars were being wrecked right and left, others fell by the
way with mechanical troubles. Foucret's Mercedes dropped out
with a seized piston; Bouriat's Bugatti burst its fuel tank. But
Bertelli's little Aston Martin snarled on deftly picking its way
among the mangled machines that smouldered in the shadows as
the long night wore on. Dawn found the field reduced by a good
half, but the Aston Martin's only trouble was fender bolts "of
unknown French origin" which kept breaking until the fenders
were simply roped in place.

At the end of the race only nine of the 26 entering cars were
left running, and Sommer's Alfa was the winner for sheer distance
travelled. The smaller Aston Martin won the equally important
Biennial Cup for the best performance for two consecutive years,
and England had gained a new champion, a new hero-marque.
Inevitably, a "Le Mans" Aston Martin was offered immediately to
the public.

This was the third model of a marque that, shortly after the
Armistice, was born of a gentlemen's agreement between a com-
petition-car designer named Lionel Martin and Europe's fabulous
Count Zborowski, a thoroughly Anglicized millionaire sportsman
who had built and raced a series of cars all named "Chitty-Bang-
Bang."

Zborowski knew Martin would build him the kind of cars he
liked to drive. Martin had designed his first one-off competition
car in 1913, and it, like the rest of his cars, demonstrated his
passion for perfect handling qualities. He was convinced that a
mildly stressed engine in a truly nimble chassis could run circles
around less subtly conceived machinery.

"The car I want to build will be small but perfect," Martin
promised the Count. "It will combine the reliability of the Rolls-
Royce with the Bugatti's agility. It will win races."

The first of the postwar machines, known as "Bunny" to intimates and always referred to as "she," did indeed win races. Bunny became the first of a series of cars that were so successful at the then-famous Aston Clinton hill-climbs near London that the marque was christened Aston Martin.

Cars of the Bunny breed are now identified as the "Side-valve" Aston Martins. They were powered by a neat little 91 cubic inch, four-cylinder engine with integral head and light-alloy crankcase. There was nothing radical about the engine but it was notable for attention to design detail and for good workmanship. The chassis was skinny but solid, used the conventional semi-elliptics, was underslung at the rear, and became famous for its light, dead-accurate handling qualities. The provision of a torque tube reflected big-car influence, and brisk performance was abetted by a close-ratio, four-speed gearbox that was suggestive of Bugatti practice. In regular road trim, peak speeds in the gears were about 25, 45, 55 and 72 m.p.h.

Motor

B. S. Marshall at the wheel of a 1920 Aston Martin.
Photograph taken at Brooklands Race Track.

H. Kensington-Moir, who later became Bentley's master pit strategist, won many races at the original Bunny's wheel. In October of 1921 he took the car to Brooklands track, where he broke the British 1.5-liter record by averaging 86.21 m.p.h. for a solid hour. This feat caused a major stir in the racing field because

Bunny, a hill-climb contender, was never expected to do so well on the level. Lionel Martin hurled a challenge at his rival in Molsheim, offering to meet the best Brescia Bugatti in a match race at Brooklands. Bugatti accepted but when the time came did not appear. Bunny had the last word. She got out on Brooklands and averaged 75 m.p.h. for 18 hours, becoming the first light car to hold world's records — 10 of them.

The trusty Side-valve continued to hack a wide swathe in small-displacement competition until the Zborowski-Martin combine passed from the scene late in 1926 and a young engineer-racing driver took over the firm. He was A. C. Bertelli, who later won at Le Mans. He had been designing and building engines for several years, and he brought to the company an original engine and chassis that were conceived with emphasis on reliability and high performance, in the Aston Martin tradition. But they were much more advanced and more highly refined than the Side-valves. The Bertelli Aston Martins brought the marque its greatest glory in the years between the wars.

The efficient new engine had a detachable head with chain-driven overhead camshaft operating in-line valves actuated by cam followers and tilted to fit wedge-shaped combustion chambers. The block and crankcase were a single casting and a magneto and two carburetors were used. Lubrication was by the dry-sump principle, with a three-gallon oil reservoir carried between the frame rails, ahead of the radiator. The four-speed transmission was separate from the engine, the torque tube was retained and worm drive to the rear axle was introduced. The chassis was low, short, fast and rock-solid.

These chassis were sold with a trim, two-seater body, Rudge knock-off wheels, and racy external exhaust pipes. The "International" four-seater was introduced in 1930 and both cars were capable of about 80 m.p.h. in standard tune. This was not a remarkable top speed, but the cars' superb handling qualities and fine brakes enabled them to maintain very high average speeds over any road course, as Bertelli proved at Le Mans in '31 and '32.

A more static firm might have frozen its Le Mans winner's design for many years, but there was another change of ownership, and R. Gordon Sutherland determined that drastic revisions would be made in his 1933 models. He eliminated the heavy torque tube and replaced the occasionally unreliable rear-axle worm drive with spiral bevel gears. He had the transmission redesigned to form a unit with the engine.

In 1934, before the introduction of the Mark II sports model, Sutherland made detail changes in the engine, all aimed at obtaining higher power output and longer service life. He adopted a counterbalanced crankshaft which was machined from a nitralloy solid billet and he redesigned the combustion chambers and went to a compression ratio of 7.5-to-1. The Mark II and its almost-twin the Ulster marked the highest development of Bertelli-based design, and an Ulster made further history at Le Mans by breaking the 1.5-liter record in 1935 — a mark that stood until 1950.

These Aston Martin models of the early Thirties were the ultimate in classic, thoroughbred sports-car design. In fact, it is likely that these are the cars which, with their low lines and cut-down doors, cycle fenders, close-coupled bodies, racing windscreens, rock-screened headlights, logically-located controls and fine instrument panels, set the form that all British sports cars were to follow for years and which some continue to reflect strongly today.

They were hard-sprung and the passenger felt every irregularity on the road, but it was that very rigidity of the chassis that gave the old Aston Martins their wonderful stability. Their steering was light, yet required less than two turns from lock to lock and was outstandingly accurate. Their acceleration was better than that of almost any other car of the time and the Ulster could do an honest 100 m.p.h. in ordinary road trim. In every way they were what their maker called them — "The Race-Bred Luxury Car."

However, in spite of these cars' enviable record in 1.5-liter competition, Sutherland was not neglecting the requirements of the average Aston Martin owner, who was just as interested in low-speed as in top-end performance. To give his customers better acceleration at low r.p.m. he increased engine displacement to 1,950 c.c. (118 cu. in.), sacrificing the marque's eligibility for its traditional racing class. The larger-engined models were introduced in 1936 in a 15/98 and a Speed Model, available with small sedan or close-coupled four-place bodywork. These cars had a moderately successful racing career at home and on the Continent and remained in production until the outbreak of the war.

Just before the war, however, an experimental model was built which was, except for the 2-liter engine, a complete break with Aston Martin tradition. Sutherland, an astute observer of consumer trends, reasoned that the medium-sized quality car would soon demand an entirely new approach to design which would combine comfort, economy and performance as never before. The traditional Aston Martins were heavy; the future promised acceptance of lightweight constructional methods. The Aston Martins were sprung like wagons; independent springing, of the front axle at least, seemed sure to become universal. The crash-box transmission had had its day; motorists were demanding easier shifting.

Motor

Clive Gallop with racing mechanic Bentley photographed at the 1922 Strasbourg Grand Prix Meeting. Note the four-wheel braking system and the large diameter steering wheel.

The experimental Aston Martin "Atom" was fitted with a Cotal preselector gearbox which transmitted the drive to an open propeller shaft and hypoid rear axle. This power train was mounted in a combined chassis-body assembly made entirely of welded rectangular-section steel tubing. The object was greatest rigidity with lowest weight. One of the most important details of this experiment was the deliberate avoidance of monocoque unit construction, where the body is made part of the frame structure and shares its stresses. The frame, around which the entire body was built, took all the stresses and permitted easy varying of the body lines. This is a technique that many Italian coachbuilders have used with great success in post-war years.

The Atom used an enclosed and quite streamlined four-place body. The coil spring independent suspension was designed so that correct steering geometry was maintained regardless of vertical travel. Acceleration, road speeds, top speed, safety, fuel economy and passenger comfort all were improved significantly. The Atom, a prototype far in advance of its time, enabled Aston Martin to repeat its early history in postwar years as one of the design and competition leaders of the automotive world.

BALLOT

THE FIRST BALLOT CAR WAS BUILT FOR POST-World War I Indianapolis competition and merged the resources of the Ballot Works—which before the war had supplied engines for such outstanding French makes as Delage—with the talent of M. Ernest Henri, a Swiss engineer who was one of the real pioneers of the industry. Henri, who died in miserable poverty in the early Fifties, revolutionized high-performance engine design; his intelligent exploitation in the 1912 Grand Prix Peugeot of the idea of four valves per cylinder, inclined to give straight-through breathing and combined with dual overhead camshafts, set the pattern still followed today.

Not surprisingly, this design was used in the 1919 Ballot, which ran second to Frontenac in 1921's Indianapolis classic and third in 1922. It was also used in the first production Ballot, a four-cylinder, 1,995-c.c. (121.7 cu. in.) sports car which appeared in 1922. Unhappily for sales, this car's superb quality was reflected in its $9,000 price tag; and in 1923 a new, less-expensive model was added to the line.

This was a high-performance touring car called the 2LT and powered by another four-cylinder engine of the same displacement but having just one overhead camshaft and two vertical valves per cylinder. Its cost was a relatively painless $4,000, and it had the additional virtues of good operating economy, an elegant lightweight fabric body and—like the earlier Ballot—

Ballot's snappiest model
for 1925 was this Sports Two
Liter, powered by a 4-cylinder engine.

Autocar

fine Isotta-Fraschini brakes which in the 2LT were soon fitted with a pioneer power-brake system, the Dewandre vacuum servo.

In 1925, the double-overhead-cam model was dropped entirely and replaced by the 2LTS, a refined and higher-revving version of the 2LT which reverted to inclined-valve layout; actuated, however, by a single overhead camshaft and short rocker arms.

By 1927 Ballot had experimented with a 2-liter, six-cylinder model, rejected it, and started to concentrate on chic straight-eights which were as classic as they were sporty. This RH series had 2.6-liter (158.6 cu. in.) displacement which grew to 2,874 c.c. (175.3 cu. in.) in 1928, and the company's last model, in 1929, was the 3,050-c.c. (186.1 cu. in.) RH3.

THE SALE OF BENTLEY TO ROLLS-ROYCE IN 1931 marked the end of an era for England. Bentley, single-handed and with a kind of relentless gallantry, in the years 1923 to 1930 gave Britain a period of almost invincible success in international competition that has been just a wistful memory in the lean years since. The battles that Bentley waged and won earned

| BENTLEY |

for the make the fierce and sometimes astonishing loyalty of its countrymen; for England they earned almost as much respect from her international rivals as they might have if road circuits had been true battlefields from which England emerged a just and generous victor.

It was not only the fact that Bentleys won races that set them apart from the herd, but also the *way* that they won. Their speed and stamina enabled carefully-casual amateurs to compete with unprecedented success against hard-bitten professionals to whom racing victory was a grimly essential factor in earning a living. So perfectly did Bentleys and their drivers represent the sometimes naive but nonetheless admirable ideals of the *beau geste* that they were the prime agent in the creation of the chivalric cult of motor racing that bloomed in Britain between the wars.

The philosophy of this latter-day knight errantry was defined most eloquently for the masses by S. C. H. "Sammy" Davis. Sammy was a member of that loose association of gentlemen drivers known as "The Bentley Boys." He was also sports editor of *The Autocar* and most of his pieces were signed "Casque"— the name for a knight's helmet. This allusion to the modern driver's crash helmet was an accurate symbol of Sammy's feeling for the sport.

Sammy did more than write inspiring prose. He was an ardent, competent and—needless to say—sportsmanlike amateur driver. With his intimate friend J. Dudley Benjafield he gave to the sport one of its most stirring tales of determination and to the Bentley make one of the most spectacular racing victories of all time.

It happened in 1927 at Le Mans. Benjafield, a mild little doctor who wore black Homburg hats, had a few years before been attacked by Bentley fever that no pink pills could cure, and had purchased a 1926 Le Mans team car for making his daily house calls and for occasional racing. When it looked as though "The Firm" could not afford to enter a factory team in 1927's race Benjy volunteered his machine and, if desired, his services. Both were accepted, along with Sammy Davis as co-driver.

Three Bentleys were finally entered that year: a brand-new 4½-l., a new 3-liter and Benjy's warhorse, which was to run third to the newer, better cars. Some 19 other machines also ran, among them the Bentleys' most serious competition, a French Aries.

The great 24-hour trek got under way smartly at 4:00 P.M. and all cars lapped the course through the afternoon and early evening almost without incident. Then at 9:30 that humid June night, with Bentleys leading 1-2-3, the excitement began at now-legendary White House Corner.

On the grandstand stretch just beyond the Arnage turn Tabourin pushed his Th. Schneider a little too eagerly through a left-hand bend, lost control, tore out a 20-foot section of roadside wall and spun to rest across the road. Bentley's great hope, the 4½-liter, screamed onto the scene at 90 m.p.h., swerved into a muddy ditch and was wrecked. Right behind the Bentley was Thelusson in a French Fasto. He managed to brake, skidded around the Schneider, and stopped, facing the wrong way. The Fasto was still in motion when Bentley Number Two, the new 3-liter, barreled in. Its driver made the same reflex decision as Number One's and took to the same ditch. With a tremendous crash and rending of metal Number Two bore headlong into Number One, struck it hard enough to bounce it into the road, and itself lay shuddering in the mud.

Hurtling through the darkness toward this wreckage was Bentley Number Three, Davis up. Scant yards away his headlights picked out a few loose stones and skid marks on the course and his instincts took over. He hit the brakes, entered the area of wreckage and at 60 m.p.h. or so slashed his way through as best he could. His best saved the car from annihilation, but as he braked to a desperate stop he nicked the tail of Bentley Number One, smashed one of his wheels, crumpled a fender, and destroyed two of the three headlights. While Sammy darted about in the darkness and determined to his relief that no one was seriously hurt, the Aries, too far behind to be touched by the incident, was left with the lead.

A deluge of rain began to pour down upon the course as Davis drove back to the pits. His was the only Bentley still remotely able to race, but it had a twisted axle, a loose battery box, a flapping fender and runningboard, and one light. By the time a new wheel was mounted a solid half-hour of racing time had been lost.

When Benjy took the wheel and drove back into the storm the lone, crippled Bentley was running third, 40 miles behind the first-place Aries. All night long the Bentley ground on with inadequate light, damaged steering, and brakes that now tended to make the car swerve. But the 3-liter engine never missed a beat through the night, then the morning, then the afternoon. And then the Aries' exhaust note began to go sour. The Bentley gained steadily until, at 2:00 P.M., with two hours of the race left, only two minutes separated the solitary British challenger from the leader. Gradually Benjy moved into the lead. The French crowd went wild with approval, its normal nationalistic passions entirely overcome by the performance of the bloody but unbowed Bentley.

Benjy increased his lead steadily until only 15 minutes were left in the race. Then, in an act of chivalry that was almost more than the crowd could bear, he pulled into the pits insisting that Sammy Davis have the honor of bringing old Number Seven across the finish line. When Sammy took the checkered flag in the battered green four-seater even the Aries pit cheered itself hoarse.

Benjafield, Davis, and *Le Marque Bentley* were fêted as conquering heroes in France and, when they returned to England, the honors and celebrations continued for weeks. The climax came two weeks after the Le Mans victory at a dinner given by *The Autocar* at London's aristocratic Savoy Hotel. The guests, splendid in white ties and tails, were Bentley executives, team personnel, and others who had contributed in some way to the success in France. After liqueurs had been served the toastmaster signalled for a pair of large double doors to be opened. There, in the banquet room, stood Benjy's Number Seven Bentley, mud-crusted and battle-scarred, just as she had crossed the finish line at Le Mans. Every man stood at attention and joined in a toast to the old warrior.

This story offers a glimpse of the tough, thoroughbred nature of the Bentley cars, of the sort of people who made history in them and of the fervent regard in which they were held at home. The Bentleys were, literally, heroic automobiles and, as was so often the case with the truly great makes, they were born of the inspiration of one man.

He was Captain W. O. Bentley, a World War I aircraft-engine designer with a background of automobile racing. His conception was of a series-produced passenger car based upon an advanced Grand-Prix-type racing chassis, ruggedly built and with engine detuned for maximum reliability. As soon as the Armistice was signed and W. O.'s government job had ended, he plunged into the designing of the first 3-liter Bentley, with the aid of H. T. Burgess, engineer, and H. Varley, draftsman. The prototype was exhibited at London's Olympia Auto Show in the winter of 1919 and production models were first offered to the public in 1921.

The frame and running gear were perfectly standard; in fact, the frame needed additional stiffness. Steering was by worm and wheel—the best. But it was primarily the four-cylinder engine which commanded every racing man's respect. The head was integral with the block, as it should be in a high-performance power unit. The four valves per cylinder in "pent-roof" combustion chambers showed W. O.'s appreciation of the excellence of that layout in the Henri-designed Peugeots. He also followed the Henri formula of a stroke-to-bore ratio of about 2-to-1. The single overhead camshaft and the finger-type cam followers indicated that W. O. had studied the 1914 Grand Prix Mercedes and isolated its best features. The connecting rods measured 11½ inches from center to center and were machined and polished all over. The five-main-bearing crankshaft was finished in the same manner and weighed just 34 pounds. Spark plugs entered both right and left sides of the combustion chambers and were backed up by twin magnetos, driven by gears from the vertical-shaft cam drive.

These engines were decades ahead of their time in many ways and their power output was, consequently, abnormally high. But equally important was the reliability which had been designed into them. Crankshaft support, cooling and general ease of maintenance were some of the vital factors that received profound attention on drawing board and test bench and consequently gave the cars matchless performance on road and track. Reliability had been built into the 3-liter chassis so well that W. O. could afford, without hesitation, to guarantee his cars for a period of five years.

The Speed Model was good for an easy 85 m.p.h. and could be tuned to do 100 m.p.h. It could lug at eight m.p.h. in top gear and average fuel consumption was in the neighborhood of 21 m.p.g. The appearance was formidable: ultra-light four-place bodywork; high, massive, vee-cored radiator; Rudge racing wheels and skimpy fenders. These assorted choice qualities caused the 3-liter Bentleys to become collectors' items at their first introduction. A cult came into spontaneous existence; eligibility for "membership" simply consisted of owning a Bentley.

The competition record of the 3-liter Bentley includes many classic exploits. In 1922 it covered 2,083 miles in the Brooklands Double Twelve (24-hour) race at an average of 86.79 m.p.h., a remarkable speed for the time and a rare demonstration of reliability. In 1923 it finished fourth in the first Le Mans 24-hour race. In 1924 it won, making pilots Clement and Duff the first British victors at Le Mans. In 1926 at Montlhery it broke the 24-hour record with an average of 95.03 m.p.h. In the same year, it took the world's record for 2,000 kilometers at 100.23 m.p.h. And it won at Le Mans again in 1927 with Benjafield and Davis at the controls of a thoroughly crippled car. This was W. O.'s first car and it was all he wanted it to be; fast, trouble-free, and as well-suited to creeping through London traffic as it was to breaking speed records.

Autocar

One of the earliest photos of W. O. Bentley at the beginning
of his career as an auto manufacturer. Car is 4-cylinder, 3-liter model of 1920.

W. O. was, however, a confirmed believer in the virtues of abundant cubic inches for competition and normal motoring alike. In June, 1925, he announced a new model which reflected these convictions. It was the Bentley 6½-liter "Big Six"—an all-purpose car in the fullest sense. Here, at last, was a Bentley with the displacement (6.6 liters or 402 cu. in.) and the torque to reduce the bottom two cogs in the gearbox to mere emergency status. Smooth starts could be made in third and a steady flow of power was available in top gear from four m.p.h. on up. Here, too, was a chassis powerful enough to carry heavy, coachbuilt sedan bodies, which had not worked out well with the 3-liter. A 5,000-pound,

6½-liter Bentley could accelerate from 10 to 30 m.p.h. in six seconds, zoom up to 70 m.p.h. before shifting to fourth gear, cruise comfortably at 75 m.p.h. Its low-speed hill-climbing abilities were as fantastic as those of a powerful steam car.

The new car's nickname derived not from its literage but from its number of cylinders. The Big Six engine's design was closely similar to that of the 3-liter; the most important difference being in drive to the overhead camshaft. While the 3-liter had used a vertical shaft and bevel gears, the Big Six resorted to a set of three eccentrics driven by one steel and one fabric gear and connected with a set of eccentrics on the camshaft by means of three connecting rods. This strange construction had the virtue of being very quiet, and Rolls-Royce owners who wanted performance as well as respectful silence began to invest in Bentleys.

But their patronage was not enough to save Bentley from a financial position that was unfortunate and almost untenable. The market for $6000 sports cars was a limited one; production was necessarily limited too, and the establishment of a self-sufficient plant was out of the question. Much of the foundry and machine work had to be farmed out, so that many costs remained more or less fixed regardless of increased production. The financial structure was tottering when one of the most famous of "The Bentley Boys" came to the rescue.

Woolf Barnato was the resounding name of a young millionaire who had become a member of the Bentley cult after several years of racing various cars, including an American Locomobile. His reaction to Bentley's plight was to invest such a sum of money in the firm that he could take over the position of chairman of the board. And he automatically gained the right to drive third-string on the Bentley team. Barnato's cash transfusion made possible the introduction of a brand-new model the following year.

Just over 1,600 3-liter Bentleys had been made when that model was retired in 1927 and the more-modern 4½-liter (4,398 c.c. or 269 cu. in.) was placed on the market. Replacing—as it did —the 3-liter, it was purely an enthusiast's car but with even greater racing promise. In addition to the added displacement, the stroke was shortened slightly and the four-cylinder engine made more compact; Mercedes-type cam drive was retained. Brakes were greatly improved, giving stopping distances of 18 feet at 25 m.p.h. and 56 feet at 40 m.p.h. The $6,800 sports four-seater weighed 3360 pounds, took five seconds to move from 10 to 30 m.p.h. and had a top speed of 92 m.p.h. This is the car that was Bentley's white hope at Le Mans the year Dr. Benjafield's runabout saved the race for England.

No wreckage got in the 4½'s way at Le Mans in 1928 and Barnato and Rubin were the victors with an average of 69.11 m.p.h. for 1,658.6 miles. Tim Birkin (Sir Henry Birkin, Bart.) scored the fastest lap with his 4½ at 79.5 m.p.h. The following year the 4½'s finished second, third, and fourth in the Grand Prix d'Endurance and first and second in the Rudge-Whitworth Cup.

Meanwhile, the Big Six was undergoing some serious grooming. W. O. was convinced that such a powerful car should be able to make a brilliant showing in competition. With engine modifications including increased compression and larger carburetors this car was rechristened the Speed Six and entered for Le Mans in 1929. This time Barnato and Birkin manned the winning machine and the Speed Six won both in the general classification and the Rudge-Whitworth Cup. In 1930, Barnato returned with the Speed Six, Glen Kidston co-driving, and repeated the double victory. In 1929 and 1930 the Speed Six also won the Six Hour and the Double Twelve (24-hour) races at Brooklands. In 1931 an old Speed Six won the Brooklands 500-mile race at what was called "the colossal average of 118.39 m.p.h." This was invincibility.

W. O.'s policy obviously was to advertise his cars by winning races with them. The policy began to pay off in 1929 when the firm realized a $138,000 profit. Gains were even greater in the first half of 1930, encouraging W. O. to release upon the market his *tour de force*, the utterly formidable 8-liter, his reply to the monster classics which were appearing in greater numbers each year on the Continent and across the Atlantic.

The chassis alone sold for $9,000. It could be had with wheelbases of 144 and 156 inches. The engine was essentially a bored-out Big Six, retained the eccentric-driven single overhead camshaft and four valves per cylinder. Two S. U. carbs were fitted and dual ignition was by Delco distributor and Bosch magneto. Cam followers were made of duraluminum and all non-stressed light-metal parts were of Elektron magnesium alloy. The big, quiet, four-speed gearbox was a unit separate from the engine and the rear springs were mounted outboard for stability, just as close to the hubs as they could be placed.

W. O. intended this machine to be an ultra-fast and silent touring sedan and not in any sense a sports car. Its top-gear speed range was from six to 104 m.p.h. and acceleration with full sedan coachwork was clocked at 50 seconds from 10 to 100, in fourth gear all the way. Only a few of these cars were made and Bentley faithfuls still boast of their prowess, of their being "the finest machine of their type ever made, anywhere." Fine coachbuilders like Gurney Nutting and Saoutchik created some of their best bodies for the 8-liters, of which 120 were made.

People who could afford Bentleys at all could afford the best and most potent, which meant that in the sports line, all the demand was now for the Speed Six. Evidently in order to make his remaining stock of 4½-liter fours more attractive, W. O. fitted the last 50 of these machines with huge Roots superchargers mounted forward of the radiator and coupled directly to the crankshaft. The blown 4½'s went very briskly, had a top speed of 98 to 100 m.p.h., but when the last one was sold, no more fours were built.

During the last half of 1930 the depression caught up with Bentley Motors Ltd. People stopped buying costly automobiles, above all costly sports cars which were, essentially, playthings. W. O.'s stockholders blamed his cars more than they blamed the world crisis. They interpreted the decrease in sales to a lack of consumer interest in—if not an actual fear of—racing cars.

They went over W. O.'s head and withdrew from racing with these public comments:

"It is inevitable that participation in races should stamp the Bentley in the eyes of a certain section of the public as a racing car. Nothing is farther from the truth. On the contrary as our racing successes have increased, our cars have become more silent, more docile, more refined."

Having thus rejected W. O. on the policy level, the shareholders dealt a final, insulting blow by rejecting him as an engineer. They felt that there was nothing wrong with the prices of their cars and that by manufacturing a completely mild-mannered thoroughbred the company could be saved. Sir Harry Ricardo was called in to design an engine that would bear W. O. Bentley's name!

Undoubtedly it was not Ricardo's decision to mount his 4-liter engine in the ponderous 8-liter chassis, but that is what happened and the resulting car was a dismal failure. It had such poor acceleration that prospective buyers who had been attracted by the Bentley name were completely repelled.

Nevertheless, considered apart from its installation in a car much too big, the Ricardo engine did great justice to its noted designer. He had been commissioned to create a six-cylinder power plant of given displacement, good power output, outstanding silence and reliability. He did just that.

The Ricardo Bentley engine had a displacement of 239 cubic inches and used an F-head valve arrangement with intakes above and exhausts at the side. Running a modest 5.5-to-1 compression ratio it developed 120 b.hp. at 4000 r.p.m., equivalent to .5 b.hp. per cubic inch. Weight was kept at a minimum by use of magnesium alloy for the crankcase and other parts that could be made in light metal. Seven main bearings were used and these, plus generous overlap of the large main and connecting rod journals, produced a crankshaft so rigid that a vibration damper was not needed.

The 4-liter Bentley was introduced in the spring of 1931 but by July the firm had already gone into receivership and Napier and Rolls-Royce were bidding for its assets. Dr. Benjafield, in his book "The Bentleys at Le Mans," echoed the bereft sentiments of countless Englishmen when he wrote:

"That the Government should have allowed a Company such as Bentley Motors Ltd. to fail for the need of a few thousand pounds, a Company that had done more genuine and useful research on behalf of the motor-car than all the other British companies put together, a Company that had done an immense amount in advancing the prestige of the British motor-car, not only in Europe, but throughout the world, must be regarded as a national disaster."

One effect of this disaster was to intensify the loyalty of the already militant Bentley cult. The cars were preserved with a sort of vengeful reverence. Parts were hoarded against wasteful loss but joyfully donated to fellow Bentley owners in need. A vigorous competition policy was preserved, with occasional surprising results. There was the time, for example, in 1950, when Forrest Lycett took his 20-year-old, 8-liter Bentley to the Jabbeke-Ostend highway in Belgium and ran for official national records. He ran with full road equipment and, without changing rear axle ratios, clocked 82 m.p.h. for the standing kilometer, 93 for the standing mile, and 132 for the flying mile. Each of these times was a new record.

Membership in the Bentley Drivers Club is still large, and includes the owners of more than 350 Bentleys of 3-liter vintage alone. The BDC's race meetings are affairs of national im-

1931 4½-liter, 269 cubic inch, supercharged Black Label Bentley.
Wheelbase is 130 inches, weight of car with minimum coachwork is 2,940 pounds.

portance, although their significance is mainly nostalgic. W. O. himself is the club's honored Patron and he frequently functions at these meets as a race steward, along with others of the grand old Bentley Boys. The club's races on the airport road circuit at Silverstone reflect a membership interest that is concerned almost solely with W. O.'s creations and the cars they raced against in the Golden 'Twenties. There is a race for 3-liters, another for 4½'s and still another for modified 4½'s. Then a great, thundering free-for-all which is open to 4½-, 6½- and 8-liter Bentleys. The 3-liter Sunbeams, old Brooklands rivals, are given a race of their own which is followed by an exclusively 30/98 Vauxhall event, also in memory of the 3- and 4½-liter days. Then comes the climax of qualifying—a hackle-raising battle between S, SS, and SSK Mercedes-Benz, in commemoration of the Le Mans Bentley victory over the Germans in 1930.

After the fastest qualifiers in each class have proved themselves, one of the most thrilling shows on earth is staged: two five-lap races for these noble, indestructible old cars. The first is between the screaming, supercharged 7-liter Mercedes, and 4½-, 6½- and 8-liter Bentleys. The second is contested by the 30/98 Vauxhalls, 3-liter Sunbeams, 3- and 4½-liter Bentleys. It is a shattering spectacle, colossal and unique. It is also a tribute to, and proof of, the deathless greatness of W. O. Bentley's cars.

B.M.W.

Germany produced little in the way of legitimate sports cars between the wars. Those that counted were built by Mercedes, but their blown sixes smacked of the road locomotives of earlier decades. The idea of the small, nimble car of great power and performance was contained in the small-displacement supercharged fours that Paul Daimler designed for Mercedes, but they died almost as soon as they were born. And that was about all—with one great exception, the 2-liter B.M.W.

It was a cheap, mass-produced machine, but its most refined form—Type 328—stands out as a monument to engineering achievement and easily ranks as one of the most successful automobiles of all time. Its top speed, in standard showroom tune, was over 100 m.p.h. It could bound from a standstill to 30 m.p.h. in 3.4 seconds, from zero to 60 in 9.5, and from zero to 70 in 13.5. A soberly respectful tester for *The Autocar* reported in 1937 that the Type 328 had the best acceleration ever recorded in the long history of the journal's road tests. Although it was conceived in 1935 its engine was still under development and setting new international records 18 years later, and in 1954 the end was not yet in sight.

The 328 was developed after B.M.W. had been manufacturing automobiles for just a short time, although the Bayerische Motoren Werke of Munich had already become famous for its record-breaking opposed-twin motorcycles. The first B.M.W. car was built in 1929, when the company took over the Dixi-Werke, of Eisenach, and acquired with its other assets the German manufacturing license for the Famous Austin Seven. Dixi had been building the Austin Seven since 1927, and B.M.W. continued to produce it according to standard specifications until 1932, when Dr. Fritz Fiedler joined the organization as chief designer. Under his supervision the displacement of the little Austin was upped from 747.5 c.c. (46.4 cu. in.) to 788 c.c. (50 cu. in.) and an exciting new feature was added—independent rear suspension by swing axles.

This was only the beginning of Fiedler's effect on B.M.W. In 1932 he designed his first overhead-valve six for the firm, and it was from this design that the Type 328 evolved. It had a displacement of 1,200 c.c. (73.2 cu. in.), which was increased to 1,490 in 1934. In-line, pushrod-operated valves were arranged in the normal manner and the engine produced 34 b.hp. in touring form, 40 b.hp. in sports form. Even in this relatively primitive form the B.M.W. gave the impression of great latent power. A Type 40 prototype was entered in the 1933 Alpine Trial, and its performance was witnessed by the Aldington brothers of Frazer-Nash. They lost no time in acquiring British rights to the design.

In 1935 the engine's displacement was increased to 1,911 c.c. (116.6 cu. in.) and two carburetors were fitted as standard equipment. The engine in this form developed 45 b.hp. and powered the Type 45 cars, which were also known as the Type 321. The next quick improvement was the Type 55-327, which ran three carburetors and pulled 55 b.hp.

Then, in 1936, came the Type 328. For this engine Fiedler created a special head that was to transform a fast pumpkin into a screaming carriage. Aside from an increase in displacement to 1,971 c.c. (119.3 cu. in.), all the significant changes were above the head gasket. The head was cast in light alloy and used vee-inclined overhead valves with spark plugs centered between the valves. The intake ports were vertical and the exhaust ports swung off to the right side. The camshaft was left in its previous position in the block below the bottom of the stroke. Pushrods actuated the intake valves directly by means of extremely compact rocker arms. Another set of pushrods worked bell cranks mounted on the intake rocker-arm shaft. Short, nearly horizontal pushrods extended from the bell cranks to the exhaust rockers to complete the valve gear.

It sounds like and it was a gadgety sort of arrangement, but it performed with a crisp suddenness that put it in the same class as the best overhead-camshaft engines. It boomed the 328's output to a conservative 80 b.hp. at 4,500 r.p.m. The four-main-bearing crankshaft provided perfect reliability, and the carefully worked-out lubrication system provided pressure oil even to the wrist pins.

The car had rack-and-pinion steering to which it responded impeccably. The solid rear axle was suspended by semi-elliptics in the normal manner, but the front wheels were sprung independently, by means of a transverse leaf and A-arms. The 328 set a standard of roadholding and precision controllability never known before in Germany.

Furthermore, it was a trailblazer in the areas of weight reduction and streamlining. The frame was made of light tubular steel and every reasonable effort was made to reduce poundage from chassis and body. The body was carefully designed to create minimum wind drag. The fenders and headlights were molded smoothly into the main body panels. The two-seater body was attractive rather than handsome, but—and much more important—it was so rationally worked out that it was considered no handicap for a 328 in full road trim to compete against stripped 2-liter cars. Its stamina and invincibility gave it a sort of noble character that somehow blended perfectly with its youthful, hell-raising exuberance. Unlike most first-rate sports cars, it was as adaptable to shopping for groceries as it was to winning races, and it sold for a price that many could afford. At just over $3,000 it was one of the better buys of all time.

Autocar

The Type 328 B.M.W. was not a costly car, but was one of Germany's best competition sports cars. These cars were imported by Frazer-Nash in England, where they were known as the Frazer-Nash B.M.W. This is a 1939 Model.

The Type 328 was, of course, entered in competitions almost from the moment it appeared. Frazer-Nash was rewarded for its early recognition of the B.M.W. potential by having its nameplate on the first 328 to win an important race. This was the 1936 Ulster T.T. over the Ards circuit, in which the team of three Frazer-Nash B.M.W.s finished 1-2-3 in their class, third, overall, and won the team prize. This devastating success was just the start of a long career. In 1938 alone the Type 328 won 125 first places in German and international events. Among these was a 1-2-3 win with two team prizes in the Mille Miglia, a 1-2-3 in the International A.V.U.S. Races, a 1-2-3 in the Belgian Grand Prix des Frontières, and a 1-2-3 in the German Mountain Grand Prix. The 328 scored fastest sports-car time of the day at the J.C.C. Brooklands Rally in 1936, '37, '38 and '39. In 1937 Sammy Davis demonstrated both its reliability and its speed by covering 102.22 miles in exactly one hour at Brooklands. The car was in full road trim, ran on pump fuel, and its engine held between 4,600 and 4,900 r.p.m. for the hour. In the 1940 Brescia Mille Miglia a Type 328 won with the extraordinary—for a 2-liter car—average speed of 103.6 m.p.h. and speeds on the straightaway as high as 130 m.p.h.

Enthusiasts were never more justifiably fanatical than those who discovered the full wonder of the 328. This marvelously versatile and powerful little car seemed to prove once and for all that although the relatively immediate action of overhead camshafts is of vital benefit to engine performance, proper combustion-chamber design, porting and spark plug location go a long, long way toward determining top power output. The 328's prewar successes were just a trial run for its long-lived and supremely adaptable engine. Its greatest destiny lay in the postwar future, associated not only with Frazer-Nash, but also with Bristol, Veritas, A.F.M., Monopol, Cooper and E.R.A.

Ettore Bugatti built his first motor vehicle in Milan at the age of 18. Before he died at the age of 66 he had produced some 9,500 cars which fell into 74 distinct types. They all had in common the virtues of exquisite design and execution,

| BUGATTI |

exceptional all-around performance, and startling originality. Bugattis were to the automotive world what the platypus is to biology—without equal in the whole tapestry of evolution.

Ettore's cars had little direct influence on the engineering world, perhaps because they were oddly out of phase with the world in which they existed. He conceived and created machinery with a total disregard for the world and its accepted practices that expressed not arrogance but enormous self-sufficiency. As far as we can determine, Ettore let external influences alter the straight-line development of his engineering concepts only twice; once when he was reluctantly converted to super-charging and again when he voluntarily adopted dual overhead camshafts and the hemispherical-combustion-chamber principle.

The much-abused title of genius belongs to Ettore Bugatti beyond doubt. His strange, wonderful, beautiful automobiles were only one of his accomplishments. Men like Papa Daimler and Ferdinand Porsche demonstrated their claim to the title in the automotive field alone, but Bugatti had an overwhelming versatility that positively established him as a great creative mind. He invented constantly in many diverse fields, took out over 1,000 patents and sold the manufacturing rights for many with which he could not be bothered. He designed good airplane engines (his 16-cylinder job started the post-World War I straight-eight trend) and rail-car engines, and he relaxed by designing bicycles, yachts and toy cars.

Furthermore, he had flair. He was a master showman, by simply being himself. He was eloquent but not loquacious; dressed in a dashing style that was all his own; spoke with the authority of a Biblical prophet on problems of life, art and engineering—all of which he had solved in detail to his satisfaction.

One of the greatest of his creations was the baronial estate-factory at Molsheim, in Alsace-Lorraine. It was a dream-domain containing manor house, gardens, museums for his private collections, stables of thoroughbreds, kennels, aviaries, vineyards, a distillery, a private electric powerplant, wood and pattern shops, boat works, a foundry, and, finally, the buildings in which the automobiles were designed, fabricated and assembled. With his small quantities of non-conformist cars, Bugatti supported this eccentric hobbyist's paradise and made it produce profits.

Patron simply means "boss" in French; and Ettore—from the beginning of his Molsheim period in 1910—naturally was called *le Patron*. But, as a 1953 Bugatti factory release stated: *"Ettore Bugatti était un Seigneur."* The man was a consummate aristocrat in spirit and his status was always clear to the inhabitants of the village and the employees at Molsheim. *Le Patron* was admittedly the master of the land, as well as being the master artist, engineer, machinist, businessman. No titles were tolerated other than that of *le Patron;* his 1,200 to 2,000 employees knew their jobs and that was enough.

Bugatti's greatest passion aside from automobiles was fine horseflesh. Evidently the pure-bred hunter or race horse sym-

bolized for him beauty in motion and the creation of functional
perfection through skillful breeding. The association was clear
in his automotive activities. In the Twenties his advertisements
frequently consisted of his oval trademark above a photo or
drawing of a magnificent horse. Under it would be the slogan
"Le Pur Sang des Automobiles" (the thoroughbred of automobiles), bounded on each side by horseshoe outlines which, by
no coincidence, were the outlines of the Bugatti radiator.

The English, with their unparalleled appreciation of the qualities of breeding, discovered Bugatti automobiles with a vengeance
in the early Twenties. The wiry machines were ideally suited to
negotiating the Isles' winding, narrow lanes but, even more important, had that *chic* combined with performance that has always
lured small numbers of Britons from the Home Product. The
Bugatti Owners Club, still vigorously extant, was organized in
England in 1929 to help with the social, mechanical and racing
requirements of a strong and growing Bugatti cult. Throughout the Twenties and Thirties Britons were the second-most-
enthusiastic supporters of the marque. The first were the French
themselves who found in Ettore's cars that combination described
by Jules Romains of the Académie Française as: *"l'individualisme
français, avec la qualité et la belle mécanique."*

Bugatti's engines were among the finest and handsomest ever
designed but they were not world beaters in terms of producing
high horsepower for each unit of displacement. It was as a chassis
engineer that *le Patron* was almost incomparable and his subtle,
precise insight into all the problems of chassis design enabled his
cars constantly to win races from machines that were admittedly
faster on the straightaway. The Bugatti racing chassis was stable,
roadable and controllable to a literally fantastic degree and Ettore proudly supplied the same chassis in all his sports and touring
cars.

George Monkhouse, in *Grand Prix Racing Facts and Figures*
(which includes many classic sports-car events), lists 170 first
places for Bugatti in major races as compared with Alfa Romeo's
216. But Bugattis competed successfully in innumerable lesser
events and won more contests than any other make, perhaps more
than all other makes combined. This was a direct result of Ettore's radical and clearly conceived policy that current Grand
Prix and G.P.-based sports models should be sold across-the-
counter to all comers. Competition-minded amateurs and free-
lance professionals learned very quickly where they could buy

the hottest mounts, frequently for the least money. Thus Ettore had many of Europe's top independent drivers fighting on the side of his own fine teams and rolling up wins for the marque.

Bugatti produced a confusing array of automobile types. There were cars with four-, eight-, and 16-cylinder as well as single- and dual-overhead-camshaft engines which evolved according to a complex, interwoven chronology. In the following pages we shall describe the most important models and trace their development briefly.

Type 13

Most of the genes and chromosomes of the pure Bugatti strain were dominant at the very beginning. The others were not recessive long and the main points of the breed were quickly established. The pedigree of the offspring of succeeding decades was almost entirely inbred, which suited the *pur sang* concept.

Ettore's devotion to *qualité et la belle mécanique* was revealed fully in his first Type 13's. During 1910, his first year at Molsheim, five of these cars were made, followed by 75 in 1911 and similar numbers in 1913 and 1914.

The upper half of the early Type 13 radiator formed half a hexagon and was decorated with the red and white oval name-plate that always remained a feature of Ettore's cars. Half-elliptic springs were used front and rear on these early models, two half-elliptics being used side by side at each rear wheel. Around 1912 these were replaced by the reversed-quarter-elliptic springs which became a hallmark of all subsequent Bugatti construction. The butt ends of these springs were anchored to the rear extremity of the frame side members and curved forward and down to meet the rear axle.

The neat little Type 13 four-cylinder engine had two vertical valves per cylinder and a shaft-and-bevel-driven overhead camshaft. The aluminum cam cover had an arched cross-section and four brass plugs threaded into each side and the top of the cover. Each of these plugs had two small holes drilled in its flat surface to accommodate a pin wrench. Tappet adjustments could be made by removal of the plugs alone and without disturbing the cam cover. Cast in the left-hand slope of the polished cover was a big and beautiful facsimile of Ettore's signature. The cylinder block had an integral head, as subsequent Bugattis were always to have. The crankcase was an aluminum casting which included rugged beams jutting to the sides from the four corners of the case. These were the engine mounts and they also served to stiffen the frame.

Also around 1912 the hex-shaped radiator was replaced by one having a pear- or egg-shaped outline. Even the earliest Type 13's cornered with characteristic Bugatti solidity and had the crackling, modern-sounding, "firecracker" exhaust note for which the marque soon was to become famous. The 13 cruised happily at 50-55 m.p.h., had a top speed of about 60 m.p.h. and would give about 37 m.p.g. at a steady 40 m.p.h.

5-Liter — "Black Bess"

This big, 307-cubic-inch car was designed in 1908, to compete in the Prince Henry Trials, and several copies were made before the beginning of World War I. One of the most famous was the Bugatti driven by Friderich at Indianapolis in 1914. The other is the 1913 ex-Louis Coatalen, ex-Ivy Cummings "Black Bess," later owned by Peter Hampton in England. It employed chain drive to the rear wheels and had a final drive ratio of about 1.8-to-1. The four-cylinder engine was closely similar to the Type 13, its most important distinctions being its large size and its use of three valves per cylinder—two exhausts and one intake. Black Bess' suspension consisted of double, side-by-side half-elliptics for the front axle and reversed quarter-elliptics at the rear. The car's owner reported in 1951 that Black Bess could cruise all day between 60 and 70 m.p.h. and average nearly 17 m.p.g. at that speed. The car is said to have topped 100 m.p.h. on methanol fuel but 90 m.p.h. on benzole and gasoline was its most-quoted top speed. Hampton called it a fascinating, reliable and potent car. It was fitted with the egg-shaped radiator.

Type 22

By 1911, modified Type 13's were active in important competition events and in that year Ernest Friderich placed his 660-pound Bugatti second in a field of two-ton monsters in the Grand Prix de France at Le Mans. Five newly modified 13's were hidden at the outbreak of war in 1914 and resurrected for the light-car or Voiturette Grand Prix held at Le Mans in 1920. These cars retained the plain-bearing lower end of the standard 13, but were bored out 4/100-inch and their tiny combustion chambers were filled with four valves and two spark plugs each. Friderich's Bugatti came in first in this race, 20 minutes ahead of the second-place finisher. These 1914 cars are generally regarded as the first of the Type 22's.

The displacement limit for Voiturette competition had been 1400 c.c. (85.4 cu. in.) but was increased to 1,500 (91.5 cu. in.) for 1921. Taking partial advantage of the new limit, Ettore bored his small four-cylinder engine out from 2.55 to 2.67 inches, increasing its displacement from 82.5 to 88.7 cubic inches. Ball races were used for the first time on the engine's main bearings and roller bearings were fitted to the connecting-rod big ends. The engine had 16 valves, two Bosch magnetos, two spark plugs per cylinder, and two Zenith carburetors. A team of four of these cars was entered in the 1921 Italian Voiturette Grand Prix near Brescia and impressed the world by finishing 1-2-3-4. Thus was born the Brescia Bugatti, the ultimate refinement of the Type 13 strain.

Type 23 — "Full Brescia"

A very few of these cars were made after the Italian victory. They were super-sports and racing models with two wheelbase lengths, close replicas of the Brescia race-winning cars that were sold straight across the counter to the general public. Center and rear main bearings were ball races, the front main- and connecting-rod bearings were plain, lead-bronze. They had 16 valves, two spark plugs (both on the intake side) per cylinder, two Robert Bosch ZU4 magnetos, two Solex carburetors. An additional millimeter of bore raised the engine's total displacement to 1,496 c.c. or 91.3 cubic inches.

As they were raced in Italy, these little cars carried a very simple two-place body finished, of course, in French racing blue. In contrast with this were narrow, flat, polished copper strips which served as fenders, and a large cylindrical fuel tank, also of polished copper. With a top speed of about 90 m.p.h. and very fine acceleration these cars went on for years earning fame in competition. Raymond Mays' Brescia, for example, was the fastest hill-climb car in England from 1923 to 1926. But the Full Brescia was a harsh, fierce little *bolide*, suited almost exclusively for racing. So Ettore built the Type 23.

Type 23 — "Brescia Modifié"

This was a detuned and elongated version of the Type 22 and was far more practical for touring purposes, though just about as noisy. It was a popular car and sold in what were big numbers by Bugatti standards. In terms of acceleration and top speed, the 23 was one of the best cars of its day, which was 1923 to 1926. When four-wheel brakes were adopted for the final year's production, outstanding stopping ability was added to the car's virtues, the greatest of which was really superb roadholding. The most popular bodies on this petite, 93-inch wheelbase chassis were three and four-place tourers.

The main differences between the "Full" and *Modifié* engines were milder valve timing and single, rather than double, magneto ignition for the more popular model. Lower-end bearings were like those of the Full Brescia but slightly smaller in diameter. During the *Modifié's* life span, the egg-shaped radiator was replaced by the classic Bugatti horseshoe shape. The *Modifié's* chassis sold for $1,575.

Type 30

The straight-eight concept was an old one to Ettore. He had built a single car in 1913 with an engine consisting of two Type 13 blocks on a common crankcase. This was followed by two wartime aircraft engines—a straight-eight and the famous 16-cylinder "twin eight" which influenced Duesenberg in the United States and Ballot in Europe to kick off the straight-eight-automobile trend in 1919. In that same year, Ettore announced an 183-cubic inch, in-line automotive eight of his own, but the car did not materialize.

However, *le Patron's* plans for an in-line-eight automobile were pretty firmly established when the 1921 Paris Auto Salon rolled around. There Ettore exhibited a car with an engine of about 183 cubic inches displacement. Evidently convinced that four valves per cylinder was too weakening to combustion-chamber structure, he provided this engine with only three valves per barrel, as in his 16-cylinder aircraft engine.

The appearance of the new straight-eight was unlike that of any previous Bugatti, or any other engine in the world. There is good reason to assume that Cubism—the then-flourishing school of *avant garde* graphic art that had risen in Paris in the years just before the war—had made a fairly deep impression upon that erudite observer of the arts, Ettore Bugatti. Aluminum covers fitted over the blocks and heads of the new engine, giving the assembly above the crankcase the form of a clean-sided, knife-edged rectangular slab. The crankcase formed a more squat, more nearly square rectangle in transverse cross-section. The assembled power plant had a profoundly "essential" quality when viewed from any angle; its external surfaces, of relatively minor importance in the functioning of the engine, were a carefully studied facet of the design. This engine was a masterful piece of modern-school sculpture. All "sentimental" curves—meaning all those unnecessarily borrowed from nonmechanical fields to grace machines—were eliminated. This pure appearance was a major mutation in the evolution of Bugatti *pur sang* engineering.

The following year, 1922, a team of cars was built to compete in the French Grand Prix at Strasbourg. The cars were powered by 122-cubic inch "rectangular" in-line-eight engines, Vizcaya's mount finishing second. In 1923, the touring version of this car made its appearance, Bugatti's first production-model eight. The Type 30, as it was called, had the square-cut engine, 119.3 cubic inches displacement, three valves per cylinder and coil ignition. The crankshaft ran in just three double ball races and the safe r.p.m. limit was 3,800. One owner said of his well-restored Type 30 that the noise level must be experienced to be believed. He added that the suspension was magnificent, giving a post-World War II ride with Bugatti roadholding thrown in. These cars were equipped with four-wheel brakes, hydraulic on the front wheels and cable-operated at the rear. Their top speed was around 80 m.p.h.

Type 35

In 1924 a sensation was created at the French Grand Prix, which was held at Lyons that year. The excitement was occasioned by the debut of a new racing Bugatti, the Type 35. The first detail of this car to catch every eye was the radical design of cast-aluminum wheels *le Patron* had created. These wheels had broad, flat spokes cast integrally with the rims. The spokes had a slight pitch, to enable them to deflect air against the brake drums. The drums were also an integral part of the entire wheel casting, which was of help in reducing unsprung weight. Additionally, when wheels were removed during tire stops, the brake drums were automatically removed, making ultra-rapid brake-shoe changes possible.

Another highly important innovation was the replacement of Bugatti's customary, solid H-section front axle with his famous tubular axle. One notable point about this axle was the fact that the half-elliptic front springs passed not over, nor under, but through it, little box-like openings having been forged and machined for the purpose. The most unique feature of the axle and one that stands as a machining *tour de force* was the fact that the central, between-springs portion of the axle was given a much larger diameter bore than the axle's extremities. This optimum weight reduction was made possible by two machining operations. First the large bore was drilled through the piece of bar stock that was to be an axle. Then the extremities were compressed by a forging operation and bored again, using a smaller diameter drill. This axle was used on all subsequent Bugatti cars and became as much a trademark as the quarter-elliptic springs and cable-operated brakes.

The Type 35 Bugatti, including the many variants on the original, has often been called the world's greatest racing car. This claim is justified by the staggering number of events the marque was able to win: a total of 1,045 for the two seasons 1925 and 1926. One of the reasons for the high figure was the car's versatility, its ability to excel in hill climbs, road races, sprints, and track events. Another reason was that most of the Type 35 variants were catalog models that anyone could buy.

The Type 35 had a straight-eight, 119.3-cubic inch engine with a five-bearing crankshaft. The three central bearings were rollers, held in split cages, and the end mains ran in double ball races. The connecting rods had no bearing caps, being ultra-light, one-piece, H-section forgings. The rod bearings were rollers and, to make their use possible, the entire crankshaft came apart, throw by throw. The crankshaft was not assembled by means of splines as in German practice, but merely by huge pins which locked against a flat area machined on each journal. The machinists who carved these simple, perfect shafts had little latitude for error.

The webs of the crankshaft — sections which joined the various journals — were simple steel discs about seven inches in diameter. The assembled crank was a pretty thing to contemplate, consisting of a perfectly aligned series of 16 uniform discs. These discs acted

as so many tiny flywheels and permitted the use of a very small flywheel proper. The most interesting detail of the multiple-disc
clutch which operated in this drum-shaped flywheel was the
method of exerting pressure upon the alternating steel and cast-
iron plates. A light outer spring supplied enough pressure for low
r.p.m. but as revs mounted a linkage similar to a flyball governor
translated centrifugal force into pressure upon the plates, squaring
the applied pressure as engine speed increased. No means was
provided for positively separating the plates but the spring pressure upon them could of course be released.

The Type 35A was a catalog model which appeared in 1924 for
general sale. It differed from the 35 in having plain connecting-
rod bearings and was commonly known as the Imitation or Arti-
ficial 35.

The 35C was a supercharged version of the 35, with a three-
lobe Roots blower mounted beside the cylinder block. It appeared
in 1927 and was good for 130 m.p.h.

The 35T was an unblown 35 with a longer stroke, increasing
piston displacement from 119.3 to 138.0 cubic inches.

The 35B, also called the Targa Florio (which it won in 1926),
was the supercharged version of the 35T. Both of the 2.3-liter
cars were introduced in 1926.

Type 37

This car appeared in 1925 to take the place of the Type 23
Brescia. The factory was no longer interested in participating in
small-time light-car racing but a great many enthusiasts were.
This was the car for them, a beautiful and business-like little
machine with extra-narrow radiator, narrow body with pointed
tail and, for road use, trim cycle fenders. It used the Type 35
chassis but was fitted with wire wheels and larger brakes. Its
most exciting feature was its diminutive, perfectly finished four-
cylinder, 91.3-cubic inch "square-cut" engine. Three valves were
provided for each cylinder and the crankshaft had five main
bearings, both rod and main bearings being plain. The Type 37
had the astonishing top speed of 95 to 100 m.p.h. and could scoot
from zero to 60 m.p.h. in 14.6 seconds without ever getting out of
bottom gear. Its cable-operated brakes would stop it from 30
m.p.h. in 30 feet and from 70 m.p.h. in 255 feet, which is pretty
adequate.

The Type 37A — a supercharged version of this fine little

four — was released in 1927. Bugatti aluminum wheels were optionally available on the 37A and one of these averaged 122 m.p.h. around the Brooklands track.

James Talmadge

Rakish Bugatti straight-eight four-seater of the late Twenties. Louvers at base of body were a common Bugatti touch.

Type 38

This 2-liter tourer was an improvement over the Type 30, which it replaced. It had the tubular front axle, which the 30 did not, and its engine was quieter and more reliable. It was normally fitted with Rudge wire wheels and was the first Bugatti chassis to have a centrally located gear-shift lever. It is usually pointed out that the 38 was a cross between the Type 30 and the Type 44, which later replaced the 38.

In 1927 a Type 38A "Grand Sport" appeared. It was a super version of the 38 and had a full roller-bearing crankshaft.

Type 39

In 1926 a 1.5-liter displacement limit was adopted for Grand Prix racing. Bugatti modified the Type 35 engine's bore and stroke to yield a displacement of 1,492 c.c. or 91.0 cubic inches. A Roots blower was added, after the manner of the Type 35C, and the Type 39A was established.

Type 40

The Type 40 was brought out in 1926 as a replacement for

the Brescia *Modifié*, a conveyance for those with expensive appetites and lean wallets. With four-seater Grand Sport body the car sold for a mere $1,770, delivered in England. Its four-cylinder engine was essentially that of the Type 37 but with coil instead of magneto ignition and with a lower compression ratio. The Type 40's acceleration times were not particularly exciting and its top speed was only about 75 m.p.h. But it had the matchless Bugatti handling qualities, design and workmanship.

The rarely encountered Type 40A was in production briefly during 1931. It used one cylinder block from a Type 49 engine, giving it a displacement of 99.3 cubic inches as compared with the 91.3 of the Type 40. Like the Type 49, it had three valves and two spark plugs per cylinder. It was the last four-cylinder Bugatti produced between the wars.

Type 41

This was *La Royale*, which is dealt with separately in the Classics Section.

Type 43

The Type 43 2.3-liter Grand Sport was said by one critic to have all the characteristics of a racing car with a touring body. This was not an inaccurate statement, since it used the same supercharged ball-and-roller-bearing engine as the 35B Grand Prix machine. The clearance limit for the rollers was, incidentally, $1/1,000$-in. and they required replacement about every 30,000 miles. The Type 43's tremendous acceleration, speed and flexibility were outstanding, and it had race-car steadiness at all speeds on all roads. Maximum speed was around 112 m.p.h. and one car was clocked from zero to 70 m.p.h. in 30 seconds. The tester placed the parked car in top gear and turned on switch and starter, the latter grinding the car forward until the engine took over. The car actually moved from a standstill to 82 m.p.h. in 54 seconds, in fourth gear all the way.

Type 44

All authorities agree that this nine-main-bearing straight-eight was Ettore's first effort at producing a thoroughly refined, comfortable and generally useful touring machine. The sporting qualities were still there in force, but emphasis had shifted to silence, ease of control and top-gear flexibility. This was a model that women (strong, game ones) could drive, which was a lot to say for a Bugatti. The three-valve, single-camshaft engine had a displacement of 182.6 cubic inches and shared with the Type 49 the distinction of taking its cam drive from the center of the crankshaft. Top speed was in the 85-to-90 m.p.h. bracket.

Type 46

This car, which appeared in 1929, continued the Molsheim effort to produce models the average citizen could drive and enjoy. It sought to do the job with plenty of displacement and torque and was actually a smaller Royale, with 326.5 cubic inches. A modification — the 46S — was introduced in 1931. It used a 2.3-liter-engine's blower, and the compression ratio was consequently reduced. However, the small supercharger's output was so modest that the unblown 46 version was the better-performing car. The Type 46 was a classic example of Ettore's indifference to mere "detail": the rear axle and crankshaft had to be removed for inspection of the valves.

Type 47

This fabulous chassis appeared in both sports and racing form but did not go far. The engine was its outstanding feature. It consisted of two 1.5-liter straight-eight block assemblies mounted on a common crankcase which contained a nine-roller-bearing crankshaft for each block. The entire power plant, including gearing-together of the dual cranks, carried right back to the old Bugatti 16-cylinder aircraft engine. The car was intended to compete at Le Mans but did not.

Type 49

This model was another step in the Bugatti trend toward relatively quiet and luxurious passenger cars. It also anticipated the bore, stroke, displacement and performance of the Type 57, yet to come. It employed the old three-valve layout, had a displacement of 198.8 cu. in. and was remarkable only for its use of dual-coil ignition with two plugs per cylinder. It was certainly one of the best-performing cars in its rather dignified class, with top speed between 85 and 90 m.p.h. and an ability to move from zero to 60 m.p.h. in 20.2 seconds. *The Motor* reported in a road test: "The brakes . . . proved to be exceptionally good . . . better than is usually considered possible: 23 feet from 30 m.p.h. and 50 feet from 40 m.p.h. We found that many main road bends, which on the average car we would treat with the utmost respect, could be rounded on the Bugatti at such high speeds that it would be wise not to quote them in this article. There are very, very few cars capable of equalling this performance."

Type 50

According to W. F. Bradley, *le Patron's* sensitive and perceptive biographer, it was Ettore's study of an American Miller racing engine that finally caused him to decide in favor of dual overhead camshafts and hemispherical combustion chambers. Thus a full-circle was completed, because Harry Miller had derived much of the inspiration for his straight-eight from Ettore's 16-cylinder aircraft engine. Miller, who built the carburetors and fuel pumps for Ettore's engines, had worked on and tested them extensively at the old Duesenberg plant.

As much as possible of the old straight-cut purity was carried over into the Type 50, Ettore's first twin-cam power plant. It had 295.4 cubic inches' displacement and like all double-overhead-cam Bugattis, two valves per cylinder. Coil ignition was used, and a large, two carb Roots blower which was pronounced the most silent-operating ever developed. The crankshaft ran in nine main bearings and a three-speed transmission formed a unit with the differential housing.

The acceleration of these cars was truly memorable in any gear and a touring model was able to run up and down the range of five-to-112 m.p.h. in top gear with complete smoothness. However, front-end heaviness made these cars lethally unsafe in road races and their otherwise-promising competition potentialities were not exploited. The same chassis, blower-deleted, was introduced in 1932 as the Type 50T. With its longer wheelbase and modest top speed of 100 m.p.h. it did not tend to get its drivers into trouble.

Type 51

This was a variation on the Type 35B and was Ettore's first

Grand Prix car to utilize dual camshafts and V-inclined valves. Like the 35B, it was supercharged and had the full ball-and-roller-bearing lower end. In the same year, 1931, the Type 51A was brought out. It was identical to the 51 except for a much-reduced stroke which dropped the 51's piston displacement from 138.5 cubic inches to 91.0.

Type 54

This was another supercharged 4.9-liter racing machine, like the Type 50. It shared the 50's defect of poor weight distribution, was good for 140 m.p.h. or better but could hardly be controlled at 130. As a racing project the Type 54 was retired and the engines diverted to Type 50T tourers.

Type 55

This Bugatti was undoubtedly one of the finest sports cars ever built anywhere. The Type 55 was powered by a very slightly de-tuned version of the full ball-and-roller-bearing Type 51 supercharged engine installed in a Type 54 Grand Prix chassis. The performance of the beautiful Type 55 roadster was all one might expect from a road machine with such a racing heritage. Top speed was about 50 m.p.h. in first gear, 75 in second, 100 in third, and around 115 in top gear. Acceleration in all gears was equally good. Zero to 60 m.p.h. could be achieved in 11 seconds. The Type 55 was a Bugatti connoisseur's Bugatti.

Type 57

One of the most successful and desirable Bugattis of all time was the Type 57 and its several variants. It was still a relatively fierce mount to manage by normal standards, but one expects that of a thoroughbred. The 57's design, in which Ettore's intelligent and highly practical son Jean made many decisions, filled the requirements of a broader segment of sporting motorists than any previous Molsheim product. With a chassis price that ran as low as $2,860, many could afford the car. The temperament that had caused countless Bugattis to be as heartily cursed as they were loved was almost entirely gone. Engine and chassis were convenient to maintain and speed ranging from good to record-breaking could be had simply by paying for the appropriate degree of tune.

The chassis amounted to an elongated Grand Prix Bugatti, with tubular front axle, cable-operated brakes, reversed quarter-elliptic rear springs and worm-and-wheel steering. The basic engine was a beautifully made and finished gear-driven double-overhead-cam, in-line integral-head eight. With a displacement of 198.7 cubic inches it delivered 135 b.hp. The disc-web crankshaft was, as usual, turned from a solid steel billet and ran in six (two at the flywheel end) plain main bearings. This engine represented a conservative summation of all the vast Bugatti experience with Grand Prix, sports and touring cars. Retention of the non-synchromesh four-speed gearbox and provision of a far from soft, single-plate clutch demanded a moderate amount of driver skill, while the incomparable Bugatti handling qualities and fast-revving, high-torque engine kept the driver far from boredom.

The 57 Tourer, introduced in 1934, was followed by the 57S and 57T in 1935. The Type 57S proved to the world in a most dramatic manner the remarkable development possibilities of the newest Bugatti touring chassis. The wheelbase was shortened from 130 to 117.5 inches, compression ratio was increased from 6.2 to 8.3, valve timing was changed and power output was raised to 185 b.hp. at 5,500 r.p.m. This chassis, with two-seater sports body, broke 14 International Class C records in 1936 ranging from 135.42 m.p.h. for one hour to 123.93 m.p.h. for 24 hours — some of the most memorable figures ever achieved by a production automobile. The car went on to win the Le Mans 24 Hour Race in 1937 with an average speed of 85.07 m.p.h.

Jean Bugatti designed some of the most beautiful bodies in the history of the marque for the Type 57S chassis. Notable among them were the magnesium alloy *Atlantic* coupe, with fenders and bodies assembled by means of riveted flanges, and with oval-outline pointed radiator, and the equally aerodynamic *Atalante* coupe, with its horseshoe radiator and flange-less aluminum body.

The Type 57T, also brought out in 1935, was a slightly modified 57S intended for Tourist Trophy-type competition.

In 1937 "the finest road machine ever made" appeared — the Roots-blown Type 57SC. It was the 57S chassis with compression ratio brought back to 6.2-to-one, as in the original Type 57. The 57SC's power output was quoted as high as 220 b.hp. at 5,500 r.p.m. and top speed was generally agreed to be in the 130-to-135 m.p.h. range. It was equipped with a beefed-up clutch to handle the much higher torque and its acceleration was invariably described as "terrific."

The Type 57C was the ultimate development of the Type 57. Supercharged, it appeared in 1938. A two-seater version, running on 80-octane fuel, won the 1939 Le Mans race with an average of 86.85 m.p.h. for the 24 hours, during which the hood was never lifted and there was no appreciable brake wear. It was a perfectly standard production chassis, except for use of an oil cooler and a rear axle ratio giving the 142 m.p.h. at 5,000 r.p.m.

From the beginning to the end of his career, Ettore Bugatti produced outstanding high-performance automobiles which owed almost nothing to "the outside world," but everything to their sole designer. Bugatti's clarity and originality of engineering thought, and the smoothly flowing continuity with which his life's work evolved are among the many measures of the man's creative greatness. If he did not alter the course of history like Daimler, Maybach and Ford it was because those others were professional, industry-minded engineers, whereas throughout his life *le Patron* was an artist.

CHENARD-WALCKER'S LONG, RESPECTABLE HIStory stretched from 1900 to the early Thirties, and was largely one of sturdy middle-class automobiles which had little to do with competition — except for a short, mad period in

| CHENARD-WALCKER |

the Twenties, when the company produced some weird and quite successful racing machines.

They came in four sizes: the 2,978-c.c. (181.6 cu. in.) Three Liter and the 1,973-c.c. (120.4 cu. in.) Two Liter, both of which had four-cylinder overhead-camshaft engines; a four-liter straight-eight and a four-cylinder 1,100-c.c. (67.1 cu. in.) with a stream-lined, beetle-backed body.

Some of each of these models had excellent four-wheel brakes of the Perrot type, with Hallot servo-mechanism driven from the transmission. Others, probably to reduce unsprung weight, had no rear-wheel brakes at all. The front brakes were enormous and obtrusively apparent through the wire wheels, and the car at side view had a peculiarly naked and unbalanced appearance. This did not help the looks of the earliest cars of these series, which were distinctly ugly and were justly, if irreverently, known as the "Wart Hog" Chenards.

The bodies improved in subsequent models, however, and finally attained a bizarre beauty that was quite compelling. One of the handsomest Chenards was the Three Liter sports-four-seater of 1925. It was just wide enough to seat two persons front and rear; the side panels tapered down toward the running boards and swept back to form a pointed "boat tail." It had meager but graceful peaked fenders and vee windshields for both front- and back-seat passengers.

Chenard's interest in unusual bodies was most apparent in the 1100-c.c., which was equipped with slab-sided "aerodynamic" coachwork much like that which Bugatti and Voisin used at the French Grand Prix at Tours in 1923 and discarded soon after. The 1100's engine was no less remarkable than its body. As described by *The Autocar* it had a two-bearing crankshaft and "vertical valves operated by push-rods and rockers, and in addition a rotary exhaust valve, with two openings for each cylinder, turning at one-quarter engine speed. As most of the exhaust was eliminated at the bottom of the stroke, the exhaust valve in the head was very small and the intake valve particularly big." These cars were very successful in competition and won, among other things, the 1,100-c.c. class at Boulogne and the Boillot Cup in 1926, and the 1,100-c.c. class of the Spanish Grand Prix in 1926 against O.M., Mercedes and Peugeot.

The larger-displacement Chenard-Walckers became famous primarily at Le Mans. A Three Liter won the 24 Hours in 1923, and a Two Liter placed third in 1924. These performances, plus that of the 1100 c.c. in 1925 won Chenard the Biennial Cup for 1923-1924 and the Triennial Cup in 1925, awards given for the best cumulative record over the given number of years. With these and the 1100-c.c. laurels, Chenard-Walcker retired from racing and went back to building good solid cars for the middle-class market.

During the thirties no car in the world was quite as accurate a midway point between sports and classic as the Delage. The bodies usually fitted were extreme examples of the long-hood, low-chassis classics, some of them with sufficient space in the engine compartment for a straight-16 rather than the straight-eight which made up the top end of the Delage array of models. Yet during the same era there was a six-cylinder sports chassis that won the Tourist Trophy race in 1938. This chassis furnished the basis for a team of cars which won their class in 1-2-3 order at Le Mans in 1949.

DELAGE

The first Delage appeared in 1906, and almost at once the marque was living a double life, running a team of racing cars of special design and producing a series of passenger designs. The racing cars had a number of successes in the Twenties, one of the most notable being the acquisition of the title of Champion of the World in 1927. On the passenger-car side there were fours and sixes until 1929 when the fours were dropped.

The earliest postwar six-cylinder passenger engine was a push-rod-operated-overhead-valve with 3.15 x 5.91 inches bore and stroke, 276 cubic inches displacement. Dual ignition, magneto-supplied, and single carburetion were used. Reports spoke of 80 to 84 m.p.h. top speeds from the developed 88 b.hp. at 2,380 r.p.m., an excellent showing from an engine of that size in 1921.

Eighty m.p.h. was also the advertised speed of the 1930 straight-eight, though *The Autocar* could only find 72.2 m.p.h. in the large-wheelbase model tested. A Supersports model utilizing basically the same engine in a shorter chassis was introduced two years later, and this car was capable of 100 m.p.h.

In 1932 there were three engines, the eight-cylinder D8, and two sixes, the D6 and smaller DS. That year, also, the eight's rear suspension was changed from semi-elliptics to double quarter-elliptics. Another suspension change appeared on the D611 the following year, independent front suspension by wishbones and a single-transverse-leaf spring. Like the rest of the Delages, this small sporty car had pushrod-operated overhead valves, constructed in an unusual manner. The valve spring returned the valve to closed position through a lever arm, one end of which operated on a collar on the valve stem when the offset spring exerted force against the other end. The pressure exerted to close the valve could thus be varied by changing the location of the pivot point of the lever arm or by changing the spring pressure.

Between 1933 and the beginning of World War II, several modifications were made in the Delage line. The straight-eight engine was bored out to 3.15 inches and destroked to 4.21 inches, the net result being an increase in displacement to 262 cubic inches. A sports version, the D8120, could be counted upon for 100 m.p.h. though its weight was 4,250 pounds, a considerable increase over the earlier 100-m.p.h. straight-eight. Three six-cylinder chassis were made, the D6-60, D6-70 and D6-80. The D6-70 is the car which won the TT and showed so well at Le Mans. In racing trim it used three S.U. carburetors and, like most of the stock models, was equipped with the Cotal electrically-controlled gearbox.

After World War II Delage made a heroic attempt to come back to prominence, but a series of difficulties kept production down to little more than a trickle. The one car that was presented to the world market was a dressed-up version of the old, successful D6-70, now called the Olympia.

DELAHAYE

A FELLOW MEMBER WITH DELAGE IN THE G.F.A., a French auto combine, was an even older marque, Delahaye. Founded in 1896, the firm began its career with road-racing machines, then turned to passenger cars until 1936, when the first of the medium-size, six-cylinder sports cars were made. In 1937 two sports types were in the catalogue, one the Coupe des Alpes, the other the Competition. The Coupe des Alpes, though equipped with a slightly smaller engine than the Competition, could clock 100 m.p.h. and — according to a test reported in *The Autocar* — accelerated from zero to 60 m.p.h. in 13.7 seconds. With the convertible-coupe body, the Coupe des Alpes weighed less than 3,000 pounds. Though it was a touring car as well as a sports car, the independent front suspension and semi-elliptic rear were designed for stability at high speeds and in corners. Steering was quite abrupt — 1¾ turns lock to lock. The engine was an orthodox, pushrod ohv, with four main bearings and three carburetors.

In competition the most notable Delahaye sports-car victory was at Le Mans in 1938. There was a V-12 Delahaye during the late Thirties also, but it had a very brief span as a sports car before it was modified into a full racing machine. In a memorable event in England between private owners of high-performance equipment, one of the six-cylinder Delahayes beat a 2.9 Alfa Romeo and a Darracq in 1939.

The Delahayes of the post-World War II era were — like the Delage of the same period — close descendants of the pre-war designs. Types 135M, 135MS and 148L were all equipped with an engine of the same dimensions and technical features as the Competition model of 1937; types 175, 178 and 180 were similar to the bigger six-cylinder cars of the Thirties.

The two sports models — 135 MS and 175 — were nicely scaled for speed and maneuverability. For the 1952 model year, a modified Type 135M known as the Type 235 was issued in small quantities. The engine had been hopped-up to 150 horsepower, and the chassis and suspension had been changed slightly to handle the increased speed.

In America, few of the sports Delahayes and Delages exist. What we see over here are the Saoutchik or Figoni et Falaschi interpretations of what a good French high-performance car should look like. Some of these creations have been from the chrome-and-curves school of design, some have been more modest. All, however, differ widely from the accepted sports-car-ideal, yet the chassis are still distinctly sporting in dimensions and performance. Even in the postwar period, these two famous French names could not quite decide what they wanted to represent.

Fred and Augie Duesenberg were conservative men. When they built the Model A Duesenberg they designed one of the most potent and portent-loaded chassis of its or any time. Then they dressed it in a body that was far more suitable for elderly dowagers and cap-wearing, fiftyish males than for the well-heeled sheiks and flappers who were buying speedy transportation in the "Roaring 'Twenties." The Model A was an engineering *tour de force* and a financial failure.

DUESENBERG

The 11 American manufacturers who for years before and during the Model A's lifespan bought Duesenberg engines to power their own cars did not make the Duesenberg brothers' mistake. They equipped their machines with appropriately rakish bodies and the results were such dashing combinations of fleet performance and appearance as the "Racy" Revere; the light, sporty Roamer; and the Argonne, Biddle and Meteor, with their sharply pointed Mercedes-like radiators.

The engine that all these cars of the late 'teens and Twenties used was based upon a four-cylinder power plant that Fred and his younger brother designed in 1912. Fred was 33 then, an intuitive engineer who had had only a rudimentary education and had been designing and building cars for nine years. In 1913 Fred and Augie established the Duesenberg Motor Company in St. Paul, Minnesota, and began to refine and exploit their engine.

It was a radical, weird powerplant, attracting attention wherever it appeared because of its ungainly looking valve gear. The combustion chambers had a rectangular shape and were placed vertically "on edge" over the cylinders in the head, which was cast integrally with the block. Mounted horizontally in the right side of these chambers were two valves per cylinder; a spark plug was threaded horizontally into the opposite wall of each chamber. The beauty of this design, as opposed to the rambling combustion chambers of the L- and T-head engines then in general use, was its manner of creating short flame travel in the compact space and of focusing all the expansive force of the burning fuel upon the head of the piston instead of upon remote, "dead walls."

The horizontal valves were operated by vertical rocker arms about a foot long. They were generally referred to as "walking beams" and became a hallmark of early Duesenberg design. The beams had an "I" cross section, the web of which was extensively drilled to reduce reciprocating weight. The lower tip of each beam rode on the lobe of a crankcase-mounted camshaft and the upper tip bore directly on a valve stem and was fitted with an adjusting screw.

This engine's crankcase was a one-piece aluminum "barrel" casting. The crankshaft, which ran in two large ball bearings, was necessarily of heavy, rugged construction and was installed in the case from the rear instead of from below.

On the race tracks, this engine did not set the world on fire but it did enable Eddie Rickenbacker to bring his Duesenberg into 10th place at Indianapolis in 1914. Two similar cars took fifth and

10th in the 1915 "500," then second, sixth, eighth, and ninth the following year. These 1916 cars had two camshafts and a set of rockers and valves on each side of the engine, giving it four valves per cylinder.

In 1916 the Duesenberg brothers had reason to move their manufacturing activities to Elizabeth, N. J. and the walking-beam engine, well-suited to light aircraft, got them their first war contracts. It was in 1918 that the builders of the Biddle automobile decided that the publicity and performance to be gained by using Duesenberg fours in their cars made a golden opportunity. Their decision was promptly followed by the makers of Argonne, Kenworthy, Mercury, Meteor, Premocar, Revere, Roamer, Shad-Wyck, Shaw Colonial, and Wolverine. Roamer continued to use the Duesenberg four until 1927.

But something had happened in 1917 to make Fred and Augie Duesenberg look on the four-cylinder engine as a thing of the past. They received a United States Government contract to manufacture the new Bugatti 16-cylinder, 500-horsepower aircraft engine. Complete drawings, a small technical staff, and a sample engine were sent to the Elizabeth plant from the Bugatti wartime headquarters in Paris.

Fred Duesenberg, intuitive engineer, fully comprehended and appreciated the ideas and methods of artist-engineer Bugatti, some of whose peculiar concepts were to remain with Fred permanently.

The Bugatti engine was composed of two separate straight-eight engines mounted perfectly parallel to one another, on a single crankcase. Their two crankshafts were geared to a central gear which was part of the propeller hub. Each engine had a single overhead camshaft with three cams and three valves per cylinder. During the year that Fred worked with and tested these engines he became convinced that his first creative act, once the war ended, would be the designing of an original in-line-eight racing-car engine.

Their enthusiasm for four-cylinder equipment dead, the brothers sold their plant to Willys and manufacturing rights to the walking-beam engine to the Rochester Motors Company. Their plan was to build a new factory in Indianapolis, then the heart of both the automobile industry and the racing sport. But this took time to accomplish and meanwhile work was rushed ahead in Elizabeth. A drafting room was set up in Fred's home and the first Duesenberg straight-eights were designed with incredible speed and just as quickly built in the corner of a rented

garage. The first postwar Indianapolis race was held six months
after the signing of the Armistice, but in that time, Fred had
managed to build a team of cars from scratch.

The engines showed Bugatti influence in such matters as the
choice of a single overhead camshaft, three valves per cylinder,
and much greater valve-and-port area for the exhaust than for the
intake side. Instead of Bugatti's cam for every valve, Fred drove
his twin exhausts by means of a single, Y-shaped rocker arm — a
unit that often failed and later was deleted from the design. He
also used a scant three main bearings for his crankshaft, the rear
main being a large ball race. The crankshaft drove the camshaft
by means of a vertical shaft and bevel gears. The crankshaft was
of the "four-four" type, laid out as though two single-plane four-
cylinder cranks had been joined together, with their planes 90
degrees apart.

Although the Duesenberg straight-eight racing engine was not
successful in its first appearance at Indianapolis in 1919, it shared
domination of National Championship racing for the next ten years
with one other car, the Miller. Harry Miller was inspired by the
Duesenberg engine to build his first straight-eight, which ultimately evolved into the famous Offenhauser four.

The Duesenberg brothers, having seen several passenger-car
manufacturers base profitable enterprises upon the walking-beam
engine, decided to ladle themselves a share of the gravy in 1920.
With their reputation, the experience and know-how on which it
was based, plus their latest, ultra-modern engine design, it looked
as though they could not miss.

Their prototype of the Model A Duesenberg was completed in
time for the New York Auto Salon of December, 1920 and small-
scale series production began shortly after. The Model A chassis
was an up-scaled version of the racing car, the basic differences
being wheelbases of 134 and 100 inches and displacements of 183
(1920-1922) and 260 cubic inches respectively. Cam drive was
the same for both engines, but the A used only two V-inclined
valves per cylinder. The tubular connecting rods, three-bearing
crankshafts, cooling and lube systems were identical except for
scale. So were the tubular front axles, rear-axle and torque-tube
layouts, steering, and transmissions. Four-wheel hydraulic brakes
had been introduced on Duesenberg race cars and had helped
Jimmy Murphy score the first and only American victory in a
major European road race, when he won the Grand Prix of France
in 1921. These brakes were also offered on the Model A.

Thus the Model A Duesenberg was an engineering prophecy, an instigator of trends that were to sweep the industry. It was the United States' first passenger car with a straight-eight engine, first with four-wheel brakes, first with hydraulic brakes; later it was first with balloon tires.

The chassis was a legitimate masterpiece, a private conveyance for the engineering connoisseur. There was one flaw in the Model A: style. Fred and Augie Duesenberg knew that their costly passenger car could be afforded only by people of means and these, they evidently assumed, were conservative as a class. So the Model A chassis, appealing strongly to the young in heart, was fitted with staid, refined coachwork, almost devoid of any dash. As a marketable package, the car was self-contradictory and output ceased in 1926, when a total of about 70 A's had been sold. It was a technical hit and a commercial flop, with an impact upon the automotive world that was out of all proportion to its meagre production. Better things were in store for the marque.

Erret Lobban Cord bought the company in late 1926 and, combining his businessman's genius with the Duesenberg brothers' engineering talent, created America's greatest classic car. While this dynamic monolith — the Model J Duesenberg — was making luxury-car history the "pure strain" Model A was given an extension of its lease on life, a chance to demonstrate its mettle to the world. The opportunity was created when, from 1930 through 1934, relaxations in the FIA international-competition formula permitted an upping of the American National Championship displacement limit from 91.5 to 366 cubic inches. Cars powered by production-model engines were urged to compete.

This made big-time racing possible for the first time for many limited-budget competitors. Model A Duesenberg engines, having been detuned racing designs to start with, were seized as power-plants for many of the new "production-engined" racing cars. Three Model A-powered machines ran at the Speedway in 1930, Bill Cummings finishing fifth in his. In 1931, 14 cars with Model A engines reported to the Indianapolis garage area. Six qualified and Jimmie Gleason brought his A-Dues home sixth, four "pukka" race cars and a souped-up, big-displacement Studebaker ahead of him. In 1932, Ira Hall was one of the top qualifiers in his Dues A track job at 114.2 m.p.h. and he finished seventh. In 1933 four of the A's made the grade, Hall qualifying Denny Duesenberg's Model A at 115.7 m.p.h. But these engines were finally feeling their age, and their best showing was made by Willard Prentice's car in the 13th spot, with a 500-mile average of 93.6 m.p.h. Duesenberg was through at the Speedway but the J and SJ models were earning a new kind of glory for the marque.

DU PONT

THE DU PONT FAMILY, WHICH HAS A REPUTATION for accomplishing what it sets out to do, took an interest in building dashing automobiles in 1921. The cars were assembled at Wilmington, Delaware, reputedly under the direction of E. Paul du Pont. Aside from the fact that the chassis had a 123-inch wheelbase and used a four-cylinder L-head engine with bore and stroke of 3.94 × 5.0, little is known of these few-off, early cars.

The marque was brought to the attention of a discriminating few in the late Twenties, when New York fine-car dealer A. J. Miranda ran airy two-page ads in *Fortune* describing his wares: Maybach-Zeppelin, Delage and du Pont. Then early in 1929 came the announcement in horsey magazines that Miranda and Charles Moran Jr. — drivers who were gentlemen to the marrow — were entering a new du Pont in the Le Mans 24 Hour Race.

This entry, designed by Briggs Weaver (later of the Briggs Cunningham organization), revealed an acute understanding of the sort of coachwork that had been proved most desirable for the great French race, and it was one of the most imposingly beautiful sports cars ever built on this side of the Atlantic. The narrow four-place body bore a moderately close resemblance to the Vanden Plas Bentleys of the time, but the du Pont was more graceful, with raked door lines and a pointed boat tail. It also had a noble pointed radiator, knock-off wire wheels, cycle fenders, two huge hood straps, and an immaculate white paint job.

If the du Pont had run as well as it looked, it would have won the Grand Prix d'Endurance hands down. But its 322-cubic inch L-head Continental engine was rated as putting out 75 b.hp. at 3,000 r.p.m. — precious little urge for a machine that weighed in the neighborhood of 3,500 pounds even before a few dozen gallons of fuel had been taken aboard. Furthermore, it was unstable in the turns and when the massive white car had covered just over 190 miles of the race, something happened. The "official" report was that the compulsory ballast had broken through the floor boards and put a kink in the drive shaft (du Pont did not use torque tubes). There were observers, however, who claimed that the car's gearbox had jammed. So much for the Moran-Miranda overseas campaign.

It was a sad disappointment to the French, who liked the entry's name.

On the strength of this adventure, du Pont Motors Inc. introduced a Le Mans model in 1930. *Country Life* reported: "The du Pont Le Mans model, with a tiny tonneau substituted for the racing fishtail, clearly should receive a laurel wreath. It isn't just a streamlined job tricked up to be sold as something awfully fast; it is actually a racing car. That is, it has distinguished itself at Le Mans (hence the name), and is due to perform at Indianapolis."

Rather than break the spell of this prose, we will anticipate the Speedway venture with a post-event quote: "In this race . . . . there was one superb sporting gesture. The du Ponts entered a car that could be purchased in any of their sales rooms. It was a stock car. They knew they couldn't win the race. In fact, the best they hoped for was to come in about tenth, with the credit of lapping the track at the speed of 100 m.p.h. To make the thing still more perfect, they had back of the wheel a gentleman driver, Charles Moran . . . . It was one of the most sportsmanlike attempts that American racing has seen since the old Vanderbilt Cup days on Long Island."

The attempt may have been sporting and perfect, but the stock chassis with typical Indianapolis racing body weighed in at the Garage Area at 3,350 pounds, still powered by its big, heavy, 75-b.hp. engine. Only one car out of 38 starters had a slower qualifying speed than the du Pont's 89.733 m.p.h. Mr. Moran kissed the wall in the 22nd lap and thus brought the marque's racing history to a close.

Du Pont cars before 1928 generally had an uninspired appearance. Styling improved markedly in '28 and immensely in '29, and continued on a high level until the firm suspended business in 1933. The most noteworthy du Pont bodies of this period — and they rank with the best in American automobile history — were the narrow four-seaters and the doorless, two-place speedsters. These bodies were mounted on top of naked frame rails and were made both with boat- and turtle-backs. Aside from looking "all hood" the stunning feature shared by both speedsters was the one-piece fender idea. Each front and rear fender consisted of a single, gracefully flowing and narrow, sheet of aluminum mounted away from the body and giving an illusion of lightness to the entire car's appearance. Anyone who has seen one of these gorgeous cars will never forget it. Standing still, they suggested 150-m.p.h. speedometers with bent needles.

To alleviate the glare of mediocrity that confronted the raiser of the hood of one of these Series G du Ponts, the makers crafted a huge polished aluminum casket which was screwed down over the cast iron from which the vehicle's horsepower emerged. To the uninitiated, it might seem to conceal a fairyland of gadgetry. But salesmen, when taken in hand by both lapels, would admit that this device was intended to keep moisture away from the wiring.

If the du Pont chassis was not a great achievement, the bodies it wore during its last years were. Only 175 cars were made in 1929, 125 in '30, fewer in the remaining period. But if more of them had been made and seen their sheer good looks would automatically have gained them a place alongside the Bearcat, Raceabout and Continental.

| FRAZER-NASH |

THE FRAZER-NASH AND ITS PARENT G.N. WERE cars with hair on their chests. They were made in small numbers, each unit tailored to the requirements of an individual purchaser capable of salivating at the thought of drifting fast bends in narrow lanes without a differential. Archie Frazer-Nash did not make great numbers of cars — only a great name. The F.-N.'s aggressive supporters stoutly proclaimed that its chain-drive final transmission was "unique, but unquestionably the most efficient," and looked with pity upon the world of out-of-step automobile manufacturers who had capitulated to the effete if tidy shaft drive. As for the souls who bought the "chrome-Niagara gin palaces," they were hopelessly lost. They heard no music in the jingling whir of the chains, they were cowed by raining grease,

The Shelsley Frazer-Nash of 1935, powered by a supercharged version of the traditional 4-cylinder engine, was notable for its external exhaust.

Autocar

and not one in 10,000 would know how to cope with an involuntary downchange of gear at 60 m.p.h.

The beginning was in 1910, when Captain Archie Frazer-Nash and H. R. "Bill" Godfrey (who later played a principal role with H.R.G.) became interested in the then-current demand for "four-wheeled motorcycles." The nascent light-car cult demanded a vehicle that was cheap to buy and operate and as lively and manageable as the average 'cycle. Godfrey and Frazer-Nash, both ardent motor sportsmen, sailed into the problem with gusto, built their first car in 1911 and, using their initials, named it the G.N.

The little car weighed all of 950 pounds, had a simple wooden frame, quarter elliptic springs front and rear, drive by a combination of belts and chains, and power from an air-cooled J.A.P. two-cylinder motorcycle engine. These cars sold well on sight and were quickly replaced with an improved model having straight channel-section frame rails. This was followed in late 1914 by a "Grand Prix" model with rear wheels driven by four chains, no belts. These cars weighed about 900 pounds and, thanks to good power-to-weight ratio, accelerated as well as they handled — far above average. They found an eager market which was kept panting by the exploits of Archie Frazer-Nash, who earned the reputation of England's best racing driver from before the war until the middle Twenties.

Of course, Archie drove a G.N. From 1919 until 1924 this man-car team was seldom beaten in its own 1,100-c.c. class and Frazer-Nash had the pleasure of winning more unlimited-class

races during that period than any other man. He held many
Brooklands records and, for a while, almost all records for every
important British hill-climb. When he gave up driving in competition Basil Davenport and his G.N. "Spider" carried on brilliantly
for the marque. Not without reason, English authority Gregor
Grant called the G.N. "the first genuine light sports car." And
John Bolster, England's leading expert on "trials specials," credits
the examples set by Frazer-Nash, Davenport and their cars, with
being "the inspiration that has produced our finest specials."

In 1922, G.N. assets changed hands and Godfrey left, eventually to become an initial in H.R.G. Frazer-Nash left at the
same time. G.N.'s new management "brought the car up to date"
by converting to shaft drive and a water-cooled engine, then back
to chain drive when the more conventionally-engineered cars
only collected showroom dust. The marque vanished after 1928.

To be or not to be in chains was not a question that bothered
Archie Frazer-Nash. He was the prophet of a small but ardent
sect which held that there was no substitute for chain drive and
could point to a nearly unparalleled racing record to prove the
point. Promptly after leaving G.N. Archie began designing an
all-new chain-drive car embodying every improvement he had
learned and dreamed of during the 13 previous G.N. years. The
result was the first car to bear the Frazer-Nash name. It was
introduced in 1924 and hit the English automotive world with
bombshell impact.

The light chassis, actually that of a racing machine, sold for
about $1,800 and, fitted with a two-place body, was guaranteed
to do 85 m.p.h. A 1,496-c.c. (91.3 cu. in.) Plus-Power, four-
cylinder, pushrod-overhead-valve engine supplied urge to a propeller shaft which terminated at a bevel-gear housing, without
differential, mounted roughly two feet ahead of the rear axle. A
countershaft fitted with four sliding sprockets ran, axlelike,
through the bevel box. Each sprocket had a dog clutch which,
by means of an outside-mounted gearshift lever alongside the
driver, could be engaged or disengaged with fixed dogs (actually
gear teeth) on the countershaft. The rear axle itself was a solid
tube on which four larger sprockets were mounted, chain-driven
by the sprockets on the countershaft. Of course, only one chain
and one pair of sprockets were used to drive the vehicle, the various sets of chains and sprockets providing three forward speeds
and a reverse. Occasional enthusiasts chose to eliminate the reverse gearing entirely and substituted a fourth forward speed.

The frame was considerably shorter than the wheelbase, front and rear axles being located by the tips of quarter-elliptic springs and radius arms. The front axle was a simple, straight tube. As much as minimum weight was emphasized, the entire lower side of the chassis was under-panned, which must have made an important reduction in wind drag.

This utterly unique chassis design changed little until the outbreak of war, when the chain-drive F.-N.'s finally were retired. The most important modifications were always in engine specification, different power plants from perhaps half a dozen manufacturers, including Meadows and Anzani, being used in these cars, which were often supercharged. In 1933 the firm designed its own single-overhead-cam, four-cylinder, 91-cubic inch power unit.

Regardless of engine employed, all these F.-N.'s had powerful personality that was specifically their own and around which loyalties grew that were equalled only by the more ardent *Bugattisti*. The singing of the chains that gave the cars a distinct character appealed to sporting young bloods as well as to many oldtimers who had always looked askance at the universal swing of the industry to shaft drive. The Nashes had lightning-quick steering, fast shifting, really good acceleration. They were a joy to drive, if you happened to have a healthy streak of the bronc-buster in your disposition. The fact that a man was a "chain-ganger" automatically marked him as an alert, virile type. It took those qualities to cope with the sudden clutch, the often-tricky transmission, the differential-less cornering.

The Nash's spartan spirit was never disguised by inappropriate coachwork. The bodies were invariably of aluminum — narrow, light and fast-looking. The speed was there. The 1930 Fast Tourer moved from 10 to 30 m.p.h. in 5.0 seconds, had a top of 70 m.p.h. The Super Sports of the same year did 10 to 30 in 4.2, had a maximum speed of 77. The 1932 Nuerburg supercharged model could reach 108 m.p.h. easily. The 1933 TT Replica would do zero to 60 in 16 seconds and 87 m.p.h. flat-out with its 91-inch, double-overhead-cam Blackburne engine. The 1934 Sports Tourer with six-cylinder, double-overhead-cam, 1,657-c.c. (101.1 cu. in.) engine had similar top speed, would get to 60 from standstill in 14 seconds.

H. J. "Aldy" Aldington was apprenticed to Archie Frazer-Nash in the early Twenties. In 1927, the opportunity occurred for Aldy and his brother, W. H. "Bill," to acquire the firm. They shared

Archie's view of how a sports vehicle should be constructed, were as competition-minded as the founder, kept his policies intact and used his initials for the name of their new firm: A.F.N., Ltd.

In 1933, the Aldington brothers took an F.-N. team across the Channel to compete in the Alpine Trial. There they were exposed to and fascinated by the 91-cu.-in. German B.M.W. They promptly arranged for the license to produce B.M.W. cars in England and British-assembled Frazer-Nash B.M.W.'s began to appear on the market that same year. They are discussed fully in the chapter devoted to B.M.W. In 1936 the 1,971-c.c. (120.3 cu. in.) F.-N. B.M.W. Type 328 made its first racing appearance in Britain in the T.T. Race on the Ards Circuit. Honors included Team Prize, third overall, 1-2-3 in the 2-liter class and a new lap record. Although the marque had led a distinguished career in competition from 1925, when Clive Gallop won the Grand Prix des Voitures Légères at Boulogne in the F.-N., it was the German-designed product that brought F.-N. its greatest fame in international road races, hill-climbs, and mountain trials, as well as in British events. A full listing of F.-N. racing successes from 1933 to 1939 would easily fill this page.

In 1939, A.F.N. Ltd. was ready to introduce the first F.-N. B.M.W. cars manufactured entirely in England and to be called, simply, Frazer-Nash. The war interrupted these plans, but there was a bright future for F.-N. and the B.M.W. 328 engine in the postwar world.

H.C.S.

W HEN HARRY C. STUTZ SOLD HIS BEARCATS AND roadsters in 1919 he immediately made plans to produce an automobile of his own.

As the widely known guiding genius of one of America's foremost sports marques, he had no trouble setting up his project with backers and dealers — but unfortunately for him, and perhaps for the automotive world, he did not try to build another car like the Stutz. He concentrated on fortune rather than competition fame. His H.C.S. — as the new car was called — turned out to be a disappointment.

Introduced in the latter part of 1920, the H.C.S. hit the same depression that killed Leland's Lincoln chances. It was a blow from which the tiny firm never recovered, though production continued through 1924. That year the factory had an estimated 200 employees and the discouraging total of 18 dealer outlets. Production for the previous year had been only 750.

Engines for the H.C.S. were turned out by other firms. Weidley made a 3¾ × 5½, overhead-valve, four-cylinder engine for the low-price models; Midwest manufactured a 3½ × 5, six-cylinder plant for the more expensive line. Bodywork was not outstanding on either of the two models, though it was as good as most of the other small firms were producing in the same period. There was little about the car to remind the prospective buyer that its maker was the renowned Harry C. Stutz.

THE BIG, BARRELING 4½-LITER INVICTA OF THE Thirties was a handsome and intimidating sight. Its appearance was tough and massive. It had a roaring top speed of 100 m.p.h. and the immediate acceleration of a frightened horse, and it could be steered as delicately as a bicycle.

INVICTA

The 4½-liter came from a short but high-bred line of earlier Invictas. The first appeared in 1925, a six-cylinder, 2,692-c.c. (164.3 cu. in.) job which was replaced the next year by the more famous six-cylinder, 2,964-c.c. (180.9 cu. in.) car. This Invicta was equipped with two huge Solex carburetors, four-wheel brakes and a four-speed gearbox, and could leap from 10 to 30 m.p.h. in 3.2 seconds in low gear. It immediately set about creating some new long-distance speed records, including a world's 5,000-mile record at 70 m.p.h.

In 1928 the first 4½ liter Invicta was added to the line. It was a six-cylinder car too, with an actual displacement of 4,467 c.c. (272.6 cu. in.). The engine had overhead valves operated by vertical pushrods, two S.U. carburetors plus a small auxiliary starting carburetor, and dual ignition (both coil and magneto).

In 1930, this engine became available in "low" and "high"

chassis forms, the former being the rarer (only 77 were built) and better-handling version. In this chassis the frame was arched over the front axle and swept down to become underslung at the rear axle. Many of the innards customarily concealed by today's sports coachwork hung out starkly for all to see. The exhaust pipes were external. A big fuel tank sat exposed at the back of the car on the frame's side members. The honeycomb radiator core — unconcealed by shell or grille — was made small and compact so that the hood would be sufficiently low for the driver — who sat way down in the car a few inches above the road — to be able to see the corners when they came.

Invicta 4½-liter model was first sold in 1929, cost $4,775 for chassis alone.

Autocar

In both chassis versions the 4½-liter had acceleration that road testers of the time unanimously called "extraordinary." Invictas performed heroically in competition, particularly in long-distance events. The make won the 1931 Monte Carlo outright, and the next year took the first three places in the grueling Alpine Coupe des Glaciers.

Nevertheless, respected and coveted as it was, the 4½-liter cost about $5,000 for chassis alone and $7,000 with rakish sports body, and in 1931 the market for big expensive cars was getting slim. In that year Invicta began to experiment with smaller, less costly cars.

The first was a six-cylinder, 1,274-c.c. (77.8 cu. in.) model which carried a big 2,500-pound, four-seater body but was geared to give the same hair-raising acceleration as the 4½-liter cars, although top speed was sacrificed and did not go above the middle 60's. This little Invicta had a jewel-like engine, with a single chain-driven overhead camshaft and polished hemispherical combustion chambers. The exhaust valves were vertical and the intakes were inclined, an arrangement which gave the valve cover a peculiar slant. The frame was a rugged scaled-down version of the 4½-liter's, and with a good-looking touring body all this cost under $2,000.

In 1932 the "Small" Invicta was slightly increased in displacement to 1,498 c.c. (91.4 cu. in.), and in this form continued to be sold along with the 4½ until 1934. A few supercharged models were built during that time, and the firm also dabbled lightly in a twin-overhead-camshaft small car, but in 1934 Invicta production came to a dead halt. The organization changed over to production of a fast light car called the Comet, which never passed the prototype stage.

This might have been the end of Invicta, except for a final blaze of glory just after World War II. In 1947 the name was suddenly resurrected by a new business organization which began to market a remarkable car called the Invicta Black Prince. This new Invicta combined some of the most advanced design features of its time. The six-cylinder, 3-liter (183.1 cu. in.) engine had twin overhead camshafts and was equipped with three S.U. carburetors. Suspension was by torsion bars — independent all around — steering was by rack and pinion and transmission was automatic by means of the then-revolutionary Brockhouse hydraulic torque converter. Unfortunately this car carried a blistering $16,000 price tag and probably for that reason soon disappeared. Invicta met its second and probably final death.

Autocar

Invicta's Black Prince was the product of an unsuccessful effort to revive the marque between 1947 and 1949. It used dohc 6-cylinder engine, torque converter.

AMONG AMERICAN CARS OF THE TWENTIES THERE is frequently a very small distinction between the truly sporting and the merely sporty. Stutz's big, 1927, four-passenger speedster could hardly be called a sports car by modern definition, yet it made quite a score at Le Mans. Kissel's little "Gold Bug" looked infinitely more like a sports car, yet it did not appear at any of the world's racing courses. On the basis of performance, the Stutz deserves to be called a sports car; on the basis of its appearance, the Kissel can, without too much argument, be included under the same heading.

Never a major figure in the auto field, the Kissel was first introduced in 1906 and by 1923 had only 1,000 factory workers in the little plant in Hartford, Wisconsin. It was still a family enterprise, under the direction of President G. A. Kissel. All the cars in the line had the same basic engine, a Kissel-made, L-head six which was offered in two slightly different sizes. Both had the same bore, but the larger had a 5½-inch stroke while the stroke of the smaller was 5⅛ inches. It was the larger engine that powered the Gold Bug and the few other sporty bodies developed by the company. On the standard, 4.8-to-1 compression ratio the larger engine managed 61 b.hp. at 2,300 r.p.m. in 1923.

During the Kissel's career, a number of custom bodies were built for the larger chassis, one of them a speedster with the Weymann-type fabric body. Stock bodies were occasionally unusual, too. Before the Twenties there was a special Kissel with a removable hard top which could double as a phaeton for summer and a closed sedan for winter. Another was a sedan of ordinary four-door dimensions and design but equipped with only two doors, one for the driver on the left, one for the rear-seat passengers on the right. The Gold Bug had special seats which pulled out from the deck, providing room for one passenger to sit on each side of the car. That must have been the most uncomfortable and precarious seating arrangement of all time, out beyond the protection of the windshield and the body panels.

Kissel managed to withstand the reverses of 1921 and 1922, but as competition grew tougher later in the Twenties the little company began to slip. Even the introduction of a series of straight-eights in 1925 couldn't help much. By 1931 Kissel gave up completely.

I N 1935 W. O. BENTLEY LEFT THE BENTLEY CARS
to the elegant ministrations of Rolls-Royce and
began to look for new expressions for his skill and
intelligence. The niche he found was the technical directorship of Lagonda, Ltd., a firm that
had been building cars since the turn of the century and now
found itself in a design-and-policy crisis.

> **LAGONDA**

Lagonda, founded by an American named Wilbur Gunn who
died in 1920, had from 1900 moved from the manufacture of cycles
and three-wheelers to small family sedans and steadily toward true
high-performance machines. The make had its first taste of competition in 1921 with a special single-seater version of its production car which set a new 1½-liter record for the hour of 79.17
m.p.h. at the Brooklands track. This car had a 1,420-c.c. (86.7 cu.
in.), bored-and-stroked version of the four-cylinder, 1,090-c.c. (67
cu. in.), F-head engine that had been standard on Lagondas since
before World War I. The 1,420-c.c. size was further increased to
1,496 c.c. (91.3 cu. in.) and these became the engines which
powered Lagondas until 1925. The first such cars that were built
had appropriately light bodies, and became well-liked for their
vivid and nimble performance. One lady tooled about the English
countryside in a chauffeur-driven two-seater painted a bright
magenta to match her livingroom draperies. As the light-car competition from other manufacturers became more acute, however,
Lagonda countered by dressing the little car in heavier and more
luxurious bodies, until by 1925 it was so unwieldy that a top of 46
m.p.h. could be reached only with great difficulty. In that year
Lagonda management decided to abandon the 1½-liter engine
and came out with an entirely new 1,954-c.c. (118.2 cu. in.)
model.

The "Two Liter" four-cylinder engine was of true high-
performance design, with 90-degree-inclined overhead valves
operated by two overhead camshafts which were driven by a
double roller chain. The engine was fed by two downdraft S.U.
carburetors; in later forms both coil and magneto ignition were
provided instead of magneto alone, and from 1930 the car was
available with optional supercharger. Its top speed was around 80
m.p.h. unblown and 90 blown, but it had the old Lagonda drawback of too much body for its engine size and its acceleration
was on the sluggish side. Nevertheless the Two Liter became

much desired, especially by sports-minded drivers who could not afford the more expensive Bentleys and Invictas, and it is one of the *vintagents'* pets even today.

During the lifespan of this model Lagonda manufactured several other models, and by 1934 — a year before Bentley joined the the organization — had produced itself almost into bankruptcy. In addition to the double-overhead-cam Two Liter, there were a six-cylinder car of the same displacement but with pushrod-operated overhead valves, a 3-liter with the same valve layout called the "Special," and another 3-liter six called the Selector Special because it was equipped with the massive Maybach pre-selector gearbox. If all these were not enough, in 1934 Lagonda introduced two new cars, a big 4½-liter car and the little Rapier model. This last was a beautiful scaled-down version of the Two Liter, with a tiny 1,104-c.c. four-cylinder double-overhead-cam-shaft engine. The 4½-liter had the more conventional pushrod-operated overhead-valve layout, but it was capable of extremely impressive performance. A big, high four-seater 4½ was entered in the 1935 Le Mans 24 Hours and won outright, the last time until Jaguar won in 1951 that a British car was victorious in that important race.

All these models were promising cars, but apparently it was just too much of too many good things for the Lagonda organization to handle. In 1935 the company made a feeble attempt to introduce still another model, this time a 3½-liter job, and then gave up entirely. The business changed hands and a new director — A. P. Good — took over. His first acts were quick and decisive. He stopped production on all the models except the 4½-liter, and he engaged the famous and dynamic W. O. Bentley first to whip the remaining Lagonda into better shape and then to help work out a new policy for future models.

Bentley was permitted to make only those modifications to the 4½-liter that would not require extensive retooling, and the engine was changed just slightly. Nevertheless when the car that evolved was entered in the Ulster T.T. of 1936 its fastest lap speed of 83.91 m.p.h. was a significant amount higher than the 76.41 m.p.h. lap record set by a blown 4½-liter Bentley in 1931. In strict production form, the Bentley-modified Lagonda was known as the Rapide, and when it was tested by *The Motor* in 1936 it was timed at 108 m.p.h. — the highest speed of any unsupercharged production car in England at the time.

With this rejuvenated six, Lagonda temporized until a really

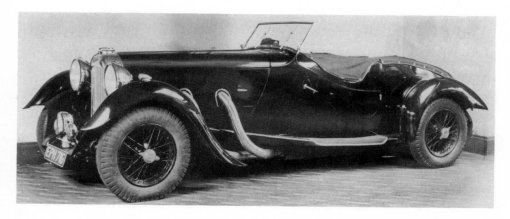

Fastest British production car in 1937
was the Lagonda Rapide, good for 108 m.p.h. in stock tune.

new, entirely Bentley-built car could be produced. At this point Lagonda stood at a crossroads. The 4½-liter six, even with its opulently rakish Rapide four-seater sports body, was still in the tradition of the violent and adventurous sports cars of the Twenties. Good and Bentley felt that the more modern concept of a sporting vehicle, especially one in the higher price brackets, had to include smooth and flexible city performance as well as open-road power and speed. The result of their thinking was the 1937 4½-liter V-12 Lagonda.

It was a suave and dignified town carriage, and at the same time had more potent performance than almost any English car of its day. The V-12 engine was remarkable in many ways. It employed an almost-square bore-to-stroke ratio which permitted top safe r.p.m. in the 5,500 region. Lightness of reciprocating parts was stressed throughout the design. The connecting rods were light-alloy forgings running in direct contact with hardened crankshaft-bearing surfaces. The valves were actuated by simple, low-weight, mushroom tappets placed between valve stem and camshaft. A single overhead camshaft was used for each block of cylinders and the valves were placed in line. This engine in standard form developed 175 b.hp., more than the six-cylinder 4½-liter Lagonda that had been specially tuned for the Ulster T. T. The V-12's coachwork was luxurious and ponderously beautiful, but in spite of its mass and weight the car lapped Brooklands at 108 m.p.h.

This was obviously a machine that could have a future in competition, and in 1939 Lagonda decided to enter a team of two cars at Le Mans. They were carefully prepared for the race but the engines were scarcely modified from standard. The compression ratio was boosted from the normal 7-to-1 to 8.5-to-1, and two downdraft carburetors were provided for each manifold instead of the usual one per manifold — an arrangement that proved so successful that it was later offered on the production cars. The chassis were encased in long-hooded bodies that had torpedo shape but were only vaguely streamlined.

The conditions of the race and the kind of cars that now competed in it had changed enormously in the four years since the last Lagonda entry, and it was decided that the two cars would perform the function of a sort of reconnaissance squad. They were to give the cars a competition test, pick up what data they could, and in the meantime keep the Lagondas running at a conservative speed.

Nevertheless, the two Lagondas finished third and fourth, averaging 83.5 and 83.3 m.p.h. — faster than the winning car at Le Mans ten years later.

The next race the two Le Mans Lagondas entered was the last held in England before the war. They ran flat out and won easily, the number one car averaging 132.81 m.p.h.

Unfortunately the war put an end to production and development of the V-12, but W. O. Bentley had by then surely proved that he had accomplished what he set out to do — design a luxurious and comfortable production car that could be rivalled in performance only by a true racing car.

LANCIA

Vincenzo Lancia was an innovator and a prophet from the start of his career as a designer. In 1908, when Europe began to rebel against elephantine automobiles with gross displacements, Vincenzo had already anticipated the coming trend. He had been head of Fiat's car-testing division as well as one of the most celebrated racing drivers of his day, quitting at the age of 25 to establish Lancia and Company "so as to think and create in freedom." His first car, built in 1908, was a sensation in the technical world. It was long, low and ultra-light and used an engine that peaked at 1,450 r.p.m. — well over 30 per cent faster-revving than almost all of its contemporaries. Critics jeered and engineers reflected. But the future proved that the path of Vincenzo's choice was a good one.

The 4-cylinder Lambda was the most famous of Lancia's vintage models. Vincenzo pioneered unit chassis-frame construction.

James Talmadge

Lancia resembled Ettore Bugatti in many ways. He was another remarkably versatile Italian: he, too, was entirely self-contained and required no outside inspiration; he formulated his personal engineering philosophy early and followed its rigid orientation to the end; he was an individualist as a racing champion, an engineer and an industrialist; what bore his name was his and he avoided debts, moral or financial; he was a dedicated man, passionately devoted to the automobile as a vehicle for artistic expression as well as for carrying payloads. His spirit of dedication and inspiration managed to permeate his factories at Turin and Bolzano. When he died, in 1937, his workers sent a delegation to Signora Adele Lancia to assure her that her husband's spirit would continue to be their inspiration.

"Non un anno senza novita" could have been the firm's motto. Each year at least one innovation from Vincenzo's drawing board rocked Italy and reverberated over Europe. Typical was his mar-

velous V-12 which was the focal point of interest at the 1919 Paris and London shows. This *gioiello di meccanica* employed the narrow-angled vee which Vincenzo always favored, and the crankcase and both blocks were cast as a unit. The car was described in the press as an engineering triumph but when it went on sale in 1920, carrying a huge price tag, it was a marketing disappointment. Nevertheless, many of its design features were applicable to a more popularly priced car.

The low-priced adaptation appeared in 1922. It was called the Lambda, following Vincenzo's Greek-letter code which had begun with his Alfa model at the very beginning and had just passed through the Kappa, Dikappa and Trikappa designs. What the Model T was to Henry Ford, the Lambda was to Vincenzo, although the Lambda was not a big-mass-production car. But it gave the engineering world food for thought that remained nourishing for decades.

The Lambda was low and light and it had no frame, in the customary sense. *Monococque* (unit-body-frame) construction was introduced with this historic car. Chassis frame and body framework were all built up out of steel stampings, the body consisting of aluminum panels fastened to this structure.

Lancia Lambda with wiry, light, four-seater body.
Car was years ahead in its engineering.

The Lambda's suspension was another revelation. Rear suspension was fairly normal, by means of underslung half-elliptics and Hotchkiss drive. But the front axle was deleted entirely and replaced by a structure the like of which had been approached only by Morgan in England — and then with just partial success. A triangular (more precisely, trapezoidal) tubular-steel framework served as the mounting for front-wheel spindles which rode vertically in steel tubes containing both coil springs and hydraulic shock absorbers. This was excellent independent front suspension, date-line 1922. The handling qualities of this chassis — never billed as a sports car — were simply excellent. Augmenting virtues already mentioned were fade-defying four-wheel brakes using aluminum drums with die-cast aluminum shoes.

Just as original and as deathless in its conception as the Lambda's body-chassis design was its engine. Although it is often referred to as a "square four," it was actually a V-4, its blocks spread at a negligible 14-degree angle. The cylinders were staggered and a four-throw, three-main-bearing crankshaft was used. This engine layout was well covered by patents, and it was made with displacements ranging upward from 2,121 c.c. (129.4 cu. in.).

The Lambda's cylinder barrels were cast in close-grained gray iron, given a preliminary machining, then placed in a mold so that the aluminum water jacket and crankcase could be cast around them. These cylinders were "wet liners" without the advantage of being removable. A detachable cast-iron head was held down by only six studs, which gave these engines a tendency toward head-gasket failure. The valves were exactly vertical, were closed by pairs of concentric springs, and were operated by a single overhead camshaft and rocker arms. The connecting rods were tubular and the aluminum pistons carried three compression and two oil rings.

The engine had no intake manifold; its carburetor was simply bolted against the rear side of the cylinder head. From there ports meandered to the various combustion chambers, and from the chambers exhaust ports made their way aft, emerging from the head on either side of the single intake "manifold" flange. The point of this utterly radical engine design was obviously compactness. From the tip of its little wooden airplane-propeller-type cooling fan back to its flywheel the engine measured just 22 inches!

The final unique feature was the Lambda's bodywork. At the start of its career this consisted of the open four-place model illustrated on Page 92. No other car has ever looked quite like the factory-bodied Lambda, which eventually was available in two- as well as four-place form. Both bodies had an aspect of delicacy and airy grace which belied their sturdy construction. Each line and small detail was drawn and finished with great taste, giving the whole a quality best described as aristocratic. Although the wheelbase was fairly long, the Lambda was a low, narrow and definitely small car. It was not precisely a sports car or a classic, but it was undeniably a rapid tourer of memorable quality and design.

A new series of Lambdas was introduced each year. Most of the changes were small ones and the bodies remained virtually unchanged, although the 1927 7th Series had a frame structure modified to permit the use of custom bodywork. The 8th and last Lambda series came out in 1928 and was followed in '29 by the much costlier Dilambda. This series used a narrow 20-degree V-8 engine similar to that which had been developed for the Trikappa of 1921 and retained the Lambda's independent front suspension. It was a light, powerful luxury car, made with the custom coach-builder in mind.

To cope with the inert market produced by the world crisis in 1931, Vincenzo wisely withdrew this new emphasis on relatively expensive machinery and brought out two new models, the four-cylinder, 1,924-c.c. (117.4 cu. in.) Artena and the eight-cylinder, 2,972-c.c. (181.4 cu. in.) Astura. With these cars he dropped the Greek-letter nomenclature and, appropriately and poetically, began giving each new model the name of one of the great roads which radiated from Ancient Rome to all parts of the then-known world.

The next historic Lancia model was the Aprilia, introduced in 1936, which carried Vincenzo's design concepts to their most advanced development. It was powered by a modernized, 1,352-c.c. (82.5 cu. in.) version of the traditional V-4 and used the unique Lancia front suspension. It also featured independent rear suspension and aerodynamic bodywork in unit with chassis. It sold, imported in England, for a tiny $1,190 but it was one of the finest cars the firm ever made.

In 1937, aged 56, Vincenzo died. His fulfilment in life would have been even greater than it was if he had known that his young son, Gianni, would carry on the pure Lancia tradition when he reached manhood in postwar years.

Augustﾠ18, 1928 was a big day for british racing. On that day the Royal Automobile Club staged the first Ulster Tourist Trophy Race at the Ards Circuit near Belfast. It soon became *the* great annual sports-car event in the British Isles,

LEA-FRANCIS

and from the start manufacturers and masses alike responded to it with wild enthusiasm.

All night long before the first race, boats shuttled across the Irish Sea landing great throngs of Englishmen at the Belfast docks. By starting time Belfast was deserted but the 13-mile triangle of the course was lined with volatile Irish and unexpectedly boisterous English milling and jamming at the best vantage points, clinging to rooftops, hanging precariously from the bridges overlooking the course — half a million people in all.

Probably not 10 of them seriously thought that Lea-Francis had more than a slim fighting chance of winning. Lea-Francis was an old, respectable English make that — four years before — had won a medal for good performance in the International Six Days trial, and since then had taken a third place in the 200 Miles Race at Brooklands. But it was not renowned either for speed or endurance, and this race required both. It was a six-hour grind over a tough course, and although the cars were handicapped for displacement they included some of the fastest, hottest makes in the world. There was a blown Mercedes, a big black Stutz, and a team of Bugattis. There were Bentleys, Austro-Daimlers, Lagondas, and teams of Rileys, Alvises and Frazer-Nashes. The four supercharged Lea-Francis entries were official works entries too, but the cars were scarcely different from the strictly over-the-counter version.

Nevertheless a Lea-Francis won by a bare 13 seconds after an hour-long duel with the second-place Alvis. It would have been a spectacular underdog win at any time, but in the feverish, tumultuous atmosphere of the first Ulster it resoundingly identified Lea-Francis as a great sports car.

It was an all-important victory for a make that had been born modestly in 1902 as the producer of a little three-cylinder chassis, had switched to motorcycles in 1907, and in 1918 had returned to automobile production with a 12/14 model and an urgent desire to make a name for itself in the sports-car field. A tuned version of the 12/14 was able to win the 1924 Six Days trial, but it did little else in competition.

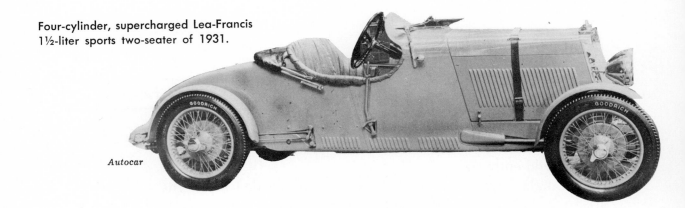

Four-cylinder, supercharged Lea-Francis
1½-liter sports two-seater of 1931.

Autocar

In 1925 Lea-Francis began to produce the four-cylinder, 1,496-c.c. (91.3 cu. in.), overhead-valve 12/40 model, and in 1927 it leaped headlong into the high-performance market with a supercharged touring car having the same engine layout and displacement. This car in sports version became the Hyper-Sports which, with almost no special preparation, won the T. T. The attitude of the British public toward Lea-Francis products immediately became, in the words of a road-tester for *The Autocar*: "... changed from 'how fast is this docile car?' to 'how docile is this fast car?' "

With a top speed of 85 m.p.h. in normal tune the little Hyper "Leaf" was fast, and it was remarkably flexible too. It was considered next to impossible for a small car to idle down to eight to 10 m.p.h. in fourth gear, crawl around a corner, and accelerate away without shifting, but the Hyper did it, thanks to its permanently engaged Cozette supercharger. It had excellent handling and road-holding qualities, and could corner very fast. Its bucket seats were equipped with a quaint sliding device which allowed them to tip sideways on sharp turns.

A businesslike Weymann body of fabric over ash sat on the 111-inch wheelbase chassis, which rode on semi-elliptic springs that used, instead of shackles, pin joints in the front and grease-packed rollers in the rear. The four-wheel Dewandre vacuum-operated brakes were firm and smooth, actual braking distance from 25 m.p.h. being 40 feet.

This was the car that firmly established Lea-Francis' reputation, and during most of the Thirties the company produced nothing to compare with it. In 1931 they marketed the six-cylinder, 1,991-c.c. (121.2 cu. in.) "Ace of Spades" model, so-called because a front view of the engine suggested the inverted Death-card. The Ace had a smooth, high-efficiency engine, but lacked the spirit and appeal of the Hyper.

By the middle of the decade Lea-Francis of Coventry was in the same financial boat as a number of other companies, and that boat was sinking fast. A quick reorganization and some new investors saved the day in 1937, and by 1938 a complete changeover had been made to an entirely new engine. Two versions were produced, both identical except for displacement — 1,496 c.c. (91.3 cu. in.) and 1,629 c.c. (99.4 cu. in.). The engine layout was very similar to that of the Riley Nine, with twin camshafts high in the block, driven by a chain and helical gears, and actuating very short, slightly inclined pushrods. Valves inclined in a 90-degree vee seated in machined and polished hemispherical combustion chambers. This engine in its smaller version produced 50 b.hp. at 4,800 r.p.m., and in larger form reached 56 b.hp. at the same r.p.m.

Suspension was by conventional half-elliptic springs all around, and bodies were handsomely designed examples of British coachwork of the prewar period. The bodies were low — the sedan was only five feet, one inch high — with smoothly flowing, attractive lines.

A handbuilt 1½-liter Super Sports roadster was offered with extras which included a higher compression engine than the standard 7.5-to-1, higher rear-end gear ratios, and Hartford shock absorbers adjustable from the driver's seat. This car's top speed was well over 80 m.p.h., and a small amount of competition work by private owners in the scant months before war broke out produced some Brooklands victories, a notable finish in the Monte Carlo Rally, and various trial and rally wins.

Like all its compatriots Lea-Francis suspended production in 1939 to meet the war emergency, maintaining only a small experimental department to prepare for the peace ahead.

Like CHENARD-WALCKER, LORRAINE-DIETRICH was a sound and solid French marque whose international racing reputation was achieved brilliantly at Le Mans. Lorraine's great days were in 1925 and 1926, just after the Chenard

LORRAINE-DIETRICH

triumphs and just before the brute Bentleys really moved in.

The Le Mans Lorraine was aristocratically narrow and carried the emblem of the four-armed Cross of Lorraine on the sharply pointed core of its radiator. It was — in accordance with Le Mans rules — a four-seater, but reluctantly; the rear seat was small and its token door was barred by the huge spare tire — also required by regulations — that was mounted on the side of the car. In 1924, two of these cars came in right behind the winning Bentley in a field that started with 41 eager contenders and finished with a weary 14. The next year Lorraine hit its stride with a vengeance: the two cars entered came in first and third. In 1926 they did even better, coming in 1-2-3, with number one setting a new world's record for the course at an average 66.08 m.p.h.

The production sports version of the Lorraine was known as the "Silken Six," and was engineered with light chassis and an abundance of power to give great flexibility and performance to spare. It became known as a car of *"grande vitesse moyenne"* (great average speed), implying that not only its top speed, but also its road-holding, steering and braking qualities were excellent. It had enormous torque and pulled like a Percheron in top gear.

The six-cylinder, 3,447-c.c. (209 cu. in.) engine, designed by the French engineer Marius Barbarou, had overhead valves actuated by thin pushrods. It remained essentially the same from its introduction in 1921 right up until the firm stopped production in the early Thirties, although modifications in the induction system and rear-axle gearing in 1928 gave the later models even greater flexibility.

MASERATI

IN THE LATE TWENTIES, THE BROTHERS MASERATI gave the best of their youthful talents and even their name to a car with which they are no longer associated. Maserati built its great prewar reputation on the efforts of these four men.

The first Maserati car was entered in the 1927 Targa Florio. It was an entirely unknown quantity, a family production designed by Ernesto Maserati, tooled by Ettore, engine-tested by Bindo and driven by Alfieri. It had no right to do anything significant in the race, but it finished third.

This was the beginning. The Maseratis began to be heard of in all manner of races, and by 1930 were known to be the equals if not the superiors of the then-current Alfas and Bugattis. These were the years when anarchy was rampant in Grand Prix racing (there were displacement rules, but they were honored more in the breach than in the observance) and the Maserati varieties mirrored the chaos. The Targa Florio car was a 1.5-liter which was subsequently increased to 1.7 liters and then to 2 liters. In 1929, a fantastic variation on this power plant was created for *formula libre* racing. It consisted of two of the 2-liter, blown, 32-valve, double-overhead-cam, in-line eights mounted on one crankcase, geared together and yielding 250 b.hp. A car equipped with this engine and a three-speed gearbox went all the way to Indianapolis in 1930 to qualify poorly and retire after seven laps with plug and magneto trouble. However, a number of remarkable sports cars based on this chassis were built on private order and in Grand Prix form the 16 went on to win its share of races and set a new 10-mile Class C international record at 152.9 m.p.h.

In 1930 the Maserati brothers designed and produced an entirely new 2.5-liter Grand Prix machine which, aided by the 16, won almost everything in sight for the marque. The year of its introduction, the 175 b.hp., Roots-blown, double-overhead-cam 2.5 snatched more Grand Prix victories than any other make — an amazing performance for a new model. George Eyston drove one of these cars in the 1931 Tourist Trophy. It was fitted with fenders, headlights, spare tire and other road equipment and although it earned him no better than eighth place it did make the third fastest time of the day. An also-ran in the same race was a 1,078-c.c. (65.8 cu. in.) blown Maserati. The "1100" fared better in Italy, won its class in the Mille Miglia that year, as well as in '32, '34 and '35.

In 1933 a blown 2.9-liter (177 cu. in.), 230-b.hp. car was introduced which the experts branded superior to the P3 Alfas and Type 51 Bugattis. But by 1934 the Germans had begun their methodical blitzkrieg of the Grand Prix circuits and Maserati, like the other great Italian marques, was eclipsed in the *Grandes Epreuves*.

In 1937 a lot happened to the firm and to the brothers. Alfieri died, and the car-building Maseratis (a fifth brother was an artist) were reduced from four to three. They sold the firm's assets to outside capital and, as salaried technicians, moved from the old barn at Bologna to the new factory at Modena. Here they continued to build racing and on-order sports cars in one corner of the great machine-tool, storage-battery and spark-plug plant that bore the name of Alfieri Maserati. In spite of the move to the new city, Maserati cars and other products carried the brothers' old trade-mark — a red Neptune's Trident, the coat-of-arms of the City of Bologna.

Under the new management Maserati cars were no longer factory-raced, although independently owned cars continued to run in sports and other events with memorable success. In 1937, '38, '39 and '40 Maseratis set the astonishing record of filling the first three places in the Targa Florio each year for four years in succession. In '39 and '40, the glories of the Grand Prix past were recalled by Wilbur Shaw's famous consecutive victories in the Indianapolis "500" at the wheel of a Maserati 8CTF.

MERCEDES-BENZ

No EUROPEAN MAKE EVOKES MORE CLEARLY THE picture of the giant, bloodless, impersonal business machine than Mercedes-Benz. The stories of its infinite efficiency in production and competition are legion, and certainly the ruthless appearance and sound of the cars themselves did little to contradict the legends.

Many of the tales are true — Mercedes engineers *did*, for example, march out to the course before an important Grand Prix race and measure everything in sight; they surveyed the entire course, plotted the radius of every turn and determined its degree of bank, calculated the pitch of every grade and the length of every straight, made operating tests of the widest possible variety of humidity and barometric pressure readings, and so on.

Nevertheless, the great Mercedes sports cars of the Twenties were the creations not of the design cells of a corporate robot but of two men — Paul Daimler and sad-eyed Ferdinand Porsche — and the heritage of a third — old Gottlieb Daimler, whose solution to the problem of the small, high-speed internal-combustion engine in the early 1880's had literally given birth to the world's automobile industry.

Daimler Motoren Gesellschaft, which produced Mercedes, was Papa Daimler's attempt at building an industrial empire, but almost before he conceived it, the firm was taken over by financiers to whom it represented a healthy piece of income property. Nevertheless, in its early days the company retained much of the character of a small "family business." Gottlieb died before the introduction of the first Mercedes car in 1900 but his young son Paul was schooled to step into his historic shoes. When the company's technical director and Gottlieb's lifelong friend Wilhelm Maybach retired in 1907, Paul Daimler became chief engineer of the company, but the memory of Papa Daimler was still a living, vital force.

The derivation of the famous Mercedes star is an unexpectedly sentimental example of this influence. When Paul needed a trademark handsome enough to be carried on the radiator of the spirited and aristocratic 1909 Mercedes, he chose a symbol that represented his father and his vision. He remembered that one night Papa Daimler, already a world-famous engineer, had taken out a photograph of the house in Deutz where the family had lived when the small high-speed internal-combustion engine was perfected, and very carefully inked in a star above the roof. Frau Daimler asked him why, and he said, "From this house a star has risen; I hope it will bring blessings to us and our children."

The graceful, balanced three-pointed star that Paul designed decorated the top center of the flat-front radiators used by Mercedes from 1909 through 1914. When the majestic pointed radiator was introduced shortly before World War I it was graced by two of the stars, one on each side of the vee. There they stayed until 1928, when a single star fitted over the apex of the vee became the permanent and unmistakable emblem of the Mercedes marque.

Mercedes-Benz SSK competition sports car, introduced in 1928. Wheelbase was 116 inches.

Paul Daimler continued as engineering head of D.M.G. until 1922, and during his fifteen years with the company was responsible for the construction of no fewer than 17 touring cars and three racing cars, plus many engines for aircraft and submarines. But his greatest achievement — one that instigated a real revolution in the technique of building fast cars — was his development of the supercharger, and this again was based on his father's inspiration.

Gottlieb Daimler conceived and patented the idea of forced induction in 1885. His drawings showed a piston-type pump mounted alongside the cylinder block, which delivered a greater supply of combustible mixture to the cylinder than mere atmospheric pressure could, and which also effected a more complete removal of exhaust gases. Paul Daimler first worked with the idea when he was confronted by the problem of fuel starvation in his wartime aircraft engines, and as soon as the war was over and peacetime production could be considered again, he set up a special research project with the object of designing a practical supercharged automobile.

The first method he tried and discarded was his father's piston-type pump. Then an eccentric-vane type was tested and rejected. The pump that finally proved to be as workable on a car as on stationary test equipment was an old American invention, the positive-displacement Roots blower. With its figure-eight cross-section meshing rotors properly made, and its thousandths-of-an-inch clearances carefully controlled, Paul Daimler found it to be a costly but reliable method of supercharging.

The first ear-piercing road test of a Roots-blown car was made near Stuttgart in October, 1919. The results were so startling that Daimler was encouraged to gamble the already great Mercedes racing reputation on this new, upstart idea. He had a blower installed on the engine of a 28/95 sports car that was entered in the 1921 Coppa Florio; and of course it won. This was the first race won by a supercharged car since the victory of a centrifugally blown American Chadwick in the Giants Despair hill-climb of 1908. The Chadwick's message about forced induction was so far ahead of its time that it was generally unintelligible, but the Mercedes *coup* electrified all designers of high-performance engines. Within four years almost every important racing marque in Europe and America adopted supercharging.

The 28/95 model that won the Coppa Florio was one of the most famous of Paul Daimler's creations. It was introduced in

1914 with a chassis that was not an important departure from conventional Mercedes practice, but its engine stirred the engineering world profoundly. Based on the firm's recent aircraft experience, it set a new standard for lightweight construction, power and efficiency.

It was a six-cylinder engine with 7,273 c.c. (431.6 cu. in.) displacement and a single shaft-driven overhead camshaft actuating valves inclined in a narrow vee. The crankcase was a light-metal casting, and the cylinders were individual steel sleeves bolted to the case and joined in pairs by welded-on water-jacketing, a construction which made possible precision control of the dimensions of cylinder walls and jacketing, and which held weight to the rock-bottom minimum. The 28/95 became the firm's prestige car in the years right after the war, and was called by the factory a *Hoechsleistungs-Tourenwagen* — a high-output tourer. It was sold in a short-chassis sports version with external exhaust pipes and dual carburetors which was raced widely on the Continent. But it soon earned the reputation of being unreliable. What had proved to be long-wearing in aircraft, which used relatively constant engine speeds, tired rapidly in use involving constantly varying r.p.m.

Although this car continued in production for a few years after its Targa Florio victory, Paul Daimler lost no time in building two new supercharged sports cars. Both were four-cylinder Roots-blown machines, one with 1.5-liters (91.5 cu. in.) displacement and the other with 2.6-liters (159 cu. in.). They were produced in tiny numbers in 1921 and 1922 and although they were impressive to the engineering *cognoscenti* they failed to perform with the necessary spirit. At the same time Daimler built a 2-liter (122 cu. in.) supercharged straight-eight racing car. It was a promising and potentially formidable machine but plugs which fouled too easily made its performance frustrating and inconsistent.

These were too many failures for the men at the top who read the financial statements. Daimler might not have known it, but he was on the way out. In 1922 the company hired an Austrian engineer named Ferdinand Porsche to come to Stuttgart on an ostensibly temporary basis and do what he could to make the 2-liter car go.

Porsche was a relatively young man who had made himself a sound reputation designing fast cars for Austro-Daimler, and he refined the 2-liter until it no longer balked and eventually won races, including the 1924 Targa Florio. The company was not unaware that he had succeeded where Daimler had failed. Late in 1922 Paul Daimler and D.M.G. parted ways. Daimler left to take charge of engineering at Horch, and D.M.G. offered Porsche the position of chief engineer of what was Germany's greatest automobile-manufacturing firm.

In April, 1923, Porsche wound up his Austrian obligations and moved to Stuttgart-Untertuerkheim, bringing with him such talented men as Alfred Neubauer, who later became famous as *the* genius of racing strategy.

The directors of D.M.G. knew very well that when they acquired Porsche they were getting one of the most prolific minds in the entire world of automotive engineering. But Porsche probably produced beyond his employers' most fantastic hopes. He was with the firm for less than six years. During that time he supervised the design of about 65 machines—trucks, tractors, military machines—and also the great K and S Series Mercedes cars, which represented then and now a peak of achievement in automobile design.

One of Porsche's first assignments with D.M.G. was the design of a brand-new supercharged passenger car which would have the reliability that Daimler's cars had lacked. Within a year he had two models in production, which, although they evolved into the K and S Series, were then known as the 15/70/100 4-liter and the 24/100/140 6-liter, the numbers representing respectively taxable horsepower, normal peak horsepower, and maximum horsepower with supercharger engaged. These cars embodied practically all of the basic design features that were eventually developed into the 156 m.p.h. SSKL.

Their speed was, of course, not in the neighborhood of this hair-raising figure, but the 6-liter in particular soon became known for its abundance of power and its excellent hill-climbing and accelerating ability. Unsupercharged, it had an inexorable torque that made a spin down the open road feel like a ride up in a fast elevator. When the blower went in a herd of extra horses hit the heads of the pistons and the car came bestially alive. The illusion of an animal gone berserk was further enhanced by the sound of the blower—a snarling bellow at moderate speed that rose to a demoniac wail at high speed. The noise always terrified the uninitiated and was stirring music to those who understood the breed.

The entire layout of the supercharger system was faithfully patterned after the system developed by Paul Daimler. The

A supremely powerful and reliable sports car:
Mercedes-Benz Model S close-coupled four-seater.

carburetor was mounted between, rather than ahead of, the
blower and engine, and the blower was engaged at the driver's
will when the foot throttle was pressed all the way to the floor.
The big vee-radiator and three external exhaust pipes gave the
Porsche *kompressor* machines a strong family resemblance to
Daimler's 28/95, but beyond these points Porsche took off on
his own.

All the K and S Series cars had the same blown single-overhead-cam six-cylinder engine, but varied in displacement and
minor details. Block and crankcase were a single light-alloy casting, a daring and probably unique feature in those days. The
layout of the top of the block was entirely unique. Instead of
having the usual smooth metal gasket-surface with occasional
water passages, its surface was reduced to a set of six slender rings
that were a part of the casting and through which the cylinder
liners were inserted in the block. This arrangement had the virtue
of providing perfect water-jacketing of the cylinder walls throughout their length, and furthermore gave such a complete view
of the interior of the block that no casting defect could pass
unnoticed.

The crankshaft was completely machined and ran in four
immense, plain, bronze-backed bearings. At its forward end a
multiple-disc clutch transmitted crank rotation to the set of bevel
gears which drove the two-rotor, two-lobe Roots blower mounted
vertically on the crankcase, ahead of the cylinder block. Long

but light tubular connecting rods had a polished finish and their caps were secured by four strong bolts. The sump was of cast light alloy, deeply ribbed on bottom and sides for cooling and machined to form an oil-tight seal with the crankcase, without requiring a gasket.

The cylinder head was of cast iron and carried two vertical valves per cylinder in fully machined combustion chambers. Instead of being arranged in a line, the valves were staggered in the chambers with intakes on the left, exhausts on the right, and straight-through porting as effective as that found in many hemispherical chamber layouts. Valve-spring surge was rendered harmless by use of two nested springs per valve. The single camshaft rode in four long bronze bearings above the valves and finger-type cam followers were interposed between cams and valve stems to absorb side thrust. The cast aluminum fan looked like a marine propeller and was driven from the front of the camshaft *via* an over-running clutch, so that the fan ceased rotating (and absorbing horsepower) at high engine speeds, when it was not needed.

A vertical shaft, driven by the crankshaft and fitted with helical gears, drove all the auxiliaries, plus camshaft and fan. Water pump, generator and magneto were mounted in a line on the right side of the engine, alongside the crankcase, and all were driven by a single gear on the vertical shaft. The Robert Bosch ZR6 magneto included a coil-ignition circuit, the mag feeding a set of spark plugs on the left side of the block and the coil distributor handling a separate set of plugs on the right side.

Until the S Model was introduced, these engines were equipped with a single carburetor of Mercedes manufacture; thereafter, dual carbs were standard, as they had been on the 28/95. The block and head were painted green or black, the auxiliaries on the right side of the crankcase were shielded from dirt and from view by attractive light-alloy covers. The cam cover, carburetor, blower, blower discharge pipe, and crankcase were left with a natural light-metal finish, the cam cover and carbs were polished with countless small circles—"engine-turned" in the inaccurate vernacular. It was a handsome and formidable-looking power plant. Transmission, steering gear, and radiator were all mounted solidly on the engine, making the three-point-mounted whole a neat package relatively immune to distortions and vibrations in the frame.

As complex as it may sound, and in spite of superb machine-work throughout, this was a simple engine to work on. Only one special tool was essential; the puller for the topmost gear on the vertical cam-drive shaft. A chain hoist was appreciated when removing the head and essential when pulling the engine. Otherwise, a set of metric wrenches, an instruction book, and average mechanical ability were enough. It was a stolid warhorse of an engine, rather than a high-strung thoroughbred.

Synchro-mesh was never a feature of the four-speed gearbox and, until the S model appeared, shifting was by means of a massive lever in a bronze gate; "popping a shift" was suggestive of crowbarring a spike from a railroad tie. The universal joint was a monument to Teutonic engineering, consisting of an incredibly massive, simple, fork-and-blade arrangement hewn from blocks of bronze, machined to fit with a scant few thousandths clearance, and making an assembly the size of a fair coconut. End-play in this joint was regulated by a nut on the torque tube that could only be coped with by a wrench peculiar to locomotive shops. The rear-end ring and pinion gears set an all-time high for hugeness.

The Merk's rear axle was built up out of light, strong steel pressings and the front axle was a thing of simple beauty. It was well-dropped and of H-section construction throughout most of its length, becoming not only tubular but forked at its extremities. The upper branch of the fork accommodated the king pin, the lower branch contained the brake-control rod. The brakes were cable-operated and could be adjusted conveniently from the driver's seat by means of handwheels. The brake drums were quite immense and early models of the series had Robert Bosch vacuum-assist. This valuable detail was scratched from the SS

All-weather sports conveyance de luxe: Mercedes-Benz Model SS with convertible coupe body by Keibl.

and SSK specifications, when potential speeds demanded more braking ability than ever. An inability to stop was the biggest shortcoming of the best of the blown Merks.

Nevertheless, they handled magnificently. Even the long-wheelbase jobs took the corners on rails and once they hit their stride steered like motorcycles. They were designed, the factory said, to make possible the maintenance of high average speeds during cross-country travel. Curves and grades were minor obstacles to the omnivorous *radmeister*, Mercedes-Benz.

Sports competition soon proved to be equally vulnerable to Mercedes power. Porsche had repeatedly proved his ability to build successful competition cars long before he joined D.M.G. and as the Mercedes sixes were developed it became apparent that he had conjured up another winning combination.

First his big touring models, the 6-liter (actually 6.2-liter, 380.8-cu. in.) cars, began to assert themselves in central-European competition. Then in 1927 the 180 b.hp. S Model appeared and Merz won the Nuerburgring Grand Prix of Germany for sports cars in an S, with two similar cars taking second and third. By 1928 the 7.1-liter (428.4 cu. in.) SS and SSK (K for *kurz*, short, referring to the wheelbase) models were available and Caracciola won the same race in an SSK, with SS models second and third. In 1929 "Caratsch" drove one of the most famous races of all time, winning the Ulster T.T. in an SS and setting a new record in driving rain. In 1930 he was first again in the Grand Prix of Ireland in an SSK and went on to win the European hill-climb championship for sports cars. In 1931, Caracciola won the Mille Miglia in an SSKL (L for *leicht*, light) and Zehender won the Belgian 24-hour race in a similar car. And "Caratsch" was hill-climb champion again. In 1932, von Brauchitsch won the Avus races in Germany with a new class record for 200 kilometers of 120.54 m.p.h. and Hans Stuck won the *Alpenmeister* title in his SSKL. This was only a tiny smattering of the racing achievements of Porsche's blown oh.c. sixes.

But in spite of all this fabulous success the solemn little Austrian engineer tired of the pressure of work in Germany's Detroit. He left Daimler-Benz (D.M.G. and Carl Benz & Cie. had combined in 1925) at the end of 1928 to go to work with Steyr, in his homeland.

Daimler-Benz promoted Hans Nibel (pronounced Neebel) to the position of chief engineer. Nibel had been *chefkonstrukteur* with Benz since 1908 and had designed the immortal *Blitzen*

Benz which, in 1909, set a world's absolute speed record of 142.23 m.p.h., which was not broken until 1924. His first exciting work at the new job was refinement of the existing Porsche designs. Nibel created the superlight SSKL by filling the SSK's frame with lightening holes, beefing up the engine with a counterbalanced crankshaft and jumping power output to the neighborhood of 300 b.hp. His next step was to build a superluxurious Porsche-type blown overhead-camshaft car called the *Grosser Mercedes* —an eight with 7.7-liters displacement (463.8 cu. in.). And that was the end of the Porsche line of Mercedes cars.

Nibel went on to create new, great Mercedes, but not sports cars. He introduced the swing-axle rear end, coil-spring suspension for all four wheels, the 500K, from which the 540K and 770K were developed, the rear-engine *Typ 170*, the oval-tubular frame, and the 3.3-liter Grand Prix Mercedes. Nibel's work is covered in the Classics Section.

MERCER ENTERED THE BETWEEN-WARS PERIOD with what was probably the finest reputation of any American sports car. Its fame rested largely on the 800-odd immortal, dashing Raceabouts built by the firm from 1911 to 1915. Seldom had

> **MERCER**

so much machinery been covered by so little sheet metal. They had a wire-wheeled chassis, a hood strapped over the engine, and a dashboard from which a brass steering column jutted. There were two skimpy bucket seats with cushions about three inches above the floorboards, and behind the seats was a huge cylindrical fuel tank topped by a great wing-bolt-operated filler cap near each end. There were meager flat fenders. Shift lever, hand brake, throttle pedal, hand pumps for fuel and oil, and even the flywheel—all hung out in public view. The total, practical effect of this nakedness was that these cars had little more than their own chassis weight to pull, and they did it in hair-raising style.

The early T-head-engined Mercers are unfortunately beyond the chronological scope of this book. A fact that was of im-

1920 Mercer Raceabout
— an American sports car in
performance as well as appearance.
This model used side-valve engine.

Jaderquist

portance to the postwar history of the company, however, was that the Raceabouts' success helped F. W. and C. G. Roebling, who had built the business with a total investment of $550,000, to realize $125,000 clear profit in 1915 and $230,000 in 1916. Even more important to the postwar Mercer organization was the fact that in 1917 F. W. Roebling died and the next year his brother did too.

The heirs put the business up for sale and in 1919 a Wall Street syndicate agreed to their price. Emlen S. Hare, former Packard New York branch manager, was made director of the new Mercer Motors Company, which then proceeded to pick up the Locomobile and Crane Simplex companies. Hare's Motors became the main managing and distributing force behind the three marques. The Hare group produced a Mercer Raceabout after the war, along with other body styles, but these lacked the distinctive flair and never achieved the fame of the T-head aristocrats.

The Series 4 Mercers of 1919 and the Series 5 of 1920 through 1922 were powered by four-cylinder, L-head engines of 298.2 cubic inches displacement. These power units were almost identical to those which had replaced Mercer's T-head engine in 1915 and were among the cleanest ever designed in the United States. Only two components adorned the smooth, left-hand side of the block; the magneto and carburetor were mounted there, the latter being bolted to the perfectly flat side of the block, in which the intake manifold was cast. The right-hand side carried only a water pump and a handsome, deeply finned exhaust manifold.

Each of the engine's four corners was mounted to the frame and horizontal webs joined the mounting extensions on each side, forming a structure that was extremely rigid and beautiful to look upon. Among the most awesome features of this power unit were its tremendous H-section connecting rods, which measured 15 inches between centers. Some of the last engines used "short" rods which had this dimension reduced to a mere 14.375 inches.

In the postwar period, Raceabout bodies—low, spare, angular and authoritative in prewar days — became steadily more chunky and conventional. By 1920, when the Series 5 cars were introduced, the Raceabout had the appearance of a well-made sports car, but a more subdued and socially proper one. The monocle windshield and hand crank of its forebears had been retired, but the new two-seater was still light, powerful and sporty, had appallingly quick steering, and could boast minimum bodywork, although abbreviated side panels constituted a passenger compartment where before there had only been two bucket seats bolted to the chassis. The Series 5 also retained the famous, thundering Mercer exhaust cut-out, but this last vestige of undisciplined violence was refined out of the Series 6 cars which reached the market at the end of 1922.

These Mercers had precisely the same exterior appearance as the last of the Series 5 cars, but under the hood many changes had taken place. The new model was equipped with an entirely new engine, a six-cylinder Rochester power plant of 331.3 cubic inches displacement with overhead valves operated by rocker arms and pushrods and having the first detachable head ever used by Mercer. The crankcase was aluminum, light reciprocating parts were used throughout and every effort was made to keep the engine light and smooth. Its worst structural weakness lay in the bolts that held the connecting-rod-bearing caps. These had a tendency to give way at high speeds, and many a Mercer owner had his engine destroyed for want of a rod bolt another $\frac{1}{16}$-inch in diameter. The engine was fitted with a single Stromberg carburetor and a three-speed gearbox, and dual ignition was an optional feature.

The Series 6 chassis was basically the same as those of the earlier Mercers, but the frame was stiffer and there was a new three-quarter floating rear axle. Suspension continued to be by semi-elliptics all around.

This new series was the result of some ambitious plans for expansion and modernization that the Mercer Company entertained in the early Twenties. Those proved to be recession years, however, and the company found that its program was disastrously timed. In 1923 the firm went into receivership, in 1924 shut down production, in 1925 started up again briefly and then lay down and died for good.

Mercer enthusiasm did not die when the factory did. The cars, above all the Raceabouts, continued to be treasured with a devotion approaching monomania, first by sportsmen, then—as the decades passed—by vintage-car collectors. The thrill of these cars' monumental low-speed torque, their terrier-like responsiveness and quickness, the growl of their gears and the virile bark of the exhaust—and one of the windiest rides ever devised—was unforgettable. In 1948, Mercer Associates was formed: "an organization dedicated to the preservation of America's most famous sports car." There were no dues, but ownership of a Mercer was essential to membership. The roster was in no danger of becoming overcrowded. Out of the approximately 25,000 Mercer cars made between 1909 and 1925, only 98 were still known to exist in 1951. Of these, 49 were timeless Raceabouts.

M.G.

MOTORCYCLISTS ARE AMONG THE MOST RABID of vehicle enthusiasts but even so most of them have to take to four wheels sooner or later. The impetus may be a firm-minded fiancée, one-too-many babies, or simply lost youth. Whatever it is the dethroned cyclist's plight is usually painful; gone are the speed, acceleration and bird-free handling qualities that he prized.

Correcting this condition was the aim of the men who founded and developed the now-famous line of M.G. Midgets. They were ex-motorcyclists, and they determined to build a cyclist's four-wheeler—a machine combining the performance and economy of the motorbike with the safety, roominess, and weather-protection of the automobile. Such were the simple beginnings of the world's best-loved sports car.

The founder of the M.G. Car Company, Cecil Kimber, was a Morris dealer (M.G. stood for Morris Garages) who built "trials specials," as hot rods are called in England. According to the splendid M.G. history, *Maintaining the Breed,* by John W. Thornley (Motor Racing Publications Ltd., London), the very first M.G., built in 1923, was one of these. It was basically a Morris chassis, rendered more potent by the installation of a 1,500-c.c., four-cylinder, overhead-valve Hotchkiss engine. Decked in a minimum of bodywork, with tiny side lamps and cycle fenders, this grandfather of all M.G.'s could turn 80 m.p.h. and proved its reliability when Kimber drove it to a gold-medal win in the 1925 London-to-Lands End trial.

This car, and the other more or less experimental models of the early years, completely captivated a hardy group of enthusiasts. The Mark IV (110 cu. in.) which appeared in 1927, was a four-cylinder, 1,800-c.c. sports model that could be purchased with two- and four-seater open bodies or as a sedan. It sold for about 50 per cent more than cars of its general displacement class and boasted a 20 per cent increase in performance; it was then that the eager young hot rodders of Abingdon recognized the need for a model that could attract a mass following from the lower-income brackets.

So the Type M Midget first appeared in 1929. It was not, however, intended as a racing car. The engine capacity of 847 c.c. (51.7 cu. in.), for instance, placed it near the bottom of the competition class that ran from 750 c.c. (45.8 cu. in.) to 1,100 c.c. (67.1 cu. in.); but the car was low, with stiff springs and tight, husky shock absorbers. With a reliable 20 hp. pulling only a little over 1,000 pounds, it demonstrated such respectable speed and acceleration that it was adopted wholeheartedly by the sporting element and soon began appearing in amateur-club competition with considerable success.

Although Kimber was not at this point outwardly planning a competition career, R. C. "Reg" Jackson (still one of Abingdon's top racing mechanics) was encouraged to work over one of the plant's new Midgets. He installed stronger valve springs, shaved the head, ported and polished, and had achieved a respectable boost in horsepower output when H. N. Charles came into the company as chief designer. Charles not only approved of Jackson's work, but worked out a new valve timing which proved so successful that it was incorporated in all Midgets immediately.

The M.G. plant was suddenly launched on a competition career by two private enthusiasts, Randall and Edmondson, who had been impressed by the high-speed reliability of the cars and dropped in at the Abingdon plant to discuss running an M.G. team at the 1930 J.C.C. Double Twelve Hour Race at Brooklands. Although no one had dared hope to win the two-day, 24-hour grind, the teams' three new cars finished with miraculous ease and polish. Out of eight teams which had started only the M.G. and Austin teams finished complete and M.G. held a healthy handicap win over their supercharged rivals.

After another of the special 847-c.c. M.G. racers placed fifth in its class in the Belgian 24-hour race, the model was considered a success. It was named the M12/12 (Double Twelve) Midget and placed in production as the racing member of the stable. This followed a practice that M.G. continued through its racing career—a sports car and a racing model, in this case the Type M Midget and the M12/12, both using interchangeable parts wherever possible, in production at the same time. This allowed the factory to present cars tuned and totally prepared for competition at an amazingly low price.

The startling success of the Midgets completely cut off a promising line of six-cylinder cars which started with the Mark I of 1929 (not to be confused with the totally different "Mark" series of previous years; early M.G. nomenclature is hopeless) and evolved to the Mark II (Model A) sports car and the Mark III (Model B) "Tigresse" competition model. The Midgets were not supposed to win races: that was the job of the Mark III. Even today the Tigresse sounds imposing. It featured a 2,500-c.c. six-cylinder, single-overhead-cam motor with inclined valves, pent-roof combustion chambers, twin down-draft SU carburetors, a four-speed crash-type gearbox, and a very high degree of balance and polish throughout. But even at the surprisingly low price of $4,340 it was obvious that competition with this model would be a rich man's sport. Then too, while observing the astonishing victory of Edmondson's team of Midgets at the Double Twelve Hour Race, the Abingdon hot rodders had observed that the Midgets cornered as fast as a bigger car on a dry track, and on a *wet* surface the light cars went faster.

The six-cylinder Marks II and III drifted out of production and before the dust of the Double Twelve had properly settled the EX 120—to be a prototype for an improved series of Midgets —was tearing up the roads around Abingdon. Although the Type M engine was changed only in minor details, and even the bore and stroke of 57x83 mm. were retained, changes were made in the chassis that set the pattern for years of future midgets. The frame was formed by two straight channels that swept over the front axle and under the rear. Strength with some flexibility was gained by cross tubes that passed through the side members and were secured by flanges brazed to the tubes. Semi-elliptic springs were shackled directly to bushes within the outboard ends of the cross tubes at the rear, and front springs were similarly shackled in boxes fastened to the frame members. The springs were nearly flat under normal loads and gave enormous lateral rigidity.

A three-point engine mounting had the rear of the power unit fastened to the two side members while the front was mounted to the foremost cross member in such a way that the member could rotate around the center line of the motor. The radiator was bolted solidly to the engine to prevent hose breakage due to anticipated vibration and frame distortion.

After thorough testing, both on the road and at Brooklands, a new 1931 line of Midgets was based on the EX 120. The Type D Midget sports model retained the 847-c.c. displacement and 57x83 mm. bore and stroke of the Type M and went on the market at the shatteringly low price of $945. The racing model —called the Type C—had the same 57-mm. bore, but the stroke was reduced to 73 mm. (2.875 in.) to bring the displacement below the 750-c.c. limit of Class-H competition. Among other advantages, this arrangement allowed the block and head to remain common to both models. Such interchangeability of C and D parts kept the price of the Type C down to $1,430.

But the EX 120 was destined to become more than a prototype. Just as the M.G. plant was beginning to tool up for the Type C and D production cars, another private enthusiast, J. A. Palmes, entered the picture. He had secured a special block in which the bore was sleeved down to 54 mm. (2.13 in.) and a special crankshaft brought the stroke down to 81 mm. (3.9 in.)—a total displacement of 743 c.c. (45.3 cu. in.). Scooping up Capt. G. E. T. Eyston as driver, he descended upon Abingdon with a gleam of devotion in his eye and expressed a desire to be the first to crack 100 m.p.h. with a Midget.

No one at Abingdon, from Kimber on down the line, could resist such a thought, so a stark and (for those days) fairly stream-lined body was closely tailored around Eyston. Preparations became frantic when it was learned that Sir Malcolm Campbell— then at Daytona with the Bluebird—also had a below-750-c.c. car — a supercharged Austin — up his sleeve and also intended a shot at the magic 100 m.p.h. figure. Working night and day at Montlhery, the M.G. mechanics and designers doctored the growing pains of the new car and, running unsupercharged, set records at around 87 m.p.h. — an increase of only three m.p.h. They decided that supercharging would be necessary, and even as they struggled to tune the car with a supercharger, Campbell's Austin boosted the records again, taking the five-kilometer at 97 m.p.h. Finally, with the M.G. crew exhausted and tempers stretched taut, on a wet track and with a wind blowing, everything was declared ready and Eyston began the run. After all their trouble, the records fell anti-climactically with the engine sweetly sustaining 7,000 r.p.m. They were: five kilometers, 103.13 m.p.h.; five miles, 102.76; ten kilometers, 102.43; and ten miles at 101.87.

With that one stroke, M.G. became a world-famous concern. The little record-breaker preserved its flair for the dramatic right to the last. Late in the summer of 1931 it was returned to Montlhery where Eyston drove it 101 miles in one hour. As he finished the insurance laps of this final record run, a hot bearing ignited the oil in the crankcase and the career of EX 120 literally ended in a blaze of glory.

Although the tooling for the Type C Midgets was largely set up before EX 120 began its record-breaking runs, and despite the fact that only minor modifications were incorporated into the design as a result of the high-speed experiments, the Type C was generally known as the "Montlhery" Midget. The little competition car lived up to the achievement of the EX 120 by finishing in the first five places in the Brooklands Double-Twelve-Hour Race of 1931 and snapping up an overall first-place victory in the Irish Grand Prix.

Cars of all displacement sizes were able to compete simultaneously in these events thanks to an ingenious and highly flexible handicapping system similar to that used at Le Mans. The Type C M.G.'s spectacular wins in these two classic races of 1931 made it immediately obvious to the rulesmakers that the art of light-car design had progressed to a point where the handicapping would have to be revised for the maintenance of competition equality. The men of Abingdon realized that the Type C could not win again in its existing form.

With only three months to go before the important R.A.C. International T.T. at Belfast, the M.G. mechanics again shifted into overdrive and, exploiting their rather limited experience with the supercharged EX 120, fitted a Powerplus blower which boosted horsepower output by no less than 40 per cent. Seven of these supercharged M. G.'s entered the T.T. and in a blistering battle Black (who had also won the Irish Grand Prix) nosed out Borzacchini's Alfa Romeo by 72 seconds and Crabstree in another M.G. finished just five seconds behind the Italian to take third.

Of course, the handicappers then reacted against superchargers, so M.G. ripped off the blower, redesigned the head, and went faster still. This bush-whacking struggle between Abingdon and the rulesmakers continued throughout M.G.'s period of active competition and is one of the reasons given by William Morris (now Lord Nuffield) for M.G.'s eventual withdrawal from competition. But at that time M.G. was not part of the mammoth Morris Motors Ltd. William Morris was only a private, though heavy, investor in the company and Kimber and his "special" builders were happily keeping a step ahead of the handicappers. During 1932 and 1933 over 10 models were produced.

The M.G. line of 1931 consisted of the Type C racing model, the 847-c.c. Type D sports model; and, to satisfy the demand for a few more horses, the small, six-cylinder, 1,271-c.c. (77.5 cu. in.) Type F Magna was added. It carried virtually a Type M engine with two cylinders added, most of its parts were interchangeable with those of the Type M, C or D models, and it was never intended as a competition car.

But even as the Type C Midgets gave the handicappers fits, a new recordbreaker, the EX 127, was being constructed. The Abingdon crew, now a group of respected although still violently enthusiastic engineers, developed this car throughout 1931 and 1932. In their effort to reduce its frontal area without trimming any appendages off the rather bulky George Eyston, they angled the driveshaft back to an offset banjo housing next to the left rear wheel. The driver sat beside the driveshaft with his hip pockets scooting only six inches off the ground. The general shape of the car was developed along the lines of other record-breakers of the day, but this time the efforts to achieve lower wind resistance were checked in a wind tunnel and proved satisfactory.

Before the EX 127's career was finished, M.G. held every official Class H record. It was the first 750-c.c. car to achieve 120 m.p.h., first to achieve 200 km.p.h. and it wound up its career with the M.G. plant by boosting the hour record to 110.87 m.p.h. The car was then sold to Bobby Kohlrausch, a German racing driver, who not only won many road races and hill climbs with it, but later fitted it with an M.G. Q-type engine and boosted the flying-mile record to 140.6 m.p.h. The car finally ended up in the hands of Mercedes-Benz and eyebrows in England raised considerably when features of EX 127 subsequently appeared — it was claimed — in the Mercedes Grand Prix 1½-liter racers.

But the EX 127 was never intended as a prototype. It served its purpose purely as an experimental and developmental car, and lessons learned during its record runs filtered down into mechanical innovations that appeared in all subsequent models.

The new line of Midgets that appeared in 1932 and replaced the Types C and D was named the J Series. At this time the plant changed its method of naming models so that a basic series would be lettered (as in the case of the J Series and K Series) and different models would be indicated by a numerical or letter suffix. Thus the J1 was an 847-c.c. model available with four-seat open and closed bodies, the J2 was the open two-seater 847-c.c. sports version, the J3 about the same but like the Type C destroked to 750 c.c. and supercharged, and the J4, also 750 c.c., was the racing model.

Mechanically the cars evolved directly from the Type C, but a new head was developed for the J Series. Whereas the Type C head had both the intake and exhaust ports on one side, the new head permitted freer mixture flow by placing the inlet and exhaust ports opposite each other, instead of side by side. A lightweight, close-ratio gearbox replaced the unnecessarily massive box used on previous models, and twin carburetors appeared for the first time on the production sports model.

The J2 is of special interest today mainly because it first set the M.G. body style that has continued through to the TF. The tapered (speedster) tail of the early midgets gave way to the squared back and slab tank that is now traditional. With these familiar features and the sharply cutaway doors, the lines of today's M.G.'s were laid down.

Especially considering the limitations of the two-bearing crankshaft common to all four-cylinder models to this time the J4 performed remarkably against severe handicapping and ever-stiffening competition; however, the series was almost completely eclipsed by the more romantic and spectacular 1,100-c.c. Magnettes which were produced at the same time.

Since M.G. had made a complete sweep of the Class H records and rules makers were bearing down on the startling Midgets, the company decided that the next racing car should run in Class G. In addition, M.G. felt the enthusiasts with heftier pocketbooks (those who had bought the Mark II sports sedans and open four-seaters) should be attended to. The six-cylinder Type L Magna, which evolved from the Type F and was introduced in 1932 with the J series, was too small; so the K Series was designed by, roughly speaking, scaling up the J-type sports car. The K1 had a four-foot track and a nine-foot wheelbase and was available as a comparatively luxurious open or closed four-seater; the K2 was a smaller two-seater version; and the K3 was the supercharged racing model. Sorting out the different K models is unnecessarily confused both by M.G. inconsistency in nomenclature and by the fact that four models of engines were developed for this line — the KA, KB, KC and KD. So one may have a K1 or K2 car with a KD engine in it. As a crowning blow to the historian, the factory took the K1 chassis and fitted it with the powerplant of the Type N Magnette (which replaced the L Magna in 1934); this mixture was named the Model KN.

The competition model of the six-cylinder line — the K3 — followed the design of the J4 fairly closely. The engine carried a four-bearing counterbalanced crankshaft and, with a standard 57-mm. (2.25 in.) bore and the stroke reduced to 71 mm. (2.79 in.) the capacity came out at 1,086 c.c. (66.3 cu. in.). Fitted with a Powerplus supercharger, the new bomb developed 120 b.hp. at 6,500 r.p.m.

The prototype for the K3 was started just six months before the Mille Miglia of 1933, but after a typical burst of activity, M.G. had a team of three ready for the big event. The canny team managers sent one car off from the starting line in a flat-out dash in the hope that the competition would blow up trying to catch it. The

The Daytona K3 Type M.G. Magnette racing car.

Autocar

plan was happily successful, for when the car went out with a burned valve after covering 220 miles at speeds that averaged between 80 and 90 m.p.h., their biggest threat — the Maserati team — was also defunct. The other two cars moved along at a more reasonable speed with the car driven by Eyston and Lurani in the lead and Howe and Hamilton right behind them. They finished in that order to take both first and second in their class and the team prize.

In spite of inevitable teething troubles, the Magnettes swept through the racing season with a dramatic flourish that oldtime racing fans have never forgotten. One of the most spectacular of the K3 wins in 1933 was the Ulster T.T. with Nuvolari at the wheel. As John Thornley records it, Nuvolari entered practice on the completely strange course at full speed and, "during the first laps of practice completely wore out a set of tires . . . Nuvolari had not got the hang of the self-changing box, selecting third but not kicking the pedal, and in consequence arriving a good deal too fast at most of the hazards. The score on the very first lap was three complete gyrations in the Square at Newtownards, a rearward visit to within inches of the famous butcher's shop in Comber, and an excursion up the escape road in the direction of Belfast at the Dondonald hairpin. Otherwise the lap passed off without untoward incident. . . ."

As soon as a stop at the pits allowed explanation of the intricacies of the gearbox, Nuvolari's difficulties vanished. He drove into the race with a complete disregard for the fact that the Magnettes had been given a handicap speed of 77.93 m.p.h. and no one accorded them a chance to win. The M.G. plant had pinned its hopes on the Midgets which, for once, were in a better position.

The latter laps of the race developed into a wild battle between Hamilton in a J4 and Nuvolari, with each breaking records at every lap. With three rounds to go, Nuvolari lapped at 81.42 m.p.h.—27 seconds less than his handicap time. Hamilton's lap (in a 750-c.c. J4, remember) was at 77.2 m.p.h. — 36 seconds under *his* handicap time. In spite of an earlier pit stop that had lost seven minutes, Hamilton was pulling up steadily, but with the end of the race in sight, he had to pull in for fuel. Nuvolari won by 40 seconds at a speed of 78.65 m.p.h. — .72 m.p.h. over the handicap speed — a feat which everyone had considered impossible.

By the end of the season, the 1,100-c.c. competition models demonstrated their worth, and during the winter they were redesigned; among other things, they were fitted with an out-and-out racing body. But only 30 of these K3's were constructed over 1933 and 1934. They were unquestionably one of the greatest of the vintage M.G.s; however, they had been designed around a supercharger and were too heavy to race unblown.

Prior to 1932 superchargers had not proved themselves in British racing to the point where their use was an absolute threat, but by 1933 there were powerful factions that considered a blower to be positively immoral. When the rules for the important R.A.C. Ulster T.T. of 1934 were published, M.G. was horrified to learn that superchargers were banned completely.

With no racing car ready to go, M.G. turned its attention to the NA Magnette sports car — which had replaced the Type L. Although, like the F and the L, it had never been designed for competition, it was light, fast and reliable. M.G. had previously hopped-up the Type L with considerable success, so they applied that experience to the Type N with such luck that a racing model called the Type NE evolved. With triple valve springs to sustain revs up to 7,000, twin SU carburetors, special manifolds which had been developed for the Type L specials, and high-domed pistons to boost the compression ratio to 9.8-to-1, the amazing NE developed 74.6 horsepower at 6,500 r.p.m. With this surprise entry at the Ulster T.T., C. J. P. Dodson won a tense hard-fought race to bring M.G. its third victory in that important event in four years.

The early Abingdon crew was very hard to beat. Time after time they rose to an occasion and overcame incredible handicaps. During 1934, the last year before M.G. withdrew from racing, they were commencing a redesigning program that probably would have revolutionized all their lines.

With the NE successfully holding down the 1,100-c.c. competition, the Midget engine was redesigned. Since the Type J engine was limited by its two-bearing crankshaft, and the K engine carried successful intermediate mains, the designers simply chopped two middle cylinders out of the K and came up with the three-bearing, four-cylinder PA power unit which was to be the basis for the last two M.G. racing cars — the Q and R types.

The PA had the usual 57x83 mm. bore and stroke, but in response to demands for more power the bore was increased to 60 mm. (2.36 in.), giving a capacity of 939 c.c. (57.2 cu. in.). This new model was named the PB in accord with the latest policy of naming a series by letter and modifications within the series by a suffix letter.

The P-type sports models were the last of the oh.c. midgets to go into production, for Morris sold out his interest in M.G. to Morris Motors Ltd., and in 1935 the axe fell. Racing was banned;

the highly successful 750-c.c. supercharged Q-type racing Midget which developed 113 horsepower at 7,200 r.p.m. (nearly as much as the 120-horsepower, 1,110 c.c. K3 Magnette of the year before), and the completely revolutionary R-type competition model with independent suspension all around, and an experimental Y-shaped rigid frame, all faded from the picture as control of the factory passed from the hands of the specials crowd.

After reorganization, all engines for the Morris, Wolesley, Morris Commercial and M.G. were assembled at one plant and were to be common to all models. The relatively expensive overhead-camshaft versions gave way to the 1,292-c.c. (78.8 cu. in.), pushrod-operated-overhead-valve engines which appeared with the TA model of the new line of Midgets and, though modified, still power the M.G. When the war brought an end to automobile production, the M.G. line consisted of the six-cylinder, 2,288- or 2,322-c.c. SA (140 and 142 cu. in.) which was produced as an open or closed four-seater; the TB Midget which evolved from the TA and was the first of the Midgets to use the 66.5×90-mm. (2.64×3.54 in.) bore and stroke that has continued right up to the latest TF model; the VA, a 1,500-c.c. four-cylinder open or closed four-seater; and the 2.6-liter WA sedan.

The last flicker of former competition greatness was seen in the famous EX 135. This car was originally built along the lines of the K3 for Eyston, who wanted to take a swing at the Class G records. With an odd-looking but comparatively streamlined body, Eyston drove the car to an hour record at 120.88 m.p.h., and in the process gobbled up the short-distance records at about that same speed. But when the racing ban was announced Eyston sold the car.

Perhaps nothing more would have been heard of EX 135 without the efforts of Lt.-Col. Goldie Gardner. He managed to interest Kimber in fitting a streamlined shell to the car for a try at lifting the 1,100-c.c. speed record up to 170 m.p.h. So EX 135 was purchased from its new owner, the now-famous Reid Railton streamlined body was constructed (without the benefit of a wind tunnel, incidentally), and the Class G records were blown wide open at an average speed of 187.61 and a one-way trip at 196 m.p.h.

The men returned to Abingdon, smugly certain that 200 m.p.h. was merely a matter of axle ratio. The following year, 1939, with the centric blower speed increased 17 per cent, the engine produced 202 b.hp. at 7,500 r.p.m. on the test bed. Armed with new gearing Gardner celebrated the opening of the autobahn at

Dessau by cracking the magic speed of 200 m.p.h. His speeds were: flying kilometer, 203.5 m.p.h.; flying mile, 203.9 m.p.h.; 5 kilometer, 197.5 m.p.h.; and the highest speed recorded was 206 m.p.h.

Not content even with that smashing triumph, engineers Reg Jackson and Sid Enever bored out the block, fitted .020 oversized pistons that brought the capacity up to 1,106 c.c. and sent the car out again to try for the Class F (1,100 to 1,500-c.c.) records. A duplication of the previous run was the only thing needed to sweep Class F, but the speeds were: flying kilometer, 204.2; flying mile, 203.9; five kilometer, 200.6; and a fastest one-way run of 207.4 m.p.h.

The highly festive group returned to Abingdon and began construction of a 750-c.c., six-cylinder engine that would mow down the Class H records, but the war broke out and, of course, all activity stopped and the project was shelved for the duration.

In the beginning, 1923, the M.G. was a group of motorcyclists' conception of a car that would be fun to drive and easy to own. By the time production was suspended in 1939, M.G. had become one of the world's most successful competition cars and a best-seller in the sports-car field. But the mighty Midget's most heroic commercial achievements were ahead in the postwar future.

IN 1950, WHEN THE HARDY SONS OF COVERED-wagon pioneers were demanding an end to the backbreaking slavery of shifting gears, Englishmen were still producing, buying and thoroughly enjoying a crude and lusty three-wheeled car. In

MORGAN

the United States motorcycles have seldom been regarded as a legitimate form of transportation; in England they are respected and used even by "blooded gentlemen," and few vehicles have been doted on more than that motorcycle with a body, the three-wheeled Morgan.

In the early experimental days of automobile manufacture many three-wheeled "cyclecars" were built. Morgan was born then, and it outlasted them all. To ensure its longevity, H. F. S.

Morgan concentrated from the first on two essentials well known
to be dear to the buyer's heart — power and economy — and
lavishly disregarded such effete considerations as comfort and
finish. From 1910 — when they were first built — until just before
World War II, Morgans were powered by violent two-cylinder
motorcycle engines which lay nakedly exposed on the frame tubes
in front of the body. They changed very little during their 40 years
of production. They used various engines, always the best available, and the buyer at any given time usually had his choice of
two or three. These always, of course, were of displacements that
seemed tiny by automobile standards, but the usual 1-liter (61 cu.
in.) was sufficiently powerful for the stripped-to-the-bone Morgan
so that the little three-wheeler eventually achieved speeds as high
as 116 m.p.h.

Morgan, like Henry Ford, would never use two pins if one
would do, and his determination to pinch pennies resulted in
simple construction that was sometimes precarious but frequently
indestructible. The vintage Morgans, for example, used the lower
chassis tubes as exhaust pipes and the vee twin engines were
braced only by a slender rod below the chassis. At the same time,
one owner vowed that when his clutch throw-out bearing shed all
its balls it continued to work every bit as well as before. Like the
old Model T Fords, Morgans were not troubled by small details
and could almost always be kept running by anyone equipped with
baling wire and chewing gum.

H. F. S. Morgan was a man who loved racing. He spent more
years driving in competition than probably any other man in
England, and it was not surprising that shortly after World War I
he began to market the three-wheelers in Grand Prix sports-car
form. These cars had the chassis construction that became standard for the make for most of the Twenties and were powered by
J.A.P., Precision and M.A.G. water-cooled engines. The wheelbase
was 84 inches and the car cleared the ground by just six inches.
The frame was tubular steel. The independent front suspension,
which had been a Morgan feature from the very first, was by coil
springs and sliding axles; rear suspension was by quarter-elliptic
leaf springs. Transmission was by a leather-faced cone clutch, and
drive was by two chains, one to a gear on each side of the rear
wheel.

The steering ratio was 1-to-1, and Morgan drivers were known
to develop strong wrists. The brakes consisted of external contracting bands on the rear wheels only. This lack of a brake for

every wheel may have been somewhat inefficient, but as one Morganophile remarked with admirable airiness, "Nine times out of ten you can accelerate your way out of trouble." Acceleration was hair-raising — the big-twin engines had a total weight of 500 pounds to cope with!

Starting was theoretically by an electrical unit but it seldom worked; most Morgan drivers admitted that starting was actually manual. These cars had no reverse gear and drivers became adept at climbing banks when they wanted to turn around. In traffic they were not unnaturally regarded by other drivers with what Sammy Davis called "a certain amount of alarm and despondency."

The G.P. series was replaced in 1924 by the Aero series, which was essentially the same but offered a different choice of engines — J.A.P., Anzani or Blackburne. The fastest of these had overhead-valve layouts, and one such Aero-Blackburne, in almost perfectly stock form, set a new record for the flying kilometer at Brooklands with 96 m.p.h. During the time that the Aero series was produced Morgan began smoothing out some of the rough edges. Steering reduction and three-wheel brakes were adopted, and in 1927 a super-Aero appeared with a low rakish body and an 80 m.p.h. guarantee. These cars grew heavier — to about 900 pounds — but retained their speed and power. They were generally fitted with water-cooled overhead-valve J.A.P. engines, and became very popular with motorists who had not lost the spirit of adventure. Anyone who drove one of these Morgans had a peculiarly intimate association with the innards of his car. The throttle controls were on the steering wheel, and by a touch of the hand the driver could see the valve gear operate at increased or reduced speeds in the exposed engine.

In the early Thirties the Morgan was produced with the new "M" chassis, which gave better stability and road-holding and had a three-forward-speeds-and-reverse gearbox. These chassis until the end of the prewar period were most often powered by optionally air- or water-cooled Matchless engines.

In the middle Thirties, Morgan began to market a lively little four-wheel car, first with the overhead-inlet-valve Coventry-Climax engine, and just before the war with a 1,267-c.c. (77.2 cu. in.), overhead-valve Standard engine. These "4-4" cars were additions to, rather than replacements in, the Morgan line. The three-wheeler continued into postwar times to provide adventurous and unconventional transportation for its numbers of faithful followers.

O.M.

O.M. COULD HAVE BEEN A GREAT AND FAMOUS sports car if Benito Mussolini had never happened to Italy. O.M. was rising in popularity and in engineering ingenuity when in 1930 *Il Ducé* — with bloodier combat on his mind than racing — abruptly directed the company to divert its operations to building military machines.

In spite of its untimely death, the O.M. (for *Officine Meccaniche*) made an impressive dent in racing during the years of its existence. It was built in Brescia, and appropriately its most resounding triumph was its victory in the first of the great Mille Miglia races, run from Brescia to Rome and back to Brescia. It is not difficult to believe that the volatile Italians achieved screaming hysteria when the "home town" make roared across the finish line 1-2-3 in that race.

The make's popularity both in Italy and abroad was enhanced by its square, clean, competent lines and the excellence of its craftsmanship throughout. Almost all the O.M.'s through the Twenties were powered by a deceptively stolid-looking six-cylinder, 1,991-c.c. (121.5 cu. in.), side-valve engine, although a pushrod overhead valve conversion later became available. Beautiful execution compensated for the engine's somewhat unexciting basic design. It had a fully machined, dynamically balanced circular-web crankshaft with integral counterweights, running in four plain main bearings water cooled by extensions in the water jackets down to the bulkheads. The crankcase was separate from the cylinder block, the superb quality of its casting indicated by its extremely thin walls.

1926 15/45 Model Italian O.M. These cars, powered by surprisingly potent side-valve engines, were often successful in major races on the Continent in the Twenties.

Autocar

Even in side-valve version, the car was capable of very snappy performance. It was offered in several horsepower varieties — 45, 60, 75 and the blown 80 and 85 which, aside from supercharging, differed primarily in compression ratios and carburetion. The least potent of these had a top speed of over 70 m.p.h. and could reach 60 m.p.h. in third gear.

In addition to the Mille Miglia *coup*, these cars won the Coupe Bienniale Rudge Cup Race at Le Mans in 1926, the Tripoli Grand Prix in 1925 and the Coppa Ciano in 1924. At the Mille Miglias of 1928 and 1929, however, O.M. had to content itself with running second to the double-overhead-camshaft Alfa Romeos; and still later, when Alfas entered the race in fleet lots, O.M. dropped to also-ran status.

Perhaps because of the Alfa invasion, O.M. in the late Twenties began to experiment with engines of more potent design. One of these was an overhead-valve, six-cylinder, three-carburetor, 2.2-liter (134 cu. in.) car, and the other a 1,500-c.c. (91.5 cu. in.), straight-eight, twin-overhead-camshaft model which was run blown or unblown and in the latter condition achieved 114 m.p.h. in an English race. Where these designs might have led O.M. in international competition will never be known. Neither went beyond the prototype stage, and shortly after their introduction Mussolini's directive brought the company's automotive production to a dead halt. From that time and into the postwar years, O.M. transferred its energies to military and industrial production, and became a pioneer in the development of high-performance diesel engines.

THE RILEY NINE WAS ONE OF THE MOST ENDURING and versatile cars of all time. Furthermore, while other cars of the late Twenties were gathering dust on the showroom floors, Riley Nine enthusi-

RILEY

asts materialized in great enough numbers to support a brisk black market even in those pre-austerity days. The Nine's numbers were, to be sure, necessarily limited by the facilities of the factory. Finally the public clamor became so great that the company was forced to suspend production of its previous model, the Eleven, even though it too still had a healthy consumer appeal. The Eleven had much of the outward grace of the new model, and was in fact widely thought of as one of the most attractive cars of its time. But its straightforward side-valve innards were far less exciting.

The Nine first appeared as a passenger car, but enthusiasts and engineers could not look at its power plant without realizing its great potentialities for racing. Percy Riley, who built the first car bearing his name in 1898 and then with his brothers formed the Riley Engine Company, put years of research into the design of the Nine, and the result was a powerful and advanced 1089-c.c. (66.5 cu. in.) engine that proved to be well worth the effort.

Cutaway of M. P. H. Model Riley of 1934. This car had 2-liter, 6-cylinder engine, did well in competition.

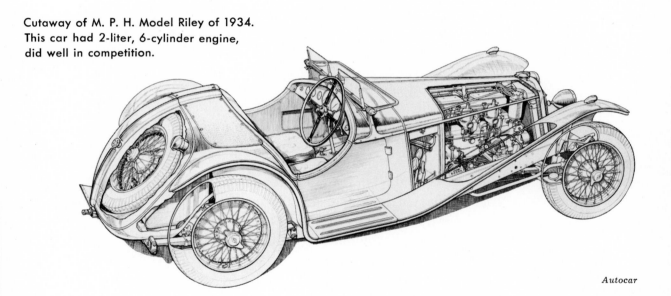

Autocar

There may have been small-displacement passenger-car engines that could compete with the Nine on grounds of originality but hardly any could match its designed-in rigidity and efficiency. The first experimental Nine engines produced in 1926 had separate block and crankcase castings, but this method was short-lived. Production for 1927 set the future pattern with a single deep, square, cast-iron structure combining both units. Riley carefully avoided the conventional split crankcase and used instead a modified barrel type which gave full 360-degree support to the two big main bearings. The crankshaft weighed 23 pounds and had unusually massive rectangular-cross-section webs, drilled for rod bearing lubrication. However, the oil was led from one end of each throw to the other by means of curved external tubes which were intended to minimize the centrifugal force acting on the oil flow. Oil pressure was generated by a novel plunger pump driven by two small connecting rods activated by eccentrics on the shaft of an idler gear which transmitted crankshaft motion to the camshaft gears.

A camshaft was located on each side of the four cylinders and as high in the block as possible. Each shaft carried an extra cam working against a spring-loaded plunger which acted as a vibration damper. The high location of the camshafts permitted the use of extremely short, light pushrods. By means of these and short, stiff rocker arms, each camshaft actuated a bank of 90-degree V-inclined valves seated in hemispherical combustion chambers. Intake and exhaust ports were short and straight, and manifolding was worked out with rational care. The engine's mounting arrangement was years ahead of its time. A tubular cross member extended through the crankcase between number one and number two connecting rods and was the means by which the forward part of the power plant was mounted in the chassis. There was no metal-to-metal contact between tube and crankcase: the tube rode in huge conical rubber bushings. A third rubber mount aft of the transmission completed the flexible support of the entire power unit.

None of these forward-looking details of design were lost on the sharp-eyed racing men who examined the Nine in its earliest form. The standard production engine developed just 34 b.hp. at 4,000 r.p.m. and the car's top speed was estimated modestly at 65

Autocar

The Tourist Trophy Model Riley of 1937.
Note "door" required by sports car regulations.

m.p.h. in a very mild degree of tune, but the knowledgeable could see that this was only the beginning. Such great men of racing design as Parry Thomas and Reid Railton took an immediate interest in the Nine, with the result that the power of the competition version was easily boosted to 55 b.hp. at 5,500 r.p.m., and running on alcohol the little engine was known to reach a shattering 99 b.hp. at 6,300 r.p.m.!

The first racing Nine was changed only slightly enginewise, a fact which paid tacit tribute to Percy Riley's talents. Its chief modifications lay in drastic but delicate surgery performed on the chassis by Railton. He cut the wheelbase from its original 107.5 inches to 91.5 inches by shortening the frame and driveshaft and moving the rear axle forward. The frame side members were bent sharply inwards from a point about in line with the steering wheel to accommodate a pointed tail. The body was lowered to a height of 36 inches at the cowl, the radiator redesigned and placed low behind the front cross-member of the frame. The aluminum bucket seat was dropped to a scant six inches above the ground and the driver sat with his elbow resting on a tunnel which housed the torque tube. This little car became the nucleus of the famous Brooklands sports version of the Riley.

The Brooklands and gradually evolving Nine-based cars which followed it earned for the marque an impressive record of competition success. In 1928 Riley set five new long-distance records at the Brooklands track with speeds from 83.34 to 87.34 m.p.h. From 1929 to 1931 Riley won its class in the Tourist Trophy race, and in 1931 also won the 1,100-c.c. class of the German Grand Prix at Nurburg. In 1933 a new Brooklands version with six cylinders and 1,486-c.c. (90.7 cu. in.) displacement, based — like the Nine — on a touring-sedan model and retaining *in toto* the engine arrangement of the Nine, began to be entered in competition and promptly won its class at the Le Mans 24 Hour Race. A modified version of this car known as the "White Riley" was raced very successfully by Raymond Mays, and had the distinction of becoming the direct ancestor of the famous E.R.A. Grand Prix racing cars later built by Mays.

In the middle Thirties the 1½-liter car was marketed again in four-cylinder form as the Sprite Series, and in six-cylinder form as the Alpine and Stelvio versions. In the last half of the decade 2-liter Rileys were produced with six- and eight-cylinder layouts; all, however, still based on the ubiquitous Nine. Shortly before the war Riley's assets were sold to the many-armed Nuffield

Organization, which put less emphasis on competition but left the car's excellent engineering almost entirely alone.

And in postwar times the black market which had thrived so nicely on the first Riley Nine found new profits in the new, sleek, ever-popular Riley — *still* powered by the engine that Percy Riley designed to last.

With amilcar, the sprightly, impudent Salmson of the Twenties was the car adored both by French enthusiasts and by those would-be expatriates who popped gaily over the English countryside sporting berets and a heavy admiration for Gallic sophistication.

	SALMSON

Their affection was amply justified by the make's competition record. Salmson probably won more races during its heyday than any car of its class.

Although throughout the Teens and Twenties they were always characteristically French in final form, the very first Salmson was actually of mixed parentage. It was a smart little car powered by an air-cooled chain-driven engine built by the Société de Moteurs Salmson of Billancourt under license from England's G. N. Company, Ltd. Salmson soon replaced this with their own engine, a four-cylinder water-cooled 1,100-c.c. (67 cu. in.) plant which appeared before World War I, was used for French aircraft during the war, and reappeared on the first postwar Salmsons.

This engine had two overhead valves for each cylinder — eight in all — but only four pushrods. One perplexed but delighted owner, writing in *The Autocar*, explained the rather startling absence of the other four pushrods like this:

"Inlet and exhaust were operated by the same rocker and pushrod. After closing the exhaust at about top center, the rocker continued to rotate, its other end bearing on the inlet valve and being pulled down by two tension springs mounted on an antler-like extension. The whole was an impressive sight, particularly when making its full 2,500 *tours*, above which speed valve bounce not unnaturally set in. Being enclosed only in free space, as it were, the valve gear was lubricated by hand, simultaneously with

Grand Prix Salmson of 1928 was petite, very cheap. It had
fabric body, traditional "X" radiator design.

the spark plugs, while other departments had little plates inscribed
'Fill with thick oil every few months,' and similar reminders of the
days before these designers went all scientific."

Scientific or not, Salmson management realized that intriguing
as this car was, it was not suited for really serious racing, and it
was through racing that they wished to advertise the marque. It
was the opinion of M. Petit, chief engineer of the Salmson racing
department, that special competition machines would wind up in
road use within a couple of years after their introduction, and
consequently the racing cars were designed so that they would
lend themselves easily to touring purposes. The first really high-
powered Salmson was equally suitable for both functions.

The four-cylinder engine had 1,087 c.c. (66 cu. in.) displacement, and double overhead camshafts which were responsible for
its fond nickname in England of "Twin-Cam Sammy." The camshafts were driven by a vertical shaft at the front and actuated
two inclined valves per cylinder in hemispherical combustion
chambers.

The sports production body was almost the same as its racing
counterpart, with the reluctant addition of little fenders and
running boards, tiny headlights and doors, and a minute vee windshield. The car's trademark for years was an "X" formed by two
nickel-plated tubes the diameter of a fat lead pencil which crossed
the rectangular radiator core and were anchored in the shell. The
car was almost single-seater narrow, but was theoretically a two-

seater, with "panels" (most often of fabric), a pointed "Grand Prix" tail, and thin, spidery wheels and tires.

This saucy "Sammy," often equipped with blowers, was entered in almost any race that was handy and seldom was beaten in its class. Salmson won the Biennial Cup at Le Mans for 1926-1927 and for 1928-1929, finished first and second in its class twice at the Targa Florio, won the 1,100-c.c. class in the Brooklands 200-miler with monotonous regularity from 1922 to 1925, and finally in 1926 succeeded in winning the J.C.C. Production Car Race outright, in the same year setting a lap record at that track of 114.49 m.p.h. These were some of its more important wins and there were literally hundreds of others.

Nevertheless, in the late Twenties the firm decided that four cylinders were too few and in 1928 introduced a 1,100-c.c. double-overhead-camshaft straight-eight engine. In spite of its exciting specifications it somehow could achieve neither the racing success nor the popularity of the four-cylinder car, and it did not go into general production.

Its predecessor represented the apex of Salmson's success in sports-car manufacture, although the company continued through the Thirties to produce cars of excellent quality, both in France and, for a few years before World War II, in England.

The British Salmson, although it harked back to the early mixed-breed days, was in some ways a complete departure from French Salmson tradition. Where the old Salmson had featured racy and piquant bodies, the new version in many cases represented dull and stodgy coachbuilding at its worst, a fact which must certainly have reinforced the anti-British feelings of the old Salmson clique. Why the British company made so small an appeal to the enthusiasts in styling was a mystery, because the engine was well designed and in a lighter, fleeter body would have been capable of really outstanding performance. It was of 1,470-c.c. (90 cu. in.) displacement and had double overhead camshafts actuating inclined valves by means of Ballot-type cup — or piston — tappets. An ingenious touch was the provision of aluminum "cushions" between the cups and cams, in the interest of silence.

Later versions of the British Salmson had larger engines, including a 2,590-c.c. (158 cu. in.) six. In 1938, production at the British works was suspended, and the car again became the French Salmson. It reappeared as an entirely French product in postwar years.

LIKE RILEY, SINGER MADE ITS NAME IN THE SPORT with a model called the Nine that was just as successful if not as long-lived. The Singer Nine first appeared in 1933. Singer had made a somewhat unsuccessful try at the sports market in the late Twenties with its little four-cylinder 848-c.c. (51.7 cu. in.) overhead-camshaft "Junior" model. This car even in its special "Porlock" sports version failed to make an impressive appearance on road and track, but its engine had a sound and potentially powerful basic design, and it was this engine, placed in a rugged, stable chassis, that became the Nine.

The same year it was introduced a nearly stock Nine was entered in the Le Mans 24 Hours, performed with good speed and perfect reliability, and won the distinction of being the first British car of under 1,000-c.c. displacement to qualify for the Rudge-Whitworth Biennial Cup. Naturally a "Le Mans" Singer model was promptly offered to a buying public now acutely familiar with the Singer name.

At the same time Singer began to produce a six-cylinder, 1,493-c.c. (91.1 cu. in.) engine for the Nine chassis. It had the by-now-standard Singer layout of chain-driven overhead camshaft, was equipped with three S.U. carburetors, and with various compression ratios achieved from 95 to 103 m.p.h. top speed. In 1934 Brian Lewis (Lord Essendon) and John Hindmarch co-piloted an example of the 1½-liter Singer to a seventh overall place at Le Mans, and brought home the second-place trophy of the Rudge-Whitworth competition for which the 1-liter model had qualified the previous year. The Lewis-Hindmarch car is still extant in England, now equipped with a banana-bunch of external exhaust pipes, and still gives newer and bigger cars a good race on occasion.

This particular car, and quite a few other Singers of the make's lusty years were given a "crab-track" chassis — the front axle significantly wider than the rear — and these dimensions added to the Singer's already outstanding cornering ability. Suspension on all the early Singers was by semi-elliptics all around, harsh and jolting at low speeds but properly firm and smooth when the car was really moving. Braking was by Lockheed hydraulics with deeply finned drums, and four-speed synchromesh gearboxes were standard.

In both 1- and 1½-liter form the Singers continued to pile up competition successes. The factory participated in racing with great enthusiasm for a few years, but in the 1935 Tourist Trophy Race three team Singers were demolished at precisely the same spot on the course when the pitman arms in their steering mechanism broke. They had been manufactured by an outside contractor, and Singer was not directly responsible for the tragedy, but the public was indignant, the press was cool, and Singer lost its taste for official racing. Nevertheless, privately owned Singers continued to offer provocative competition to the hot light cars of the time.

The 1½-liter Nines had a short life span — only about 50 were built — but the one-liter Nine continued in production basically unchanged until the war, although a highly tuned version called the "Replica" was added briefly to the line in 1936. Singer had, of course, been marketing quiet family-style sedans all along, and for 1937 introduced one that lasted only for a short time, and inexplicably was adapted to only a few sports chassis. It had a 1½-liter four-cylinder engine, with the usual chain-driven overhead camshaft, a dynamically balanced three-bearing crankshaft, twin S.U. carburetors and the unusual feature for a four-cylinder engine of a torsional vibration damper mounted on the front of the crankshaft. This engine, like the Nine, was later modified for use in the H.R.G. competition cars.

The last Singer sports model before the war was the 1,074-c.c. (65.5 cu. in.) Roadster, a somewhat subdued version of the Nine which retained the overhead camshaft but developed just 36 b.hp. at 5,000 r.p.m., and had a top speed of 68 m.p.h. This car continued in production until the war broke out, and reappeared after the war as Singer's answer to the new appetite for high-performance machinery that blossomed overseas.

The Singer Junior Sports model of 1930 was highly popular in England. It deserved to be, with a retail price of $800.

Autocar

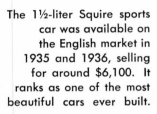

SQUIRE

Eᴠᴇʀʏ ɴᴏᴡ ᴀɴᴅ ᴛʜᴇɴ ᴀ ᴄᴀʀ ᴄᴏᴍᴇꜱ ᴀʟᴏɴɢ ᴛʜᴀᴛ makes no particular mark in the world but is so seductive in form and style that it just can't be ignored. The Squire was not an outright competition machine and it never won a race. Fewer than 20 were built, and their effect on the industry as a whole was negligible. Yet Squire needed to do nothing more than simply exist.

Courtesy of the Henry Ford Museum, Dearborn, Michigan.

The 1½-liter Squire sports car was available on the English market in 1935 and 1936, selling for around $6,100. It ranks as one of the most beautiful cars ever built.

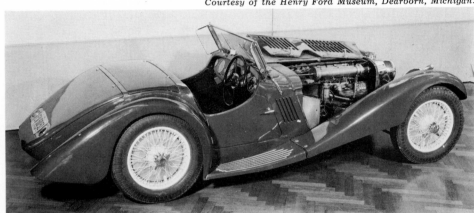

It was essentially a toy — an exquisitely engineered, impeccably finished toy designed to please that somewhat limited group of drivers who had little interest in such an energetic pastime as racing, but who nevertheless would pay $6,500 for a tiny four-cylinder two-seater that offered spirited performance and a more thoroughbred look than many true competition cars. This market, especially in the middle Thirties, soon proved to be a small one, a fact which was one reason for the short life span of the Squire Car Manufacturing Company. Another reason was that, expensive as the car was, its price was not high enough to pay the cost of its production. A. M. Squire did not cut corners when he built his car, and it was consequently both a financial failure and an automotive masterpiece.

The Squire's 1,496-c.c. (91.3 cu. in.) engine took full advantage of some of the most advanced engineering practices of its time. It had double-overhead camshafts, driven by a gear train and actuating V-inclined valves in hemispherical combustion chambers. At the forward end of each cam was a water pump. A vertically-mounted Roots blower was geared to the front end of the crankshaft and drew fuel through a single S.U. carburetor. The sump level was kept constant by automatic replenishment from a 2½-gallon supplementary tank on the firewall, and a handsome finned oil cooler and filter was mounted below the radiator, between the frame rails. The back of the left camshaft drove the distributor, the back of the right one drove the tachometer. The fine exhaust system consisted of a gently curving pipe running from each of the four ports to a big exhaust pipe under the car. The Squire was equipped with a Wilson four-speed pre-selector gearbox and hydraulic brakes. The brake drums were huge and there were airscoops in the brake backing plates for cooling the internal brake mechanism.

Even without all this, however, the Squire would have been a difficult car to overlook, because its Vanden Plas body was one of the most beautiful ever built, and had that perfect simplicity of line that any woman will tell you characterizes a $2,000 Paris gown. It was very low, with beautifully flaring fenders rising as high as the hood and sweeping back in a long, graceful curve. The line of the rear fenders was a perfect repetition of the subtly humped rear deck. In profile view the sharply slanted lines of the radiator, the hood louvers, the windshield and even the driver's seat were precisely parallel, a careful detail that gave an air of great harmony and integration to the whole.

All the Squires were sold with a certificate guaranteeing 100 m.p.h. top speed, and their gasoline economy was probably fine, but these details are as immaterial as knowing that Helen of Troy could cook. The Squire was a thing of beauty, and the few still extant are a joy to this day.

THE FIRST S.S.I. (SWALLOW SPORTS) OF 1931, THE grandfather of the potent double-overhead-camshaft Jaguars of today, had a wickedly extravagant air about it that immediately proved irresistible. It was only 54 inches high, with a long, long hood line that made the cab look tiny; and — in an age when one climbed precariously up on a running board to enter almost

S.S. JAGUAR

all production cars — the slinky S.S. needed no running boards
and had none. Long, low and handsome, with flowing, full cycle-
type fenders tucked demurely around racy wire wheels, it created
a sensation when it first appeared.

One startled newspaper gave it banner headlines: "The Car
With the £1,000 Look." But a thousand pounds sterling in those
days was close to $5,000; and this particular bit of fast living
could be purchased for only $1,509. Britain's largest firm of dis-
tributors immediately offered to buy all of the first year's production.

That first year's production, however, was small, for the
Swallow Company was nothing more at that time than one energetic young man, William Lyons, and a modest manufacturing
plant devoted chiefly to the production of motorcycle sidecars.

Lyons entered business in 1922 at the age of 20 with, as he
described it, "a partner, an idea, a heap of enthusiasm and a small
overdraft." Since he had named his sidecar the "Swallow," he
named the business "The Swallow Sidecar and Coachbuilding
Co." The addition of the word "Coachbuilding" was pure opti-
mism at first; but it was not long before the company took its first
step in the automotive field by designing and building special
bodies for the Austin "Seven."

These baby Austins occupied about the same spot in England,
economically and sentimentally, as the Ford Model T did in
America. They were tiny, ungraceful economy cars that sold well
within popular price ranges. Lyons contracted to buy chassis and
engines of these little cars in lots of around 50, and, with the
uncanny eye for line that never deserted him, designed special
bodies for them. The Swallow-bodied Austins were attractive,
comparatively luxurious, and sold for only $50 more than standard
models; business boomed to such an extent that in 1928 the little
Blackpool plant was bulging at the seams. With gamecock reck-
lessness, Lyons and his partner scooped up their business and
moved into part of a large factory building in Coventry — the
Detroit of England. Given this extra breathing room and constantly improving financial circumstances, Lyons was set free to
design and build a car of his own.

His first step was an arrangement with Standard Motors to
deliver chassis and engines constructed to Lyons' own design.
One was a 109-inch-wheelbase chassis with underslung suspension
front and rear giving a very low center of gravity and permitting
the design of bodies with an extremely low silhouette. The engine

was the stock Standard in-line six with a bore and stroke of
65.5×102 mm. (2.58×4.02 in.) and a modest 43-horsepower delivery at a peak of 3,400 r.p.m. This chassis, equipped with the
Lyons body, became the fabulous S.S.I.

The other car of that initial S.S. line has been totally eclipsed
by its big brother. The chassis was simply the stock "Little 9"
Standard, a four-cylinder, 1,005-c.c., 90-in.-wheelbase affair with,
of course, the sensational Swallow body added.

The enthusiasm that greeted the premier showing of the S.S.I.
at the 1931 London Annual International Automobile Exhibition
has already been described, and the bulging order books that
resulted dramatically launched the Swallow company into automobile production.

The S.S.I. was actually a one-man triumph. Lyons had exactly
determined those automotive features that the public wanted and
could not find: daringly racy and beautiful lines, luxurious finishing, and a low price tag. Although at least two of those demands
seemed mutually exclusive, they were not to a person like Lyons.
That he was an artist with a nearly perfect eye for line, his
products proved. But the man was also a demon of energy, a
salesman with a rare understanding of publicity values, and at the
same time a forceful, cold-headed businessman.

The real key to his success perhaps lay in his ability as an
administrator. Strong enough to keep the reins of management
tightly in his grasp, yet astute enough to delegate authority and

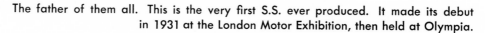
The father of them all. This is the very first S.S. ever produced. It made its debut
in 1931 at the London Motor Exhibition, then held at Olympia.

responsibility to his executives, he built an organization that was both resourceful and loyal. But although he inspired respect and even devotion among his subordinates, he was no easy taskmaster. Many of his pictures emphasized a jaw like an iron wedge and an eye capable of a hard cold glitter guaranteed to encourage workers along the paths of virtue and energetic accuracy. In later years, signs on the walls of the plant bearing such flatly final statements as "Damage Means Dismissal" helped drive the point home. From the efficiency engendered by this managerial firmness came the economy that made the S.S. and Jaguar cars so incredibly inexpensive.

With characteristic drive, Lyons saw in the astonishing success of the S.S.I. not an end, but an opportunity. Moving rapidly to cash in on the publicity created by the S.S.I., he began planning new models.

The S.S.I., while beautiful, developed only 43 horsepower and was far from sensational in performance; but it looked so fast just sitting still that, at first, no one really seemed to care. Lyons realized, though, that once the novelty of the car wore off, public reaction would turn against its comparatively sluggish performance. Within months he had a larger, 2,663-c.c. (163 cu. in.) alternative engine ready for the market.

By 1933 Lyons was able to form a company carrying the name of "S.S. Cars Ltd.," the plant had expanded to cover 500,000 square feet plus about 13 acres of the land around it, and employed about 1,000 workers. The S.S., too, went through some changes. The lines were generally cleaned up, and long, gracefully sweeping fenders replaced the cycle-type fenders of the earliest models.

With the constant need to improve the overall performance of the cars in mind, Lyons hired a young engineer from the Humber plant, W. M. Heynes. Heynes did his best to hop up the Standard side-valve (L-head) engines by adding a special dual-carburetor manifold, aluminum head and pistons, and light-alloy connecting rods. He raised the compression, polished up the engine throughout and redesigned the combustion chambers; but as any engineer can tell you, the L-head power plant has decided limitations. Although the hopped-up engine allowed the standard models to pull a 4.25:1 axle ratio as compared to 4.66:1 in earlier models, and top speed was thereby boosted to over 85 m.p.h. it became apparent to everyone that entirely new departures would be necessary.

This additional horsepower was put to work, though, in an entirely new line that had been Lyons' dream for years. He had wanted to produce a smaller car with a high power-to-weight ratio. The S.S. models had always been luxuriously appointed cars with a "sporting flavor": Lyons wanted to produce a car that would interest sports-car enthusiasts.

The finished product, the S.S. 90, actually founded the line that culminated in the postwar Jaguar. It had a 104-inch wheelbase, a track of four feet six inches, weighed 2,184 pounds and, powered by the hopped-up S.S. engine (with a high-lift extreme-overlap cam added), could turn an honest 90 m.p.h. The all-aluminum body managed to look stark and functional while still retaining the extremely graceful Lyons lines. The runningboards swept forward and upward into a regally flowing fender line which terminated well ahead of the radiator in the impressive classic fashion. Enormous chromed headlights added a final touch of efficient arrogance to the car.

But Lyons was not yet happy. The model had been named the S.S. 90 specifically because it was capable of a speed of 90 m.p.h. But the figure 90 m.p.h. means little; it is the magic 100 m.p.h. that is impressive. The publicity value of a car named the S.S. 100 because it *was* a 100 m.p.h. car would be enormous.

The side-valve Standard engine had been developed about to its peak, so Heynes was turned loose with a drawing board, a wealth of ideas, and 100 m.p.h. as his goal. Within a year he had developed a six-cylinder, pushrod-operated-overhead-valve engine of 2,663-c.c. (163 cu. in.) capacity that would produce 102 b.hp. A little later this same power unit was scaled up to 3½ liters (214 cu. in.) and the power output lifted to 120 b.hp. All this developmental activity was, of course, carried on behind locked doors and under a cloud of secrecy.

While Heynes sedulously closed in on the 100 m.p.h. goal, Lyons prepared to enter the market with an entirely new model. Rather than being a warmed-over Standard, he intended that it should be an entirely new car that was unmistakably his own. An entirely new name, then, was felt to be necessary. Cars had already been named after a Noah's Ark of living creatures — "Hawk," "Tiger," "Viper," "Hornet," for instance — so Lyons demanded that his publicity department prepare a list of all the beasts, fish and fowl that had not as yet been honored by the automotive industry. With such possible names as "Sloth," "Toad," "Polecat," and "Hog" omitted by the prudent publicity depart-

The 1934 S.S.I. 4-light 2-door saloon. This was the last model to be produced under the name of S.S., the next following model being the first of the Jaguars.

ment, a final list of 500 unsung creatures was completed on a crash-priority schedule and duly transmitted to Lyons. One writer states, "His decision was characteristically swift and uncompromising. 'We'll call it the Jaguar,' he declared."

The unveiling of the S.S. Jaguar sedan in a 1935 showing at London's swank Mayfair Hotel before 200 dealers and reporters was enlivened by another glossy-smooth publicity stunt. As soon as the initial squeals of admiration had subsided, Lyons passed around slips of paper and asked that everyone write down what he felt the sales price would be. After another look at the luxuriously appointed sedan which was later to be called "The Poor Man's Bentley," the figures were recorded and the slips collected. There was a period of carefully calculated tension. Then the actual selling price of the model was announced, and the audience gave a satisfactorily-astonished gasp. The price — only $1,700 — was far under the average of all the guesses.

There you have the secret of Lyons' success: as an artist, he produced beautiful cars; as an administrator, he delivered quality at popular prices; and as a showman, he knew how to drive his point home to the public.

With the S.S. Jaguar nailing down the more conservative end of the market, Lyons turned his attention to the 100 m.p.h. model, and finally the S.S. 100 was a reality. Outwardly, the first models were identical to the S.S. 90, but they contained the new ohv powerplants and, with the 3½-liter engine installed, could turn an honest 105 m.p.h.

In spite of its top speed, the S.S. 100 has been considered a "soft" sports car by the more hardy enthusiasts. The semi-elliptic springing was more than firm enough for ordinary high-speed motoring, but there was a tendency toward front-end instability at high speeds. Still, it handled remarkably well and developed its own hard core of enthusiasts. It certainly *wasn't* in the Bugatti class, but it was one of the most beautiful cars ever produced, and its rakish, classic lines are guaranteed to stop traffic to this day.

The difficulty was that the S.S. models were never tested by the factory in competition. Lyons pointed out with considerable historical accuracy that heavy concentration on factory competition was the quickest possible way for an automotive firm to lose money. "Let the customer do it" was his stand, so without the advantage of lessons directly learned in competition — the greatest proving ground of all — the S.S. models left something to be desired in handling.

Driven by private enthusiasts, though, the cars did bring home some impressive victories. S.S. cars won or placed high in the Marne Grand Prix, the International Alpine Trial, the Monte Carlo Rally, the R.A.C. British Rally, and in many Brooklands events.

By 1936 the S.S. company was in a sound position with an imposing line of merchandise including 1½-, 2½- or 3½-liter sedans or convertibles as well as the 2½- and 3½-liter, 100 m.p.h. sports cars. Feeling that a time of reorganization and consolidation was in order, Lyons incorporated the company (at this time his original partner, Walmesley, elected to resign), and with the fresh capital gained, he proceeded to expand the factory, modernize equipment and generally plan for the future.

No additional models were produced, but existing cars were smoothed out and improved. Just as Lyons realized that an entirely revolutionary line of models would be necessary, and the first prototype of the X.K. 120 reached the drawing board stage in development, the war broke out to put an end to all automotive activity without military purpose.

I F THE POST-WORLD WAR I STUTZ HAD NEVER done another thing, it would still live in history for having given the great W. O. Bentley one of the grimmest 24 hours of his life. While he watched, a lone Stutz entry in the 1928 Le Mans endurance race methodically chewed up two of his best cars and looked well

STUTZ

on its way to digesting the third. Brisson, driving the Stutz, had worked his way to first place and held it till 1:00 A.M., lost it during a pit stop, then come back to regain the lead for what looked like the rest of the race. Not till 2:30 that Sunday afternoon, just an hour and a half before the end of the event, did the Stutz run into serious trouble. The American three-speed transmission had had it — Brisson couldn't hold the car in gear by using both hands on the shift lever. The Bentley passed him to win. Stutz, however, came through with a solid second, averaging 66.42 m.p.h. for the 24 hours, traveling a distance of 1,594.1 miles.

The Stutz accomplishment received its full measure of applause in Europe. Americans today, more than 25 years later, look back on it with a feeling of pride and wonder. If those same feelings had been evoked in the American citizen of 1928 there might be a Stutz on the market today. As it was, only the friendly interest and fat pocketbook of Charles M. Schwab kept the Indianapolis concern solvent.

In the beginning of the marque's career, a good showing in a single race — the Indianapolis 500-miler of 1911 — had meant financial success. The one Stutz entered had finished 11th. Cars were introduced to the public the next year with the slogan: "The Car That Made Good In A Day." Designer and executive chief was Harry C. Stutz, operating under the name of Ideal Motor Car Company. In 1913 he formed, and became president of, the Stutz Motor Car Company, and in the same year his cars won the United States road-racing championship plus a third place at Indianapolis.

With this successful background of competition, Stutz presented, in 1914, what is perhaps the most famous American automobile of all time — the "Stutz Bearcat." With its top speed of somewhere between 75 and 85 m.p.h., its rakish styling (everything that wouldn't rust, including the passengers, out in the open), and the glamor of its name, the Stutz Bearcat cut heavily into the sales of the previously introduced Mercer Raceabout. The owner had his choice of a six- or a four-cylinder engine, both huge. The four had a displacement of 390 cubic inches; the six, 377 cubic inches. Both were of T-head design.

A major engine change occurred in 1915 when the racing-team cars were fitted with overhead cams and four valves per cylinder, a prophecy of things to come 15 years later in the DV32.

Harry C. Stutz abandoned his competition program shortly after the introduction of the four-valve engine, and finally sold

Autocar.

Stutz special Tourist Trophy model with close-coupled four-place coachwork,
photographed in London. The knock-off hubs are not standard Stutz equipment.

the company in 1919. From that year on he was not connected
with Stutz, though he did stay in the auto industry, introducing
his own H.C.S. car in 1921. Beginning in 1920 Stutz turned out
cars based on the original designs, adding small improvements
from year to year. In 1924 came the first overhead-valve-push-
rod engine — the Speedway Six — running as a companion model
to the traditional T-head four. The Speedway Six was the beginning of the transition to the overhead-cam eights that were
eventually to make up the entire line. It had the very common
3½x5 bore and stroke, 288 cubic inches displacement and developed 80 b.hp. at 3,000 r.p.m.

The first overhead-cam eight arrived in 1926. This Series
AA was the basic engine retained by Stutz till its demise, though
it went through numerous modifications as a result of the competition experience the company began to acquire when racing
was resumed in 1927. It was difficult to find the correct type of
racing in the United States. There were two choices — both on
track-type courses — stock cars or all-out racing cars. In the
first category, the Stutz Black Hawk mopped up everything in
sight; in the second, the company raced Miller equipment under
the Stutz name and did fairly well in 1928. Frank Lockhart's
highly publicized record attempts in a Stutz were also done with
Miller engines.

The 1928 Stutz used by Brisson in the Le Mans race was a
Model BB, a bored-out, hopped-up continuation of the AA. For
1929 the BB gave way to the Model M, which turned out to be
a bored-out BB. With this additional power plus a new four-

speed transmission a team of three Stutz cars returned to Le Mans for the 1929 running of the event. In addition, Brisson's car had a Roots-type supercharger mounted in front of the radiator between the frame rails. The blower drove through the carburetor and furnished a maximum of four-pounds pressure. Five Bentleys faced the Stutz team, one of them with a 6½-liter engine. The race turned out to be a disappointment for two Stutz drivers, Brisson and G. E. T. Eyston went out with split fuel tanks, a technical shortcoming that evidently hadn't been anticipated. The third Stutz finished fifth.

For 1930, Chief Engineer Charles R. Greuter revamped the entire engine from the combustion chambers up. His new head had twin overhead camshafts, chain-driven, and four valves per cylinder. Called the DV32, it is easily the most famous of the Stutz engines, though its actual competition performance was so limited that it is difficult to rate it. At Le Mans in 1930 two of them went up against *six* Bentleys, three of them 6½-liter models and the other three the blown 4½-liter competition specials. Also very much in the running that year was a lone supercharged Mercedes-Benz driven by Caracciola. Brisson's Stutz, hounded by incredibly bad luck, literally exploded on the course, and the other DV32 went out with a broken axle.

Thus ended the last brave attempt by an American company to win an internationally famous sports-car road race until the advent of Briggs Cunningham after World War II. For its struggle Stutz was paid poorly. Even the reintroduction of the Bearcat and the inauguration of the light and powerful Super Bearcat could not turn the public's apathy into interest. America's last, and perhaps best, sports car was forever dead after 1934.

"IT BEHOOVES ALL PATRIOTIC ENGLISHMEN TO know their Sunbeams."

| SUNBEAM |

Thus wrote an earnest *vintagent* in England's organ of the hobby — *The Vintage Car*. The statement was only slightly an exaggeration. Sunbeam was, to be sure, a member of the intricate Anglo-French

Sunbeam-Talbot-Darracq combine, and its designer was a Frenchman. Nevertheless, Sunbeam *was* essentially a British marque, one always regarded with great pride by Englishmen, and it produced most of England's few successful all-out racing cars. Grand Prix cars and land-speed records are not within the scope of this book, but it is difficult not to mention such Sunbeam successes as its victory in the 1923 French Grand Prix and its distinction, in 1927, of exceeding 200 m.p.h. on land for the first time, an achievement for which the driver of the 1,000-b.hp. twin-engined monster, Henry Segrave, was promptly knighted.

Chief designer for all the S.T.D. cars in their greatest days was Louis Coatalen, a man who believed passionately in racing. He designed many, many competition cars, and simultaneously designed many touring cars. And yet, although the difference between racing and sports design was not nearly so vast in the early decades as it is today, he produced only one true sports Sunbeam, the Three Liter.

The Three Liter appeared in 1925, and in spite of its high-performance, G.P.-derived design it competed successfully in just one important race during its lifetime, the 1925 Le Mans. In that event, co-piloted by the appropriately Anglo-French combination of Davis and Chassagne, the Sunbeam placed second, thoroughly defeating the 3-liter Bentley whose smashing success in the previous year's race the Sunbeam Three Liter may have been built to eclipse.

At any rate, the Three Liter continued in production until 1931, and during that time became by far the most admired and desired model of the otherwise relatively unsporting Sunbeam line. Very few basic changes were made in it during its years of existence. The six-cylinder engine had vee-inclined valves in the head operated by two overhead camshafts driven by helical gears. The camshafts and crankshaft each ran in seven bearings, and there were two Claudel-Hobson carburetors. Body and chassis were carefully crafted and finished, and the engine developed about 105 b.hp. at 3,800 r.p.m. and gave the car a top speed of around 90 m.p.h.

In 1928 Sunbeam introduced a supercharged version of the Three Liter, and that proved to be a mistake. Only a few of the blown models were built, but one was raced by Sir Malcolm Campbell in 1929 and another by B. O. Davies in 1930. On both occasions Sunbeam retired ignominiously, the blower basically at fault. In 1929 the clutch proved unable to cope with the increased (to 138 b.hp.) power, and in 1930 the blower's inadequate mounting caused it to shift and shatter its casing. The supercharged Three Liter was quickly discontinued, the one reminder of its existence in later models being the rear-axle ratio, which was retained at the 3.9-to-one initiated in the blown cars.

From 1930, a year before the Three Liter was discontinued, until 1932, the Sunbeam organization found itself in an executive crisis. The Coatalen-trained chief designer, Hugh Rose, had left the company and for two years Sunbeam struggled along with no one to take his place. This interim was the most barren, sportswise, in Sunbeam's recent history. In 1932, however, another Coatalen student, H. C. M. Stephens, joined the company, and under his supervision a new semi-sports Sunbeam was produced, the "Dawn." It was a small four-cylinder car of 1,627 c.c. (99.3 cu. in.) displacement with a pushrod-operated overhead-valve layout. It was the first Sunbeam to have independent front suspension, but the transverse leaf-spring arrangement it used proved to be more of a headache than an advance.

In 1935 Sunbeam's financial troubles became so acute that the company's assets, along with those of the British Talbot company, were acquired by its principal creditors, the Rootes organization. Under the new management the Sunbeam name disappeared for years, to be resuscitated finally as part of the Sunbeam-Talbot name borne by the sports-type touring cars of the late Thirties and the postwar era. Thus the great racing name of earlier days met its hyphenated future.

VAUXHALL

ALDOUS HUXLEY, IN "THOSE BARREN LEAVES," creates a hero who vacillates between dashing manhood and cowering mousehood. The catalyst that turns a callow, lisping aristocrat into a swashbuckling youth is a 30/98 Vauxhall, driven hard. As long as the car is devouring dirt roads at 70 or 80 m.p.h. and the wind is tearing at his goggles, His Lordship is capable of the bravest, brashest deeds. When the ride ends so does his courage. Huxley's book was written in 1925 and he put his man in a 30/98 for the good reason that it was the lustiest sports car of its time.

Its life span stretched from 1913 to 1927 and even today it is the yardstick against which a vast number of British enthusiasts gauges the quality and performance of vintage sporting machinery. One member of the Vauxhall cult says the 30/98 typifies "motoring-carved-from-the-solid"; others boast of "its sheer animal ferocity." A king of thoroughbreds, it was and it remains a connoisseur's treasure.

The 30/98 sprang from the Vauxhall Iron Works, established in London in 1857. Their business became the manufacture of marine engines, and in 1903 the first Vauxhall car was offered for sale. Two years later the firm acquired the services of Laurence H. Pomeroy, engineer and father of the great automotive writer of the same name. The elder Pomeroy designed a series of brilliantly successful cars including the "Prince Henry Vauxhall" in 1910, often called the first true production sports car produced in Britain.

In 1913 a hill-climb enthusiast asked the firm to build him a car that could break the record at Shelsley Walsh. Pomeroy agreed to meet his needs and designed a modified 4.5-liter (270 cu. in.) Prince Henry which effortlessly slashed the record from 63.4 seconds to 55.2. In the same year the same machine *averaged* 108.03 m.p.h. for a lap at Brooklands — an impressive speed today for a medium-sized car.

This car was the first of the breed that came to be known variously as the 30/98, the E-type 30/98 and the Velox. There was little in its basic design to suggest outstanding performance. It used a straightforward sidevalve engine as prosaic as the Model A Ford's, with, however, generous valve and port areas, centrally located spark plugs and beautifully machined H-section connecting rods. This careful attention to detail and a fairly radical camshaft were responsible for the car's impressive behavior.

In the interest of greater flexibility throughout the r.p.m. range, the E-type engine was revised in 1922 to the OE 30/98. The OE's stroke was shorter and it had pushrod-operated overhead valves; it revved fast for 1922 — 112 horsepower at 3,500 r.p.m. compared to the E-type's 90 at 2,800. But in spite of all this apparent progress, no 30/98 ever improved on the original prototype's times at Brooklands and Shelsley Walsh, not even when a counterbalanced crankshaft was added in 1926.

In that year another body style was added to the 30/98 series.

It was the "Wensum," a boat-tailed two- or three-seater that was handsome and rakish but never quite replaced the traditional Velox four-seater in the public regard or in competition.

The racing success of these cars was truly phenomenal. At Brooklands alone the E-type 30/98's had by 1936 captured 13 firsts, 19 seconds, and seven thirds, and the OE's had 14 firsts, nine seconds, and seven thirds. The factory's enthusiastic support of racing was a potent factor in keeping sales of the medium-price 30/98 at a high level until the early Twenties, when the automotive industry as a whole tottered from the effects of world-wide economic depression.

In 1926 Vauxhall was sold to General Motors. G.M. kept the 30/98 current only so long as it took to convert the plant to the production of automobiles with a more universal appeal.

But the 30/98's adherents, if few in terms of mass production, were fervent. The death of the model in 1927 made extant examples even more precious, and many are carefully preserved today, not only in England, but also in Australia and New Zealand. They seem to be indifferent to age and many are entered regularly in competitions. As recently as 1953 one 30/98 owner casually performed a feat that can only be termed extraordinary.

This was a T. H. Plowman, who in August of that year shipped his old two-seater across the Channel, drove it from Dunkerque to Montlhery autodrome and arranged to make some speed runs under the accurate supervision of the official timers of the Auto-

Touring model of the 30/98 Vauxhall: comfortable and violently fast.

mobile Club of France. They may have muttered something about "mad dogs and Englishmen," but Plowman paid his fee and set about removing from the car such bric-a-brac as fenders, license plates, and door handles. He changed spark plugs, added a richer needle to the single S.U. carburetor, and told the timekeepers to wind their watches; he was ready.

Within a couple of turns around the concrete saucer, Plowman began lapping consistently at about 104 m.p.h. He came in and announced to the now wide-eyed French timekeepers that he would like to be timed for exactly one hour. After three warm-up laps he was given the flag for his flying start. For the first half-hour, every lap the old 30/98 turned was within a few 10ths of 105 m.p.h. Then the car hit its stride and rapidly picked up speed until it achieved a top of 108.78 for one lap. The average for a solid hour was 106.91 m.p.h., with 120 m.p.h. exceeded consistently on the straights.

Plowman was not running for a record or for a show. His car was 29 years old, hadn't been opened up since Brooklands closed before the war, and Plowman wanted to see how fast it still would go. When he found out, he replaced fenders and the rest of his hardware and quietly motored back to the Channel ferry. Without saying a word he had created a Critique of Progress which will long be cherished and cited by the vintage cult.

M. GABRIEL VOISIN WAS A WEALTHY AND WONDER-ful Frenchman who made his fortune in aircraft during World War I and after the war spent it gorgeously indulging his passion for building extraordinary automobiles. In a sense all the

VOISIN

Voisins were experimental cars, and most of them were in one way or another wildly unlike anything seen before or since.

One of M. Voisin's first cars appeared in 1921, and in 1922 won the distinction of snaking over the twisting Alpine road from Paris to Milan in record time — a good two hours faster than the Orient Express. This Voisin's aspect was — like most of them — bizarre. The two-seater body was made entirely of aluminum, including a sort of skeleton version of fenders which consisted of two perfectly flat sheets of aluminum attached to each side of the hood, flush with the radiator at the front and extending back a bit beyond the hood at the rear. Just below and behind these were three square aluminum baffles, which looked very much like cupboards without sides. Both of these arrangements had practically no wind resistance and furthermore gave excellent protection from mud and rocks on the road. The driver of the Paris-Milan run, one Dominique Lamberjack, vowed that he drove through pools of water at 60 m.p.h. and, even though this Voisin had no windshield, got not a drop of water in his face.

1930 Voisin 12-cylinder
had traditional fender braces,
unorthodox body. It sold for $7,800.

Autocar

The engine of this car had the sleeve valves that most Voisins used, regardless of size and number of cylinders. All Voisins of this period also had bodies that reflected M. Voisin's preoccupation with the challenge of wind resistance. Some of these were crude and almost comical, but they were also among the first attempts of their kind.

One of the most fantastic embodiments of M. Voisin's anti-wind prejudice was a car entered in the 1924 Grand Prix de Tourisme, run for passenger rather than racing cars. Its performance in the race made no headlines but its appearance certainly did. It was a four-seater, so narrow that the front doors were, out of sheer necessity, bulging curved panels. The rear doors coped with the problem of fitting two people into an impossibly small area in another way: their upper halves slanted outward from the rest of the body like the arms of a "Y." In any case the rear seat was not intended for human passengers. Instead it carried a large vertical cylindrical fuel tank which was distinguished by a contents gauge with huge, seven-inch dial, screwed into its top. This was typical of the interior decor; the dashboard was a looming mass of gauges and controls.

By far the most improbable feature of the car, however, was its front end. It had the sloping profile of a locomotive cowcatcher and consisted of flat knife-edged metal panels on the top, bottom, and on both sides. A rectangular opening was left in the upper slope of this sheet-aluminum wedge, through which air could reach the recessed radiator. In front of the radiator spun a four-bladed propeller measuring about a foot from tip to tip, which acted not only as a somewhat incongruous reminder of Voisin's aircraft background, but also used wind velocity to drive a small, extra oil pump. Above this, affixed to the hood, which ended in a canopy projecting some six inches beyond the radiator, was the Voisin mascot, a great aluminum bird with vertically raised bolted-on wings. In spite of its somewhat ludicrous appearance, this car was an earnest attempt at streamlining and light-alloy construction. Almost all of the engine was built of light metals, and the torque-tube and rear-axle casings were of built-up dural sheet.

The next Voisin that made history had a far more discreet and professional look, and was in fact as slick and smooth a job of streamlining as could be found in its time. It was powered by the usual sleeve-valve engine, this time a 7,939-c.c. (485 cu. in.)

Of all Gabriel Voisin's radical creations during almost two decades of automobile manufacture, one of the most fantastic was his in-line twelve of the late Thirties.

Autocar

straight-eight. This car in 1927 broke the world's 24-hour record with an average speed of 113.4 m.p.h., and scooped up six records of lesser importance at the same time. The same year the same car, this time equipped with underslung-chassis-frame construction, set a new world's one-hour record at 128 m.p.h.

These spectacular achievements must have been utterly intoxicating to M. Voisin, for few manufacturers had such a proud and fatherly attitude toward their products as he did. He frequently rode with the testing crew in newly-assembled Voisins, and those that met his own impeccable standards he personally crowned with the Voisin bird.

His flair for drama continued to be expressed in the Voisin cars throughout the Thirties, particularly in their luxurious and advanced coachwork, and one of the last Voisins in 1936 was one of the most unlikely of all. It was a *straight-12*, so long that the hood extended a foot beyond the fenders and two of the cylinders were extended through the firewall, warming the feet of the front-seat passengers.

Voisin ceased to be produced in 1938. Gabriel Voisin must have been content. He had added a vivid chapter to the proud legend of *l'individualité française.*

PART TWO

Classic Cars

DE GRAND LUXE

IN 1953, IF YOU HAD AN UNLIMITED CHECKING ACCOUNT AND A passion for automobiles, you could take your choice of a vast number of exotic and expensive machines. Saoutchik would build you a body on almost any chassis you preferred, a body as fantastic as your taste dictated. Pegaso would take your order for a sports car that would reputedly do everything any high-performance car had ever done and more. Any one of a large number of Italian coachbuilders would turn out a high-fashion body shell and sew it on a Ferrari or a Cunningham or a Cadillac. But you couldn't buy a Phantom IV.

There was one exception to that last statement — you could order a Phantom IV if you were of sufficiently high rank. Some

157

eight were made, as of the beginning of 1954, and more were slowly being fashioned for the few aristocrats who could afford them. But the average man hadn't a chance.

The Phantom IV, of course, was the official title of the postwar, king-size Rolls-Royce, a direct descendant of the Silver Ghost and Phantoms I, II and III. It might be called the big brother of the small, postwar Rolls-Royces that were sold in America, but it was essentially far more than that. For it was almost the world's last out-and-out *voiture de grand luxe,* as anachronistic in the post World War II era as a horse in a mechanized cavalry unit. In size, styling, performance and craftsmanship the Phantom IV was a product of the decade and a half that preceded the war — the classic period.

Between 1925 and 1942 the skills and special knowledge required to make a great luxury automobile were abundantly available in the five important automobile-producing nations. From the past had come craftsmanship, the ability to work with the metal and wood and fabrics that made up the custom and semi-custom bodies. From the past, also, had come the tradition of quality as an end in itself, an intangible but essential part of the finished product. Both had been a major part of the luxury automobiles of earlier days, perhaps to a greater extent than during the classic period, but the chassis and engines of those early cars had been primitive. Not till after World War I did the engineers catch up with the craftsmen. It was during the classic era that luxury cars first became the smooth, silent, trouble-free servants they had long been advertised as being. A 1920 Locomobile or an earlier Crane-Simplex cost many times more than a 1932 Packard Twelve, and represented at least five times as much careful, skilled hand labor, but the Packard was a better luxury car.

Engineering and craftsmanship are important, but the determining factor in the establishment of the classic period as the golden era of luxury cars was styling. Up until about 1925 automobile-body design was essentially functional. Fenders were honestly intended to do little more than live up to their old name of mudguards. The engine was enclosed in the smallest compartment that could be built for it, and hood lines were straight and square. At the front of the engine was the radiator, at first bare and later covered by shutters designed not for beauty but to function as a control for the amount of air admitted to cool the engine. Invariably the radiator was positioned over the front axle. Headlights — not yet incorporated into fender or body — stood nakedly in front. In the rear, the body customarily ended directly over the axle in a sharp vertical line, with the rear fenders extending beyond it. On this bare and simple framework was frequently positioned the craziest and most impossibly complex tonneau imaginable. Its design bore no relation to the chassis, and the inevitable result was a completely unharmonious, bizarre and ugly vehicle. If the tonneau was as plain as the rest of the body the effect missed being ludicrous, but it was still far from beautiful.

The artistic revolution of the Twenties made a tremendous impression on the shape of the automobile. Early in that decade, the traditional bodybuilders began to lose control of their monopoly of the field, primarily because customers wanted something in keeping with the times. The story of Le Baron is symbolic of the changes that took place. Tom Hibbard and Ray Dietrich left the greatest coachbuilding firm in America, Brewster of Long Island, to establish their own firm in Manhattan in 1920. Both were young stylists, full of ideas. After a year they were joined by Ralph Roberts, a young enthusiast fresh from university. The three men almost starved for two years while they submitted drawings to anyone who would look at them. Since they had no body plant, they had to be content with their fees for drawings alone. Gradually their designs caught on, and they built up an architect-like arrangement whereby they took the order from the customer and sub-contracted the actual building of their design to a body plant. In another couple of years they had built themselves up to the point where they could merge with the Bridgeport, Connecticut body works and take the profits from the entire process. This was only the beginning. There too much creative ability in each of the men to make for a stable relationship between the three. Hibbard left first, setting up his firm of Hibbard and Darrin in Paris — Darrin being, of course, Howard "Dutch" Darrin, another American designer. Dietrich went to Detroit under an arrangement with Murray — a builder of stock production bodies for cheap cars — that permitted him to set up a separate branch of that firm for custom bodies. His designs were later some of the most famous in the United States, seen on Packard, Lincoln, Pierce-Arrow and other classics. Roberts went to Detroit, too, on a similar arrangement with Briggs Manufacturing Company, another builder of stock, cheap bodies, and established the Le Baron division of that firm.

The move to Detroit of both Roberts and Dietrich was occasioned by the rise of the semi-custom body in the luxury field. For an explanation it is necessary to go into a brief discussion of the relation of bodymaker to chassis builder. There were many of the classic manufacturers, Rolls-Royce being a good example, who did not make their own stock bodies for their chassis. Instead, the customer ordered a chassis from the maker and had it shipped to a bodybuilder. There, after discussions between the body firm and the customer, the body was built. It was customary with most of the established coachmakers, as they were still sometimes called, to design for the salon each year a few sample bodies. These could be ordered placed on any chassis. Since their dimensions had already been thoroughly worked out they cost the customer less than a custom body made to his individual specifications. Within the framework of the coachmakers' standard designs the customer still had enough options to give him the comfort of receiving a body that would not be quite like anything else on the road. He could choose upholstery colors and fabrics, accessories both inside and out, exterior finish, top covering material, interior hardware, etcetera. The manufacturer of the chassis dictated none of the details of the body except, usually, the hood, fenders, cowl and instrument panel.

Though most of the customer contact was necessarily with the bodybuilder, the chassis manufacturer was the one that "maintained sales rooms and offices in principal cities throughout the world for the convenience of the purchaser." Frequently one office served more than one manufacturer. For example, the A. J. Miranda firm in New York handled Minerva, Maybach-Zeppelin, and Delage for America.

While the automobile was still young, this continuance of the old carriagemaker system benefited all parties to the contract. The chassis builder was relieved of the expense and responsibility of maintaining a body plant, the coachbuilder served so many chassis builders that he was able to build and keep a large inventory of materials and a permanent staff of skilled workers, and the customer was able to select and combine his favorite body and chassis.

As the automobile became a more important part of the world's economy and the individual companies grew larger, chassis builders gradually took over the functions of the bodybuilders. It was during the final stages of this process that the semi-customs became so popular. A chassis maker would ask to have design sketches and models submitted to him by the body-builder each year. From those submitted he would select the few he wanted and order from 50 to 200 bodies made for delivery to the factory, or in some cases for fitting to factory chassis at the bodybuilder's plant. Assured of this volume of work the body-builder could quote a reasonable price far below the cost of the same body built singly. The customer lost a little in individuality but he gained much in price. The chassis maker could control his product from start to customer. This is the arrangement Le Baron had with Lincoln before Roberts moved to Detroit.

Both Briggs and Murray had built up a tremendous volume business in low-cost bodies for Fords, Chryslers, Dodges and other popular cars, and they saw an opportunity to cash in on the luxury-car trade as well. With such mammoth corporations as these in the competition, the smaller independent bodybuilders, most of which were still located far from Detroit, lost a major portion of their business.

The situation in Europe was entirely different. There, semi-customs never reached the status they did in America and the bodybuilders remained strong — so strong, in fact, that they were still around after World War II, proving more durable than many of the chassis makers.

For America, then, the classic period was one of major change in the relation of the bodybuilder to the chassis maker. Even more significant was the change within the body industry, where styling of the traditional type fought a losing battle with the young ideas of Le Baron's founders and others like them. The new style was lower, with more emphasis on the length of the hood. Sharp corners were rounded, fenders were brought down in front to, finally, the bumper line. In the early Thirties, the use of slanted windshields and V-shaped radiator grilles became standard practice. Passenger compartments were now built as a logical extension of the front part of the body, only a few wildly unorthodox carriage-type bodies remaining in the catalogues. Right in the middle of the classic period came the rash of experimental bodies like the Pierce-Arrow Silver Arrow, bodies which were to fail miserably in sales but which drew sufficient publicity to warrant the expenditures made on them.

Classic styling was so positive in its effects on the automobile world that it eventually set the pattern for all the cheap production cars. Never before, or since, has there existed a group of designers so powerful as the semi-custom and custom body builders of the Twenties and Thirties. Darrin, in speaking of the effect of the designers of the period on future styles, points out that there is no way a mass manufacturer can experiment with the appearance of his product safely. An engineering laboratory can test engines and chassis, can even measure the durability and aerodynamic efficiency of a body, but is helpless when faced with the job of finding out whether the buyer wants fadeaway, clamshell or cycle fenders. The only method of testing public taste is to show the designs and let the people make the decisions. The bodies built on classic chassis by Dietrich, Castagna, Hooper, Saoutchik and others were widely publicized in the newspapers and magazines, and then sent on a tour of the great auto shows. If the public liked them, their distinctive design features would be picked up by the mass manufacturers.

It is, of course, entirely subjective to say that the designs of the classic era are more beautiful than those of the post-World War II period. They do represent the highest development of the traditional school of automobile design. A long hood, the symbol of power and speed, was indispensable to a classic car, and was one of the design elements that differentiated the expensive automobile from the cheap one. Packard made the hood of its 12-cylinder classic longer than the hood of the eight, though the eight engine was considerably longer. This meant that much of the space under the hood of the Twelve was devoted solely to prestige. The French Delage had one of the longest hoods in history, though the engine was not as large as most of the classics had. The prestige of the long hood was gained at the expense of passenger capacity and comfort. Modern practice is to shorten the hood as much as possible to gain extra passenger space.

The long wheelbase went with the long hood, and was the inevitable result of traditional chassis design. Overhang was almost non-existent, except for bumpers and fenders. A 144-inch-wheelbase Packard V-12 is about the same in overall length as a modern Buick or a small Cadillac, though the wheelbase of the modern cars is almost two feet less. Other traditional features of the classics were the narrow bodies with running boards and the location of the rear seat over the rear axle. The very impracticality of the classic designs shows that the stylists were sacrificing everything to fashion and appearance. Thus, beauty and stability of design joined engineering and craftsmanship in this era to create the finest luxury automobiles the world had ever seen — better luxury cars than the world would see for at least the first decade after the war.

None of the great cars would have been made if economic conditions had not been favorable. In the beginning of the classic era, 1925, the United States was in the midst of its decade of greatest prosperity to that date. The frantic days of widespread stock-market speculation were yet to come, and jobs were plentiful in comparison with times past. Consumers were buying more "hard" goods than ever before, thanks largely to installment-plan buying, or, as the makers of classic cars liked to say, "purchasing out of income." With all this prosperity there was still a vast disparity between the income of wage-earners and employers, a state of affairs that did not disturb the average laborer unduly. He went right along with his wealthier fellow citizens and elected Calvin Coolidge in 1924, though Coolidge's platform was dedicated to maintaining the status quo.

There were minor depressions during the Twenties, but none so severe as the first one which began late in 1920 and lasted through 1921. The general trend of the economy was so solidly upward that gradually an almost super-confidence was bred in the people, particularly in those who had made their fortunes during that decade. This was the feeling that boosted the investment in personal luxuries like big cars, big houses, and jewelry.

Automobile manufacturers had yet another factor operating in their favor. This was the era of the automobile's coming-of-age. Not only was it reasonable to spend money, it was fashionable to spend it on cars. As in the post-World War II period, there was almost a seller's market during the late Twenties. In Hollywood and New York the craze for expensive foreign cars brought Rolls-Royce, Mercedes, Hispano, Isotta and a few others into the United States in larger numbers than ever before or since. Most of the foreign classics in collectors' hands today date back to the late Twenties. Those who could not afford to jump to the $10,000-and-up class bought Packards, Cadillacs and other United States compromise classics.

Compounding the automakers' happiness was the fact that the all-purpose luxury car had not yet become supreme. People still bought town cars, phaetons, seven- and five-passenger sedans, roadsters, convertible sedans, victorias, and a few others in a variety of weights and sizes. A Packard dealer who handled extremely wealthy customers did not consider a transaction a success unless he sold two or three cars to each one.

Nor did the customers expect yearly model changes. It was possible to use the same patterns and dies till they sagged with age and justify the lack of progress by advertising that the car would not look out of date in five years. The fact that it looked five years old when it was new made no difference. It was the maker's name the customer bought, not newness.

Between 1925 and 1930 the 3½x5 bore and stroke, eight-cylinder, L-head was the standard fixture on the American classics. Eights and sixes were both popular in Europe. Displacement was seldom less than 300 and seldom more than 400 cubic inches. An honest top speed of 80-to-90 m.p.h. was considered plenty, and many of the cars could not reach even the lower mark. The classic was not judged on its acceleration or top speed, but on its comfort, reliability and silence. As long as the big car could outrun a Ford or Chevrolet or Buick, the owner was satisfied.

In 1929, the most insane year of the prosperous decade, American manufacturers began a battle in their research and development laboratories. Out of this fight came the tremendous 12- and 16-cylinder classics, cars so vast and powerful that they at once made obsolete the products of the Twenties. Duesenberg was first in 1929, followed in 1930 by Cadillac, followed in turn by Marmon and Lincoln in 1931 — and then in 1932 the remainder of the companies swamped the market with new entries. In Europe Maybach-Zeppelin, Hispano-Suiza and eventually Rolls-Royce fell in with the trend. Daimler's V-12, introduced earlier, had not set off the power race because there were few Daimlers competing for customers outside of England. Bugatti's Royale eight, also earlier, was of such formidable proportions and price that it would have been sheer folly to try to match it.

Duesenberg and Cadillac showed a change in American thinking that might have developed into a pattern for the rest of the industry if the Wall Street debacle had not occurred. The Duese was the most expensive and luxurious American vehicle, in comparison with the competition, to be introduced since 1920; Cadillac's V-16 was the most expensive automobile ever to be manufactured by a major producer in the United States, considering that there were at most a very few major producers anywhere before 1920. Both cars were introduced in the hope that the runaway prosperity of the late Twenties would continue, Duesenberg appearing nine months before the crash, Cadillac less than three months after. But the Depression did intervene before the other manufacturers could put their models on the market, and what might have been a first-class luxury-car race soon became simply a power struggle.

The year 1932 is the high point of the classic era from the

standpoint of the number of outstanding cars in production. In the four years since 1928, average engine displacement had risen from approximately 350 cubic inches to almost 450 cubic inches, horsepower output had nearly doubled, top speed and acceleration had improved remarkably. An honest 90-to-100 m.p.h. was not unreasonable to expect from both top-grade and compromise classics. What variety had been lost by the failure of a few manufacturers was more than compensated for by the increased number of models offered by each remaining marque. Body design reached the height of its excellence in 1931 and 1932 and remained uniformly magnificent until the end of the decade. The single jarring note, and it was noticeable only in the compromise classics, was the absence of much of the interior luxury of before. Gone was the abundance of handworked wood, metal and cloth that used to be an essential part of these fine cars. In its place were mass-production facsimiles, made of excellent materials but lacking the exquisite detail and finish.

This was 1932, after all, the most wretched year of the Depression. Unemployment estimates ran as high as 18 million, and even the conservatives grudgingly admitted that the figure might be over 10 million. Trying to sell classic cars in this market was as impossible as growing orchids in an open field in a North Dakota winter. In 1932 and the following few years many old-line companies withered and died — Marmon, Franklin, Duesenberg, Auburn, Cord, Pierce-Arrow and Stutz in the United States; Maybach-Zeppelin, Hispano-Suiza and others in Europe. To make it tougher, the United States passed the Smoot-Hawley collection of highly restrictive tariffs and other nations quickly retaliated with tariffs of their own. Sales of foreign cars were all but killed in all the Western European nations and America. With little or no market to shoot at, most of the manufacturers of classics froze their designs and limited output drastically. Cadillac's new V-16 engine in 1938 and Rolls-Royce's V-12 in 1936 are the two notable exceptions. Those who had the money to invest in new models were trying desperately to wedge into the lower-price classes.

But it wasn't only the depression that forced the eventual abandonment of classics. Engineering advances had gradually made the big, heavy cars obsolete. In a car of much lower price the buyer could find comfort, speed and reliability. It was partly in recognition of this fact that Packard built its first Model 120 and Lincoln introduced the Zephyr.

As the end of the Thirties drew near, the death of the classics was a foregone conclusion. The war cannot be blamed for their demise. Newer types of luxury cars appeared — the Lincoln Continental, commonly considered the last classic, being the foremost example. The Continental was smaller and less of a palace on wheels than Lincoln's Model K, which saw its last year of production in 1940. If it had been fitted with a high-performance engine it would have been considered the first of the American sports touring cars rather than the last of the classics.

From the standpoint of sheer luxury there never will again be cars as fine as the classics. Today's standards do not require the craftsmanship or the majestic bulk once thought necessary. Nor can the conditions which made the styling of the classics so outstanding be duplicated. Fashions in automobile design are changing constantly, and thus far they have never gone backward. The Golden Age of the Luxury Car is over, and nothing short of a time machine can take us back to it.

THE CORNERSTONE UPON WHICH E. L. CORD BUILT
his empire was one of the most unusual automobiles ever produced in the United States. Not
unusual technically — the Auburn did not essay
anything as strange as a rear engine or front-
wheel drive. What distinguished it from the others in its price
class was its proportions.

From the beginning of the classic era until the demise of the
Auburn Supercharged Eight in the mid-Thirties, the buyer could
get more for his money in an Auburn than in any other automobile.
In 1933, for example, there were three different models of 12-
cylinder Auburns, the most expensive of which sold for $1,745 as

| AUBURN |

a four-door sedan. The cheapest V-12 Auburn that year cost $1,145, about one-third the price of 12's made by other manufacturers. Judged by price alone, these cars scarcely deserve to be called classics, but by the more rational standards of performance and styling, they must be included.

The Auburn first appeared in 1900, and when E. L. Cord took over in 1924 it was in failing health. Cord embarked on a long-term policy of engineering a top-quality low-price car, during the course of which he hired Fred and August Duesenberg as engineers, Gordon Buehrig and Phil Wright as stylists and introduced both the Cord and the Duesenberg. As a sideline, he built up the Lycoming engine plant to the point where it was making all his automobile engines plus engines for other automobile companies, plus a full line of aircraft engines. Another allied venture was the Le Grande body plant where a few of the Duesenberg bodies were built.

The first Auburn Lycoming Eight appeared in 1925. By 1930 the model which had developed from it was still about the same size and carried the same-displacement engine, but the price had dropped $400 and horsepower had been increased almost 85 per cent. In 1927, Auburn was 25th in the nation in sales; in 1930 it was 23rd; and in 1931 E. L. Cord added another cause for worry to the Depression jitters of other auto executives by taking the Auburn abruptly into 13th position. In making this leap, Auburn passed De Soto, Hudson and Packard among others. Flushed with this success, Cord issued the first V-12 in 1932, but that was not the way to get rich. Sales slumped immediately and stayed down for the remainder of Auburn's existence, hovering between 16th and 20th in rank in the nation. The decline was no fault of the V-12 — the trade press of that day and present-day owners of restored Auburns confirm that the engine was fast and reliable. Aside from the valve arrangement it was a thoroughly conservative piece of machinery. The valves were called "horizontal" and were arranged somewhat like the valves of the Packard V-12. Above the camshaft, which was located in the block, was a hollow rocker shaft which operated the valves, which entered the combustion chamber from the side.

Structurally the Auburns were not as beefy and solid as the more expensive classics, but they were better looking than many. Today's classics collectors are anxious to get their hands on a good V-12 speedster, and the price of a restored example is well above the original factory list of $1,345.

The V-12 speedster proved itself early in its existence by capturing a series of stock-car speed records under A.A.A. supervision. In June and July of 1932 the Auburn clocked 100.77 m.p.h. for the flying mile, 92.16 m.p.h. for 100 miles, and 88.95 for 500 miles. These records stood till after World War II. During the same year an Auburn with a closed body had registered another series of record speeds, which were wiped out by the Chrysler Airflow in 1934.

One of the major reasons for the Auburn's high top speed was the dual-ratio rear axle which was available on the more expensive models. The driver could choose between a final ratio of 3.04- or 4.55-to-1, the former for high top speed and the latter for acceleration or hill-climbing.

In 1934 the Six was returned to the Auburn array and the V-12 was on its way out. Cord was cutting costs to meet the continuing unpopularity of the cars. Beginning in 1934 the six-cylinder and eight-cylinder engines had exactly the same bore and stroke — $3\frac{1}{16} \times 4\frac{3}{4}$. Pistons, connecting rods, valves, etcetera were interchangeable between the two engines, an effective way of lowering manufacturing expenses.

The next model year opened disastrously in September, 1934 when the new cars were poorly received at the shows. Cord called in his top talent — stylist Gordon Buehrig and engineer August

Every line of Auburn's 8-100 Series Cabriolet indicated speed and dash. The two-passenger sports model with rumble seat was used either as a closed or open car. Wheelbase measured 127-inches and the engine was a 100 horsepower Straight Eight Lycoming. This model also offered exclusive Dual Ratio as well as silent transmission, selective ride control shock absorbers, L.G.S. free wheeling, automatic Bijur lubrication, and Startix.

Duesenberg — to perform a drastic operation. Buehrig gave the '35 models a complete face-lift and Duesenberg added a supercharger to the eight-cylinder engine to make a separate line of Auburn Eights. One of the Buehrig-designed, supercharged eights is today the most famous of all Auburns — the Model 851 speedster. It had everything — long, low hood; tiny cockpit; rakish boat-tail deck; and a plate on the instrument panel which stated that the car had been driven at a speed greater than 100 m.p.h. This last was not a difficult job at all. The speedster weighed slightly over 3,700 pounds, had a horsepower rating of 150 at 4,000 r.p.m. With the dual-ratio rear axle's high gearing of 3.23-to-1 on this model, 100 m.p.h. was, as the British say, "easily at hand." To prove the point beyond question, Cord sent a stock Auburn for another series of speed runs through the A.A.A. clocks. The 851SC not only topped its own class (Class C Supercharged) but went on to post a higher speed than any other car in any class for all distances attempted between 0.62 miles and 1,864.11 miles. For the first 1,242.74 miles the average was 102.90 m.p.h.

The speedster cost $2,245 and that's about what a restored one will cost you today. Unfortunately the market for supercharged, 100-m.p.h. cars was slow in 1935 and 1936. Auburn never could recover the magic formula that had once raised it to 13th place. In 1936, when E. L. Cord introduced his new Model 810 Cord, Auburn began its last year. The models offered were the same as the previous year.

BENTLEY

WHEN ROLLS-ROYCE TOOK OVER BENTLEY IN 1931, its firm intention was to replace the tradition all-out sports line with a light and lively luxury car. But all through 1932 and most of 1933, the builders of "The Best Car In The World" refrained from sharing their plans with the public. The suspense was excruciating for tens of thousands of British enthusiasts and almost unbearable for lovers of the Bentley marque. With few facts to go by, they created fantasies.

It was known that W. O. Bentley himself had been retained to help Rolls engineer the new Bentley. That was enough to intoxicate the imagination of any enthusiast: what a supremely perfect sports car this combination of genius would produce! For all the satin smooth and exquisite refinement of their cars, Rolls-Royce engineers were also masters of high-performance design. Witness the R.-R. Schneider Trophy engines which had shattered records on water and in the air and weighed only 1,630 pounds but developed 2,350 horsepower. The greatest British sports car of all was on the way, rumor ran. The talent and resources now joined would produce a wonder car combining the classic perfection of the Rolls-Royce with the hairy violence of the Le Mans Bentley.

When the Rolls product was revealed late in 1933 it brought roars of rage from supporters of the old, fire-snorting Bentley. The new Bentley *did* combine the performance of the "W.O." models with the best traditional qualities of the Rolls-Royce, but the harsh mechanical ferocity of the old cars, so alien to R.-R. practice, had been eliminated. Members of the Bentley cult registered righteous fury when they saw the new car's coachwork and general lines. Only the radiator shell was reminiscent of the great old Winged B. Bentley had lost its aspect of potent authority; instead it had acquired a look of modest opulence underlying a deliberate and unrelenting unobtrusiveness. The Bentleys made by R.-R. were never to rival in splendor the appearance of the Rolls itself, as the old Bentleys often had. Nevertheless, the R.-R.-made Bentley — "The Silent Sports Car" — was a superb machine. It was recognized as such by the world at large and its success was immediate and lasting.

When W. O. began working on this car he was given the run of the R.-R. factory, including its experimental department, and was asked to see what he could do with existing components. The final combination consisted of a super-tuned 25/30-hp. R.-R. engine installed on the chassis of an experimental 18-hp. Rolls.

This was the foundation of the 3½-liter (actually 3,669 c.c. or 224 cu. in.) Bentley which was first exhibited to the world at London's Olympia show in the fall of 1933. The chassis was base-priced at $5,320 and four standard, coachbuilt bodies were available. A two-door sports sedan sold for $7,915; Park Ward's four-door sedan and convertible coupe sold for about $7,200; a Vanden Plas four-seater brought $6,700. In addition, Britain's finest coachbuilders honored the new chassis with exceptional designs in which the newly combined themes of elegance, sport and silence were blended.

The plated and polished show chassis that was displayed at Olympia was by far the most exciting part of the Bentley exhibit. It was actually a miniature Rolls-Royce, including all the uncompromising perfection of the immense Phantoms. To make the little jewel even more intriguing, it was a hopped-up Rolls, with dual carburetors and a high-compression head. Staid old Rolls-Royce was limbering up. After well over a decade of shunning lively performance, the grand old firm was kicking up its heels.

Output of the little pushrod-operated-overhead-valve engine was claimed to be 120 b.hp. or .54 b.hp. per cubic inch, a good figure for the times. The factory suggested not exceeding 4,500 r.p.m. but even at this high speed the "Baby Phantom" power plant retained its smoothness and silence, with some thanks due the seven-bearing crankshaft.

With the Vanden Plas four-place body the car weighed 3,300 pounds, giving a weight-to-power ratio of 27.5-to-1. This, plus a 4.1-to-1 final drive and close-ratio four-speed gearbox gave the car an ability to "tear away in exhilarating bursts . . . always a delight for the driver and always handling well." Zero to 60 m.p.h. could be reached through the gears in 18 seconds. The silent performance was uncanny; it was almost impossible to tell which gear the car was in from sound alone.

The 3½-liter was capable of an easy 90 m.p.h. but had far better brakes than its equally fast pre-Rolls ancestors. It was fitted with R.-R. power brakes, one of the first and still one of the finest assist of its kind in the world. Toetip pressure on the brake pedal engaged a mechanical Servo motor on the transmission and sufficed to bring the 3½ to an even, screaming stop in unusually short distances.

The performance and swank of the 3½-liter Bentley made it one of the most coveted cars of its time. It was generally referred to by the *cognoscenti,* as a "sporting car" rather than a "sports car," which implied race-worthiness. But it was as a luxury car — a smart town carriage and fast tourer — that the 3½ was most outstanding. Still, every now and then and just often enough, Bentley Motors (1931) Ltd. let the world know that the old fires still burned in the Bentley chassis.

One of the first 3½'s sold went to an E. R. Hall who was racing M.G.'s with considerable success. He was interested in using the Bentley as a practice car for the 1,000-mile Italian Mille Miglia race in order to save wear and tear on his competition Midget. When an individual buys a Bentley, he agrees not to race it without company permission — a radical departure from the old firm's policy — and Bentleys are rarely raced because the company seldom approves. But Mr. Hall was so impressed with his Bentley's performance that he asked for and was granted permission to race the car in the forthcoming 1934 Tourist Trophy. Bentley Motors actually agreed to carry out chassis modifications requested by Hall, another case of R.-R. management "frivolity" without recent precedent.

Modifications on Hall's car included raising the gearbox and rear axle ratios, raising compression to 7.75-to-1, installing larger intake valves, adding a straight-through exhaust system, friction shock absorbers and a bigger fuel tank. This special Bentley no longer could claim silence but it did develop a genuine 130 b.hp. and would do 110 m.p.h. Hall started the Tourist Trophy from scratch and finished second in a field of 40 with a 78-m.p.h. average. He was fastest in the race and nine m.p.h. faster than the best average ever made by a supercharged 4½-liter Bentley!

The factory was most cooperative toward Hall for the 1935 race. Up went compression to 8.35-to-1; larger carburetors than the stock twin S.U.'s were added and still larger intake valves were installed. This time the engine pulled 155 b.hp. and, with wind-tunnel-developed streamlined fenders, Hall was able to take another second place. He lost on handicap to a Riley but his 80.36 average was again the fastest in the race. What Hall found particularly gratifying was beating a pair of potent 3.3-liter Bugattis.

A new model was introduced for 1936. The chassis was essentially the same with the exception of hydraulic shock absorbers which varied their damping effect in accordance with road speed through a gearbox-driven pump. The driver had an additional master control on the steering wheel for instant increase in damping in case of rough roads, sudden encounters with sharp corners or other emergencies.

The most important change in the new car was the engine, and that consisted chiefly of a displacement increase to 4,255 c.c. or 260 cu. in. Output was raised to 125 b.hp. at 3,800 r.p.m. and performance was improved significantly. With sedan body and weighing 3,750 pounds the 4½ was good for 96 m.p.h. in top gear and could scoot from zero to 60 in 14.8 seconds.

The popularity of the 4¼-liter Bentley was even greater than that of the 3½. To drive one of these cars was to fall under its spell. After investing in two of them Sir Malcolm Campbell, holder of countless world's speed records said, "The engine, steering, and brakes are absolute perfection . . . I have never driven a car that holds the road so well . . . the 4¼-liter Bentley is the most amazing proposition which it has ever fallen my lot to handle."

That same year E. R. Hall applied again to the factory for permission to race his Bentley — this time at Le Mans. The approval was granted and, as before, it included collaboration. The old 3½-liter engine was removed from Hall's chassis and in its place went one of the new 4¼-liter power plants modified to give 9-to-1 compression ratio and develop 167 b.hp. Before installation the engine was run on the test bench for a solid 24 hours at full throttle, then torn down and found to show absolutely negligible wear.

Hall appeared at Le Mans in 1936 with a new, more streamlined body which enabled him to hit 120 m.p.h. on the straights during practice. But the Grand Prix d'Endurance was cancelled at the last minute because of French labor troubles and Hall had to content himself that year with running once more in the Tourist Trophy.

It was another second place — lost again on handicap to a Riley. Hall drove the 478 miles nonstop in a thunderstorm and averaged 80.81 m.p.h. — a magnificent tribute to both car and driver. Three consecutive Tourist Trophy races and three second places by the car that made the fastest time in each race seems to be the ultimate in long-term hard-luck racing experiences, but it may not have been hard luck at all.

Hall was racing with factory approval, factory help, and was largely under factory control. A first place win would have concentrated the racing limelight on Bentley — embarrassing to a management that held unobtrusive good taste sacred. An outright win in a classic race would almost certainly bring pressure from many quarters urging that the company "show the flag" in international racing through official team participation. That kind of activity was appropriate for The Bentley Boys of old but in total conflict with R.-R. policy. So there is reason to assume that when E. R. Hall raced, he did as he was told. He always finished second, he always turned the fastest lap — just enough to remind the world that The Silent Sports Car was truly fast, as well as aristocratic and reliable.

The bigger 4¼-liter engine enabled heavier and more luxurious coachwork to be fitted to the Bentley chassis without sacrificing performance. In 1938, a special streamlined body was built for a private owner who desired the ultimate in a high-speed touring car. He got it. The car did 112 m.p.h. on a German autobahn and Captain George Eyston later took it around England's bumpy Brooklands track, covering a distance of 114.7 miles in one hour. The remarkable endurance of Bentleys and of this car in particular was well illustrated by the present owner, Mr. H. S. F. Hay. In 1949, with the car's odometer registering a mere 60,000 miles, Mr. Hay proposed to enter his machine in the first postwar 24-hour race at Le Mans. He not only entered, but finished sixth in the general classification and second in the 5-liter class with an amazing average of 73.3 m.p.h. — this when most 11-year-old cars are limping through their last stages.

When this streamlined body was made in 1938, the factory thought well enough of it to plan a modified version as a standard model. Van Vooren of Paris was elected to build the prototypes and production would have been by London's Park Ward. This new "Corniche" Bentley had been through a 15,000-mile road test in Europe and was on the dock at Dieppe awaiting shipment home. Unfortunately, the war broke out and a German bomb destroyed the tested Corniche. Two prototype chassis had, however, just been completed at the Derby factory, oddly enough fitted with straight-eight, 5½-liter engines (actually forerunners of a future Rolls-Royce), and these were shipped to safety in Canada for the duration.

The last prewar modification of the 4¼-liter occurred in 1939 when the overdrive model was introduced. The car had come along since 1936 with no important alterations and this was an attempt to extract the last ounce of performance and economy from an otherwise completely satisfactory automobile. Previously, fourth gear had been a direct 1-to-1 ratio but this was now revised so that third gear was direct and fourth was an overdrive of .84-to-1. This did not increase the maximum speed of the car, but rather made it possible to use the maximum speed over any distance and time at the discretion of the driver. In overdrive, an easy cruising speed of 80 m.p.h. was possible at 3,500 r.p.m., a full 1,000 r.p.m. under the maximum engine speed. Acceleration from zero to 60 m.p.h. was accomplished in the short interval of about 15½ seconds, with 4.3-to-1 final drive. The overdrive transmission — called an over-direct drive to distinguish it from overdrive units separate from the gearbox — did produce a slight amount of noise in top gear. It could not be corrected and, since noise in any form had no place in Bentley machinery, the new transmission was soon withdrawn from production.

The prewar R.-R. Bentleys were amazing cars in every respect. They were absolutely outstanding in the areas of performance, handling, braking, stability, dependability, coachwork, appearance and comfort. Rolls-Royce did not make of the Bentley a snarling Grand Prix challenger. Instead, it produced a perfect machine that remained true to the somewhat conflicting traditions of England's two greatest marques, a car which W. O. himself could look upon with pride.

BUGATTI

Ettore's bugatti royale, the type 41, is unquestionably the most incredible vehicle of them all. If it were possible in this volume to reserve special categories for individual cars, the Royale would be in a section all its own. For it is no ordinary classic. It is at once the mightiest of the great cars and the most ridiculous.

Bugatti's ability is not in question here, only his judgment and good taste. The Royale lived up to Molsheim standards in all its details of workmanship and design. It was so well constructed that *le Patron* proudly guaranteed it for the life of the owner. But it was just too much. It was too big, too powerful, too finely constructed, too expensive. It belonged in the era of twenty to fifty years before, the period when private railroad cars were in vogue and a country estate of less than 50 rooms was considered cozy. By 1927, when the Royale appeared, sheer size had ceased to be fashionable. The landed gentry of Europe had arrived at the point where they no longer tried to outdo their neighbors by owning bigger things. Too many of them were already reduced to living in one small wing of the ancestral castle, and no one in his right mind, except an American, would think of trying to buy and restore a complete castle.

What was or was not fashionable did not seem to interest Ettore Bugatti. He went ahead with the construction of the proto-type Royale, which eventually became his personal car. As a beginning he laid a heavy frame, 10 inches deep at the center, on a

180-inch wheelbase. The track was 66 inches. To power the world's biggest luxury car he built the world's biggest straight-eight automobile engine. With its 125-mm. (4.92 in.) bore and 150-mm. (5.91 in.) stroke, it had a displacement of 14,726 cubic centimeters (898.6 cu. in.). The entire engine block and cylinder head was a single, 238-pound aluminum casting, four feet seven inches long. Each cylinder was completely surrounded by a water jacket. The crankshaft was machined from a solid steel billet, and weighed 220 pounds when ready to install in the engine. It ran on nine main bearings, each of which was water cooled. The pistons were aluminum alloy, the connecting rods forged steel. A single overhead camshaft, which also ran on nine bearings, operated the valves. There were two spark plugs per cylinder, two coils to supply them.

Despite the huge proportions of the engine and the low r.p.m. which were demanded of it, Bugatti insisted on workmanship equal to that of the most delicate of his competition cars. Parts were fitted with zero tolerances throughout. That was not enough for Bugatti. Though he only intended to make a very few Royales, he set up jigs and tools to make all the parts interchangeable. Any rod and any piston could be changed with any other.

Installed in the chassis, the complete engine weighed 770 pounds, less than the weight of the 1928 Cadillac V-8 engine which had less than half the displacement and not even a third the power output. Lightweight aluminum construction was the reason; though he was building a huge engine Bugatti saw no reason to make it heavy as well.

For this first car, Bugatti used a Packard Eight body. The total weight of the car was a surprisingly low 5,600 pounds, the engine output a solid 300 b.hp. at 1,700 r.p.m. This power-to-weight ratio permitted extremely high gearing. The rear axle gearing was 2.5-to-1, just about half that of the ordinary luxury car. Coupled to the rear axle was a three-speed transmission. First gear gave an overall ratio of 4.5-to-1; second gear was direct, giving an overall ratio of 2.5-to-1; third gear was an overdrive, 1.5-to-1. In third gear the car would go 72 m.p.h. when the engine was turning over at 1,000 r.p.m. A speed of more than 140 m.p.h. was theoretically possible, though the frontal area may have precluded an actual speed that great.

Bugatti was so pleased with the performance of his first Royale that he ordered the plant to turn out 25 chassis. These were somewhat different than the prototype. The engine was left largely as originally designed, but it was destroked 20 mm., giving new dimensions of 4.92×5.12 and a displacement of 12,760 cubic centimeters (778.7 cu. in.). Wheelbase was cut from 180 inches to 170 inches and the track narrowed to 63 inches. Just why the subsequent Royales were smaller and less powerful than the first has not been recorded, but it is not inconceivable that Bugatti deliberately planned it that way. It must have given his undemocratic soul a tremendous boost to know that four kings were riding the highways of Europe with Royales smaller than his own. He was literally the king of the road.

Fewer than 10 Royales were sold, the price tag being one of the reasons — $30,000 is a lot of money no matter what currency you change it into. The survivors are cherished by their owners today, and one of them inspired a labor of extreme devotion during World War II. The French resistance group in Paris took it underground with them and put it up on blocks in one of the sewers of Paris so the Germans couldn't find it.

One Royale is definitely known to be destroyed — Ettore's prototype, the biggest of them all. Ettore wrecked it himself five years after he built it, in an accident on one of the highways of France. One shudders at the thought of that beautiful giant lying smashed by the roadside. One also wonders what the other fellow's car looked like.

J. Lemon Burton's Bugatti Royale was still in almost daily use in 1955, in England. Wheels are cast light alloy, with integral brake drums.

J. Lemon Burton.

WHEN A CARTOONIST LAMPOONS A CORPO- ration he customarily represents it as a slug- gish, heavy-footed oaf, either simple or menacing depending on the point being made. This ties in with the popular miscon-

ception of a large business organization as so mired in paper work, red tape and directors' meetings that it must make decisions deliberately and execute them slowly — that once the decisions are made only complete catastrophe can swerve the monolith from its course. The point most people seem to miss is that a corporation which stumbles over its own feet eventually falls flat on its face in bankruptcy court. A successful firm, like General Motors, learns to move swiftly and surely despite its size.

Among compromise classics, General Motors' Cadillac has a greater string of successes than any other. In 1914, during the pre-classic era, Cad pioneered the V-8 engine in American produc- tion automobiles; in January, 1930 the company put the first V-16 on the market, thus anticipating the trend toward myriad- cylindered design that highlighted the Thirties and neatly scoop- ing Marmon by one full year; in October, 1930 there appeared the Cadillac V-12, which effectively stole the limelight from the many other V-12's being readied for introduction during the next two years; in 1941 there was another properly timed innovation — Hydra-Matic transmission; in 1948 there were the famous tail fins; and in 1949 came the first postwar overhead-valve V-8 engine. The cumulative effect of this series of triumphs (and the tail fin, however unimportant it may seem, was a positive design victory) is apparent today. Cadillac has been the nation's number one luxury car since the end of World War II.

No one car in the General Motors group is a unit unto itself. Each is planned to complement the other makes in price and style, and frequently shares body, chassis and engine features with them. While this fact robs the Cadillac classics of some of the individ- uality that characterizes Packard, Marmon, Pierce-Arrow and a few others, it also enabled the company to take chances and stay in business. Cadillac classic history, when interpreted in this light, makes much more sense than when it is considered alone.

The one vital point about Cadillac is that the division did not necessarily have to show a profit during the classic era. Other firms were not that lucky; if their models were not financial suc- cesses, bankruptcy loomed very near. Two or three consecutive bad or mediocre years could kill Packard or Pierce-Arrow quickly, or force them to a slow death by eating up the cash reserves intended for modernization and new-model changeovers. Cadillac could go on losing money year after year and be supported by the low-priced cars produced by General Motors. Lincoln was in the same position. The yearly loss was written off to prestige and advertising, on the theory that publicity garnered by the luxury cars also benefited all the other products of the corporation.

This is why Cadillac could introduce the V-16 and take the loss that would almost certainly occur during the period required to sell the idea of 16 cylinders to the public; why the V-12 could be added to a line that already had two entirely different engines in production, and kept in the line at a steady yearly loss for the simple reason that it stole much of the advertising thunder of the principal competitor, Packard, and helped block the rise of the other V-12's — Lincoln, Auburn, Pierce-Arrow.

But huge and wealthy General Motors did not end its assistance to Cadillac there. It also permitted the division to put out such a variety of models that prices on the eight, the 12 and the 16 could overlap. In 1932 there was approximately $700 difference between the basic eight and 12 chassis, about $1,000 difference between the 12 and the 16 chassis. By varying the body types widely, it was possible to market some of the 12's for less than some eights, some 16's for less than some 12's. Against this interlocking production structure, competition was difficult. The overlap was not great, but in the top price classes during the Thirties it did not have to be. Those who could afford a $3,500 car in that era could usually afford to spend $5,000.

Cadillac had not always been a high-priced car. The first (1903) model sold for $850. When H. M. Leland took over in 1905, the first expensive Cadillac was offered, but the cheaper car was also retained. Until 1917, when Leland left to form Lincoln, Cadillac went through a period of innovation and greatness. In 1908 it quite literally became the "standard of the world" when it became the first make successfully to prove the interchangeability of its component parts, both engine and body. For this accomplishment Leland and Cadillac won England's Dewar Trophy. Then, in 1912, the first modern self-starter was perfected by Kettering and Cadillac engineers, and Leland and Cadillac won the Dewar Trophy again. In 1914 came the first production V-8 in America.

General Motors acquired Cadillac by purchase in 1908. At

this time the G.M. stable consisted of Cadillac, Buick, Oakland and Oldsmobile, with Buick and Cadillac the cheapest and Oldsmobile the most expensive. By 1921, the year after Durant was eliminated and the directorship stabilized in much its present form, Cadillac had risen to the top of the list, which then consisted of Scripps-Booth, Sheridan and Chevrolet in addition to the original makes.

At the beginning of the classic era the Cadillac, powered by basically the same V-8 engine it had pioneered in 1914, cost up to $5,000. In keeping with the rising health of the national economy, it began to enlarge in 1926, when General Motors bought Fleetwood Body Corporation to build custom bodies for Cadillac. Then, in 1928, a more modern V-8 engine was designed and installed, upping horsepower to 95. This engine began a trend that has continued to this day. It was more compact, more rigid, had a smaller bore/stroke ratio. Displacement was increased to 341 cubic inches to create a potential of more power to be drawn upon when necessary, but the other popular classics of the period still had considerably larger engines.

Automobile Manufacturers Assoc.

1925 Cadillac 7-passenger custom touring car, Series 314.

The 1930 V-16 put Cadillac at the top of the compromise-classic category. Basically, it was two pushrod-operated-overhead-valve straight-eights mounted in a V on a common crankcase, driving a common crankshaft. Each bank of eight cylinders had its own manifolding, carburetor, water pump and ignition circuit.

It was possible to run the car on one bank of cylinders. For silence, hydraulic valve lifters were used.

Structurally the V-16 was exactly what you'd imagine — solid, massive and square. The carbon-steel, channel-section frame was nine inches deep at its strongest point; the rear springs were five feet long. In appearance the car looked so much like the V-8 that a special curved molding was added to the hood so the customers could tell the difference between the big and little Cadillacs at a glance. "Madame X" models had a V-shaped slanted windshield. A bar across the front of the flat radiator carried a big V with the numbers 16 written through it. Sometimes, after a V-16 had been through a paint job which had not respected the hood-molding lines, it could only be spotted by this identification badge on the front.

The Cadillac price range now spread from $3,295 for the V-8 coupe to $9,700 for the V-16 town brougham. A year after the introduction of the V-16, the V-12 was shown to the public. Its price range fell about halfway between the two existing models. Now Cadillac was doubly covered all the way through the fine-car field.

The new V-12 engine looked as if it had been cut from one of the V-16's. Both engines used the same length stroke, the same connecting rods, the same intake and exhaust valves, and so on. Both cars used some of the same Fleetwood bodies, though there was a top-price line on the V-16 chassis that the V-12 did not have. One price book lists 11 body styles on the V-8 chassis, 21 different bodies on the V-12 chassis, and 30 on the V-16 chassis — a total

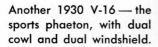

Another 1930 V-16 — the sports phaeton, with dual cowl and dual windshield.

Cadillac Division, General Motors

of *62 choices from the stock catalogue!* Maintaining an inventory like this through good years and bad in the early- and mid-Thirties was not easy for the independents, though most of them did their best to keep up with Cadillac.

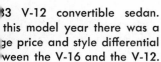

33 V-12 convertible sedan. this model year there was a ge price and style differential ween the V-16 and the V-12.

Cadillac Division, General Motors

Between 1931 and 1937 Cadillac marketed all three lines, but V-16 production was soon sharply limited. Advertisements appeared in *Fortune* and other magazines of similar appeal, stating that only 400 V-16's would be produced during 1934. All of them were to bear custom bodies, and they would be made only on order. So, advised the copywriter, the customer who wanted one had better reserve it as soon as possible after the beginning of the model year.

Nineteen thirty-six was a year of change for the V-8 engine and chassis. Again the change was to a shorter, more compact, more rigid engine. A new, cheaper series called the 60 shared the new engine with the larger Series 70 and 75, the sole difference being that the 60 had a ⅛-inch-smaller bore. For the first time with Cadillac, the V-8 had hydraulic valve lifters. Important chassis changes included a new box-section front cross member, a double universal joint connection between steering column and steering gear. Bodies were completely different than the previous year, and all the Cadillacs except the low-price Series 60 had Fleetwood bodies.

None of these innovations was carried up as far as the V-16's, which remained unchanged mechanically. The V-12's evidently went through the changes simply because they were the same as the V-8's except for the engine.

Cadillac's next big year of change was 1938, and at this time they made one of the strangest moves of the classic era. They actually introduced a brand-new 16-cylinder engine, one that represented major re-tooling expenditures. Considering that almost all the producers of compromise classics had either gone out of business or were in the process of switching to smaller and less expensive models, this move is difficult to explain.

The new engine had two radical features. One was the bore-stroke ratio, which was exactly 1 to 1 — smaller than any United States stock car then on the market. Bore and stroke were each 3¼ inches, giving a total displacement of 431 cubic inches, 21 cubic inches less than the previous V-16. The other revolutionary aspect of the new engine was the angle between the blocks — 135 degrees — which made it the closest thing to an opposed engine that had been seen in automotive circles since the very early, experimental days. The reason given for the large angle was that it permitted the use of a 45-degree crankshaft (crank throws at every 45 degrees), which in turn meant that the crankshaft received eight power impulses per revolution rather than four, making the engine theoretically the smoothest it was possible to create without adding more cylinders.

In the same year, Cadillac made two moves in what was to prove to be the right direction. On the low-price Series 60 chassis a special body was built, incorporating a few of the design features that later were adopted by most builders. This was a wider-inside, same-width-outside type of body, made possible by expanding the body sides over the running boards. The car was called the 60 Special, a series that has been continued to this day. For its other right guess, Cadillac abruptly cancelled its 12-cylinder line.

During the next two model years, the V-16 was allowed to diminish in importance and in 1941 disappeared forever. Built up at the same time was a wider variety of V-8's, all looking almost exactly the same. By 1941, Cadillac was in excellent shape for the post World War II years: it held a firm position as America's largest producer of luxury automobiles; it was solidly in the forefront of the trend toward clutchless driving with the excellent Hydra-Matic transmission. There was no longer any need for General Motors to support the production of prestige classics within the Cadillac division, because the other American companies no longer were able to afford to make classics. Those that had survived — Lincoln, Chrysler, Packard — were now following the Cadillac lead rather than showing the way.

La Salle

At best a semi-classic, the La Salle is still popular with a number of collectors today for its sheer good looks. Its history is divided into three distinct periods and the car itself might be considered three different automobiles, so radical were the changes that took place in 1934 and 1937.

When it was first introduced, during the 1927 model year, the La Salle was a small Cadillac in body, chassis and engine, made to compete with the inexpensive Packard. The division could have manufactured the same car and called it a Cadillac, but this might have detracted from the prestige that gradually was being built into the Cadillac name. The engine was a V-8 of exactly the same specifications as the smallest Cadillac with the single exception of the cylinder bore which was $3/16$ inch larger in the Cadillac. In appearance it was virtually impossible to distinguish baby brother from big brother, since Fleetwood built special bodies for both chassis, and the stock Fisher bodies were also the same.

This state of affairs continued, with little change, until the 1934 model year, when La Salle ceased to be a small Cadillac and became a luxury Oldsmobile. The Olds engine was used exactly as manufactured for the Oldsmobile Eight without change in horsepower, bore or stroke.

This permitted an abrupt slash in price that must have taken both Packard and Lincoln unawares. La Salle went down to about the same price as next year's Packard 120, and when the Lincoln Zephyr came along in 1936 it had to compete in the same price class. General Motors came to the rescue of the "luxury Oldsmobile" in 1937 and once again made it a small Cadillac mechanically by installing the Cadillac Series 60 V-8, the only difference being a $1/8$-inch smaller bore in the smaller car. With this engine, La Salle rode the rest of its way to oblivion, which came unceremoniously after the 1940 model year. But if ever a car had a quick reincarnation it was the La Salle — the 1941 Cadillac Series 61 was precisely what the La Salle would have been if it had stayed around another year.

In the handling of Cadillac and La Salle, General Motors exhibited the astute policies that have won it the undisputed leading position in the automobile field. In the five years between 1926 and 1931 the parent corporation invested lavishly in the future of Cadillac by buying the Fleetwood Body Company, introducing the La Salle and developing three new engines — the improved V-8, the V-12 and the V-16. This money could not have been spent in anticipation of immediate return, but rather to give Cadillac a large advantage, costwise and prestigewise, over the other luxury-car manufacturers in the future. Thus it was no accident that Cadillac entered the post classic era with the strongest position in the field. The foundations of its popularity had been solidly laid more than 20 years before.

| CHRYSLER |

From its beginning just one year before the opening of the classic era the Chrysler has always been an unpredictable car. The first Chrysler had to be featured in a private showing against the mass competition of the New York auto show in January, 1924 because Chryslers were not yet in volume production and the show directors would not give the prototype official floor space. Despite this handicap, that Chrysler made history as the first United States medium-priced production car with a high-compression engine, which in turn became the grandpappy of the present Chrysler engine.

By 1926 Chrysler had made enough money to expand the line to include a classic — the Series E-80. Like the other Chryslers, the E-80 was powered by an L-head six-cylinder engine which differed from the others in the line only in its dimensions. It was not an unusually large engine, having a bore and stroke of $3\frac{1}{2} \times 5$, but it could produce as much power — 92 b.hp. at 3,000 r.p.m. — as all but the lustiest engines of its competitors. Nor was the E-80 an expensive car, as classics were then measured, with its modest selling price of $3,095 for the four-door sedan.

Chrysler kept the E-80 in production for two years, then followed it with the L-80 and L*-80 for the succeeding 19 months. In keeping with the rising prosperity of the times, the new 80's were bigger, more powerful and more expensive than their predecessors. The six-cylinder engine had been retained but it had been bored out to 3⅝ inches and the compression ratio raised from 4.7-to-1 to 6-to-1, with a resulting increase in brake horsepower to 112 at 3,000 r.p.m. Wheelbase had grown from a former maximum of 133 inches to a minimum of 136. While the prices of the stock bodies on this chassis were about the same as the E-80's, a series of semi-custom bodies by Locke, Dietrich and Le Baron gave the buyer his chance to spend up to $6,795. In basic styling, the L-80 was very much the same as the E-80, but the L*-80 marked the adoption of a new pattern resembling very closely the English Vauxhall with its narrow-profile radiator.

During the early years of the company, another Chrysler model made history of a slightly different sort. One step below the series E-80 in 1928 was a Chrysler called the 72, a light, fast, medium-priced car powered by a 3¼×5 version of the six-cylinder engine. To the surprise of everyone, three of these small cars showed up for the Le Mans endurance race in France in 1928, each of them piloted by a pair of experienced racing drivers. They faced the formidable opposition of the three team Bentleys (which were managed by the great W. O. Bentley and driven by equally capable pilots) plus the Stutz team — with their overhead-cam straight-eights — and various Lagondas, Aries and assorted sports competition cars. The Chryslers, which didn't figure to scare anybody at all, got off to a good start and carefully maintained their pace for the entire race. When the clocks reached the end of the 24 hours, Chryslers were solidly in third and fourth positions. Foreign auto writers who watched them run commented that the Chryslers had performed magnificently, experiencing virtually no trouble whatever and sounding every bit as sweet and mellow after their nearly 1,600 miles as they had at the beginning.

That same year, a Chrysler placed second behind an Alfa Romeo at Spa, Belgium. In 1929 Chryslers were sixth and seventh at Le Mans, this time running against supercharged 4½-liter Bentleys. The displacement of the "72" was only 4.074 liters.

This was the kind of endurance and quality built into the 80 series, though the bigger cars were too heavy to make a good showing in competition. Good as it was on the road, however, the design had fallen too far behind current fashions by 1931, so Chrysler made a decided change. That year saw the introduction of the greatest classic of Chrysler history, the '31, '32 and '33 Custom Imperial.

Almost all the classic Chryslers in the hands of collectors today are from this series of cars. Their principal appeal is in the semi-custom bodies Le Baron — then a division of Briggs — built for them. Nothing from that period, except the L-29 Cord which the

Chrysler resembled, had lines that were so low and rakish. On the '32 and '33 phaetons, the belt line sloped gently downward from cowl to rear, leaving the upper part of the rear-seat backrest exposed when the top was down, a notable deviation from the customary square, high bodies of the Packards and Lincolns of the time. The Chrysler was closer to the European mode of the Thirties than any other American car, and might be said to be the forerunner of the Lincoln Continental and other later bodies that were derived from luxury cars abroad.

Under the long, low hood of the Custom Imperial was Chrysler's first and largest straight-eight, a 3½×5 L-head which was available in two slightly different versions — "Red Head" and "Silver Dome." The Red Head developed ten more b.hp. for a total of 135 at 3,200 r.p.m., and it could pull the sedan along at close to 90 m.p.h. top speed or cruise quietly at speeds up to 75 m.p.h.

If it hadn't been for Carl Breer — one of the three engineers who had helped develop the first Chrysler — the early Custom Imperials might have continued through the '30's. But Breer had been working behind the scenes at Chrysler on a radically new body and chassis design which was destined to change the face of Chrysler for the next four years. This was the Airflow.

While the Airflow is scarcely a classic in the ordinary sense, it is included here because of the tremendous effect it had, not only on Chrysler, but on the industry as a whole. What the public saw first was a strange-looking, experimental body bearing the Chrysler emblem, and the public quite definitely didn't like it. Few people were willing to get close enough to see all the solid

1933 Chrysler convertible coupe,

Chrysler Corporation

1937 Airflow.

Chrysler Corporation

engineering improvements that had been embodied in the Airflow.

What Breer and his engineering staff had done was to start with four wheels and build an original car. Passengers were cradled between the axles, the engine and steering mechanism were hung over the front axle, the spare tire was placed out of the way of the windstream, the headlights were buried in the fenders. the body skeleton was designed to assume some of the stresses usually handled by the frame and softer and heavier springs were used in front. In its basic chassis design, the Airflow was a sound prediction of the cars of 20 years in the future. Unfortunately it was not a car of the present, not in 1934. It lived for just four years, growing weaker in sales year by year until the company replaced it with a conventional car.

The biggest Airflow of them all — the Series CW — was in every way a more luxurious automobile than the '33 Custom Imperial, but of course its lines were far from classic. Less than 100 of these were sold in the two years they were offered. One style note on the CW caught on in later years — the curved one-piece windshield. It was not on the cheaper Airflows because it was too expensive to make.

After the Airflows, Chrysler remained conservative until 1941, when the factory commissioned Le Baron to build two special bodies to drop on the New York chassis. One, a roadster, was the Thunderbolt; the other, a phaeton, was termed the Newport. Neither car was ever intended for production in anything like commercial quantities. The bodies were hand made of thin sheet aluminum; both cars, but particularly the Thunderbolt, were equipped with a number of gadgets that were still in the experimental stage. One memorable Thunderbolt plaything was the convertible hard top. When the driver wanted to put the top down, he pressed a button and: (1) a metal cover opened, exposing a well behind the seat; (2) the metal top arched up and then down into the well; (3) the metal cover dropped back and clicked shut.

In styling, the Thunderbolt's body was a fair prediction of the Italian bodies of the 1950's. The exterior was little more than a single, unbroken shell which enveloped wheels, engine and frame. There was a refreshing lack of chrome and decoration, and the bumpers were small and cinched in tight to the body.

Of all the major manufacturers in the classic era, Chrysler emphasized its luxury cars the least. That is why the firm produced fewer cars of collector interest than Packard, Pierce-Arrow and the others. But Chrysler's unpredictable qualities — as illustrated by the Custom Imperials of the early Thirties and the CW Airflow — make it a rewarding marque for study. On the Imperials the stylists experimented with a Continental-type body; on the Airflow they flouted the classic fashions entirely yet stayed in the classic price range. Then, abruptly, Chrysler dropped all its expensive models. Packard, Lincoln and Cadillac proved the wisdom of this move when they followed suit a few years later.

CORD

A LESSON WELL-LEARNED BY AUTOMOBILE MANUfacturers is that you can't get away with extreme deviations from the normal pattern. Almost all the road machines manufactured today are powered by a front-mounted, poppet-valve, internal-combustion engine driving through the rear wheels, a combination which almost 70 years of evolution has shown to be the most practical and easiest to manufacture. Engineers have tried ideas as far afield as steam and electric propulsion, even eight-wheeled chassis, only to return to the orthodox design. There are just two major variations which continue to pop up in cars from time to time — the rear-mounted engine and front-wheel drive.

The Cord was easily the most successful front-wheel-drive car manufactured in the United States. Its final versions — the 1936 and 1937 Models 810 and 812 — are almost as popular today as the Lincoln Continental in the classic-car market. This is only partially due to the front-wheel drive, however. Gordon Buehrig's unusual styling and the high-winding Lycoming V-8 engine get most of the credit. Indeed there are some enthusiasts who go so far as to say that the Cord would be with us today if it had only been equipped with conventional, rear-wheel drive.

Front-wheel drive has distinct advantages and disadvantages. On the credit side is the absence of the driveshaft, thus permitting a lower center of gravity without the inconvenience of a high tunnel through the center of the passenger compartment, and the inherent stability on corners. Power applied to the front wheels tends to *pull* the car through a corner, or out of a skid, while applying power to the rear wheels under the same conditions will *push* the car into deeper trouble. When you take a corner with a front-wheel-drive car, you keep power applied during the curve; when you turn a rear-drive car the accepted method of handling the situation is to drift the car through the first half of the corner and apply power to straighten out on the last half.

There are some operational conditions where front-wheel drive is not the answer. During the Twenties many of Harry Miller's highly successful racing cars were equipped with front-wheel drive, and the pilots of these cars had nothing but praise for the design. Since that time, however, there have been virtually no front-drive designs on the tracks. Today there are the Novi Specials, but their success has not been notable. In 1953 Chet Miller, one of the world's finest drivers and certainly the most experienced in handling front-wheel drive, crashed to his death during a practice run at the Indianapolis Speedway in a Novi. Old Indy authorities who were there say that Chet Miller made the mistake of putting his left front wheel too far inside on the corner. In a rear-wheel drive car he might easily have pulled out -- in the front-wheel drive Novi the loss of traction on the one driving wheel caused him to lose control and he spun clear across the track into the outside wall. Ralph Hepburn lost his life in almost exactly the same way in a Novi years before.

There is another drawback, too. While the front drive can pull you around a corner, you have to keep the power turned on all the way around. Once you back off the throttle, the weight shifts to the front of the car and the rear wheels get that dancingon-ice feeling. A good driver who is familiar with the course can pace himself to keep power on during cornering, but if he underestimates his speed entering the corner and has to shut off, he can get into trouble more easily than the driver of a rear-drive machine.

Steep hills are also a poor place for front-wheel drive. The first L-29 Cords could not pull hills beyond a certain steepness because, with the weight of the car applied to the rear on the slope, there was not enough traction on the front wheels. One owner recalls that his L-29 was always good for one trick to frighten passengers away from front-wheel drive forever; he'd point the nose of the car up his steep driveway in wet weather and then apply power. The front wheels would break traction and slip gently off onto the grass. Later, when the Model 810 was developed, this annoying characteristic was largely eliminated by moving the center of weight of the car farther forward.

Technically, a front-wheel drive is complex because the front wheels must do everything. They must be so sprung that they transmit power to the ground without bouncing or hopping; they must have differential action on corners; they must steer with the same lightness and control as if power were being applied to the rear wheels. Cord's original design was derived from the Miller racing cars. What had worked well for Miller also worked well for Cord.

For the most part the L-29 was a conventional car, but from the firewall forward the changes are noteworthy. To begin with, the engine was reversed, with what is normally considered the front placed next to the firewall. Moving frontward toward the bumper there were, in order: the rear of the engine, the clutch, transmission and differential housing. The last three were bolted together to form a single unit. From the differential an axle went to each wheel, and on each axle were two universal joints. Two universal joints were required because a single universal joint would have given a disturbing variation in the speed of the driven shaft when it was at an angle to the driving shaft, as it would be while cornering. By adding a second universal, the variations of the first were automatically corrected.

Caster and camber of the front wheels were 1½ degrees. Dual quarter-elliptic springs carried the front axles. Steering was Gemmer worm-and-roller. An interesting difference in the drive train was the location of the pinion gear, which was two inches *above* the ring gear, rather than below. The Cord differential was situated lower than the engine's crankshaft, and there was no long, slanting-downward driveshaft to make up the difference in height.

An advantage of front-wheel drive was the relatively low unsprung weight. In the rear end, where conventional cars have the most unsprung weight, the Cord had no driveshaft or differential to support. They were carried in front, mounted on the frame.

An unusual problem was posed by the reversed engine. All cars in 1929 were equipped with an emergency gear for manual cranking of the engine, and drivers were accustomed to cranking clockwise. So that Cord owners would not be required to remember to reverse cranking direction for their reversed engine, the engineers placed a reversing gear between the hand-cranking shaft and the engine's crankshaft.

The L-29's engine was a Lycoming straight-eight, the same engine that powered the Model 125 Auburn that year. Though smaller than the comparable Packards and Pierce-Arrows of 1929, it produced as much power as any — 125 b.hp. at 3,400 r.p.m. — and more than some.

The dashboard was slightly odd, the shifting mechanism

Detail of L-29 Cord front-wheel drive. Axle curves forward, around front of car. Live axle shaft can be seen with universal joint at wheel. Tiny louvers ahead of fog lamp are to admit air to brake drum, mounted inboard against differential-transmission unit.

Borgeson

Borgeson

Cord 810 convertible phaeton sedan. Car was introduced in 1935, had 125 b.hp. V-8 engine.

frankly unusual. There were two distinct groups of instruments, one in front of the driver, the other far over to the right of the panel. In front of the driver were the speedometer, oil-pressure gauge and water thermometer. On the opposite side were the gasoline gauge, oil-quantity gauge and ammeter. All were moving dials with stationary pointers. All were so small it required a spotlight and 20/20 vision to read them from the driver's position in the front seat. The gear-shift lever was a knob protruding from the lower center of the instrument panel. To shift into low gear, the operator pulled the knob forward and moved it to the left; second, rearward to the right; high, forward to the right; reverse, rearward to the left.

Styling was one of the L-29's memorable virtues. It won a series of awards in European Concours d'Elégance and was awarded the highest flattery by being copied by other manufacturers in America. One of the reasons for its superiority was its low overall height, 61 inches, which was made possible by the front-wheel drive.

Introduced at an inopportune time (August, 1929, just two months before the stock-market crash), the Cord never had a chance to prove its sales value in a good market. Only 4,429 were sold in the three model years of its existence — 1930, 1931, 1932.

But Cord was not ready to die quite yet. After the country had worked its way back to a semblance of prosperity, E. L. Cord tried again. This was in 1935, and the car he introduced was the Model 810, the car most people think of when the name Cord is mentioned. This was the weirdly beautiful, coffin-nose Cord. To some it is a sports car; to others it is a classic; to yet a third group it is simply a freakish stock car. Each definition is partly correct. The front drive and venetian-blind louvers were decidedly freakish; in price and luxury the Cord was equal to the minor classics; and in its supercharged form the performance of the car was as good as any in its price class. The factory claimed a top speed of 112 m.p.h. and *The Autocar* obtained a top speed of 102.27 m.p.h. under "adverse" conditions. In 1937, a supercharged Cord set a series of stock-car records at Bonneville, under A.A.A. sanction, that were not broken until 1953. Yet with all this speed and power, the Cord was too big and bulky for sports competition.

For the new 810, Cord had made a decided improvement in the front drive. The old, double-universal system, necessary on the L-29, was replaced by a single, constant-velocity universal which had proven itself in industrial applications. This was the

Rzeppa invention, wherein a third member was added to the universal, placed between the driving and driven shafts. In the Rzeppa design the third member was a series of six balls in concentric inner and outer race grooves. The front suspension had also undergone a change. Gone were the two quarter-elliptic springs on each front axle, and in their place was independent suspension of the trailing-arm type, utilizing a single, transverse leaf spring 34½ inches long, bolted in the center to the front crossmember.

Two other brand-new items were the engine and the transmission. Lycoming had developed a V-8, a cylinder arrangement which fitted the requirements of the front-wheel drive better than the old straight-eight. More weight could now be concentrated over the front axles for improved traction. Like the car, the engine was light and fast. It was rated at 125 b.hp. at 3,500 r.p.m., and could be turned up to 4,500 r.p.m. for top speed. The crankshaft ran on three main bearings, each 2½ inches in diameter.

The transmission, which later proved to be not quite as reliable as had been hoped, was operated by a Bendix finger-tip pre-selector mechanism. To operate it, the driver dropped the selector into the slot he desired, then disengaged the clutch and took his foot off the throttle briefly. The shift was made by the force of the engine's vacuum. There were four speeds forward, the highest being similar to an overdrive with its 2.75-to-1 final drive ratio. One of the best arguments against the Cord as a sports car lies in this transmission, which was not as responsive to the driver's control as a manually operated transmission can be to the touch of an expert driver.

But it is not for its engineering features that the Cord is primarily remembered today. The 810 and 812 could have been marketed with a small, four-cylinder engine and rear drive and still be famous after 17 years out of the picture. Gordon Buehrig is the man who really put the Cord on the pages of the history books. He was, and still is, an automotive designer with talent and ideas. Whether he would have been allowed to work them out elsewhere is another point — probably E. L. Cord deserves much of the credit for bringing Buehrig's design to production.

Development began in 1933, but the body that was later to be the Cord was then intended as a medium-price Duesenberg. An experimental chassis was built, but before it could be made into a workable design, Buehrig and Duesenberg were both transferred to Auburn to brighten up the line for the introduction of the '35 models. After this task had been successfully accomplished, Buehrig went back to his baby Duese and discovered it had been changed to a Cord front-drive.

There were a couple of other interruptions and false starts before the decision to produce the Cord was finally solid. This was in the middle of 1935, four and a half months before the show deadline, November 1. If there was to be a '36 Cord it had to be completed fast. Furthermore, since the show authorities were skeptical of one-off prototypes, 100 models had to be built. With only four and a half months, there was not time to set up large-scale production. So the first 100 models were hand built.

They arrived at the show complete except for transmissions. Response — surprising considering the revolutionary character of the design — was more than excellent. Cord won an informal poll of showgoers as the most beautiful automobile on exhibit, with the Packard 120 placing second. Salesmen on sentry duty at the Cord booth took cash orders every day, promising delivery by Christmas.

Actually it was months after Christmas before the first Cords reached the public. And then there were two bugs — overheating and a tendency for the trick transmission to return to neutral unexpectedly. By the time these were corrected, Cord popularity had diminished from the first enthusiastic response at the show. Sales never did reach a sufficiently high level to ensure a profit, staying at an average of less than 100 per month. Just 2,320 of both models — 810 and 812 — found buyers.

In its overall concept, the Buehrig design was a brilliant synthesis of many different ideas current at the time. This era, to repeat a previous statement, was one of extreme experimentation in body styling and chassis layout. Many special cars had been built previous to the appearance of the Cord, cars of such interest as the Chrysler Airflow, the Pierce-Arrow Silver Arrow, the Cadillac aerodynamic sedan, the Packard aerodynamic coupe, the Briggs rear-engine car. Of these, the Chrysler Airflow was the most significant, since it successfully anticipated the automobiles of the future. The most radical was the Briggs rear-engine car; the most luxurious was the Silver Arrow. The Cord's chief distinction was its unorthodox beauty. Of all the cars-of-the-future exhibited to the public in the Thirties, Buehrig's Cord is the only one that looks good today. Considered as a design alone, it was, and is, a success. In every other way it turned out to be a failure.

There are many Cords in existence today in the hands of collectors. Most of these are the Buehrig Cords, and the things some owners have done to them are valuable as criticisms of the original. In many cases the Lycoming V-8 engine has been discarded in favor of a Mercury or a Cadillac. Frequently the entire front-drive system has been thrown away and at great expense a rear-drive system installed. Another common casualty is the electric-vacuum shift, which is replaced by a standard, three-speed transmission. Only one owner of record has touched the body, however. Most Cord fans feel that to do so is almost sacrilegious.

O F ALL THE CARS WHICH HAVE ASPIRED TO THE title "The American Rolls-Royce" the one that probably came closest during the classic era was the Cunningham. As with Rolls, no stock bodies were made — the factory would build a special body to your order. The simplest sort of roadster cost $6,500 and prices ran straight up from there.

| CUNNINGHAM |

Few automobiles in the Twenties were built in such small numbers as the Cunningham. Not over 500 were sold after 1924,

Automobile Manufacturers Assoc.   **1920 Cunningham V-8 roadster.**

yet the company managed to stay in business while Locomobile and others were forced to drop out. In 1931 about 75 cars were sold, approximately equalling Rolls-Royce's sales for the same year.

There was never anything cunning about the classic Cunningham. From the first model in 1912, it was as solid and conservative a piece of equipment as there was available. Under the hood was America's largest V-8 engine, which was made larger after the 1931 model year by opening the bore up to 3⅛ inches from its previous 3¾ inches. The stroke remained at five inches. This gave it a displacement of 471 cubic inches, larger than the Cadillac V-16. At the same time it had one of the lowest compression ratios in America, 5-to-1, and reached a mild peak horsepower of 140 at the loafing speed of 2,800 r.p.m. Due to the low peaking speed, only three main bearings were necessary, but these were the largest that could be made. The rear main bearing was almost four inches long. Rod bearings were also exceptionally husky, as they had to be to handle the heavy thrust on each of the big pistons.

Few of these vintage Cunninghams have been saved, but one, not surprisingly, is owned by Briggs Cunningham, manufacturer of a modern sports car which is also named Cunningham. It would be difficult to think of two more dissimilar cars than the slow, heavy, classic Cunningham and the Le Mans contender of the post-World War II period.

| DAIMLER |

H.R.H. EDWARD, PRINCE OF WALES, WAS INtroduced to the pleasures of motoring in 1897 when a Daimler was demonstrated to him at Buckingham Palace. During the next year he took his first ride in a car, also a Daimler, and in 1900 he put the royal seal of approval on the automobile by ordering one for his personal use. Acceptance by the Prince of Wales automatically meant acceptance by the entire generation of nobility in England. The automobile had passed its stiffest test.

In 1901 the Prince of Wales ascended to the throne and became Edward VII. For nearly half a century from that date Daimler was the royal car of England. Members of the royal family owned other cars as well, but Daimlers have been used consistently for state occasions.

Such recognition did not hurt Daimler at all, but the firm would unquestionably have prospered whether or not it had received royal approval. First founded in 1893 as Daimler Motor Syndicate Ltd. for the purpose of selling the English patent rights of Germany's Daimler company, it is today the oldest automobile firm in England. In 1896 the company was reorganized as the Daimler Motor Company, Ltd. and began to manufacture cars. Ten years later the company was in the midst of its first major engineering squabble. It had adopted the Knight sleeve-valve engine, and not until the Royal Automobile Club had thoroughly tested the engines and found them completely reliable did the criticism of outside engineers die out.

In 1910 Daimler and Birmingham Small Arms Company, Ltd. joined forces. B.S.A. — as it is familiarly known throughout the world — was at that time manufacturing bicycles and motorcycles as well as weapons, so the acquisition of an automobile company was a logical forward step.

At the opening of the classic era, Daimler offered a series of automobiles, all of them with six-cylinder, sleeve-valve engines of varying sizes. The smallest carried a factory rating of 16 taxable hp. and had a displacement of 1,872 c.c.; the largest was rated at 45 taxable horsepower and had a considerably larger displacement — 8,458 c.c. All had semi-elliptic springs all the way around, as well as four-wheel brakes.

The sleeve-valve design, of course, had already been adopted by a number of manufacturers in various countries, the Willys-Knight being one American entry. In the ordinary internal-combustion engine, fuel flow into the cylinders and exhaust-gas flow outward are controlled by what are generally called poppet valves, which are lifted and closed by the action of a camshaft. A Wisconsin inventor, Charles Y. Knight, worked out an alternative method which he patented in the United States in 1905. Under his system, when the piston was on its intake stroke, the cylinder moved until a port in its side near the top matched a port leading to the carburetor and the fuel-air mixture was drawn in through these ports. During the compression stroke the cylinder moved third, or power, stroke. On the exhaust stroke, the cylinder again to close the intake ports and kept them closed throughout the moved, this time matching two ports to exhaust the gases. The cylinder was moved up and down by the crankshaft through a complicated linkage of gears and drivers.

Knight's first engine used a modification of this principle, two cylinder liners, or sleeves, moving up and down instead of the entire cylinder. It was this improvement that Daimler adopted in 1906, keeping it virtually unchanged until 1926, when the original cast-iron sleeves were replaced by lighter, thinner steel sleeves. That same year the Daimler Double Six, a 12-cylinder sleeve-valve car, made its first appearance as one of the pioneer, classic passenger-car 12's. The first Double Six was just what its name implied — two six-cylinder engines each with its own magneto and carburetor and operating on a common crankshaft. As 12-cylinder engines later went, it was not extremely large with its 7,136-c.c. displacement, but its price was forbidding. The chassis alone cost £1,850 (about $9,000).

For the next jump into the unknown, Daimler experimented with a new transmission and clutch. Lawrence H. Pomeroy became managing director of the company in 1929, and one of his first official acts was to adopt a preselector gearbox and replace the clutch with what Daimler called a "Fluid Flywheel." This latter item was nothing other than an early version of Chrysler's "Fluid Drive." British auto magazines of 1930 welcomed the new method of coupling the engine to the driveshaft, though other manufacturers did not hasten to adopt it. Daimler, however, not only made both features standard equipment on its luxury models but extended them all the way down through the line within two years.

The Daimler system should not be confused with an automatic transmission. To drive a Daimler, one had to select the gear desired and operate the clutch. But the car had the smoothness that only a liquid clutch can give, plus the ease of operation on hills and in traffic that still appeals to most buyers. One writer commented particularly on the fact that the planetary transmission would not object to the roughest handling; a fast shift could be made from any one of the four forward speeds to any other, the liquid coupling taking up the difference between crankshaft and driveshaft speed.

Almost coincidentally with the introduction of the fluid flywheel the Daimler group — operating still within B.S.A. — acquired the Lanchester Motor Company Ltd., one of the oldest and most respected of British automobile companies. Two years later, in 1933, a new Lanchester model appeared with a poppet-valve engine coupled to the Daimler transmission, marking the first return by Daimler to poppet valves, and making the Lanchester the first inexpensive production car to be fitted with this type of transmission.

Between 1933 and 1936 Daimler gradually changed over from sleeve valves to poppet valves, the biggest cars in the line being the last to be converted. In 1935 came the first straight-eight, which was eventually to supplant the Double Six as the luxury Daimler.

During its long history, Daimler styling had undergone even less change than Rolls-Royce design, impossible as that may seem. The fluted radiator had been adopted at the beginning of the company's history and it has never been abandoned. A big Daimler does not have the formidable, cold look of a Rolls-Royce, but it somehow manages to look more conservative, more unassuming. (This general rule does not apply, of course, to those Daimlers which have been fitted with special bodies for Maharajahs and other moneyed buyers with an eye for ostentation. Since the Daimler's biggest model has usually been the largest British-made private passenger car available, some of the examples of coachwork turned out for the very wealthy and the eccentric have been about the size of small bus bodies.)

Daimler performance has always been smooth rather than sensational. Even the Double Six models were not built for speed. The Rolls-Royce Phantom III, also a 12, was considerably faster and more lively. State occasions, however, do not demand *autobahn* speeds, and the Daimler classics cannot be surpassed for comfort and formality.

Long-wheelbase, 12-cylinder Daimler "50" chassis fitted with very custom, close-coupled sedan coachwork.

THE E-SERIES DOBLE STOOD ALONE AMONG THE world's fine automobiles. It was the only truly classic machine that was not powered by an internal-combustion engine. Furthermore, there was probably not a single car made during the Doble's life span that could match its combined flexibility, smoothness, silence and speed.

Thanks to the Doble, thousands of motorists rediscovered the virtues of what had been a dead issue, the steam car. A moribund cult of steam was revived and it survives vigorously today all over the world. Esoteric magazines are devoted to the subject and treasured by enthusiasts who *believe* in steam with an intensity verging on the maniacal. Pressed, they may admit the manifold failings of the less-perfect steam cars. But their clinching argument is always the Doble.

By the time the first E-series Doble appeared, well over 100 lesser steam cars had been made in the United States alone, most of them following a pattern popularized by the Stanley in the 1900's. Steam was generated in a boiler housed under the car's hood and fed through a pipe to an engine which lay on its side between the frame rails at the rear of the car and which was geared directly to the differential. The layout was good but the engineering, in most cases, was based with stubborn pride on century-old theory. The upstart gasoline engine was engineered aggressively from scratch and soon bettered the steam car's performance in almost every way. When White tried to market a steam car with more modern engineering in the late 1900's, he found that public acceptance of steam had all but vanished. In order to stay in business, he switched to internal-combustion cars. The American motoring public felt a great apathy toward steam until Doble started the ball rolling all over again.

The first E-series Doble was sold in 1924, the last in 1932, and about 42 were made in all. They were big handsome noble machines and could be identified by two trademarks: immense louvers in the hood side panels and a huge radiator crowned with a delicately made, positively sealing cap which was repeated on the gasoline and water storage tanks. The Robert Bosch horn and Carl Zeiss headlamps imported from Germany and the Rudge-Whitworth wire wheels obtained from England implied to the discriminating motorist that here was a car of quality.

Four factory bodies, made by classic coachbuilder Walter J.

Murphy of Pasadena, California, were available for the Doble chassis. An open touring car sold for $8,800 and the coupe and two sedans were all priced at $11,200. Some Doble owners found that the standard bodies missed their requirements so they bought the bare chassis for $6,800 and had it shipped to the coachbuilder of their choice. The Maharaja of Baratpur had his sent to Hooper of London to be fitted with a shooting-brake body for use on tiger hunts. A Pasadena matron made her social calls in a graceful, razor-edge town car on a Doble chassis. But the hand-built "stock" bodies were usually adequate. Movie prominents Norma Talmadge, Joseph Schenck and Howard Hughes were among those who found them so.

The big Doble's performance meant all things to all men. The banker's town car gave him complete satisfaction because of its total absence of any mechanical clatter and its matchless smoothness of operation — an attribute of steam power. At the same time, the Doble gave the flaming youth of the Roaring Twenties what it wanted — a car that would out-accelerate and outrun the fastest police phaeton in the country. It was claimed by the factory that the car would climb with ease any grade on which it could get traction. This is probably true, and it gives an indication of the surging, not throbbing, power developed by this machine. In stock trim, the Doble was good for 90 m.p.h., which it attained rapidly. One of Howard Hughes' Dobles, with higher rear-axle gear ratios and higher steam pressure, is said to have been clocked at over 120 m.p.h.

The Doble's handling qualities were remarkable also. The car used a full ball-bearing worm-and-wheel steering gear that was almost identical to the costly units fitted today to Indianapolis racing cars. This type of steering is the best of all in terms of zero play or backlash, easy adjustment, light and precise action and minimum reaction to road shock. A low center of gravity, perfectly balanced chassis and 52 per cent of the total weight on the rear wheels gave the Doble handling qualities that remain unforgettable for those who have known the car.

Consider this: as the huge, heavy car cornered at high speed under power, all its bulk steered as lightly and positively as a bicycle. But what was most impressive was the uncanny silence. There was not a trace of engine noise at a time when any other car would be roaring. The car remained flat in the corners and the only audible accompaniment to its passage was the purr of firm rubber on pavement and the whish of wind. Its weight and bulk were forgotten as you were wafted along. The sensation of cruising in a Doble was the same as that of coasting in an ordinary car with the engine turned off. Accelerating was much more uncanny. You felt the thrust but there was no sign or sound of a powerful engine at work.

This was the effect when the fire was not burning around the boiler. As boiler pressure dropped, automatics ignited the fire and brought into action a blower which fed air to the flame. The result was a low, mellow roar, which corresponded to the exhaust note of a powerful internal-combustion car but was steady rather than staccato. The fire cut off and on constantly and automatically, holding the boiler pressure within narrow limits. To this extent the Doble — like any steam car — falls short of the ideal of the machine as a completely silent, completely inoffensive servant.

The Doble gave its passenger one other small clue to its power source. Since the firebox was part of the boiler and the boiler was ahead of the passengers, there was usually an aroma of burned fuel in the passenger space. But it was very faint and was not toxic.

Aside from that, all of the old disadvantages of the steam car were abolished in the Doble. While the Stanleys commonly erupted clouds of reeking, blinding fumes, only a wisp of odor clung to the Doble. While the old steamers took half an hour to fire up and involved several messy manipulations, you could drive the Doble away within 30 seconds. All you had to do to fire it up from cold was turn on an "ignition" switch. Its condenser — generally held to be the most efficient ever used on a steam car — converted most of the engine's exhaust steam back into water, giving the car an unprecedented cruising range of many hundreds of miles between refills.

This performance was accomplished with a largely traditional layout of components but with a new and modern conception of details. The steam generator was under the hood and the engine and rear-axle housing were assembled as a unit. The condenser was located where it belonged, at the front of the car where White had placed it on his aristocratic steamers of the 1900's.

The ability to get up steam with such rapidity was a virtue of the unique Doble boiler which heated its water in a single, tapered tube. The tube was actually 576 feet long but was coiled into a compact mass 22 inches around and 13 inches high. The tube was the boiler; in it water was converted to high-pressure

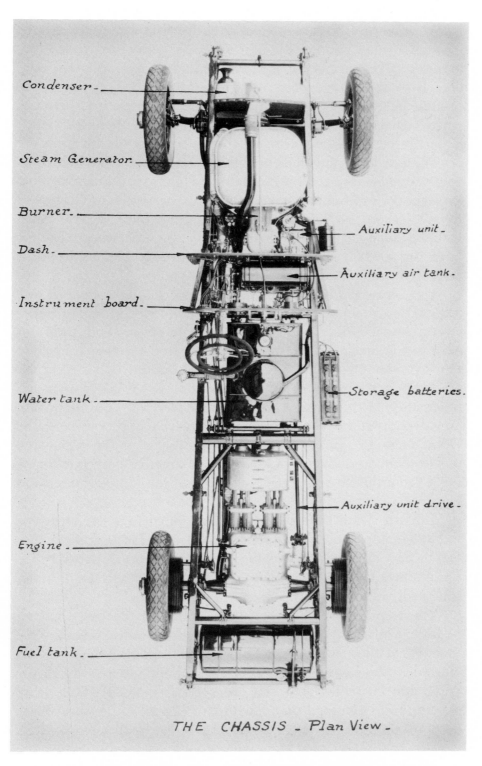

Condenser

Steam Generator

Burner

Dash

Auxiliary unit

Auxiliary air tank

Instrument board

Water tank

Storage batteries

Auxiliary unit drive

Engine

Fuel tank

THE CHASSIS - Plan View -

Doble chassis layout was standard for steam cars: boiler under hood,
engine built into rear axle.

steam. Over the coil was a combustion chamber and around and below it a firebox. An electrically driven turbine forced air through a small venturi, where it mixed with the fuel while picking up terrific velocity; then it was ignited by a spark plug. The fiercely swirling flame was guided down through layer after layer of coil, heating the water to steam. The process was arrested when boiler pressure reached 750 pounds to the inch, automatically beginning again when there was a significant drop.

These reliable and efficient boilers were tested to 7,000 pounds cold-water pressure before assembly. This was to guard against leakage, not explosion; we have found it impossible to locate any reliable record of boiler explosion in steam cars of any make. Doble's complete steam-generator unit was guaranteed against fault for 100,000 miles. The entire chassis carried a sweeping three-year guarantee.

The four-cylinder engine had two small, high-pressure cylinders from which partially expanded steam was exhausted to the larger, low-pressure cylinders. Steam acted on both sides of each piston, making each stroke a power stroke and enabling the four-cylinder engine to do the work of a 16-cylinder internal-combustion engine, with similar smoothness. While a four-cylinder internal-combustion engine would normally be fitted with 16-valves, two valves of unique, patented design were all the Doble engine required. It was a simple but cleverly engineered power plant consisting of a minimum number of parts, each part made from the best materials available in the United States and Europe.

Exhaust steam from the engine was piped to a standard-type radiator made entirely of copper. A 24-inch fan geared to turn 3200 r.p.m. at 60 m.p.h. provided enough air circulation through the radiator to ensure complete condensation of the steam under practically all conditions.

The wonderful Doble steam car embodied the best thinking of four brothers and their father — each one an engineer. One member of the team, Abner Doble, overshadowed the rest. He elected steam his life work as a child, built his first steam car while still in high school. He went East to M.I.T., built more steam cars in his spare time, finally quit school so he could build them all the time. In 1915, at the age of 20, he drove one of his cars to Detroit and went from factory to factory until the General Engineering Company bought his design. They manufactured the Doble Detroit until America entered World War I. After the war, Abner Doble returned to his native San Francisco, in-spired his well-to-do family with his plan to build the finest car that could be made. The firm of Doble Steam Motors was established, the drawings were made, and in 1921 the factory was built at nearby Emeryville. Three years and 11 pilot models passed before the first car was considered perfect enough to sell.

The Doble brothers were gifted men, but no match for the financial jungle; they experienced a series of economic crises until the depression put Doble Steam Motors out of its misery. Abner Doble stayed with his life work. There were automotive-fuel shortages in other parts of the world, which meant there was work for a clever steam engineer. Abner worked in Germany, in England, even in New Zealand but always on light steam power. Today he probably knows more about the subject than any man alive. He is no longer young, but his hard-driving personality and his devotion to steam may make history again.

FRED DUESENBERG DID NOT KNOW HOW TO BUILD a slow car; E. L. Cord had no taste for the ortho-dox. Therefore it was fated that the cooperation of the two men would create a machine both swift and unusual. Few, however, expected any-thing as overwhelming as the Duesenberg J.

| DUESENBERG |

A very average man was driving a very average car — a new Chevrolet, in fact — from Indianapolis to Chicago in the early months of 1930. It was past midnight and he had the road vir-tually to himself, so he brought the little car to a roaring 55 m.p.h. on the tar-streaked two-lane highway. Suddenly two pairs of headlights sprang into sight over the hill ahead. Both cars were coming toward him at a speed he reckoned at something like 100 m.p.h. Before he could react positively they had passed him and, as he tells it: "It felt like two engines of the Twentieth Century Limited class barely missing you in a narrow tunnel." It was 30 minutes before the Chevrolet owner recovered sufficiently to reach for the pint of bootleg strapped under the front seat.

When he talks about it today, this average driver states em-

phatically that he recognized both cars in the brief moments when
they were outlined in his headlights. "Duesenbergs," he swears.
Whether they were or not is hardly important. It is certain that
the big J's had become so famous by 1931 that any heavy, roaring,
wildly speeding car was assumed to be a Duesenberg until proved
otherwise.

The J was conceived in 1926. Fred Duesenberg — its designer
— was a mechanic, a racing enthusiast, a top designer of Indianapolis cars and perhaps a genius. He had already designed engines
for a number of stock automobiles, and his Duesenberg A, introduced in 1921, was the first car in America with a straight-eight
engine and four-wheel brakes. He was not primarily a business
man, so his previous ventures had paid off in prestige rather than
in fortune.

By 1926 E. L. Cord had been on his way up in the executive
ranks of the automobile industry for two years. Taking a moribund
Auburn in 1924, he shook it into a semblance of wakefulness, then
proceeded to boost it to a position where it was returning a profit
to the stockholders. They reciprocated by giving Cord a free
hand. One of his first moves was to buy the services of Fred
Duesenberg.

Slowly the J took shape. There is good reason to believe that
Duesenberg himself wanted to build a lighter, smaller engine and
fit it with a small body, somewhat as Bugatti was doing in France.
But Cord, supposedly, nixed the idea because it would not be as
popular with the clientele he had in mind for the Duese. Ameri-

Gordon Buehrig designed this Rollston
"convertible torpedo victoria" for the Duesenberg J chassis.

James Talmadge

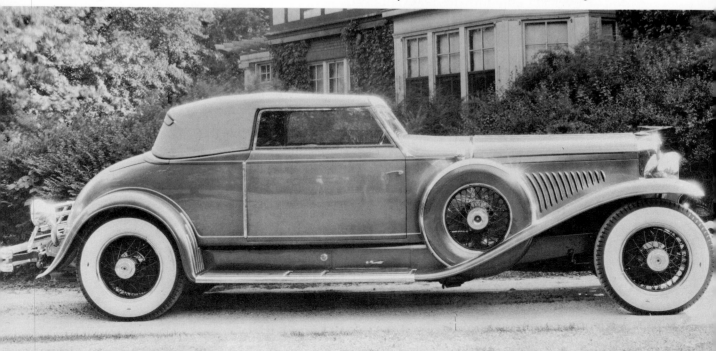

cans were not road-race conscious — they expected and got size and power for their money.

To appreciate the final product, one must quickly survey the United States market at the time. There was only one car — the Doble — which was in the same price class and it was a steamer. The most powerful American passenger-car engine available was the Auburn or the Pierce-Arrow at 125 b.hp. Most of the engines in even the most expensive United States cars were L-heads, since that design was the cheapest, quietest and smoothest that could be produced. Two valves per cylinder were considered perfectly adequate. And performance — 100 m.p.h. for a heavy, luxury body was out of the question.

Into this sane and normal world was born the twin-overhead-cam, four-valves-per-cylinder, 265-b.hp. Duesenberg, carrying a price tag of $8,500 for the stripped chassis and boasting a top speed of 116 m.p.h. At least it had attained that speed on the track at Indianapolis, running a standard phaeton body (There were hints that on a really long stretch where the car could be let out completely, 116 would prove to be a conservative figure.). At the auto shows early in 1929, the car made a deep impression on the public. The grille design looked fresh and modern in that period of flat radiators. If the engine had been an L-head it would have been large; with the added bulk of the twin overhead cams it seemed enormous. Though evidently heavy, the Duese carried its weight with grace, thanks to the long, low, narrow lines of the bodies.

Fred's engine was then the largest straight-eight ever put into a passenger-car body, but it followed the practices current on much smaller straight-eight racing engines. The nearly hemispherical combustion chambers were highly machined; connecting rods were made of aluminum alloy; the four valves per cylinder were completely surrounded by large water passages for fast and effective cooling; the valve train weight was kept to a minimum (there being only a tappet between camshaft and valve stem); valves were made of silichrome steel to withstand the high temperatures generated in the fast-revving engine. Maximum brake horsepower was developed at 4,200 r.p.m., about 1,000 r.p.m. higher than most of the other straight-eights in passenger cars in 1929. To handle the terrific blast of exhaust gases the engine produced, a special muffler had to be designed, 6½ inches in diameter and 54 inches long.

To keep the weight somewhere within reason, much of the

Duesenberg was made of aluminum, especially heat-treated for strength. Bodies, of course, were customarily constructed of aluminum when they were made — as they were for the Duese — either to order or in small lots. In addition, the oil pan, dash panel, differential housing, flywheel housing and other parts were made of aluminum. Weight of the bare chassis was given as 4,450 pounds, about the same as a big Packard four-door sedan.

One of the J's more unusual features was the vibration damper. Two containers, each 94 per cent filled with mercury, were attached to opposite sides of the crank cheek between the first two cylinders. When vibration began, it was absorbed by the friction of the mercury against baffles in the containers.

The instrument panel of the J is one of its most telling design points. A 150-m.p.h. speedometer, a revolution counter and a handsome chronometer were the centerpieces, and they were surrounded by the usual gauges. Then there was the system of warning lights. At 700 miles a light flashed on, notifying the driver that it was time to change the oil. At 1400 miles a second light flashed, this one to recommend the driver's attention to the battery water.

Most of the bodies ordered on the Duese chassis were either frankly sporty or of the owner-driver, closed-sedan type. Murphy's roadster was the most popular, some 50 of these being built before the last Duesenberg was delivered. Other Murphy bodies were also in demand; altogether about 125 of the total number of Duesenbergs built were bodied by Murphy. There was one thing no coachbuilder could do, however, and that was make a town car look natural on the Duese chassis. No matter how beautiful the job, no matter how many Elizabeth Arden vanity cases and other niceties were added, the combination of that huge, roaring engine and a quiet, sedate body jarred the sensibilities. No magic that Fred Duesenberg knew could silence the clatter of dual overhead cams operating 32 valves, each with twenty-five thousandths clearance.

This was a part of the Duese's split personality, something it inherited from the widely differing views of the men that built it. Fred wanted a sports car; E. L. Cord wanted a luxury car. Together they had constructed an anachronism, more than 20 years removed from its proper period. The Duese was similar to the great Mercedes and Mors of the pre-World War I era when the big engine in the big car was considered proper for both sports and luxury use. It was impossible to build such a combination for

1929 and the Duese, in trying to be both, turned out to be neither. It could not possibly compete with a Bugatti on a road course, because the low, light Bug had superior cornering ability, just as much speed and better acceleration. And when it came to the silent, velvet-smooth comfort of the true luxury car, such as Rolls-Royce, the Duese again had to take a position far down the line.

Despite its unusual composition, Duesenberg might have been a successful marque if the depression had not intervened. As it was, approximately 470 were sold before the end came in 1937. Largely, the last Duese sold was quite similar to the first, the engine remaining almost unchanged during the period. Only one development of importance came after the car's introduction in 1929, and that was the supercharger.

If there was anything the Duesenberg did not need it was more power, yet advertisements in 1932 claimed 320 horsepower for the supercharged J. The blower itself was of centrifugal type and located on the exhaust side of the engine. It took the mixture from the carburetor and blew it into the intake manifold with an eight-pound pressure boost at 4,000 r.p.m. An outside exhaust manifold, fully chromed, channeled the gases away efficiently, and added a feeling of power to the appearance of the car. There was also a cut-out, just in case the owner wanted to serenade the citizens on his way through town at 100 m.p.h.

Both horsepower claims — 265 for the stock J, 320 for the supercharged model — have frequently been questioned by experts, despite the acknowledged efficiency of the basic design and the large displacement. Since there are no stock J engines in factory prepared condition today, the doubts cannot be laid to rest. Detractors point out that the fuel available in 1929 was something less than ideal, and the compression ratio of the engine was low — 5.2-to-1.

During the latter part of 1935 a hopped-up version of the supercharged J appeared on the Bonneville Salt Beds in the hands of Ab Jenkins. With its special streamlined body, this Duesenberg Special averaged 152.145 m.p.h. for one hour, then continued the run for a 24-hour average of 135.47 m.p.h. On a more informal desert run, Phil Berg's Duesenberg beat Zeppo Marx's blown Mercedes in a 25-mile match race in California. Whether Fred Duesenberg's handiwork actually produced its rated horsepower or not, it was basically one of the finest passenger-car engines built in the history of the automobile industry in the United States and certainly the finest of its period.

FRANKLIN

For 32 years the franklin automobile company of Syracuse, New York tried to sell the American public on the advantages of the air-cooled engine. In the beginning there were others, like Marmon, who adopted the same cooling principle, but finally Franklin was left by itself as competitors who had formerly favored air-cooling shifted to water. Today, only European cars — and not too many of them — operate without a liquid cooling system. Owners of these cars report that they operate reliably and well, and the little Porsche's racing record proves that an air-cooled engine can sustain high speeds without damage to engine parts.

The first Franklins appeared in 1902, and by 1906 they were beginning to set cross-country records. That year a Mr. L. L. Whitman drove from New York to San Francisco in 15 days 15 minutes in his Franklin, and in succeeding years others completed similar journeys. The real advantages of air cooling were especially evident on long desert journeys, at high speeds. The Franklins, which were made to extract every possible cooling benefit from the air that rushed through the grille, could romp ahead while liquid-cooled cars were standing by the side of the road, steam billowing out from their overtaxed radiators.

By the time the classic era began, the inherent faults of the air-cooled engine began to weigh heavily with the buyers. There was the matter of noise — there is no way a blast of air can be prevented from sounding like a blast of air, although it can be muffled to a great extent (which is what Franklin engineers finally managed to do). In addition and by contrast, the water jacket on a liquid-cooled engine absorbs much of the noise set up by the valve gear and the steady explosions in the combustion chambers; the Franklins lacked this friendly insulater. In the days before liquid-cooled engines were extremely quiet, the additional noise did not matter. But the Packards and Pierce-Arrows of the late Twenties and early Thirties ran very smoothly and quietly compared to the Franklins. Not that the noise of the air was ever extremely loud (it manifested itself as a breathy roar) but it did not seem quite necessary to the people who could afford quality. Then, too, the Franklin had become the only air-cooled car in existence in America, and this tended to drive away those who knew nothing of mechanics and who operated on the principle that: "If nobody else does it, then something must be wrong."

But Franklin went right ahead, not only making air-cooled cars but advertising the fact proudly.

The advertising pitch used was a good one. Such personalities as Amelia Earhart — the famous aviatrix — were photographed with their Franklins, and the copy hammered home the fact that most aircraft engines were air cooled. And aircraft engines had to be reliable; when they weren't, usually somebody was badly hurt. Amelia Earhart, it seemed, liked the reliability of air-cooled engines in the sky so she stuck to them on the ground despite the fact that the cooling problems were entirely different.

For 1925, Franklin set a new standard for itself in styling with a stock line of bodies by de Causse. The engine was an in-line six with pushrod-operated overhead valves. Each cylinder was cast separately and heavily ribbed on the outside for cooling. On the top of each head was a metal cowling which funneled the air onto the hottest parts. Air was supplied by a high-revving fan driven by the crankshaft.

Beginning in January, 1930 the Franklin was available with a number of special bodies. The most famous of these was Dietrich's "Pirate," a five-passenger coupe with decidedly advanced lines. There were also a couple of stock touring cars called Pirates, but these sold for much less. The Dietrich Pirate was the most expensive car in the Franklin listings for that year at $8,300; the stock Pirates cost a maximum of $2,970. By now the engine had been bored and stroked to 274 cubic inches and was producing 95 b.hp. at 3,100 r.p.m., although it was still essentially the same as the '25 engine in its design details.

Franklin's two chief competitors in 1931 were La Salle and Marmon and those two companies took most of the customers. Estimated sales for Franklin were a little over 3,000 while La Salle sold more than twice that many.

Like most of the other manufacturers of classics, Franklin could not resist the drive toward bigger engines that was taking place in the early Thirties. In 1932 he brought out the Supercharged Airman Twelve with an overhead-valve, 398-cubic inch, 150-b.hp. V-12 engine. Supercharged though it was, not much pressure was developed. No moving parts had been added, only a special duct which channeled some of the fast-moving air through the carburetor and into the combustion chambers. Approximately seven additional horsepower were claimed as a result of this ingenious invention.

Like the sixes, which were still being produced, the 12's had individually cast cylinders and heads with large cooling fins. There was a major cooling system change, however. Where, before, air had been concentrated on the top of the engine, now it was directed to the sides. Despite the modest size (for a 12) of the engine and its rather low peaking speed, the crankshaft had seven main bearings.

With the 12, Franklin switched to semi-elliptic springs, though the six still carried the full elliptics that had been standard for many years. The bodies were a special design by the Le Baron division of Briggs Manufacturing Company. Low, long and rakish, they are the most attractive stock-Franklin bodies ever built, though few of them were sold.

For its first year, the 12 was priced at $3,885 for the four-door sedan, but this was reduced by $1,000 for the 1933 models. After two years the 12 was withdrawn, and only the six was available in 1934. That was the final year for Franklin. America's last air-cooled automobile had not been able to survive.

That cannot be blamed on the principle of air cooling, of course. Many liquid-cooled automobiles were dropping out of the production picture at the same time. And in all fairness to the Franklin engineers it must be admitted that they had gone far toward beating the noise problem. Judging from the price of the 12, they had also managed to make the engine as cheaply as much larger companies could make liquid-cooled 12's. The money saved by eliminating the radiator and cooling-system parts must have paid for the added expense of casting individual, finned cylinders.

No current manufacturer is reported at work on anything resembling an air-cooled engine. The last cooling-system experiment was Preston Tucker's flat-opposed six with a sealed-in special liquid coolant, and this did not bring any response from Detroit either. The American enthusiast has to look to Europe for leadership in air-cooled-engine design.

HISPANO-SUIZA

THE DEATH OF MARC BIRKIGT IN 1953 RAISED A small blip on the editorial pages of the world's motoring press, but nothing commensurate with the stature of the man in the automotive field. His accomplishments undoubtedly looked less imposing, viewed from a generation and more away, than they had in the period between 1910 and 1925 when he was in his prime. Then, too, he had the misfortune, in this special sense, to be working creatively at the same time as the incomparable Bugatti, whose cars captured 20 headlines to Birkigt's one. Finally, the car he produced was not named after him, but for the countries of its origin.

Every authority concedes that the Hispano-Suiza was one of the world's few truly heroic automobiles. From the first successful model, the Alfonso XIII, to the big V-12 of the Thirties, there appeared a series of tight, masterful designs, some sports cars and others classics. It was Birkigt who planned and executed them all.

Birkigt was a Swiss who went looking for backing to produce an automobile in the early years of the century. He found his money in Spain and he set up a factory there in 1904. Production lagged until the first appearance of one of the new cars in a race in 1909 and the first Hispano-Suiza victory in 1910. Wealthy buyers, when convinced that the light, multi-cylindered cars of M. Birkigt were really as fast as they looked, began to support the marque. As early as 1907 there had been a Hispano six, and the car that won in 1910 for Birkigt was a four-cylinder voiturette. It beat the strong favorite, a two-cylinder Peugeot, by maintaining an average of 55.6 m.p.h. for 280 miles. In 1910 that was surprising endurance for a "small" car of only 159 cubic inches.

1911 saw two major Birkigt accomplishments. One was a strange supercharged car prepared for a race which was never run, the 1912 Voiturette Grand Prix. This is generally considered to be the first supercharged automobile built in Europe. The other accomplishment was the introduction of the first 15T model, a T-head four with a bore and stroke of 3.15×7.09 inches and a displacement of 221 cubic inches. This was a development of the victorious 1910 racing machine, and one of the first models was delivered to Alfonso XIII for his personal use. Consequently it was named the Alfonso XIII, thus beginning one of the oldest and most famous stories in car history. Today there is scarcely a Hispano collector who does not own at least one car which was "formerly the property of Alfonso." Usually the car in question was spirited out of the country just after or before the civil war either: (a) over the Pyrenees at night or (b) into Portugal then over the ocean to freedom. If all the stories were true this would have been the greatest mass mechanical migration in history.

The Alfonso model continued, with modifications, until the

beginning of World War I. At first it had semi-elliptic suspension front and rear but this was later modified to semi-elliptic front and three-quarter-elliptic rear; the three-speed transmission was replaced by a four-speed box; the disk clutch was replaced by a cone clutch.

It was during the war that Birkigt had his greatest single triumph. He designed a light, powerful V-8 for aircraft, an engine which immediately proved so reliable and efficient that it was placed in full-scale production not only in France but in America and Britain as well. More Allied planes used Hisso engines than any other. It is estimated today that 50,000 were built before the end of the war.

One of the satisfied users was a Captain Guynemer, the ranking French ace. After the war he permitted Birkigt to use the insignia of his squadron, a flying stork, as the mascot for the postwar Hispano-Suizas.

According to W. Boddy, editor of the British *Motorsport*, the Hisso aircraft engine was derived from a four-cylinder automobile engine Birkigt was in the process of designing when the war broke out. The six-cylinder car introduced at the 1919 Paris show was, then, a logical continuation of Birkigt's prewar thinking, but it also incorporated all the lessons learned in the building and testing of the aircraft engines. The block was of a light alloy, with the six steel cylinder liners screwed in. A single overhead camshaft, driven by a vertical shaft, operated the overhead valves. Dual-plug, dual-coil ignition and four-wheel brakes were two features not common to most of the new postwar cars. Brake drums were designed for efficient cooling, with a finned outer shell of aluminum over steel liners. This single design, and its two offspring, the Monza and Boulogne models, constitute the best of the postwar sports classics produced by Hispano-Suiza. Above all else, they could *go* with a verve and responsiveness unusual in road machines. Some of them were successful in competition. The Monza was named for a good showing at that Italian event in 1922; the Boulogne twice won the Boillot Cup race in that city. No one quite agrees about the engine dimensions of these special racing models but Boddy quotes the Monza race cars as having a bore and stroke of 4.02× 5.91 inches and gives the Boulogne's measurements as 4.33×5.5 inches.

The specifications of these historic vehicles make them sound somewhat like big French Bentleys, but that impression is not correct. There never was a chic Bentley, a fact that most Bentley enthusiasts will hasten to confirm, but it is difficult to discover a Hisso that did not possess this quality. Some of the most beautiful classic bodies ever made were on the Hispano chassis. The unusual combination of sports-car performance and classic elegance threatened the dominant position of the Rolls-Royce for the first decade after the war, particularly in the International Set where owning a Hispano-Suiza was almost a rule.

During the Twenties, the section of the company that was still devoted to the production of aircraft engines had been busy. Hispano-Suiza speed, altitude and distance records were being set yearly, and Birkigt was improving his engines as quickly as he could work. One of the engines was a V-12, which became quite successful. As Birkigt invented variations on the V-12, he took time out to design one for his passenger cars.

It appeared in 1931, simultaneously with the demise of the overhead-cam sixes. Except for the incredible Bugatti Royale, the Hispano-Suiza V-12 was the largest engine of the classic era with its square, 3.94×3.94 bore and stroke giving a displacement of 575 cubic inches, about 9¼ liters. As in the previous sixes, the cylinder blocks were cast aluminum with wet nitralloy liners screwed in. Birkigt had thrown over the overhead cam in favor of pushrods, but dual ignition was retained. The crankshaft ran

Baby Hisso of 1934 was the 4½ liter model. With a displacement of 278 cubic inches, six-cylinder ohc engine, the bare chassis cost $5,080.

on seven main bearings. Side-by-side tubular connecting rods were used. The company rated the output at 220 b.hp., a conservative figure.

Suspension was entirely orthodox, with semi-elliptic springs front and rear. Four chassis sizes were available, varying in size from 124-inch wheelbase to 158-inch wheelbase. Bodies were built by the leading carriagemakers of the world, but most of the catalogue stylings were by Kellner, Saoutchik, Million-Guiet, Franay, Vanvooren, Fernandez. The weight of the car was determined by the chassis selected and the type of body ordered, but 4,000 pounds was the minimum. The cheapest chassis price was about $13,000 delivered in England.

Acceleration and top speed were, as might be expected, exceptional. *The Autocar* reported 100 m.p.h. in top (third) gear but there was 80 m.p.h. in second. Top speed could have been boosted by a little juggling of ratios. From rest to 60 m.p.h. required only 12 seconds through the gears. Fuel consumption was 10 m.p.g.

In 1934 a pushrod-operated-overhead-valve, 300-cubic-inch, six-cylinder car was added to the Hispano line, but its performance was mild compared with the V-12. There were a few products issued by the Spanish factory, too, but none of them incorporated new features of design. During the entire classic era most of the best cars came from the Paris factory, and today the Hispano-Suiza is invariably thought of as a French car. Only a devoted Hissophile remembers the small sixes and fours that emanated from the works in Spain.

When the luxury market folded, Birkigt turned back to aircraft engines again. After World War II there was the usual crop of unreliable rumors about a new Hispano-Suiza, but nothing had come of them by the time of Birkigt's death.

ISOTTA-FRASCHINI

THE BIG NEWS IN THE UNITED STATES AUTO PAPERS during the introduction of the 1924 models was the dawning popularity of four-wheel brakes in the industry. Duesenberg had introduced them on American production cars in 1920, but they were still in the development stage in most of the big factories.

One small matter that generally escaped attention was that Isotta-Fraschini had incorporated four-wheel brakes as stock equipment in 1909 for the 1910 model year.

Failing to credit the old Italian marque was an understandable oversight. Few could even pronounce the name and fewer yet had ever seen one of the cars. Though it was in the same price and quality class as Rolls-Royce, Mercedes, Bugatti and Hispano-Suiza, and despite its excellent reputation in Europe, the Isotta was never popular in America. A few stars — Gloria Swanson and Rudolph Valentino were two — owned formal Isotta town cars, but they were in the minority.

The Isotta was first shown in 1901, but the company did not become incorporated until 1904. Almost immediately production was concentrated on big, heavy cars, and — like most of the other expensive autos of the era — these were raced. There were wins in the Targa Florio and the Coppa Florio and a series of respectable showings in other events. In World War I, Isotta manufactured aircraft engines, including a notable V-12 and an 18-cylinder, inverted-W type. The latter was designed by one Giustino Cattaneo, the man who was to make Isotta famous after the war with his memorable straight-eight automobile engine.

As early as 1918 the prototype of the postwar Isotta was undergoing tests, and by 1920 it was ready for the public. Known as the Type 8, it was, with subsequent modifications, the foundation of all of the company's postwar productions. In its earliest form it had a bore and stroke of 3.35×5.12 inches, a displacement of 360 cubic inches. The cylinders were cast in a single block, but the engine was actually two fours placed end to end. The two 180-degree crankshafts were so positioned that the crank throws of one were 90 degrees apart from the throws of the other. Overhead valves were operated by pushrods, and the camshaft was driven by a chain at the front of the engine. Tubular connecting rods were used, but the reciprocating parts of the engine were generally heavy. Peak horsepower of 80 was reached at the low speed of 2,200 r.p.m.

After five years a sports model — the Spinto — was added to the line. The engine received a general going over to increase performance: dual exhaust system; dual carburetion; a boring-out to 450 cubic inches; higher compression ratio. Most of these improvements were carried over into the Type 8A which was introduced in 1926. It was this type which was usually exported to America, since the United States market was in its healthiest condition in the years the 8A was available. Most of the bodies were made in Italy by Castagna but a few chassis were shipped to the United States and other nations for local craftsmen to embellish. The Castagna bodies were generally about as conservative as could be made, despite the leopard-skin-and-wicker-work decorations of the famous Isotta town car in the movie "Sunset Boulevard." Those gaudy improvements were "strictly from Paramount." Castagna's original had plain broadcloth upholstery and severe, black finish.

A faster and better Spinto model was added after the introduction of the 8A, and the engine for this semi-sports car was rated conservatively at 135 b.hp. at 2,600 r.p.m. As a final effort in 1931, the Type 8B was developed. This is unquestionably the finest of the group from a purely classic standpoint. The engine had again been worked over. Valves were larger, the crankshaft had been stiffened and valve gear was lightened, with the result that the peak-horsepower point had been boosted to 3,000 r.p.m. A four-speed, preselector gearbox similar to that of the Daimler was offered to those who wanted it, marking the first time since the war that a four-speed transmission had been available on the Isotta.

Little had been done to the chassis other than stiffening the frame and making minor changes to the steering and springing. Softer springing (the rear semi-elliptics had 25 leaves) and easier

Autocar

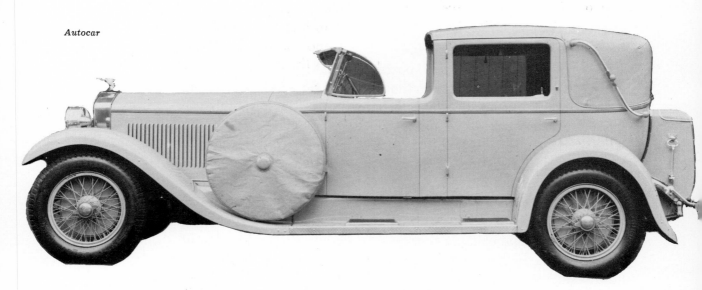

This 1930 Isotta-Fraschini straight-eight chassis cost $8,500. Town car "sedanca de ville" body was by English coachbuilder Lancefield.

maneuverability were gained. Better sales were not. The high
tariff and the depression combined to keep the Isottas in Italy, and
the market there was suffering from a severe attack of Mussolini.
With the 8B, Isotta-Faschini finished out its classic production life.
A daring, new 8C model — the Monterosa — was promised after
the war but it did not get past the exhibition stage. Isotta, however, can never be quite counted out of the Italian picture. It
exists today, though not active in auto production, and may spring
a surprise any year.

IF YOU WERE SHOPPING FOR A LUXURY CAR IN
October, 1939, you probably made a routine stop
at the local Lincoln agency to have a quick peek
at Henry Ford's senior models for the 1940 model
year. You were shown the Zephyr (four-door

LINCOLN

sedan, $1,470), the big model K (Brunn Brougham, $7,184) and
a newcomer — the Continental. Chances are you didn't pay much
attention to the Continental because it was evidently a poor value.
The chassis and engine were the same as the Zephyr, yet the club
coupe cost $2,883. Measured for prestige, the Continental's small
engine and light chassis were no match for the three-ton, 414-
cubic inch Model K. There was only one reason for buying a
Continental; it was the most beautiful automobile in America.

Today the Continental is generally considered to be the last
classic. It was not removed from the Lincoln line until 1948,
making it the only postwar remnant of the era that ended in 1942.
If you'd bought that Continental in October, 1939, it would be
worth approximately 10 times the value of a stock Zephyr of the
same year and about twice the value of the biggest K of that year.
If you wanted to sell it today you could park it on any street in
the United States where a reasonable number of people would
pass it during the day, put a "For Sale" sign on it, and buyers
would begin knocking at your door within a few hours. It is absolutely safe to say that there is no hamlet so buried in the woods
that it does not contain at least one Continental enthusiast.

To the completely devoted Continentalphile, no automobile in
the history of the self-propelled land vehicle is as desirable as his
favorite. Give him a choice between the best French custom bodies of the Thirties, the most advanced Italian bodies of the Fifties.

and a Continental, and he'll ignore the $10,000 and $15,000 imported hardware for the domestic product. Few automobiles in the world have inspired such passionate and enduring appreciation in so many people. Fewer yet have accomplished this feat on beauty alone.

The Continental was created by Edsel Ford, one of the two key men in Lincoln history. His connection with the company began in January, 1922, when his father acquired control of Lincoln from the other principal participant in the Lincoln story, Henry Martyn Leland.

Leland had started making automobiles under the Lincoln name in 1920 after converting his Lincoln Motor Company from an aircraft-engine manufacturing plant to an automobile factory. He was 77, but still sharp-witted and active. Before he could sell his first-year's production the depression of 1921 closed in on him. He offered the firm for sale and, inexplicably, it was the Model T genius, Henry Ford, who came forward to buy.

Within a few months, the Lelands had been moved out of control and the Fords were in. The car remained basically the same, and all Lincolns produced between the founding of the company and the end of the 1927 model year are frequently called "Leland Lincolns" to differentiate them from the "Ford Lincolns" which followed.

The design was conservative and simple, the workmanship the equal of anything in America. Since his highly successful years at Cadillac, Leland had changed. There he had been one of the foremost innovators in the industry, but now he was content to forego experimentation to concentrate on the perfection of the existing design. His engine — 348-cubic inch, L-head V-8 — was basically similar to the Cadillacs he had built. The Leland perfectionist touch was visible in the finish of the engine, both inside and out. Blocks and heads were *polished,* then painted with engine enamel. The crankshaft and connecting rods were machined all over rather than being left partly rough. Connecting rods were of the fork-and-blade type, a more expensive and satisfactory way of coupling to the crankshaft than the usual side-by-side construction. After the engine had been completed an exhaustive and costly testing procedure showed up any errors that might have been made. Here was proof of the integrity of the car, and of the man who had set up the manufacturing procedures in the plant.

If anything, there was too much emphasis on the non-visible features of the Lincoln and not enough on the visible. In exterior appearance early Lincolns were as stark and forthright as the Yankee character of H. M. Leland. They were pure quality without elegance; though they were often referred to as the "American Rolls-Royce" they did not possess the majesty and grace of the English car.

Between 1928 and 1932 the V-8 was modified for higher power output, first by enlarging the cylinder bore ⅛ inch, later by raising the compression ratio, changing the valve timing and re-designing the combustion chamber. Nineteen thirty-two was the last year of the first series of V-8's (they were resumed after World War II) and the first year of the V-12's. It was also the year that all of Detroit mourned the death of H. M. Leland.

That first V-12, the Model KB, is one of the high points of Lincoln history. Mechanically it was a car Leland might have manufactured. Carried over from the V-8's were the fork-and-blade rods, the careful finishing of interior engine parts, the heavy, indestructible frame. The KB was built to last. It had more main-bearing area than any other American V-12, an important factor in crankshaft rigidity and thus in smoothness of operation and durability. The engine was conservatively rated at 150 b.hp. at 3,400 r.p.m. and ran at the moderate compression ratio of 5.25-to-1. Performance was excellent for the car's weight and size. Top speed was just under 100 m.p.h., 80 m.p.h. was a comfortable cruising rate, and high-gear acceleration had the authentic steam-locomotive sureness and steadiness that was the goal of all classics builders.

Technical excellence is only half the story of the KB. The bodies that were fitted to the big chassis were the finest in the history of the marque, possessing all the style and grandeur that

Lincoln aerodynamic phaeton built in 1929 by Le Baron; polished aluminum finish.

the earliest Lincolns had lacked. To Edsel Ford must go the credit for this improvement.

Edsel had long been fascinated by luxury cars and fine coachwork. In the early Twenties he loved to visit the Le Baron office in New York and talk with designers Ray Dietrich and Tom Hibbard, and business manager Ralph Roberts. They built him a special phaeton body for his first Lincoln. Gradually Edsel began building a rational attitude toward styling within the Ford plant. When Ford switched from Model T to Model A, it was Edsel who put through some of the more unusual Model A bodies like the baby town car. As the Lincoln line expanded, Edsel selected designs from Brunn, Willoughby, Judkins and Le Baron to be offered in the company's catalogues. Occasionally he suggested changes in the stock bodies produced by Lincoln, but he did not actually design any of the cars. He was becoming not a stylist, but a styling executive. By the time the KB arrived he was ready to take charge.

His influence was evident in the design of hood, fenders and grille, all of them supplied by Lincoln to the body builders along with the bare chassis. Those three basic elements of the KB were constructed to complement the semi-custom bodies which the coachmakers had established for the Lincoln, and the result was a unity of design rarely found even during the classic era. In the Lincoln story it was more than that. It marked the end of the first phase of Lincoln history and the beginning of the second. This was the last Leland-type chassis, and the first of the series of Edsel's experiments in design.

After only two years the KB was retired in favor of the Model K. Outwardly the engines were quite similar. Each was a V-12, each produced the same horsepower at the same r.p.m. Inwardly the changes were great. Displacement had been reduced from 448 cubic inches to 414; main bearing area had been drastically lessened by cutting the number of mains from seven to four. The equality of horsepower had been achieved by raising the compression ratio of the Model K. This K engine continued virtually unchanged from its first year, 1934, to the end of the big Lincolns in 1940. Also retained in almost exactly the same form as previously were the semi-custom bodies.

Almost from the day of its introduction the K was a doomed model. No more money was spent to improve it, because Lincoln was preparing to move in another direction. Briggs Manufacturing Company, the body builder that made bodies for stock Fords and Lincolns, showed Edsel a special rear-engine car which had been designed and built by John Tjaarda. It represented a radical departure from accepted practices in both design and engineering. Edsel liked it so much he put the weight of his authority and prestige behind it, finally persuading his father to send it out on tour as a road-show attraction at Ford and Lincoln agencies all over the United States. While it was away, Ford production engineers ran an estimate on the selling price of a similar car to be mass produced.

They discovered that there was no way to fit it into either the Ford or the Lincoln price ranges, even if the rear-engine principle were to be dropped. This automatically eliminated it as a Ford, since competition in that depression era was based heavily on

1932 KB Lincoln V-12 roadster body by Murphy of Pasadena.   *James Talmadge*

price. There were three alternatives: (1) enlarge it and put it in the K Lincoln line as Pierce-Arrow had done with its Silver Arrow; (2) make it a cheap Lincoln; (3) produce it as a new line under a new name. Looking back at the situation from 1954, it strikes the observer as odd that the company did not choose the third alternative and inaugurate a new series, as was done later in 1939 when the Mercury was produced. Instead the original Briggs design was modified extensively and finally entered the market in November, 1935 as the Lincoln Zephyr. In price it competed directly wtih the Packard 120, Chrysler Airflow and La Salle.

The Zephyr is not a classic but it is an important car in Lincoln's past. With its advent the company embarked on a definite policy of low-cost luxury and abandoned the classics almost entirely. Critics today call the Zephyr's styling one of the first

successful, modern examples of streamlining — proof that it was
Edsel's designs, rather than the Ford Motor Company's engineering, which made the Zephyr the success that it was. This may not
be quite fair, since the chassis, exclusive of the engine, was of
advanced design.

The Zephyr engine won no prizes in its day and calls forth
fewer compliments today, but it deserves closer attention. Everyone assumed it was a scaled-down K Lincoln, since it bore the
Lincoln crest, and judged on that basis it gave disappointing
performance. But it really was a Ford V-8 with four cylinders
added — and not even that in size. The Zephyr's stroke was the
same as the Ford's — 3¾ inches — but the bore was only 2¾
inches as compared with the Ford's 3⅟₁₆. The displacement of the
Zephyr V-12 — 267 cubic inches — gave it an average displacement per cylinder of 22.25 cubic inches, smallest in United
States production (Ford later applied this same principle to the
Ford V-8 60, which had a displacement per cylinder of slightly
under 17 cubic inches). A design of this kind has a much higher
piston area per cubic inch of displacement, and theoretically will
produce more urge from less capacity. For competition vehicles,
like the Ferrari, an engine of this construction is excellent but for
a utility vehicle which must operate at a low average r.p.m. greater
displacement per cylinder is more practical. The latter design is
cheaper to maintain and easier to handle at low speeds.

In 1936 and 1937 the Zephyr body was built by Briggs, but by
1938 Edsel had his Ford styling department built up to the point

Post-World War II Lincoln Continental V-12 convertible.

where it could take over. Here Edsel was the undisputed boss. His father, and most of the plant's production executives, cared little for styling, leaving Edsel free to work out his own projects undisturbed. His next project was the Continental.

In the beginning the Continental was nothing more than a plaything for Edsel. It was to be his personal car, a one-off job for the styling chief. No thought was given to making a car that could later be adapted to cheap mass production on the Lincoln Zephyr assembly lines. This is why the Continental was so expensive. It is also the reason for the Continental's greatness.

Here was a car that did not have to please anyone in the company but Edsel Ford. Into it he poured all the lessons he had learned during his years in automobile styling. Into it also went the natural artistic talent and good taste of the man. Seldom has a single individual been so completely represented by a single product of his imagination. And seldom has that product gained such immediate and lasting public favor as did Edsel's Continental.

Just as it showed his strength, so did the Continental exhibit Edsel's weakness. Mechanically it was completely uninspired, a typical, production-line Detroit job, no worse and no better than its contemporaries. Edsel could have insisted on special engine and chassis improvements — since this car was intended for his personal use — but he didn't. He just didn't care.

From 1940 through 1948 the Continental underwent minor face-lifts on the same chassis. A total of 5,320 were sold, most of them in the postwar period. Prices ranged from a prewar $2,640 to a postwar high of $4,260, the increase representing mounting production and sales costs, not improvements. When the V-12 chassis and engine were dropped, the Continental had to be discontinued or completely redesigned. The company was anxious to put the entire Lincoln plant on quantity production and eliminate such operations as had to be performed by hand, so the Continental was chopped off.

Not till 1955 did the new Continental appear; it hardly resembled its predecessor. It was no longer a Lincoln, but the product of a separate Ford Motor Company division. It had borrowed little from Edsel's original design, except the basic concepts of long hood and blind rear quarter. And where the old Continental had been merely expensive, the new one was exclusive. The price kept all but the richest from the showrooms.

The New Continental had a definite appeal. Like Edsel's Continental, it was clean, graceful, distinctive. Whether it will go down in automotive history as a modern classic is something that only time and public can decide.

MARMON

ONE OF THE GREAT ENGINES OF THE CLASSIC ERA — the Marmon — died three years after its birth, never to be resurrected. Such was the condition of Marmon's finances that this engine was lucky to reach the market at all. Howard Marmon, top executive and chief engineer of the Marmon Motor Car Company, could never seem to find the right combination of prices and models to make his business successful.

What he lacked as an executive he made up in his engineering. The V-16 he introduced in 1931 was, in both body and engine, an unusual and stimulating design. It was the biggest-displacement engine in an American passenger car since the days of the pre-classic mastodons but it weighed less than some of his competitors' eight-cylinder engines; it was satin-smooth in performance but carried the highest horsepower rating of any classic except the Duesenberg. In New York, the Metropolitan Section of the Society of Automotive Engineers awarded Howard Marmon a gold medal for "the most notable engineering achievement of 1930" for the development of his V-16. The award mentioned: (a) high power-to-weight ratio; (b) compact and highly refined design; (c) new and apparently practical method of introducing cylinder liners; (d) consistent and well-studied application of light-weight alloys; (e) further development of economical block construction.

Marmon's inspiration for the V-16 dated from 1917. He had gone to France that year as a member of the Bolling Mission to study problems of supplying materiel to the United States Air Forces in World War I. There he found Ettore Bugatti in the act of testing a 16-cylinder aircraft engine which produced the astounding total of 500 b.hp. Not only was Bugatti's creation powerful; it was also smooth and light. Marmon, as civilian expert for the Mission, insisted that the United States Government adopt the engine for use in American aircraft. His recommendation was accepted, and the contract for the engines was let to the Duesenberg plant in Elizabeth, New Jersey.

After the war, the Duesenberg brothers introduced their own straight-eight, not copied from but inspired by the Bugatti engine. Marmon was not immediately in a position to take advantage of the lessons he had learned from Bugatti, but the memory of that engine stayed with him. He never forgot the incredible smoothness and power that 16 cylinders could give. And he also admired the extensive use of aluminum in the Bugatti design.

Marmon was no stranger to aluminum. He had built his first car in 1902, and by 1904 he was beginning to switch from steel to aluminum in his designs. When Model 32 appeared in 1909, Marmon established the policy that was to guide the firm for the rest of its existence; others could build the big, heavy, expensive cars but Marmon would give its customers light, fast, expensive cars. To keep weight low, he used aluminum alloys wherever possible. By the time his Model 34 was introduced in 1916 he was making his engines almost entirely of aluminum.

Model 34 continued as the standard bearer of the line until the introduction of the first eight-cylinder Marmons in 1927. It was a pushrod-operated-overhead-valve, six-cylinder engine, with the block cast in two separate pieces. Displacement was 339.63 cubic inches and horsepower rating was 84 at 2,700 r.p.m. Total curb weight of the entire car was 700 to 1,000 pounds lighter than other cars of comparable quality and price. The four-passenger roadster weighed only 3,600 pounds.

With that successful background, and the added knowledge gained from his war experience, Marmon went to work on his V-16. He shrouded the entire project in secrecy by setting up a separate enterprise, Midwest Aircraft Corporation, and confining all development of the new engine to this branch of his empire.

It must have been a nasty shock when Cadillac beat him to market by a year with a V-16 of its own, but Marmon did not change his plans. His car was introduced in January, 1931. It was apparent that he had borrowed little from Bugatti other than the concept of a lightweight 16-cylinder engine. Where Bugatti's engine had been a parallel 16, Marmon's was a V, with the two blocks set at a 45-degree angle. Bugatti had used one overhead camshaft per block, but Marmon did not need this much power so he used a single camshaft in the block and operated his overhead valves with pushrods. Marmon did employ double valve springs, a dual exhaust system and a relatively high (6-to-1) compression ratio.

One feature mentioned in the S.A.E. award is Marmon's method of installing the steel sleeves in the engine. Each sleeve was seated firmly at the top, but the bottom was attached to the block through three rubber rings. This took care of the different coefficients of expansion of steel and aluminum insofar as the liners were concerned. Not only was this technique successful, it was also inexpensive and practical for quantity production.

There was little of special interest in the remainder of the

Marmon V-16 chassis. Suspension was by semi-elliptic springs all around, and the frame was of typical massive classic construction. But the body that Walter Dorwin Teague designed holds a lot of interest for the student of American classic design. Though its dimensions were roughly the same as other American classics, it looked smaller and less truck-like because of its almost complete lack of ornamentation. The grille design was a sharper V than was common in 1931 but otherwise the lines were, if anything, more conservative than other cars of the period. Marmon's financial distress was indicated by the absence of a variety of body styles for the big chassis. No other manufacturer would have dared restrict his $5,000 cars to stock bodies only. Even Pierce-Arrow, which was suffering with Studebaker through a severe case of depression jitters, retained its varied line of semi-custom bodies.

The fact that Le Baron built the Teague-designed bodies gave Marmon owners the right to use a prestige nameplate, but this did not impress customers so much as a selection of 20 or 30 bodies would have.

In performance, the Marmon V-16 was just as smooth as a 16-cylinder car should be, just as powerful as 490.8 cubic inches

Marmon's V-16 used a 145-inch wheelbase chassis with 491 cubic inch engine developing 200 b.hp.

can hardly help but be. You could balance a coin on the engine while it was running and the factory spoke frequently of 100 m.p.h. as a certainty. On October 15, 1931 the Marmon company put their new car to a rigid test under the watchful eye of the A.A.A.'s Contest Board. A closed Marmon V-16 went on the track at Indianapolis and ran for 24 hours to set all the American Class A (488 cu. in. and over) Stock Closed Car records which have been set. For 100 miles the car kept up an average of 78.9 m.p.h., but at the end of the 24 hours this speed had dropped to an average of 76.43 m.p.h., which still was good enough to capture the Stevens Trophy from Stutz. The Stevens Trophy is awarded to the stock car maintaining the best 24-hour speed regardless of engine class. Marmon held the trophy until a Chrysler averaged 89.89 m.p.h. for the 24 hours in October, 1953.

With the Marmon Eight and 16 both falling dead in the market place, Howard Marmon went to work on a V-12. This was to be a revolutionary car, the only holdover from previous Marmons being the basic engine design. The V-12 was the V-16 with the four middle cylinders chopped out. The frame, from the transmission rearward, consisted of a single central tube. From the transmission forward, the tube branched into two box-section side members. The independent front suspension employed coil springs and vertical guide posts. Independent rear suspension was also used, but here the coils were replaced by two transverse semi-elliptic springs. Since there was only the single tube frame in the rear, the springs were mounted on the top and bottom of the differential housing, as were the brake drums. The body was attached to the frame at only three points.

For the prototype, which was the only V-12 actually built, Teague designed a radically experimental body, one that probably would not have survived intact if the car had reached the production stage.

The only styling features copied from Teague's V-16 body were the grille shape and the lack of ornamentation. Headlights had been molded into special pontoon-shaped front fenders; the hood vents were long, horizontal louvers like those on the '36 Cord; body sides were high, and the top had been lowered so far that the impression was that of an armored car with slit windows and windshield.

With this last brave gesture, Marmon gave up altogether. Of all the classics manufacturers, he had been one of the most adventurous and talented.

MAYBACH-ZEPPELIN

IT WAS IN 1900 THAT COUNT FERDINAND VON ZEPpelin, then 62 years old, set up his plant at Friedrichshafen, Wurtemburg, Germany, to manufacture lighter-than-aircraft. The good Count had spent a long and difficult life in the service of his country as a soldier, taking time out only when he served in the Union Army in America's Civil War.

In the first years at Friedrichshafen, he called for assistance in technical matters and Wilhelm Maybach, technical director and chief designer at the Daimler factory, was the man who went to Friedrichshafen to help. Maybach, who was 54 years old, had been one of the pioneers in the development of the gasoline engine. He had worked with Gottlieb Daimler for 13 years before Daimler took his historic ride through the streets of Cannstatt. To Maybach are credited the honeycomb radiator and the spray carburetor among other important automotive inventions.

In 1909 Zeppelin and Maybach formed the Maybach-Zeppelin company to manufacture aircraft. Into the firm came another Maybach, Wilhelm's son, Karl. Karl had designed and built a lightweight, six-cylinder engine, the first six to be used in the Zeppelins.

As the company progressed, most of the production went into war projects. During World War I, in an era when bombing raids were only made on the most essential targets, the Zeppelin works and hangars at Friedrichshafen were frequently hit. In one memorable retaliatory raid, the Zeppelins tried to bomb London, but with little success.

After the war, the firm branched into the manufacture of engines for marine, rail-car, industrial and automotive use. According to Karl Maybach, there was no intention to build complete automobiles until it was discovered that other vehicle manufacturers preferred to make their own engines rather than buy them from a specialist manufacturer.

Once in the automobile business, Maybach-Zeppelin unhesitatingly turned to the manufacture of expensive cars. There was first a six, and then the big 12, one of the most impressive engines of the classic era.

It was during this period that the Zeppelin airships were seriously being considered as passenger and freight transportation units. Even the United States Navy had two — the famous U.S.S. Los Angeles and U.S.S. Akron. Maybach's 12 was originally designed to power these monster gas bags, and the publicity derived therefrom was used in the promotion of the smaller engine in the passenger car.

Thus, like a few of the other classics — the Marmon V-16, Peerless V-16, et cetera — the Maybach-Zeppelin engine was derived directly from aircraft practice. The two aluminum blocks were set at an angle of 60 degrees, the overhead valves were push-rod-operated, two double carburetors were used. The crankcase and pistons were made of light-alloy metals to cut down weight. The crankshaft rode on eight, not seven, main bearings. There were actually two rear main bearings, one on either side of a large gear which drove the camshaft. And it was a big engine, one of the largest of the classic era. Bore and stroke were 3.62x3.94, a displacement of 487 cubic inches. Rated horsepower was 200 at 3,200 r.p.m., but the top quoted speed of 100 m.p.h. was not reached until the engine had wound up to 3,600 r.p.m.

It was in 1930 that the first Maybach V-12 appeared, making this one of the pioneer 12-cylinder cars in Europe. Only Voisin and Daimler had preceded it.

Among the unusual items on the car was the transmission, which had five speeds forward and the usual one in reverse. The driver had two entirely separate shifting mechanisms to operate.

Aerodynamic body on V-12 Maybach-Zeppelin chassis of late Thirties.
Horsepower was 200, displacement 487 cubic inches.

One was the usual floor lever, which engaged only two gears — the compound low and reverse. Most of the driving was done with the other control system, which consisted of two levers located under the horn button on the steering wheel. By moving the levers the driver could change gears without using the clutch and without danger of stripping the gears. All four of the commonly used gears were in constant mesh.

The Maybach used a torque tube and full-floating rear axle. All springs were semi-elliptic. The wheelbase was 147 inches, but the overall length was a modest 216 inches. The bodies were clean and honest, and had that rugged Teutonic look common to the other German quality automobiles.

MERCEDES-BENZ

ONE OF THE MOST COMMON ERRORS OF THE BEginner enthusiast in the automobile field is to call the Duesenberg a German car. The fact, of course, is that the Duese was conceived, designed and built entirely in America by Americans. But it is uncanny how closely the Model J Duese resembles the Mercedes-Benz classics in spirit. The Duese stood out among American luxury cars for the very violence of its engine and its considerable sacrifice of smoothness and silence to performance. It was also the most formidable-looking classic ever made in America, a car that looked as if it would run a competitor right off the road for the sheer pleasure of being brutal. Only one car in the history of the classics has ever been more savage in appearance and performance — the Mercedes-Benz.

If that statement seems to demand proof, consider for a moment the Roots-type supercharger which was standard equipment on the big Mercedes from 1924 until World War II. It was to be used sparingly, only for maximum acceleration or hill-climbing, so it did not cut in unless the accelerator was floorboarded. Without the blower, the engine had a rich and heavy rumble, but when the driver engaged the supercharger there came forth a sound that can only be described as a scream. It began as a low snarl and wound up to an ear-splitting screech as the engine quickly picked up revs. A former resident of a small village in Prussia remembers how, in the mid-Thirties, the son of the local baron would signal his approach to the village's main street by cutting in his Mercedes' blower. Women, children and even strong men removed themselves from the street and sidewalks quickly at the eerie sound. The young man would hurtle through the town at maximum acceleration, slide the turn at the end of the street and disappear into the distance. There was no thought of complaint — most of the villagers were actually grateful for the slight warning they received.

The pre-World War II Prussian officer was known for a hard self-discipline which was only surpassed by the spartan endurance he demanded of his troops. He usually rode in a Mercedes, if his rank was high enough. It would have been unthinkable for him to own a Rolls or a Daimler or an Hispano-Suiza. The Mercedes was built for him, almost to his specifications. If there was ever a perfect case of the man matching the car, this was it.

The first Mercedes classics were the K series (K for Kompressor), introduced in 1924 and continuing, with modifications, to 1927 when the S replaced them. Both the K and the S were more famous for their sports versions, largely the same as the classics except for body style and weight (technical details have already been covered in the First Section).

In America the Mercedes classics were popular, at least as popular as any other foreign car except the Rolls-Royce. Al Jolson bought three of them, one a $21,500 open model which was a gift to his wife, Ruby Keeler. Another he presented to movie executive Joe Schenck. It was a town car with gold-plated hardware and a bird-of-paradise motif woven into the upholstery. It cost $28,000. The third was a Saoutchik SS roadster. A very famous Mercedes in America was the one owned by Zeppo Marx which figured as one of the two principals in the Duesenberg-Mercedes match race at Muroc Dry Lake. The Duese won, but the man who was the mechanic and driver for the Mercedes blames his defeat on spark plugs which were of the wrong heat range. He swears the Mercedes was by far the better car.

In the early Thirties the gap between the racing Mercedes and those sold as luxury cars grew wider. In 1932 the first 500K appeared, a sumptuous car on a chassis intended for fast transportation. It had a pushrod-operated-overhead-valve, in-line-eight engine with a displacement of 306 cubic inches, and the price of the chassis alone was just under $7,000 delivered in England.

In the latter part of 1937 the bore was increased to 3.46 inches and the crankshaft stroked to 4.37 inches, raising the displacement to 330 cubic inches. This model, merely an up-scaled 500K, was called the 540K. It only stayed in production for a brief period before the beginning of World War II and is regarded as one of the world's greatest classics.

All coachwork for the 500K and 540K Mercedes cars was designed and built by the company-owned Sindelfingen body plant. There were exceptions, such as the passionate Figoni roadster built for one of the M'dvani princes. However, for all but the most flamboyant tastes, Sindelfingen products left little to be desired. Their greatest shortcoming, in American eyes, was the padded tops with which they equipped convertible models. Instead of disappearing when retracted, these tops formed a huge pile of fabric and framework — a German convention — that trans-Channel or trans-Atlantic motorists found hard to take. Aside from that detail, the bodies were utter perfection. Their lines were flowing and exquisitely graceful. The materials used — leather, wood and metal — were the best. Seven body styles were available on the 540K chassis, among them the last of the close-coupled, two-door touring cars and a vee-windshield roadster that ranked as one of the ultimate high points of classic-car design.

Though the 540K was a luxury car, Mercedes could not entirely eschew racing practice and performance in its design. Despite its weight (the bare chassis weighed 4,000 pounds and a fully equipped car weighed about 2,000 pounds more) the 540K could clock 107 m.p.h. according to the factory figures of the period. Acceleration times were amazingly good, as read from a Mercedes factory curve. The transmission had five forward speeds, fifth being an "overtop" with a ratio of less than 1-to-1. This "overdrive gear" permitted an overall drive ratio of 2.8-to-1 and an engine speed of merely 2,700 r.p.m. at 90 m.p.h. A sports roadster was driven for maximum acceleration as follows: from rest to 20 m.p.h. in first gear, four seconds; from 20 m.p.h. to 42 m.p.h. in second gear, five more seconds; from 42 m.p.h. to 65 m.p.h. in third gear, 10 more seconds; from 65 m.p.h. to 93 m.p.h. in fourth gear, 34 more seconds; from there to top speed in fifth gear, time not recorded. All this from an engine rated at 115 b.hp. normal, 180 b.hp. with the supercharger engaged (figures given by the Mercedes factory have invariably proved to be conservative). In 1951 *The Autocar* tested a used 540K, a car with almost 50,000 miles recorded on the odometer, and timed the acceleration from zero to 50 m.p.h. as 10 seconds, slightly faster than the factory curve shows. The braking system was hydraulic as in the Mercedes Grand Prix cars, but had vacuum-power assist and all four drums were deeply finned to facilitate cooling and resist distortion. In addition, all backing plates had screened openings to admit and exhaust a stream of cooling air through the internal braking mechanism. The front wheels were mounted at the tips of heavy, forged A-arms, all four arms being anchored to a massive H-section forging which formed the front frame crossmember. The rear wheels were driven by swing, or pendulum, axles, each having a single inboard universal joint. This four-wheel independent suspension, again reminiscent of Mercedes Grand Prix practice, was completed by two coil springs for each rear wheel and one coil for each front wheel. Double-acting hydraulic shock absorbers were fitted all around.

Type 500K Mercedes-Benz was introduced in 1932. Engine developed 160 b.hp. Beautiful body was actually a mass-production item. Body was built by Sindelfingen.

Obviously, no expense was spared in achieving a smooth, flat ride, no matter how brutal the road surface. This suspension system was supremely satisfactory on the first 500K and was still Mercedes' pride on the postwar 300S.

Mercedes made it clear to luxury-car buyers that the 540K could turn out its high speed and good acceleration for as many years as the owner cared to give the car competent maintenance. All the parts in the chassis and engine were designed with a huge safety factor. The crankshaft, which was fully machined and balanced, rode on nine main bearings. The box-section frame was heavy enough to carry much larger bodies than were usually fitted to 540K's. It was a very similar frame, in fact, to the one that was used on the bigger Mercedes, the "Grosser" 770K, which was first made in 1938.

Few of the Grossers were ever seen outside of Germany and not many were sold there. Hitler's car, which was on tour in America for a few years after the war, was a good example of the type. It, too, was an overhead-valve, pushrod-operated, straight-eight, but the engine was larger than the 540K. Bore of the Grosser was 3.74 inches and stroke 5.31 inches, giving a displacement of 467 cubic inches, very close to that of the Packard V-12. Horsepower rating was 155 normal, 230 with the blower operating. Weight, with a standard body, was a minimum of 7,500 pounds which is much heavier than any American classic of the period. Top speed was given by the Mercedes factory as 107 m.p.h. — the same as the 540K.

The ideal combination — and some one of the Nazis undoubtedly tried it — would have been the big Grosser engine in the small 540K chassis. Unfortunately no reports of a road test of this combination have filtered through.

The most unorthodox feature of Mercedes design was the supercharger, hardly a piece of equipment one expects to see on a luxury car where silence and smoothness are to be desired above performance. But Mercedes offered both — silence without the blower, a Valkyrie's battle-cry with it. Like the rest of the car, the Mercedes blower was built to give long and satisfactory service. It was a positive-displacement, Roots-type two-rotor instrument which blew through the carburetor and, as was mentioned previously, was put into operation by floorboarding the accelerator. Very deep cooling fins on the blower case and on the air duct leading to the carburetor cooled the compressed fuel-air mixture. Two exhaust pipes led from the exhaust manifold out through the hood panel. Both fed into a common pipe under the running board which fed two separate mufflers.

During the same period, in the late Thirties, Mercedes produced several other models — the types 170V, 230, 260D (a diesel), and 320 — but these were not all-out luxury cars. Two had four-cylinder engines, the others were sixes. None was supercharged. Prices (delivered in New York) ran from a minimum of $2,450 for the 170-V sports roadster, to $5,300 for the 320 convertible club coupe. Compared to the 540K's cost — the sports roadster was $14,000 — these smaller Mercedes were almost economy cars.

Advertisements of the years before the beginning of World War II called Mercedes-Benz ". . . the world's oldest and leading motor car makers." There isn't much that can be added to that description.

In 1931 A DISCERNING CRITIC COMMENTED THAT the 1931 Packard looked more like a 1925 Packard than it did like a 1931 Cadillac. He had illustrated one of the guiding principles — conservatism — of the company that made more money on classic cars than any other manufacturer. What he failed to add was that the traditional Packards looked better than most of the modern, 1931 competition.

PACKARD

By the time the classic era came along, Packard was beginning to coast on its reputation. Earlier, the firm had been adventurous enough to string together a long series of "firsts." Such items as the steering wheel and the H-slot transmission were originated by Packard for United States production cars. The great Ralph de Palma had driven the Packard Gray Wolf to a series of competition successes, and Packards were among the first cars to cross the continent. Having built its name, Packard was content to turn its attention to sales.

One of the last advancements credited to Packard was the introduction of the in-line-eight engine to mass production in the 1924 models. Duesenberg had already marketed a few of his straight-eights, introduced in 1921, but Packard was the first to work out a low-priced version of the basic design. By 1925 the Packard eight was beginning to replace the six, and all the big and expensive Packards had the new engine. Throughout the rest of the classic era, up until 1955, the straight-eight was the mainstay of the Packard line.

In this day of V-8 popularity it seems difficult to realize that there ever was a period when the straight-eight was the preferred engine, but in the mid-Twenties the public was well aware of the successes of the Miller and Duesenberg straight-eight racing engines in America and the Ballots and Bugattis in Europe. After Duesenberg and Packard had broken the ice, most of the other manufacturers switched to the in-line-eight as fast as they could afford it. Cadillac and Lincoln were two notable exceptions.

Basically, all the Packard eights have been similar to the first one — large-displacement, long-stroke L-heads built for smoothness and dependability rather than speed or acceleration.

The 1925 straight-eight had a bore of 3⅜ inches and a stroke of five inches, giving it more displacement than the Model A Duesenberg. In 1927 the bore was enlarged to 3½ inches, and this engine went through subsequent modifications all the way up to 1936 when it was discontinued. A third straight-eight, the 3³⁄₁₆x5 engine began in 1929 and continued up through 1939. In 1940 and 1941 the last classic Packard eights were destroked to 4⅝ and the bore was brought back out to 3½. As late as 1950 this same bore and stroke was available in the big Packard engine.

During these years, horsepower increases kept pace with the rest of the industry. In 1929 the 3½x5 eight was rated at 106 b.hp. at 3,200 r.p.m. By 1941, the 3½x4⅝ engine was producing 160 b.hp. at 3,600 r.p.m.

Madge Evans with her Packard. Picture was taken in 1932, but this is a 1931 model.

Packard reached its pre-Depression peak in 1928 when the entire production was devoted to straight-eights and the styling was as stiff and uncompromising as that of the Rolls-Royce. Not only was this a record year for sales — 50,000 units — but also for profits. The factory made $350 per car and the dealers were clearing up to $800 per car. Sales were not difficult to make, since 90 per cent of Packard owners were repeat customers. What most of them came to the showrooms to buy was prestige, the reputation of Packard being second to none in the United States. Along with the prestige they got a big, square, solid automobile that was as good as anything America could produce.

As far as anyone at Packard could see, the 1928 model should have been good for years to come. Given a stable economy and less competition, it would have been. But the depression and General Motors combined to shatter Packard's dream of uninterrupted ease and prosperity. People ran out of money, and the few who were still wealthy had a Cadillac V-16 to buy in 1930. Persuading a non-technical public that eight cylinders could be as good as 16 can be done, but it would have required an advertising technique Packard had never had to acquire.

Caught between these two forces, Packard started on the downhill road economically. On the one hand there was less demand, but on the other hand Cadillac was in the market with more and more models each year and Packard had to stretch its resources thin to keep up.

An exceptional Le Baron phaeton on the 1934 V-12 chassis.

This is why Packard, after two years of falling sales and one year of operation at a loss, introduced a V-12 in 1932. It gained the company little, but it gave the United States one of the finest classics of its history.

During the development of the V-12 there was a long period when the engineers were strongly in favor of a frontwheel drive car. Van Ranst, who had been the chief engineer behind the Cord L-29 (q.v.), worked with Tommy Milton under Packard's engineering chief Colonel J. G. Vincent on the car, and a front-drive design was thoroughly tested at the Packard proving grounds. One of the men who did the test driving recalls that it was an exceptionally fine job of design, and would probably have done much to push acceptance of front-wheel drive in the United States, but the company could not iron out all the difficulties in time to introduce the car at the showings of 1932 models. Alvan Macauley, then the active manager of Packard, wouldn't permit the introduction to be delayed. So the 1932 Packard V-12 appeared with orthodox rear-drive units.

The same period saw the testing of another Packard which

The interior of the special Packard own by Alvan Macauley, Packard's presid for many years. Body was built Brewster.

Borge

1934 Packard Twelve 2-4 passenger coupe sold new for $3,820 at factory.

never appeared on the market — an in-line 12. One was built and tested, then fitted with a special body. "Longest hood I've ever seen," recalls one of the men who drove it. The car was loaned to a friend of a Packard executive and stockholder, who drove it until his death, whereupon his widow returned it to the Packard company. It was promptly broken up for scrap.

Upon its introduction, the 12 was rated conservatively at 160 b.hp., but in 1935 the stroke of the engine was increased ¼ inch and horsepower rose to 175. In its final form the displacement of the engine was 473 cubic inches, making it the second largest in the United States during the Thirties, larger than the Cadillac V-16 but smaller than the Marmon V-16. Like all Packard engines before it, the 12 was a solid, heavy, durable piece of machinery designed to operate without noise or vibration at any speed. Valve layout was termed "modified L-head" because the valves were in the block, but positioned at about a 45-degree angle to the axis of the cylinder. They were operated through hydraulic valve lifters which were tiny masterpieces of workmanship and so durable they would never wear out if treated properly.

For the first year, 1932, the bodies of the 12's were adapted from the eights, and to a certain extent this interchangeability continued throughout the life of the 12's. There were, however, a few bodies unique to the 12's, memorable styling successes like the '34 Le Baron speedster and phaeton, the '38 and '39 Brunn cabriolets, and the aerodynamic coupe built for the New York Auto Show in 1933. Television star Herb Shriner owns one of the '34 Le Baron phaetons and a midwest collector has the only other one known to exist. Such unusual bodies had already fallen into disfavor in the Thirties, as had big cars of all types. Only 5,744 12's were sold.

After the demise of the biggest engine, the eight was promoted to the top of the Packard family. For the last years of the classic era, Darrin, Rollston and Le Baron contributed some interesting bodies on the 160 and 180 chassis. Darrin's victoria, a sporty but not little four-passenger runabout with cut-down doors, is still one of the most desired classics of Packard's history.

To the purist collector, Packard's greatest mistakes were the inexpensive cars that saved the company from bankruptcy during the mid-Thirties. In the Series 120, and the even cheaper six, Packard gambled everything and won. It is difficult to see how the company could have survived without entering the low-price field, but it is undeniably true that survival cost Packard its lead in the luxury-car field. Quite literally, the Packard name was put on the open market for the cash it could bring in. The company exchanged its reputation as a fine-car manufacturer for a doubtful future as a maker of automobiles for the masses. History has proved the wisdom of the move. If there had never been a Packard 120, there probably would not have been a post-World War II Packard at all.

PEERLESS

IT WAS IN THE FIRST FEW YEARS OF THE TWENTIeth Century that the Peerless lived its brief period of glory. Those were the days of blazing Barney Oldfield and the "Peerless Green Dragon," for a time the hottest car-driver combination on the racing circuits of America. Every world's record for circular tracks from one to 50 miles was captured; the best imported machinery was beaten. The public applauded and, most important, bought. On the strength of its early performance, the Peerless looked like a car that would be around for years to come.

Under the impetus of its strong start, Peerless remained prominent through the first decade and a half of the century. In 1913 the company brought out its own self-starter, and in 1915 entered the market with a V-8 engine. But there the drive stopped. For the next 17 years Peerless limped steadily downhill. There was no more competition, no innovations, little consumer interest.

End of the venerable Peerless line was the experimental "all aluminum" V-16 built in 1931. Wheelbase was 145 inches. Body by Murphy of Pasadena.

James Talmadge

Through the classic period Peerless continued to make automobiles of little more than casual interest. Gradually, as sales dropped further, the company began farming out parts of the car to other manufacturers. Continental made both a six and a straight-eight engine to replace former Peerless designs. Then, unaccountably, something happened. After a thorough factory shakeup in 1928, Peerless started to turn out a series of good designs. One of the first steps was the hiring of Alexis de Sakhnoffsky to design the bodies; this was followed by an engineering development program that resulted in the Peerless V-16.

In concept it was very close to the Marmon V-16. Like the Marmon it was constructed almost completely of aluminum; the Murphy body, like Teague's Marmon body, was almost completely clean of chrome or other brightwork. Though the wheelbase of the car was 145 inches, the aluminum frame reportedly weighed only 42.6 pounds, less than the weight of a Model T Ford frame. The engine had an almost equal bore and stroke ($3\frac{1}{4}$ x $3\frac{1}{2}$ in.) and a displacement of 464 cubic inches. Horsepower rating was 173 and top speed was recorded as 92 m.p.h., a low figure considering that the total weight was 4,000 pounds. In weight-cutting, Peerless had gone even farther than Marmon. Such parts as the front axle and the connecting rods were made of aluminum, as well as frame, body, engine block and crankcase.

Unfortunately the Peerless V-16 never appeared on the market, although if it had there is little reason to believe that it would have succeeded where the Marmon failed. Only one car, as far as is definitely known today, was ever built. It was the property of James Bohannon, former president of Peerless, who presented it to the Thompson Products Museum in 1946. If you're curious, you can see it there today.

IF THERE IS ANY SINGLE DISTINCTION PIERCE-Arrow deserves, it is the rather dubious one of producing the most successful *un*successful classic in United States history. Successful, because there was never any doubt as to the quality and excellent performance of the senior cars in the line; unsuccessful

PIERCE-ARROW

because nothing the executives could do to improve the financial condition of the company could stave off the gradual descent into insolvency.

Pierce-Arrow entered the post-World War I era in extremely healthy condition. Business had been so good in the previous few years that the plant at Buffalo, New York had been greatly enlarged until it encompassed 45 acres. In the public mind the Pierce was one of *the* finest automobiles made for luxury motoring in the world.

There had been, among others, the battleship-class Model 66-A-3, one of the biggest cars ever produced anywhere. To power it, Pierce had built a six-cylinder engine of almost 825 cubic inches displacement. That engine had been finally abandoned during World War I, but the power plant that replaced it was not exactly small — six cylinders, T-head, four valves per cylinder, 414.7 cubic inches. As originally designed this engine should have been good for another 10 years, but the technical developments during and immediately following the war soon made it obsolete. Other luxury cars at the beginning of the classic era were powered by eight-cylinder engines of advanced design — Pierce was still struggling along with its archaic six.

By 1928 things were going so badly with Pierce-Arrow that the company's directors and stockholders were happy to accept Studebaker's offer to buy. Under new management, Pierce immediately dropped its old engine and came out with a brand-new eight, not as heavy as previous engines but more powerful. The big eight — first seen in 1929 — produced 125 b.hp. at 3,200 r.p.m. as compared with the 1928 big six, which produced 100 b.hp. at 3,600 r.p.m. The new eight was an L-head, like all but a minority of American classic engines. During the three years — 1929, 1930, 1931 — when Pierce-Arrow produced eights exclusively, the basic engine went through minor modifications, most of them aimed at separating the production into three distinct lines of cars, to bracket the luxury price range. The cheapest Pierce in 1930 — Model C — had a bore and stroke of 3⅜x4¾ and sold for a maximum of $2,875; the middle Pierce — Model B — that same year had a bore and stroke of 3½x4¾ and a maximum price of $4,125; the best Pierce — Model A — had a bore and stroke of 3½x5 and was priced up to $8,025.

Potential customers were not impressed. For the first four months of 1930, Pierce-Arrow ranked 28th in the nation in sales, well behind Packard and Cadillac but ahead of Lincoln, Cord and

Peerless. Visible in the immediate future was the need to spend
every cent in the treasury on the development of a new engine to
fight the competition of the V-16's and V-12's that were either on
the market or in the last stages of development at factories in
Detroit. Studebaker money was running low, Pierce-Arrow money
was almost non-existent. Yet Pierce-Arrow went to work and
developed a V-12 of its own.

This was, literally, the last hope. For the first time since the
introduction of the Dual Valve Six during World War I, Pierce-
Arrow offered a product equal to anything the competition had.
There was little difference between the Pierce 12 and other multi-
cylinder cars, a fact that furnished the sales, advertising and publicity staffs of the company good ammunition for their battle
for a satisfactory share of the market. Nobody today can say why
Pierce didn't manage to sell more cars and evidently no one in the
Thirties could properly diagnose the trouble. Sales continued to
drop.

For a publicity boost the company decided to try a few runs on
the Bonneville Salt Beds. With Ab Jenkins as driver, a Pierce 12
averaged 112.91 m.p.h. for 24 hours around the 10-mile circle.
To make sure it ran well, factory engineer Omar J. Diles journeyed
from Buffalo to the Salt with it. Ab, asked to recall the event
after 21 years, remembers that the car was virtually stock except
the fenders were removed. Further, he says, "The car was stable
at all speeds, more like a racing chassis . . . tires were Firestone

1927 Pierce-Arrow limousine. The 6-cylinder engine has dual valves, develops 100 b.hp.

Automobile Manufacturers Association

smooth racing . . . four tires did the job . . . gas about nine miles per gallon."

Whether the publicity from the speed run was the reason or not, the company managed to show a profit in the second quarter of 1933 — only $4,770 but still a welcome relief from the regular deficits that had been posted previously. To show that the first speed run was no fluke, another and larger Pierce 12 was sent to Bonneville in 1933 and Ab Jenkins drove this around the circle for 25 hours and 30 minutes at an average of 118 m.p.h., this time under the supervision of the American Automobile Association. One final run was made the following year with an all-out special 12 (the engine had six carburetors among other modifications; the body was a streamlined, racing special) which toured for 24 hours at 127 m.p.h.

The 12 that did all this was, even without extreme modifications and factory pampering, a superb automobile. The engine came in two sizes — 398 and 429 cubic inches in 1932, 429 and 462 cubic inches in 1933 — for two years, after which only the large engine was used. Brunn and Le Baron were responsible for most of the custom bodies on the Pierce-Arrow chassis, with Brunn predominating after 1933. While the car was everything a classic should be, it did not introduce new mechanical principles into the field. Years before the Pierce-Arrow policy of conservatism had been established and the company was not going to break it now.

The only major experiment that was tried — the Silver Arrow — was nothing more than a streamlined body on the conventional chassis. In an era of experimental bodies, the Silver Arrow did not come as a shock to the showgoers, but it was evidence of the willingness of the company to try anything in its fight to stay alive. Phil Wright designed the car, which was made in very limited quantities the first year (1933) and sold for $10,000. The two succeeding years the car was listed at a more modest price: on the eight chassis it cost $3,495; on the 12 chassis the price was only $400 higher. Essentially the Silver Arrow was little more than another "aerodynamic sedan," similar to those being made by Packard, Cadillac and Briggs. Its most notable construction points were the absence of the running board, the 12-inch thick doors, the spare wheels completely enclosed within the front fenders, the skirted rear fenders. The company claimed 115 m.p.h. as top speed for the car on the 12 chassis and this may have been possible despite the still-large frontal area and the tremendous weight of 5,100 pounds.

The year that saw the Silver Arrow also saw the rebirth of Pierce-Arrow independence when Studebaker, in financial trouble due to overexpansion and the Depression, sold its unprofitable subsidiary for $1 million to a group of Buffalo businessmen. The new owners tried to keep the business alive by cutting production to a figure more consistent with actual sales. Three thousand units per year was considered the break-even point. Unfortunately, low as these sights were they weren't low enough and the losses continued to pile up. Another reorganization in 1935 changed the name of the firm from Pierce-Arrow Motor Car Company to Pierce-Arrow Motor Corporation. The new corporation was geared down from 3,000 to what seemed to be the safe level of 1,770 units per year.

As it turned out, there was no level low enough to be safe. Pierce-Arrow was through unless a miracle happened, and miracles weren't happening to luxury-car manufacturers. Various re-organization schemes and plans were gossiped about in the trade papers, some of them naming James A. Farley as possible executive chief, but nothing came of them. In 1937 came the last desperate suggestion — produce a low-price car. But by then there was no money available for tooling or even for basic parts. The company was through.

The final auction in 1938 was anticlimactic, bringing a quiet close to the story of a company that had tried to carry 1915 policies into the post-World War I era. The miracle was that it had lasted as long as it had, since other luxury-car manufacturers like Locomobile, Marmon, Stutz, Franklin and Cunningham who were facing the same problems had succumbed much earlier. The fact that Pierce-Arrow remained in production, however small that production was, until 1937 was a major victory, an excellent indication of the tremendous reputation that had been established during the earlier years and a tribute to the quality of the product. Pierce enthusiasts like to tantalize themselves with the thought that the company might be alive today if it could have survived until the big war contracts came along just prior to World War II. That infusion of money might have been exactly what Pierce needed to produce the low-price car that might have saved the company.

ROLLS-ROYCE

THE ROLLS-ROYCE MADE A FEW ENEMIES IN ITS long and enviable record as the world's foremost luxury car. One of these was reputed to be Ettore Bugatti, who did not understand how an automobile built to Rolls' specifications could be the favored vehicle of the discriminating. No more could Hispano-Suiza, Isotta-Fraschini and other manufacturers understand why they failed while Rolls continued to profit. Even today, with all the advantage of 15 to 30 years of hindsight, the appeal of the Rolls is impossible to analyze with anything like precision. All one can do is accept the fact of Rolls' success and reason from that.

At no time in its existence has the Rolls been superior in any one capacity. It has never been the fastest, or the most powerful, or the most luxurious, or the best built, or the most advanced in design or — but the list is endless, and one need not string details over many closely written paragraphs. Nor has the sum of Rolls' virtues ever added to a clear superiority over the finest automobiles of other makers, despite the company's slogan: "The Best Car in the World." The executives have otherwise been careful in their claims for the car during the last 35 years by citing, in direct and indirect publicity, only two virtues — silence and dependability. The first is a proper attribute of a luxury car; the second a quality that is more important in commercial than in passenger vehicles. Since the beginning of the classic era, few luxury-car owners have used their cars to the point of mechanical failure. What Rolls-Royce cannot advertise, and what it does have to the greatest degree of any automobile ever manufactured, is correctness.

James Talmadge   P-I (Phantom I) Rolls-Royce with custom, convertible coupe coachwork by Murphy.

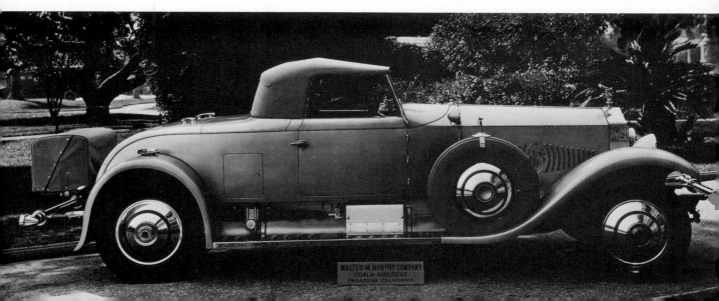

A Rolls-Royce resembles very closely an English gentleman. It is quiet, well-mannered, conservative. Just as the well-bred Englishman is prepared from birth to assume the responsibilities of Empire, so the Rolls, from its natal day on the drafting board, is designed to serve its master faithfully and forever. The analogy can be followed farther before the basic difference between man and machine asserts itself. The British are traditionally unemotional; the Rolls is a placid performer: the British detest ostentation; the Rolls chassis, fenders, hood and grille — all of which are supplied by the factory to the bodybuilder — are free of gadgets and gimmicks. (The fantastic bodies that have been publicized heavily are usually created for Indian princes and Arab rulers, and on good authority it is reported that old Rolls employees utterly disapprove of them.) The British respect stability; the Rolls has not been radically modified in appearance in more than 35 years.

The British have somehow managed to combine such unexciting qualities into a beautiful and majestic automobile. No other country has ever been able to do it, and many have tried. There is an air of authority about a Rolls-Royce, a self-assured and thoroughly noble mien that has not been duplicated.

Rolls and Royce were two of the most dissimilar men it would be possible to find. Frederick Henry Royce fought his way up from poverty working successively as newspaper boy, mechanic's apprentice, electrician. Eventually he and a partner began a small electrical-equipment business which prospered almost immediately on the strength of Royce's inventive talents. When this business began to suffer, Royce shifted to automobiles and, in 1904, finished his first car.

That same year he met The Honorable Charles Stewart Rolls. Rolls had been born with a comfortable amount of money and an adventurous spirit. He had bought his first car, a Peugeot, in 1894, and since that time had been closely connected with automobiles. When he met Royce he was the part owner of an automobile agency in London, specializing in luxury cars.

The two men worked well together. Rolls insisted on performance; Royce demanded flawless workmanship. Together they made near-perfect, high-performance automobiles. Rolls won the Tourist Trophy — then as now one of England's major races — in 1906, beating his nearest competitor by 27 minutes. In other events in France, England and the United States, he built the name of Rolls-Royce, supplementing his performances with the entire repertoire of the gifted press agent. The Prince of Wales was one of his passengers, and Rolls unobtrusively saw to it that whenever a newsworthy member of the aristocracy wanted to go anywhere, there was a Rolls-Royce waiting to take him.

Royce kept up his half of the bargain by keeping Rolls supplied with a variety of models, all of them in the finest mechanical condition. Both men, in company with hundreds of others, early saw the need for the automobile to become not only dependable and fast, but also clean and silent. Royce could make the quietest automobile in the world, and he did, sacrificing other qualities where necessary to achieve his goal. Rolls' noble passengers found for the first time that they could converse in normal tones while riding in an automobile. One could ride in a gentlemanly, or ladylike, manner in this car where it was impossible in others.

And so Rolls-Royce prospered, though tragedy early occurred to its founders. Rolls was killed in an airplane accident, Royce broke down from sheer exhaustion and had to go into semi-retirement from which he was never able to return. But Royce controlled the factory-and-design department from his own home until his death in 1933, and every Rolls-Royce manufactured prior to that date has something of its progenitor in it.

At the opening of the classic era in 1925, Rolls-Royce's sole model was the Silver Ghost, then completing its 19 consecutive years of production, the longest record in the past, and probably the future, of automobile production. It was named "Silver" because the first racing version of the model was painted approximately that color; "Ghost" because of its silence. Other than the silence of its engine, the "Ghost" did not merit its name. It was one of the most substantial pieces of merchandise on the market. The engine was a 454-cu. in., L-head six with the cylinders cast in two blocks of three. The crankshaft was a magnificent piece of jewelry, ground to an accuracy of a quarter of a thousandth of an inch on its bearing surfaces, which were then further polished to remove the microscopic scratches left by the grinder. The forgings from which the connecting rods were made weighed eight pounds; the finished rods weighed two pounds. The helical timing gears, made of phosphor bronze and nickel steel, were ground and polished by hand. They cost enough to keep an average non-Rolls-owning family in groceries for a year, but they were completely soundless in operation and, said the factory, grew more silent as the years went by.

With this literally perfected engine went a heavy four-speed gearbox and two-wheel brakes. The fourth speed in the gearbox was direct, 3.7-to-1. Rolls has always been squeamish about publishing performance figures, but some of the advertisements of the early Twenties speak of the glories of cruising at 80. This may be taken as close to the top speed.

The rear suspension of the Silver Ghost was an unusual sight, since the two cantilever springs were placed outside the frame rails and frequently were not covered completely by the coachwork. These springs and much of the undercarriage were exposed and fronted by the stark, nickel-plated radiator. Rolls' plating process is also worth noting; instead of using the customary electrolysis method of depositing nickel on the surface of the metal to be plated, Rolls laid a thin sheet of nickel over the piece and bonded the two together. With the usual, conservative body fitted, the Silver Ghost had little of the chic or beauty of a premium-priced luxury car of the Twenties. This fact was evident not only to the public but to the directors of Rolls-Royce as well. At the London Auto Show in the fall of 1935, the successor to the Silver Ghost appeared. This was the Phantom I.

Barker sports touring body on early Phantom II Rolls-Royce.

The basic changes between the Ghost and the first Phantom were in the engine. In keeping with the trend of the times, the stroke was increased to 5½ inches, the bore diminished to 4¼ inches. From the resulting eight per cent displacement increase, Rolls' engineers had accomplished a 33 per cent increase in power. Part of this was due to the changeover from the old L-head valve arrangement to a new pushrod-operated, overhead-valve setup.

A new single head replaced the old twin heads, but the cylinders were still cast in blocks of three.

There were a few other changes, such as the shift to four-wheel brakes, but there remained a strong resemblance between the Phantom I chassis and the old Ghosts. This was changed in the fall of 1929 when the Phantom II hit the market. This car had the Phantom I engine but a different suspension, semi-elliptics replacing the old cantilever rear springs. In other respects there had been little change.

During this period the Rolls' prow underwent almost imperceptible alterations. The huge slab of chrome that was the radiator-shell-and-shutter combination was built up higher, extended down lower, and also narrowed somewhat. Fenders were slimmed down, too. Thus the Phantom II, while resembling very closely the Silver Ghost, had changed with the times to become higher, more massive, yet less square in appearance.

The Phantom II can safely be called the last Rolls-Royce to be manufactured. Sir Henry Royce died in 1933. At his death the red R.R. insignia on the radiator shell turned to a sombre mourning black which it will probably remain until Royce's resurrection. But the death of the co-founder and chief engineer did not stop Rolls' progress, because in the fall of 1935 a brand-new Phantom appeared, one that was radically different from anything which had gone before. Scrapped forever, as far as the Phantom series was concerned, was the traditional six-cylinder engine. In its place was a slightly smaller V-12 with all the concomitants of the typical classic 12. There were hydraulic valve lifters (replaced after two years by solid tappets), pushrod-operated overhead valves, the customary low bore-stroke ratio (0.72). Rolls connoisseurs are split on the relative merits of the P-III and earlier models, some saying the P-III handled like a truck and lacked the reliability of the old sixes, others remarking on the tremendous speeds the P-III could reportedly achieve and its improved smoothness. At the maximum of over 100 m.p.h. which some P-III's could attain, it was possible for the passengers to speak with each other in normal tones, not a feat one would wish to try often but one that gave Rolls a little extra glamour.

Another radical innovation on the P-III was the independent front suspension, which was accomplished with typical Rolls thoroughness and attention to maintenance. Each front wheel was controlled by a horizontally mounted coil spring with a shock absorber mounted inside. This entire assembly was encased in a

Barker convertible sedan body on early P-II (Phantom II) Rolls-Royce chassis.

heavy steel container filled with oil. Thus neither spring nor shock absorber was exposed to dirt, snow, sand and other abrasive or corrosive elements. The shock absorbers could be adjusted by a control located near the driver, and it was Rolls' boast that the car could be handled almost like a sports car. The rear suspension consisted of semi-elliptic springs and a stabilizer bar.

Except for the higher top speed of the sports models, the P-III's performance was similar to that of other classics. Acceleration of a P-III limousine from zero to 60 hovered between 16 and 17 seconds, not at all bad for a total weight close to 6,000 pounds. Peak horsepower of 165 at 3,000 r.p.m. has been reported, unquestionably a conservative figure. Fuel economy, one of the Silver Ghost's most impressive points, was not as good on the P-III, about 10 or 11 m.p.g. at high cruising speeds on the road, dropping to between eight and 10 in the city.

The Baby Rolls

In 1922 Rolls-Royce produced the first of the "baby" models, small-engine equivalents of the big cars. These were not built down to a price, but rather down to a size, Rolls recognizing that city dwellers scarcely needed, or desired, a huge body and chassis. Few of these smaller cars found their way to America, since road conditions in the United States have always been more favorable to larger automobiles.

The first small car was rated at 21.6 (R.A.C.) horsepower and it was joined in 1929 by a slightly larger model, rated at 25.3 (R.A.C.) horsepower. These models — called, respectively, the 20-horsepower and the 20/25-horsepower — used an overhead-valve engine quite similar in design to the first two Phantoms. In 1936 the small car again received a boost in horsepower and became known as the 25/30-horsepower model. Then, in 1938, came the Wraith, also with the 25/30-horsepower engine, the forerunner of the postwar Silver Wraith. The prewar Wraith is known as one of the finest of the vintage Rolls models, since it had all the advantages of the fine chassis of the Phantom III without the gas hunger and problems of the big V-12 engine.

Road tests of these junior editions proved them to be as silent and well made as the big cars, but with noticeably less acceleration and top speed. They were mildly popular for a time in England as women's cars, because the ladies could handle them without developing wrestlers' biceps. Base price was about $8,000, so it was evident that there was no intention to produce an economy car. Further proof of this lay in the fact that the baby cars were permitted the Rolls-Royce nameplate, hood and grille.

Military Production

In 1914 World War I forced Rolls-Royce into the production of aircraft engines. As always, Henry Royce did the designing and his factory did the building and testing. The end-product was so good that by the close of the war Rolls-Royce engines powered over half the British air fleet. Between the wars Royce designed a series of exceptionally fine racing engines which set records on land and sea and in the air. When a Rolls-Royce engine won the Schneider Trophy in 1929, Royce was made a baronet.

During World War II Rolls-Royce Merlin engines were used extensively in British and United States aircraft. Rolls set up new plants at Glasgow and Crewes to make the engines in sufficient quantity. Another major project was a tank engine to replace the old World War I Liberty, which was still in use at the beginning of World War II. Toward the end of the war, Rolls' automotive division began a new series of experiments directed toward designing a basic pattern from which engines of various sizes could be built. These were the famous B series of engines which eventually turned up, in their six-cylinder and eight-cylinder forms, in the postwar Silver Wraith, Silver Dawn and Phantom IV.

The success of Rolls-Royce in every project it has attempted has often been traced directly to F. H. Royce and his devotion to workmanship. But other automobile manufacturers have been devoted to this same principle, yet have not been able to sell their products to the public. Even Rolls-Royce went through one awful experience in the Twenties, when the Springfield, Massachusetts manufacturing plant was set up to make cars for the American market.

The theory behind this move was excellent. So much of Rolls' business was being done with American luxury-car buyers that a considerable saving could be realized by making cars in the United States. Rolls-Royce was careful to send an élite crew of workmen to the Springfield plant to train American workers. The same materials were used, the same standards of excellence maintained; in short, the American Rolls was virtually a duplicate of its English brother. The only differences were in the position of the steering wheel (left-hand drive for the Americans) and in the engine accessories, which were made by American suppliers for the American Rolls.

This was a good test. If the Rolls-Royce had been popular for its appearance or its silence, for its technical excellence or workmanship, then the American-made product would have sold as well as the English version. The two were virtually indistinguishable in performance and design. But the appeal lay elsewhere. Americans preferred the imported model. Call it snobbishness, social climbing, whatever you will — Americans and Continental Europeans consider the *British* Rolls-Royce *the* automobile. It was the correct car for people who could afford the best. So it must have been "The Best Car In The World."

EXCEPT FOR ITS PRICE AND SIZE, BOTH OF WHICH were considerably smaller, Stutz closely compares with Duesenberg as one of the truly great classics produced in the United States. Both firms manufactured high-performance chassis, both had a

STUTZ

successful racing background, both fitted their chassis with some of the most beautiful and unusual custom bodies seen during the classic era.

The resemblance does not end there. Duesenberg's huge

engine was justly praised because it followed good racing practice in the use of dual overhead camshafts and four valves per cylinder. In 1931 Stutz brought out its DV-32 which, surprisingly, had dual overhead camshafts and four valves per cylinder. The Stutz was a much smaller engine, though — 322 cubic inches compared to the Duesenberg's 420. And the Stutz was cheaper — $3,190 for the bare DV-32 chassis as compared to Duesenberg's $8,500.

The DV-32 chassis was the only United States sports-classic ever produced. In the later-day Bearcat body it was guaranteed to better 100 m.p.h.; in the Super Bearcat body it could move at a yet more lively pace. Other bodies, being heavier, were not quite so nimble but they were still the fastest heavy cars of their displacement class available on the American market. Other American compromise classics with displacements above the 400-cubic inch mark could not match the Stutz on the open road. Only the Duesenberg was faster, and the customer paid a tremendous premium for that extra speed and power.

From the first days of its existence (see Stutz chapter in the First Section) the Stutz had been a violent machine. This was originally due to the inventive genius of Harry C. Stutz, whose great love was racing. He left the firm in 1919, however, and from that date until the opening of the classic era the marque rested in a state of indecision as to its competition future.

New blood and new engineering entered the picture in 1926. From that date, Stutz maintained a pattern that included limited but rugged competition on the one hand and the production of Packard-class luxury cars on the other. It is the luxury cars we are concerned with here, since the competition story has been told in the previous section. These were, necessarily, based on the competition chassis and used the competition engine, but they were detuned for average driving.

Rather than base its sales pitch on competition, the Stutz Motor Car Company of America, Incorporated, began the classic era by trying to sell its product as the "Safety Stutz." In an advertisement in *Vanity Fair* in May, 1926, the company quoted acceleration figures of 10 to 50 m.p.h. in "less than 15 seconds," then went on to point out that this agile performance was a good safety factor. Also mentioned was the worm-drive rear axle which permitted the body to be hung five inches lower than on cars with the conventional axle, thus lowering the center of gravity and giving the car more stability in skids and on corners. Another boast was the frame which was claimed to be the most rigid of any passenger automobile.

This might have been fine material to give the low-price car buyers but it failed to bring in the high-paying customers. The automobile had become so well established that any car with a price tag in the $3,000 range was assumed to be safe mechanically.

So Stutz began to offer rare and wonderful bodies with strange and exotic names, a policy continued till the bitter end in 1933. Chief among these were the Weymann fabric bodies, the Chaumont, Monte Carlo, Longchamps, Chantilly, Biarritz, Riviera, etcetera. Other tailors to the Stutz chassis were Le Baron and Rollston. In 1932, one of the finest years for the marque, there were 15 stock bodies, eight Le Baron bodies, one from Fleetwood, three from Rollston and one from Brunn on the DV-32 chassis. The SV-16 chassis the same year had all but two of these — the Bearcat and Super Bearcat — and one of its own, a convertible coupe by Waterhouse. Prices ran from $2,695 for the SV-16 five-passenger coupe to $8,495 for the DV-32 Fleetwood town car, a spread almost as great as that offered by Cadillac.

A star of December, 1931 New York Salon was this Waterhouse "Continental Coupe" body on Stutz DV-32, 134.5-inch wheelbase chassis. A rare forerunner of the Lincoln Continental.

By this time Stutz had modified its safety appeal, and had gone back to glamour to try to sell its wares. The Bearcat was chosen as the bellwether of the line, and it was put through an intensive series of runs in more than one city to prove to dealers and prospective dealers that it could really deliver its 100 m.p.h. and keep delivering it. At the Long Island Motor Parkway one rugged little Bearcat flashed back and forth through a measured mile at 103 m.p.h. for six and a half hours, carrying a driver and one passenger each trip. Only a few of the current Bearcat legends date from this period, rather than from the days of the really famous original Bearcat almost 20 years earlier. The old model had captured the fancy of a generation; unfortunately the new one couldn't.

The purpose of all this razzle-dazzle, of course, was to hide the fact that the Stutz had only eight cylinders. All the compromise classics in the same price range with the Stutz were blossoming out with 12- and 16-cylinder cars, and Stutz could not afford to follow suit. Hence, also, the catchy DV-32 and SV-16 tags hung on the cars. More than one unschooled buyer came into the showroom with the idea that he was going to see 16- and 32-cylinder cars. Only after he'd had his demonstration ride did he find out that V stood for Valve, not for the shape of the engine.

Financially, the company had been on a rocky road ever since 1922, when Charles Schwab had rescued it. Despite Le Mans showings that were not at all bad considering the rugged competition Stutz faced there, sales had been very disappointing even in the boom years of 1928 and 1929. In 1930 three creditors filed claims for $2 million. Schwab again came to the rescue, enabling engineer Charles Greuter to build the DV-32 series and return to Le Mans, but that was the last year of optimism. After 1931, the company went down rapidly, some estimates of production running as low as 700 cars, total, for the period between the introduction of the DV-32 and the end of the company's existence. As to the actual termination date, this is somewhat cloudy, though there seem to have been no 1934 models actually marketed, and 1933 sales were so few as to bring business almost to a standstill that year.

When Stutz died the entire concept of the classic body on the sports chassis went out of existence in the United States. Europe was left with a monopoly on that pattern for the remainder of the classic period.

IF YOU TAKE THE TROUBLE TO DIVIDE THE WILLS Sainte Claire's weight by its rated horsepower you will be confronted by a ratio that would hardly pull the skin off the proverbial custard pudding. But power-to-weight is not the only criterion of performance; torque and gearing are factors too.

WILLS SAINTE CLAIRE

The overhead-camshaft V-8 W.S.C. was one of the most spirited cars of the early Twenties. It was one of the most interestingly engineered machines ever produced in America. Although it was no match in size for Cadillac, Lincoln, Lafayette, Locomobile and Pierce-Arrow, it was very bit as much a "snob" car. The W.S.C. sport roadsters and phaetons led the elite of their class and day.

They were produced by a man romantically named Childe Harold Wills. He had worked as a draftsman with Henry Ford before the Ford automobile was born and to keep warm in the cold barn where they worked the two had used to spar together between sessions at drawing board and lathe. When the Ford Motor Company was organized in 1903 Mr. Ford, the president, made Mr. Wills his manufacturing manager. As a metallurgy-conscious engineer Wills contributed heavily to the success of Ford products and was responsible for many of the unorthodox features for which the Model T was famous. In 1919 Mr. Ford decided to become sole owner of his company and bought out the other stockholders. Wills was one and he became a multi-millionaire when he turned in his shares. He decided to build a car as uniquely and appropriately engineered as Mr. Ford's. It was intended not to compete with the Model T but, by its equally well-conceived design and styling, to lure the luxury class as successfully as the T had charmed the American proletariat.

Wills needed a factory site and, armed with his millions, bought up 4,400 acres of the State of Michigan around the Sainte Claire River town of Marysville. He invested heavily in projects that would make the town attractive to skilled workers, and even more heavily in the automobile plant itself. The first cars produced by C. H. Wills and Company, rolled out of Marysville in the spring of 1921, precision-timed to meet a major economic depression.

The car was the really magnificent Model A-68, one of America's best-engineered, best-performing and most significant automobiles. It was inspired by one of Europe's finest cars, a fact implied frankly by the Wills trademark — a wild goose in profile with wings down in flight that was almost identical to the famous Hispano-Suiza stork. The Gray Goose appeared on the rear-mounted spare-tire cover and on a radiator shell which also took its lines from Hispano.

Wills felt that the quality cars of the moment were too heavy, too difficult to handle and too hungry for fuel, so he designed a chassis that was considerably lighter and smaller than those of his competition. The car's most memorable feature, its V-8 engine, had a general layout patterned after the famous Hisso oh.c. V-8 aircraft engines which were built in great numbers during World War I not only in France but also under license in this country by the Wright Aeronautical Corporation. Its light-alloy crankcase mounted two detachable, interchangeable blocks in a 60-degree vee. As in most racing practice, the cylinder heads were non-detachable, integral with the blocks. Over each head a shaft-and-bevel-gear-driven camshaft operated in-line valves, finger-type cam followers being provided to relieve the valve stems of side thrust. The combustion chambers and piston heads were highly polished to inhibit carbon deposits and the H-section fork-and-blade connecting rods and three-bearing crankshaft all boasted a completely machined finish.

Ralph Roberts

Town car body by Le Baron on Wills Sainte Claire chassis of early Twenties.

Although this engine, with all its emphasis on quality, used thermo-siphon cooling instead of a water pump, overheating was never a problem. The intake ports, on the inside of the vee, were fed from a dual-throat Zenith carburetor and the exhaust ports, on the outside of the vee, discharged into a separate exhaust system for each bank of cylinders. A nice touch was in the cooling-fan drive, which was by gears with an automatic clutch that took the fan out of operation at speeds above approximately 40 m.p.h. It was a beautiful engine to look upon and had a minimum of exposed bric-a-brac.

The chassis' suspension was by four semi-elliptic springs, the rear set being slung below the axle. The compactness of the small V-8 engine made for low body lines and a low center of gravity, and its shortness permitted mounting well aft of the front axle while leaving plenty of payload room on the short 121-inch wheelbase that was most popular for this model. Thus the car's handling qualities were the pride of discriminating fanatics, who constituted a long-lived W.S.C. cult. Racing-car-type worm-and-gear steering gave the Wills an ultimate measure of precision controllability. The chassis was equipped with concave disc wheels of Wills' own design. It was famous for its pioneer use of molybdenum alloy steel wherever possible and the W.S.C. was often termed "The Molybdenum Car."

These cars had excellent acceleration for their time and a top speed of about 75 m.p.h. Their reception by the American public was properly appreciative, but hard times restricted sales. Wills' millions were soon exhausted, and the firm went into receivership in November, 1922.

The next year, however, Wills rallied and repurchased his company. He resumed production of the V-8's and simultaneously busied himself with a new engine. This one, too, showed strong Hisso influence. Like the big Hisso passenger-car engine, it was a single oh.c. in-line six and even used the same 5½-inch bore. The W-6, a transition model, was introduced in 1925 and retained the low, flat lines of the V-8. It was a thrilling car to drive, comparable to the eight in acceleration and capable of about 80 m.p.h. at frightening piston speed. It had great low-speed torque and smooth, fast starts could be made in top gear from a standstill. The W-6 was later replaced by the T-6, which differed chiefly in having a higher hood line, the better to accommodate the new engine.

This engine used seven massive, 2½-inch diameter main bearings in a crankcase that was water jacketed in the interest of oil cooling; the thermo-syphon principle was still retained. Cam drive and valve gear followed the pattern used on the eight, but a detachable cylinder head was adopted. One of the beauties of this engine was its easy serviceability. Two screws on the vertical shaft coupling and about ten in the head were all that held the camshaft and its housing in place. The engine could be made ready for a valve grind in 20 minutes and one owner reported that tappet adjustment could be carried out in a few minutes while wearing one's Sunday clothes. The engine was famous for its clean, uncluttered appearance. This was aided by such steps as mounting the generator on the transmission housing, a gear drive being provided for the Delco-Remy unit.

The T-6 Wills Sainte Claire was produced through 1927, when the marque, along with scores of others, disappeared in the titanic competitive struggle which gathered momentum in the middle Twenties and by the middle Thirties had narrowed the nation's once richly varied automotive industry down to a handful of survivors.

Automobile Manufacturers Association   1920 Wills Sainte Claire roadster.

PART THREE

Mid-Century Phenomenon— Automobile Mania

IF THE AVERAGE AMERICAN WAS CONCERNED AT ALL ABOUT AUTO-mobiles at the end of World War II, he was usually thinking only of the length of the waiting list for a new Chevrolet or Plymouth. At the end of 1945 the sight of an M.G. or a Jaguar was so rare as to bring traffic to a momentary halt. If any one had predicted then that 100,000 people would gather at Watkins Glen, New York for the sole purpose of watching a sports-car road race in the near future he would have been dismissed as harmlessly unhinged.

Magazine counters from New York to Los Angeles stocked no American automobile magazines that were slanted toward enthu-siasts or consumers. Professional automobile racing was still in the doldrums, although during the following year interest began to revive slightly. It would have been a rare American who could have explained what Grand Prix or sports-car racing in Europe was, let alone give you the name of a single make of automobile involved in those races.

There are a number of excellent explanations for what happened during the ensuing years. According to one interpretation, United States soldiers stationed in Britain brought the sports-car movement home with them. Certainly this did have its effect. Those Americans who had had experience with sports cars in England usually enjoyed it. Not many people in Britain, however, United States soldiers or not, had much chance to wheel merrily through the countryside, thanks to the severity of petrol rationing over there during and after the war, so it is doubtful that much of a wave of enthusiasm could have been created by the few who did. But there were millions of Americans who grew accustomed to the sight of the small English and Continental two-seaters, and this familiarity undoubtedly accelerated the growth of the sports-car movement.

Trying to explain the simultaneous increase in enthusiasm for other types of autos and auto sports is more difficult. A 1934 Packard Twelve, little more than a candidate for the scrap heap in 1939 regardless of condition, increased to more than $1,000 in value when the classics craze hit its peak in 1952. This is not a sports car. The A.A.A. Contest Board, America's top professional-racing sanctioning group, ran 322 races in 1940; in 1948 there were 530. Attendance jumped even more sensationally, as did income. There was so much interest in racing that another sanctioning body, N.A.S.C.A.R. (The National Association for Stock Car Auto Racing) was formed and grew to the point where it was sanctioning more events than the A.A.A. The dozens of so-called "outlaw" racing organizations which have been in existence for a number of years reported similar increases in attendance and income.

And then came the automobile publications. *Speed Age, Road and Track, Hot Rod, Motor Trend, Motorsport, Speed Mechanics, Cars, Auto Age, Hop Up, True's Automobile Yearbook, Sports Cars and Hot Rods* were only some of the titles. The home mechanics' magazines which formerly ignored automobiles except to advance a few tips on simple repairs that could be done to the family car at home, started to run road tests of current American production cars and foreign cars. Some of the auto magazines were hole-in-the-wall operations, others were quite the opposite. Robert Peterson and Robert Lindsay put out their first issues of *Hot Rod* on a shoestring with almost no outside help. Five years later they owned a publishing company which published four monthly magazines — *Hot Rod, Motor Trend, Auto* and *Cycle* — and news-stand books as well.

There is no single explanation for this sudden increase in car consciousness, just as there never was a specific reason for the popularity of Mah Jongg or miniature golf. One of the most striking proofs of this is found in the simultaneous nature of the revival. Hot rods didn't just become popular in Southern California where the climate and the terrain favored them; they became popular all over the nation. *Hot Rod,* at its peak, had a circulation of about 500,000, much of it ouside the Los Angeles area. Sports cars found buyers everywhere in the nation despite the difficulty of finding proper service in non-metropolitan areas. The first classics articles that appeared brought dozen of letters from readers, nearly half of them observing, "I'm amazed to find that there are others who happen to share my particular enthusiasm. . . ." Racing boomed in Georgia, New Jersey, Illinois, California and many other states at the same time.

Three factors, all economic, aided the revival. One was the dollar-hunger of Great Britain. When it became apparent that United States citizens were willing to pay dollars for sports cars, the British skillfully and intelligently built up the demand. They advertised extensively, they cooperated whole-heartedly with American journalists, they made a sizable capital investment in United States dealerships and distributorships and helped to set up large parts depots. If Clark Gable bought a Jag, the British played the fact to the hilt. So successful were the British in this, and so insistent and regular was the American demand, that the United States has absorbed the major part of British auto production since World War II.

The other factor was the drastic auto shortage in the United States after World War II. Almost all the readers of this chapter will remember the frantic scramble for new and good used cars during that period. Previously we had been a nation that had taken automobiles for granted; now we began to look at them with a new interest.

Finally, the purchasing power of the average man was at an all-time high. For the first time in history almost everyone could afford the new car of his choice. Given this dazzling new choice, many people decided to get a little more information about their alternatives. So they bought car magazines, visited showrooms, went to races. Most of them eventually bought their new American cars and promptly lost interest, but there was a sizable minority, the extent of which has never been established, that adopted cars as a hobby. It is the hard nucleus of this group of car-conscious Americans which has bought and raced sports cars, contributed members to antique- and classic-car clubs, and supported the special auto shows that featured cars of unusual interest.

Their influence proved to be out of all proportion to their number. The strength of their interest, combined with the support of the many Europeans who have always regarded the machine as a delightful toy, was instrumental in developing a postwar sports car vastly superior in performance to anything of the prewar period.

LOWER, LIGHTER, FASTER

THE EARLY POSTWAR SPORTS CARS CAN BE SUMMARIZED IN TWO letters — M.G. Major manufacturers in Europe had no money to invest in experiment and research in those years, and even if they had there was little reason to alter existing designs. Demand far exceeded supply, just as in America during that period, which meant that anything produced could be sold. Nor was there an active market for sports cars at any price; Europeans and Britishers wanted transportation first and were willing to wait for their mechanized playthings.

It was the American dollar and growing enthusiasm for automobiles that first brought the sports cars out. Happily, the Americans were not overcritical of mellowed designs, being rather used to them in their own transportation cars, so prewar styling and engineering, as exemplified by the hardy little product of Morris Garages, was all that was necessary to crack the market. It mattered not that the M.G. had far less top speed and acceleration than an American car, nor that the 1¼-liter engine necessitated constant shifting in traffic, nor that a minor gradient reduced cruising speed to approximately that of a loaded truck — the car was cute, it could corner and steer quickly, it was available.

It was not good enough, however, to satisfy the parallel interest in road racing in the United States and a world-wide revival of enthusiasm for sports-car events of all kinds. Enzo Ferrari, who was to become the driving force behind most of the major advances of the next six years, sent his two-liter V-12 sports model into competition in 1947 and stunned the sports-car makers all over the world. It was only too evident to engineers who watched the Ferrari in action that new engines, bodies and chassis would have to be developed to surpass the Italian fireball even in unlimited racing.

The Ferrari was a mutation from the evolutionary line. Enzo had done everything at once — lightened the chassis, streamlined the body into aerodynamic efficiency and lightened it at the same time, developed a high-revving, overhead-cam engine that could, within limits, stay together long enough to finish a race. The car had descended from earlier Grand Prix experience and was even paralleled by a Grand Prix car of similar displacement and dimensions. That it could never be placed in mass production, or even economical limited production, was a certainty. Ferrari's factory was too small and his manufacturing techniques too precise to permit the adoption of an assembly line. This put him out of direct sales competition with Jaguar and the other companies just beginning to consider selling to the American market, but Ferrari performance kept them from making the kind of showing in competition that was necessary to sell cars.

It was under this Ferrari pressure that the truly remarkable Jaguar XK120 was developed in England. A mass-produced car capable of 132 m.p.h., it revolutionized sports-car thinking all over the world, particularly in America where Jaguars were an instant success. With the surprising top speed there was reliability, economy, comfortable low-speed performance and attractive styling — all for approximately $4,000, delivered in America. The Ferrari was a faster car and the M.G. was cheaper, but the XK represented the most satisfactory compromise between price and performance yet developed.

Within the next year the pattern of postwar sports-car production had been set. Most notable was the growing schism between competition sports cars and touring types. Again it was Ferrari leading the way; he turned out a stream of models, gradually increasing displacement and power output without raising weight or adding to frontal area until his "sports" cars could be clocked at 170 m.p.h. and more. If they could have been depended upon to sustain this speed for the distance required to win the major sports-car races consistently they would have been unbeatable. Their relative undependability, however, would not operate in favor of opponents unless they were pushed hard. So there was no alternative but to develop special competition sports cars which could reach almost the same speeds as the Ferraris.

By 1954 Alfa Romeo, Mercedes-Benz, Jaguar, Allard, Cunningham, Gordini and Lancia had models which could top 150 m.p.h. It was in the struggle to make a 150-m.p.h. vehicle that might reasonably be termed a sports car that most of the important developments in chassis, body and engine construction came about.

To give all the credit to the big cars would be unfair, however. During the same period an intense performance war had been fought by cars of less-than-2,000-c.c. displacement. M.G. sensibly stayed completely out of the fight. Chiefly involved were Porsche, OSCA, Lancia, Jowett and Gordini-Simca. As in the bigger cars, speeds rose to incredible heights. By 1954 the high-winding little cars were going as fast as the largest prewar sports cars. Porsche emerged as one of the most successful, a feat the more remarkable in view of the fact that it was a closed car which could conveniently be used for high-speed touring.

There is little doubt that frame and body design improvements were chiefly responsible for the increase in performance in all displacement classes. For the first time there was a concerted effort to build genuinely efficient bodies. Frontal area was sharply reduced by lowering the overall height, wind drag was partly eliminated by rounding off the sharp corners. Under the leadership of the Italian stylists the so-called "envelope" body was refined to the point where it was suitable for both touring and competition.

Frames progressed rapidly from the orthodox box or channel-section rails to tubular constructions, some of them so complex they defy verbal description. The tubes were made of extremely tough chrome-moly steel, thus could be made thin and light. But lightness was only one benefit. By re-designing the position of the principal members of the frame and devising new methods of bracing, rigidity was increased by as much as five times. While rigidity had no effect on flat-out speed, it contributed much to the usable speed, particularly on curves and rough roads.

Suspension systems underwent similar modifications. Independent front suspension by coil springs and wishbones became as popular as the solid front axle had been in prewar days. The Porsche's unusual four-wheel, independent, torsion-bar suspension was not widely adopted, though Jowett tried it for awhile in England with good results. Jowett later went back to coil-spring front suspension in the R4 model, retaining the torsion bars in the rear only.

The C Jaguars publicized another improvement when they won the 1953 Le Mans race partly on the performance of their disk brakes. Braking efficiency had long lagged behind the speed increases of the new cars.

Engine design changed little, but there was the already-noted boost in output. As the postwar years rolled on, engine size went up as much as 150 per cent. The first successful Ferrari sports car fitted in the under-two-liter class; the next winning model was the 2.6-liter; then came the Jaguars, Mercedes, Lancias and later Ferraris with displacements varying between 2.9 and 3.5 liters. Larger engines — the 3.9-liter Lancias, the made-over Grand Prix 4.5-liter Talbots — have been successful. The 4.1 and 4.5-liter Ferraris had a habit of losing clutches, but in 1954 an even larger Ferrari, the 4.9, won at Le Mans and Jim Kimberly's 4.9 Ferrari was the U. S. champion. In general, the successful engines in unlimited competition have either one or two overhead camshafts, the only notable exceptions being the pushrod American engines in the Allards and Cunninghams.

While the competition-slanted sports cars were developing speeds that put them beyond the talents of the average driver, there was another group of sports cars growing up. These are variously called sports, or fast touring, cars. Most of them are made in England and they are largely special versions of standard family cars. Typical of the manner in which these cars are put together is the Healey group. The four Healeys which have appeared have used, in the order of their appearance, Riley, Nash, Alvis and Austin engines. In each case the engines have been of the traditional pushrod, long-stroke design popular before the war. On paper the Healeys should not have been capable of anything more than comfortable high-speed touring; in competition their sheer dependability has made up for what they lacked in top speed and acceleration. A Nash-Healey finished third behind the two Mercedes in the 1952 Le Mans race, and the Austin-Healey team finished intact, though farther down in the order, in the 1953 running of the same event. Both cars are capable of 110-120 m.p.h. in touring trim and higher speeds with finer tuning. Once again, weight slashing and body redesigning paid off in better performance.

While sports cars were improving faster than in any similar period since the birth of the automobile, luxury cars were being produced slowly. The great international common denominators of luxury in the postwar era have been the American Cadillac-class vehicles, which are as esteemed in Europe as they are here. Only Rolls-Royce, Daimler, Bentley, and later Mercedes-Benz made attempts to market postwar classics.

Of the products of these four marques, the Rolls-Royce Phantom IV and the Daimler Straight Eight are the closest to prewar classics. Two others, the Mercedes 300S and the Bentley Continental, may be prototypes of the best luxury cars of the future. The most notable difference between the old and the new is in size and performance. Both the 300S and the Bentley Continental are relatively small, very fast machines, differing from cheaper sports-touring cars in quality of construction and luxury bodywork and interiors.

Postwar styling has been highly experimental. In the early years after the war there were four different approaches — American, British, French and Italian — but later these merged into two separate schools. Because Italian styling was the most efficient for high speed, the sports cars intended for competition soon adopted it. Touring cars generally followed an American-British slant. The French, whose contributions at first consisted mostly of fanciful, over-complicated bodies on sports-touring chassis, eventually turned to refining the Italian ideas. Except for M.G. and Singer and a very few other holdouts, the vintage British box-body, cycle-fender sports car is out of the picture. High-speed touring cars, however, are not practical in the Italian form, since there is too little provision for luggage and the rear seat, when provided, is a cruel joke on the luckless passengers consigned to it. Hence the British-American school, which combines the roominess of the American sedan with such British styling tricks as notched doors, exposed wire wheels, the long hood, and minimum overhang.

Some of the speeds achieved by the bigger sports cars have prompted serious reflection on the part of buyers. Just what does one do with a 170-m.p.h. machine except race it? If it is geared down to a considerably lower top speed, then the violence of the acceleration becomes a problem to anyone not well experienced in the handling of a dangerous vehicle. Burying the throttle foot in the floorboard in one of the lower gears can cause nothing but trouble. Granted, the sports-car owner expects thrilling performance, but he does not bargain for a sitting-on-top-of-a-volcano feeling. It would seem that the competition sports car has almost outgrown its market.

In its place has risen the sports touring car. The Austin-Healey, just to single out one of many, has the kind of performance formerly associated only with competition sports cars. For city and highway cruising it is as much car as the average enthusiast wants, and is far less expensive than a detuned version of one of the competition cars. Judging from the trends in family cars, and the two ultra-modern luxury cars produced by Bentley and Mercedes, the sports-touring concept is behind much of modern automotive development. The Lincolns in the Mexican Road Race came through with faster times than some of the sports cars, and there are few American passenger cars incapable of an honest 100 m.p.h. and more. To keep up with these speeds, the suspension systems and brakes of the passenger cars are being improved year by year.

The credit for postwar auto improvement goes first to the engineers and stylists who have so efficiently transformed the traditional sports machines of the prewar period into the sleek, swift lightweights of today, and second to the unexpected revival of interest in sports and touring cars as personal possessions and competition tools. Without the enthusiasts and amateur race drivers, there would have been little market for the new products.

A.C.

ALTHOUGH A.C. WAS BORN IN 1900 AND AMPLE time had passed for the firm to have forged a mighty industrial empire, it continued in postwar years to be what the English call "a producer of specialist cars." Its production was still small, its quality high, and its cars' specifications were delicately balanced between the requirements of a tradition-loving clientele and the irresistible trends of the modern world.

These policies were carefully calculated before they were pursued. Before resuming production after the war the company made a survey of the desires of its customers and dealers, many of whom had been devoted to A.C. cars literally for decades. The results vastly simplified the task of building a new A.C.

Nobody, for example, wanted the engine changed. The inclined-overhead-valve, overhead-camshaft power plant that John Weller designed during World War I was still one of the best after World War II. Hardly a car in the world in its price class had as many design virtues as the A.C.; consumers were well satisfied with such features as its three carburetors, aluminum block and crankcase, and the once-controversial wet cylinder liners. As lively as it was, the 74-b.hp. engine was not highly stressed, being called upon to yield only .61 b.hp. per cubic inch of displacement. Top piston speed was just a shade high at 2,950 feet per minute, but the long stroke and small bore kept taxes down, and most buyers were happy to make the compromise.

The company had assumed that the time was over-ripe to make the change to independent front suspension, but the survey's results indicated otherwise. The people who had chosen to live with A.C. liked the car's precision handling qualities. Sacrificing the beam axle would mean losing a degree of control. A.C. management was soon convinced that chassis modifications had better be confined to spring rates and improved shock absorbers.

About coachwork there was no question; traditional techniques and quality were what everyone expected of the A.C. car. It was perfectly permissible to give the lines a more modern look. But the sub-structure must be of fine woods and the panelling of aluminum, both hand-formed by craftsmen whose employed lives had been spent with the firm. The finish must be meticulously applied, then painstakingly hand rubbed. Walnut and good English leather must dominate the interior appointments.

The resulting postwar A.C. was, therefore, a rather unique car. The layout of its entire chassis was stubbornly traditional, deliberately and frankly preserving the better qualities of the vintage period. The new body had graceful, flowing lines and vast window areas reminiscent of the carriage of an Edwardian aristocrat. Its styling ignored Continental and American influences. No lures were cast at the overseas market. The car's appeal was slanted at a tiny segment of the English market consisting largely of buyers who had learned through the years to appreciate and demand the custom-tailored product that bore the A.C. brand.

The first two-door sedans began to leave A.C.'s Thames Ditton, Surrey plant in October of 1947. The cars retailed in England for $3,340 (before tax) and the company's urge for profits was satisfied when in 1950 production averaged five units per week for the entire year.

Many of A.C.'s purchasers required open bodies for their cars and this demand soon was met with the Sports Tourer, built in small quantities by the Buckland Body Works. This body style combined a tonneau reminiscent of the Cord 810 convertible with front fenders and hood suggestive of the Jaguar XK-120. A true open four-seater, it used side curtains rather than roll-down windows and its windshield was hinged to fold forward. The fenders of this car, like those of the Thames Ditton bodies, were made of heavy, 18-gauge aluminum.

Two new body styles were revealed at Earls Court late in 1952. The first of these was a convertible sedan with three-position top: up, down or "coupe de ville." Seating accommodations were identical to those of the five-passenger hard-top but luggage space was considerably increased by the removal of the gas tank from the rear of the car and the installation instead of a seven-gallon tank in each of the front fenders. The second body style offered was a four-door version of the standard, two-door sedan.

These cars all had the reputation of feeling and handling as though they were "one piece of machinery," with a flat, firm ride that was never harsh and a wonderfully quick "old fashioned" steering that went from lock to lock in just two-and-a-half turns. The suspension was starkly traditional, using four half-elliptic springs, with the rear set slung below the axle. These cars, combining the best features of the vintage period with modern styling and comfort, were designed for touring, not racing. Their top speed was in the low 80's and acceleration from zero to 50 took about 14.5 seconds; zero to 60, 21 seconds.

Except for an increase of compression ratio from 6.5- to 6.75-to-1 and a switch from hydro-mechanical to full-hydraulic brakes (12-inch drums), there were few changes in A.C. cars during their first six years of postwar production. Then a basic change in policy took place and A.C. decided to court the modern-minded sporting motorist.

In October, 1953 the company scored one of the sensations of the Earls Court Show with the "Ace," an addition to the line that broke away from all the old A.C. practices. The power plant, in its fourth decade of service and still modern in concept, was the same highly refined oh.c. six, but the new Ace was an all-out sports car capable of a good 100 m.p.h. and what the English call "really vivid acceleration." Typical English lines were abandoned in favor of typical Italian ones and the businesslike aluminum two-seater was easy to mistake for a Ferrari.

Conservatism in chassis construction was tossed to the winds and the Ace was given one of the most advanced chassis in British production. The frame consisted of parallel, three-inch steel tubes, joined amidships by a cross member of the same material and at each end by box-like structures of steel sheet which also served as suspension supports. The front suspension was independent, by tubular A-arms below and a transverse leaf spring anchored to the top of the truncated triangular box which also served as the front cross member and a support for the accurate rack-and-pinion steering unit. The similar triangular box at the rear was also topped by a transverse leaf and did double duty as a housing for the differential and final drive. An improved suspension was carried out at the rear by means of short axle shafts with inboard and outboard universal joints which, with tubular A-arms again, added up to a modified De Dion rear end.

Most manufacturers could learn from A.C. in the matter of designing reliable and effective braking systems. The Ace used aluminum backing plates and vented, 11-inch, Al-Fin bonded-aluminum drums. The brakes themselves were Girling hydraulics and two master cylinders were used to preclude total brake failure — a remote possibility. Splined-hub knock-off wire wheels were standard.

1955 A.C. Aceca ctoupe.

This ultra-light chassis was based on the few-off Tojeiro sports cars which had already made numerous successful showings and demonstrated very superior handling qualities at British speed events. Transformed into the Ace it resulted in a car with the highly sporting weight-to-power ratio of 20-to-1, with performance to match, and with a price that kept it nicely in the middle range.

In 1954 the company took still another step away from British traditionalism with a coupe version of the Ace. The appearance of the car, with its slab sides, low flat sloping hood, and elegantly curved top-rear deck line, was no less advanced and aerodynamic than that of the most radical Italian jobs. The coupe had the additional innovation (for A.C.) of cam-type steering gear in place of the rack-and-pinion of previous models, the object being better stability at high speeds. With this car A.C.'s divorce from hidebound conservatism seemed complete.

ALFA ROMEO

Alfa Romeo's two plants — the old automobile factory at Milan and a new aircraft engine factory near Naples — were as a matter of course dedicated to the necessities of wartime. Both were destroyed; the Milan factory was bombed in 1940, the Naples plant in 1943. But Alfa executives had taken care to choose well the cover in which they hid their best racing machines for the duration. Thus, when in 1945 — with the country still a smoldering ruin — Italians again began to stage races, Alfa was ready. The 1½-liter Type 158 Grand Prix cars which had been introduced at the Coppa Ciano in 1938 proved unbeatable wherever they raced during the first unproductive years of postwar rconstruction. By the time the Milan factory was sufficiently rebuilt to produce a few cars per month, the 158 had made Alfa once again the sensation of the sporting world.

The first postwar Alfa was not, however, designed to devastate the enthusiasts, who now had little time or money for such frivolity as racing. The company astutely disregarded its traditional market; the car it exhibited at the 1947 Turin Salon was aimed directly at the solid upper-middle-class. It was called the 6C 2500, and its 2,443-c.c. (149 cu. in.) engine was a direct descendant of the

19/68-76 six-cylinder models with chain-camshaft-drive and four-wheel independent suspension which had first appeared in 1934. The 6C 2500 came in two versions — the 90-b.hp. Sports and the 105-b.hp. Super Sports.

These promising names notwithstanding, both versions, handsome and well-engineered though they were, were intended to supply practical transportation for the well-to-do, and little stress was placed on performance. Although the Super Sports had a claimed top speed of about 103 m.p.h., its most favorable weight-to-power ratio was a somewhat staid 29.5-to-1, with acceleration qualities well below prewar Alfa "sports" standards. In the heavier body styles on the less-powerful chassis, pounds-per-horsepower plummeted to a sluggish 37.4 to 1. Nevertheless, as late as 1954 the 6C 2500's were Italy's leading prestige cars, as unmistakable a symbol of means and status as the Cadillacs in America. The chassis were consistently the favorite of the fine coachbuilders and carried some of the postwar period's most inspired bodywork.

These cars were largely hand-produced, and fewer than 50 units were built each month. Alfa's directors, headed by Ing. Antonio Alessio, soon became convinced that the time had come for the firm to enter the mass-production utility-car field. The sporting enthusiasts were appalled by this announcement. Even those whose faith in the marque had survived the blow of the bourgeois 6C 2500 were convinced that the new policy would mean the final scuttling of the traditional standards of performance in favor of just another profitable but mediocre people's car. But when it was revealed in 1950, the new mass-produced Alfa turned out to be anything but drab. It was intended for a new market, but was still a product entirely worthy of the dashing Alfa Romeo name. The Type 1900 appeared while a seller's market prevailed in Italy, and the need for hard currency was not, unlike England's, painfully acute. Its appeal for export markets was therefore a question of only academic interest. It was created primarily to satisfy purely domestic requirements, and this it did extremely well.

To the urban Italian who had to cope with dense, hectic traffic, the 1900 offered excellent maneuverability and acceleration. Its four-cylinder power plant — Alfa's first four since the middle Twenties — was designed like a racing engine, with dual overhead camshafts, chain-driven, and inclined valves in hemispherical combustion chambers. Its 1,884-c.c. (115 cu. in.) displacement gave, in the two available stages of tune, 80 to 100 b.hp. at 5,400 r.p.m. In the 1900, Alfa for the first time adopted unit-body-frame construction, and this plus the simplification of many parts made for a total car weight about 30 per cent less than that of the similarly powered six and gave the 1900 a weight-to-power ratio of about 24-to-1, roughly that of a 1953 Oldsmobile 88. This was, of course, remarkable for a car of such small dimensions, and performance was further enhanced by the new engine's good torque output at high engine r.p.m., which permitted unusual acceleration almost up to top speed, which was 112 m.p.h. in the case of the 100-b.hp. version. It was obviously a car that could compete in traffic with great agility.

The 1900 had equal attractions for the rural Italian, to whom, since a large percentage of Italy's roads are in mountainous country, good hill-climbing, braking, and handling are of prime importance. No production car ever had better cornering qualities than the 1900 (and few could compare with it) and the same was true of the little Alfa's brakes. Coil springs were used at all four wheels, the front wheels were independently sprung, and the whole suspension was beefed up with anti-roll bars and torque arms. The brakes were provided with an unusually large amount of lining per ton and the drums themselves were fitted with bonded aluminum muffs, deeply finned. The steering was remarkable in that the front wheels were joined in such a way as to remain perfectly parallel during the three turns from lock to lock. The result was a "power steering" effect so strong that, once in motion, the car required only fingertip pressure to take it around the tightest corner. Such sensitive steering, a terror to the ham-fisted driver, was sheer delight to the sports-car connoisseur.

The cost of the 1900 — $3,830 — was not cheap, but with gasoline selling for around 75 cents per gallon at the time, fuel economy was as important in a car as selling price, and buyers were frequently glad to make a heftier original investment if they could get the sort of quality engineering that would stretch their gasoline *lire*. On grounds of economy the 1900 left nothing to be desired; 26 m.p.g. could be averaged easily on cross-country trips if 60 m.p.h. was set as the top speed limit.

With all this emphasis on engineering, performance and economy, the interior appointments of the four- and six-passenger sedans were necessarily on the side of austerity. However, special chassis units without the factory-made bodies were produced specifically for Italy's custom-coachwork specialists, who executed more elegant and luxurious envelopes for the 1900 both on series and one-off bases.

Such was Alfa Romeo's conception of a moderately priced family car, and it was received by the public with great enthusiasm. This success in a new market did not, however, deter the company from making plans to re-enter the racing field. Late in 1952 great international excitement was generated by the announcement that Alfa was building a new competition sports car, the *Disco Volante* or "Flying Saucer." The engines for the two prototypes were based on the 1900 and thus perpetuated the long-standing Alfa pattern of a racing model based on a production model which was, in turn, derived from past racing experience.

The Flying Saucer had a very low, flat, wide two-seater body which had been developed in Carrozzeria Touring's wind tunnel around a modified 1900 chassis. Two- and three-liter versions of the engine were built, both with stroke increased from the 1900's 88 mm. (3.47 in.) to 92 mm. (3.67) but with bore left at the original 82.5 mm. (3.25 in.). This brought the two-liter's displacement up to its competition-class limit, and two more cylinders were added to the three-liter engine, giving it an exact volume of 2,995 c.c. (244 cu. in.). Both cars weighed about 1650 pounds;

"Superleggera" coachwork by Carrozzeria Touring on Alfa Romeo 6C 2500 short chassis.

lo Milanta

1953 Alfa Romeo 2-liter competition two-seater *Disco Volante*, or "Flying Saucer."

the 128-b.hp. two-liter's claimed top speed was 134 m.p.h. and the 200-b.hp. three-liter's was 155 m.p.h.

They were soon offered with fully enclosed coupe bodies, and in 1953 a 3,493-c.c. (213 cu. in.), 230-b.hp. version was introduced. As promising as the Flying Saucers appeared, they still lingered in the development stage as this book went to press.

Nevertheless in 1954 Alfas — mostly 1900's — racked up a stunning list of competition victories, including class wins in the Mille Miglia and no fewer than 84 other European events. In the fifth Carrera Panamericana Alfas swept their class, the small European stock category, and finished in diamond formation around the Dodge that won the "small" U. S. stock class.

By this time the 1900's had been refined and specialized into three types — the standard, the super (with two-throat carburetor and displacement slightly increased to 1,975 c.c.) and the super-sprint T.I. sedan, which with twin exhausts, twin carbs and special manifolds and brakes was capable of better than 114 m.p.h.

Late in 1954 still another superb Alfa was introduced. This was the Giulietta, a 65 b.hp. 1,300 c.c. (79 cu. in.) four-seater sedan. The tiny engine provided enough urge for a solid 100 m.p.h. top speed, and the car's lines were lean, elegant, and aerodynamically sound. The aptly Shakespearian-named car appeared as the prototype of what was apparently designed to be Alfa's mass-produced "economy" line. By presstime this new Alfa had not yet been authoritatively road-tested, but its traditionally outstanding quality was suggested by the fact that the well-known driver Stirling Moss placed his order for one after a 10-mile spin.

ALLARD

THE BRITISH DO NOT BUILD HOT RODS, AS THE term is understood in America, but their "specials" are reasonable facsimiles. Where the American home craftsman builds solely for acceleration and speed, however, his English counterpart has quite another objective in mind. Occasionally it is amateur road racing, but more often it is to compete in that thoroughly British form of sport, the Trial, where the contestants are required to mush through mud, sand and water. Frequently there are difficult hills to climb and impossible turns to negotiate. Clearly the automobile was never intended to serve under most of the conditions which are encountered during a Trial, which is why the best machines for the purpose must be custom built.

Sidney Allard's first car was just such a special. The engine and chassis were derived from the Ford, and he used a Bugatti body and steering assembly. That was in 1936. By the time World War II began, Allard had modified his original car and built others for his friends. Allard and two of his closest associates became known as "Tailwaggers" because of the characteristic rear-wheel hula of the specials as they slogged through mud, up hills and around corners. What was important was that the wagging tails were visible to most of the contestants most of the time. Sidney Allard had found the right combination of high torque at low r.p.m. with weight heavily concentrated on the rear wheels, the same principles that were later to govern the design of some of the "winningest" road racers ever made in Britain. His specials were an unqualified success.

In the first few years after the war, Allard went after the hill-climbing championship of Britain, with a chassis closely resem-

Borgeson

Typical scene in American sports car races of early 1950's: big Allards out in front. Car in front row, left, is the long-unbeatable Carstens Cadillac-Allard. Scene is Pebble Beach Road Race, 1953.

bling his prewar specials, powered by an air-cooled V-8 Steyr engine. In 1947 and 1948 Allard finished among the top three in Britain, and finally won the championship in 1949. Throughout this period he had been steadily improving his original design.

While Allard was climbing hills for sport, he was manufacturing more orthodox machinery for money. In 1946 he formed the Allard Motor Company, and introduced three models. There were two fast touring cars, the K and the L, and a smaller, lighter, more powerful competition model, the predecessor of the J2. Both the K and the L were powered by Ford engines but the third model was equipped with a hopped-up Mercury. The suspension system of all three consisted of independent front suspension by means of a split axle and a transverse semi-elliptic spring; in the rear there was a single transverse semi-elliptic spring. The British, known for their devotion to small engines and light cars, reversed themselves to praise the new cars with the American-size V-8 engines. They were quick to recognize not only the excellent performance obtained from the engines, but also the economy. Ford parts were available everywhere, and repairs to an Allard were not only easy to obtain but inexpensive any place in the world.

Despite their appeal to the British press, the first Allards did not sell in America. The most frequently given reason is that the styling was not exactly in accord with the American idea of beauty, and that may well be the fact. Allard realized he would have to make a few major changes.

In 1949 the J2 Allard appeared. In appearance it was not

Stripped chassis of J2X Allard with Cadillac engine shows details of frame construction, engine installation. Note two honeycomb oil radiators at front of car. Chassis had De Dion rear end.

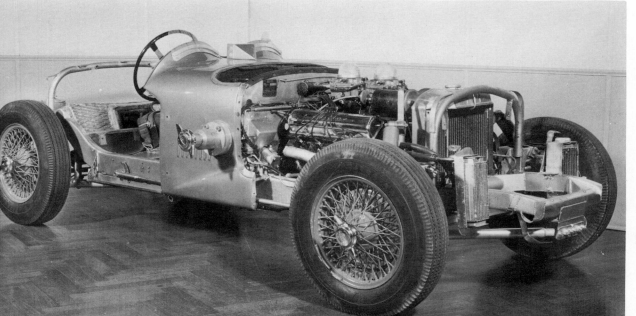

Henry Ford Museum

beautiful, but it had the virile, almost savage look of a true competition car. The engine compartment had been designed with either a Ford or a Cadillac specifically in mind, and the American versions almost always were equipped with the larger engine. Before long the Cadillac-Allards began to score on United States road circuits. Erwin Goldschmidt won the 1950 Watkins Glen race. Tommy Cole, Fred Wacker and others showed up with Allards. On the West Coast, the magnificent black Cad-Allard of Tom Carstens, Bill Pollack driving, won eight races in nine starts, regularly outrunning the best Jaguars and even managing to stay in front of a few Ferraris. When it finally was beaten, a 2.9 Ferrari did it.

The Cadillac engines used in these Allards were anything but stock. Goldschmidt's was pulling just under 300 b.hp., and Carstens could not find a dynamometer big enough to hold his engine at peak horsepower. It accelerated from zero to 60, in five to seven seconds; zero to 100 in 12 to 14 seconds; and delivered a top speed on the straightaways of 150-170 m.p.h. To go with this power there was a redesigned Allard suspension system. In the front were coil springs to replace the old transverse leaf, though the rest of the setup was much the same. In the rear, Ford parts had been adapted to form a De Dion system.

Sidney Allard celebrated the introduction of the J2 by driving it into third place in the 1950 Le Mans race. He was now ready to go into sports-car competition in earnest, having made his championship rating in Trials and hill-climbing. But along with Sidney there were a lot of others. In the United States in 1951 the Allards couldn't keep up with the Cunninghams on the East Coast; in Europe the Ferraris were too fast. So Allard kept improving his car. In 1952 he appeared at Le Mans with the J2X prototype, and the following year he introduced the JR. Neither car did well at Le Mans due to mechanical troubles.

The J2X marked a turning point in Allard's thinking. He deserted the rearward weight distribution that had stood him so well in Trials and hill climbing and changed to the approximately 50-50 distribution, long a favorite of competition sports-car builders. No more wagging tails for Allard! During the period leading up to the introduction of the JR, the front suspension was modified to include trailing links. Body design also changed radically. The lusty J2X was first dressed with an experimental envelope body for the 1952 Le Mans race, and the JR was almost Italian in concept. Weight was stripped down to 2,200 pounds, wheelbase chopped to 96 inches. One of the first United States JR owners, General Curtis LeMay, was reported to have clocked close to 170 m.p.h. In the '53 Le Mans race, Sidney Allard was timed at 145 m.p.h. before his brakes gave out.

As Allard's sports cars matured, so did the other models. In 1954 the small factory was giving its customers their choice of the JR for competition, the K3 for high-speed touring, the Palm Beach for economy, the Monte Carlo for fast, closed-car comfort and the Safari for those who demanded a station wagon. All were built around a new tubular frame Allard developed to replace the modified Ford unit he had used previously; all had very modern bodies. Of the group, the K3 and the Palm Beach were the most likely to appeal to the sports-car enthusiast.

The K3 came equipped with a Cadillac engine, with Hydra-Matic optional, yet was light and small. Its little brother, the Palm Beach, was built to a price to compete with the growing number of fast, aggressive, economy sports cars in the Austin-Healey class. Under its hood was a Ford Zephyr overhead-valve six capable of 100 m.p.h. speeds.

And with this flurry of models, Allard retrenched to build up strength for a frontal assault on the general market. During 1954 Allards began to disappear from sports-car racing, and when the 1955 models were shown at Earls Court in London there was no JR on the stand. In its place was a highly streamlined fast tourer on the Monte Carlo chassis.

Of all the models available at this writing, the closest to the original Allard is probably the Palm Beach, though it too has progressed far from the original "Tailwaggers." Allard has learned the hard way that there isn't much money in building competition sports cars for sale.

| ALVIS |

THE ALVIS FACTORY AT COVENTRY WAS BOMBED TO rubble in 1940. In 1946, devastated by war and subdued by the resignation and then the death of its founder, T. G. John, the Alvis company struggled back into automobile production. The theme now was not daring innovation, as it had been in

John's memorable front-wheel-drive days, but conservative progress toward re-establishing Alvis' popularity and reputation for fine, carefully crafted machinery. Neither the basic mode of operation nor the first postwar cars differed greatly from prewar years — Alvis was still a more-or-less-handmade specialist product, and the 1946 "Fourteen" car was based on well-tried formulae. It was offered in both sedan and sports form, with a four-cylinder overhead-valve engine of 1,892 c.c. (115.5 cu. in.) displacement, the sports version being provided with dual carburetors and a higher-than-standard rear-axle ratio. The appearance of the sedan was stubbornly traditional, but the sports-car body reflected more advanced styling.

The company's brochure literature referred to the "galaxy of new and advanced styles . . . hastily conceived" which surrounded the Alvis at its first postwar Earls Court appearance, but staunchly claimed that, in spite of the last-decade look of the car, the "company's order book has never been so full." It was, at any rate, full enough so that Alvis was able to retain the Fourteen as the sole product of the marque until 1950, when it was discontinued and the six-cylinder Three Liter took its place.

Alvis' first post-war sports car was this "14" two-seater. 1949 model is shown.

The new model was staid in appearance but sprightly in performance, soundly engineered and handsomely finished throughout. The overhead-valve engine had a close-to-square bore and stroke, 3.30×3.54 inches, and possessed good qualities of flexibility and acceleration. The Three Liter was further developed and the model introduced for 1954 and retained in 1955 was able to claim an honest 100 m.p.h. top speed (this with the determinedly unstreamlined body that Alvis adhered to) and developed 100 b.hp. at 4,000 r.p.m. It had a rugged box-section chassis frame with coil-spring independent front suspension, and two S.U. carburetors were standard equipment. Its acceleration was good in all gears and its stability and handling were outstanding but, in spite of its good performance, it was notable for its lack of temperament.

The Three Liter was designed primarily for touring use, and although it had a sports flavor, it was not what the Alvis enthusiasts of two decades before had found really inspiring. In 1953 the company released a broad hint that a car was in the works so potent that "one or two factories on Italy's famed Plain of Lombardy, who have hitherto believed themselves to have a monopoly on a certain kind of car, may find that they have it no longer," but at this writing no such Alvis threat has appeared.

ASTON MARTIN

DAVID BROWN, A TRACTOR AND GEAR MANUFACturer with a lust for flying, foxhounds and fast cars, became the fourth owner of Aston Martin in 1947. Like his predecessor Gordon Sutherland, he was fascinated by advanced design. But he was far more devoted to racing as a means of perfecting the breed than Sutherland had been. Sutherland liked to think of his cars as exemplifying a Matthew Arnold quotation: "The great aim of culture — the aim of setting ourselves to ascertain what perfection is, and to make it prevail." David Brown's administration sought perfection with fresh zeal, and what it found has prevailed. Brown set out to build a car that would win races.

In doing so he made a clean break with the conservative, often hide-bound past and introduced a new era of British sports-car design.

Brown did not have to start from scratch, although the new four-cylinder, two-liter engine he acquired with the firm reflected Sutherland's interest in a salable rather than a raceable automobile. It had pushrod-operated overhead valves instead of the prewar overhead camshaft, was slightly heavier than the prewar engines, and was frankly designed for long life and easy maintenance rather than stunning performance. But Brown also became heir to the lessons learned from the prewar experimental Atom, which had been created to measure the gains made by improving suspension and reducing wind and weight drag. The first postwar Aston Martin cars, which appeared in 1948, represented the first break with traditional British body-chassis practice.

The 1948-49 Two Liter Sports was based on a superlight but rigid chassis-and-body frame made of welded-up rectangular steel tubing. The front wheels used a trailing-link type of coil-spring independent suspension, and the solid, hypoid-bevel rear axle was sprung on coils too, its twisting effects eliminated by torque arms anchored to the axle and chassis frame. In the design of the convertible-coupe body a distinct effort was made to retain the flavor of prewar sports lines, but the aerodynamic improvement was enormous. With the 90-horsepower pushrod engine a top speed of about 90 m.p.h. was possible. That was the DB1, and it was good, but not good enough for a man with a passion for racing.

Brown had already acquired one of the great competition makes of England in the Aston Martin. When he learned that the fine old Lagonda firm was going on the block he bought it too. One of Lagonda's major assets was a W. O. Bentley-designed 2.6-liter (158 cu. in.), six-cylinder, twin-overhead-camshaft engine which had been introduced in 1945. This engine developed 105 horsepower in very mild tune; its power and torque curves were better-contoured and its development potentialities far greater than those of the A.M. pushrod engine. Brown had three closed cars set for entry in the 1949 Le Mans, and he decided to put the Lagonda engine in one of them.

This was the prototype of the DB2 Aston Martins, and it was no exception to the almost-inflexible rule that a new competition machine, no matter how impressive its history-to-come, is not successful in its first race. The new engine called for a completely revised cooling system which failed at Le Mans from complications that did not appear during prerace testing. The pushrod A.M.'s fared better, one of them finishing third for the Rudge-

1954 3-liter Aston Martin DB3S competition model.

Whitworth Biennial Cup and seventh overall. But two weeks later in the Belgian 24-hour race at Spa, cooling problems had been solved and Leslie Johnson finished the long haul by bringing the DB2 in second in the four-liter class.

The car had not yet been shown to the general public, and when it was, at the April, 1950 New York show, its effect was devastating.

The light-alloy two-seater body that had been created for the Le Mans-team cars broke the last link with conventional British design. It was 53 inches high and looked as aerodynamically perfect as a passenger car's envelope can be made. The entire body from cowl forward was a single panel — fenders, hood, grille and all. This panel was hinged at the front so it could be raised to give almost perfect accessibility to engine and forward running gear. The removal of two hinge pins permitted the entire panel to be lifted off for total accessibility.

Under the panel was the Lagonda engine, a jewel in any enthusiast's eyes. In spite of its relatively long stroke and high piston speed the engine soared up to top revs with perfect smoothness and did not vibrate even at its peak. Much of this smoothness could be credited to the rigid barrel-type crankcase which provided 360-degree support for the four main bearings. Twin overhead camshafts, chain-driven, actuated inclined valves which seated in liberally ported hemispherical combustion chambers. Excellent cooling was achieved by such devices as wet cylinder liners and valve guides in direct contact with the coolant.

The David Brown-designed-and-built four-speed transmission rapidly became the object of enthusiasts' unbounded affection. The close ratios were selected with racing in mind, and the third was a particularly useful gear. The car could be run up to 95 m.p.h. in this gear without protest and the synchromesh design made it sheer delight to pop down to third going through a corner at any speed.

No other production car could top the DB2's stability and handling qualities. The ride was on the firm side and rough roads could be felt; but the chassis remained almost vertical during high-speed cornering.

Brilliant proof of the DB2's superb racing orientation came in the 1950 Le Mans, only two months after its New York unveiling.

That was the Grand Prix d'Endurance in which a Jowett Jupiter driven by Wisdom and Wise ("The Sagacious Two") succeeded in topping by a scant 83 m.p.h. the Le Mans 1.5-liter record set by Aston Martin in 1935. But Aston's team did not have to mourn past greatness that day. The DB2's ticked off each of the 24 hours of the great, grueling race without a trace of mechanical failure and with dazzling speed. George Abecassis and Lance Macklin piloted their coupe to a new three-liter record, set a new single-lap record, placed fourth regardless of displacement, and tied with a German Monopol for first place in the Index of Performance Cup.

In spite of the steady stream of racing successes which followed, the DB2 continued to undergo refinement. Actually, only minor details lent themselves to improvement, including the engine. In standard tune, with 6.5-to-1 compression ratio, the DB2 was offered as an ultra-fast tourer, a mount for occasional competitions and a lively town carriage. For buyers who were interested in competition alone, the more-highly tuned "Vantage" engine was made available with 8.16-to-1 compression ratio and an additional 20 horsepower.

Another competition challenger was added to the line in 1952 — the DB3 open two-seater. Except for its lighter, open body the mechanical specifications were those of the Vantage. In their first major event, the Silverstone Production Sports Car Race, the DB3's finished 2-3-4 overall, running against many cars of greater engine capacity. In 1953 the DB3 was replaced by the DB3S, which was more streamlined and had its engine bored to nearly three liters (178 cu. in.). This car was an immediate success in competition, winning the 1953 British Empire Trophy, the '53 and '54 Silverstone Sports Car Race, the '53 Goodwood International, and the '53 Tourist Trophy at Ulster. In September '54 it set a new three-liter record for the Prescott Hill Climb that equalled the unlimited record for the hill.

Early in 1954 the standard model DB2 was replaced by the DB2-4, the code referring to its new passenger capacity; two in comfort or four in a pinch. Perhaps reflecting Britain's recently-acquired access to premium fuels, the 6.5-to-1 compression ratio was dropped entirely and the Vantage engine became standard equipment. Later in the year the company's trend toward more power became even more evident. The stock 2.6 engine in the DB 2-4 was, as in the competition model, enlarged to three liters, giving a hefty 140 b.hp., 118 m.p.h., and fine acceleration. At the same time the sensational 180 b.hp. DB3S was offered on sale to the public.

In the years that have passed since the end of World War II, fewer than 10 production sports cars of the first rank have appeared. Of that select group Aston Martin was one of the very first; it was and it remains one of the most advanced. The proof of its excellence and the vindication of David Brown's uncompromising dedication to progressive design lie in Aston Martin's brilliant racing record.

BENTLEY

LIKE MOST OF ITS COMPATRIOT MANUFACTURERS after the war, Bentley's national duty was to get hard currency for the British economy. Strategy toward this end was indicated in the use of factory-made bodies for the first postwar Bentley, the Mark VI. The slow, personalized attentions of the independent coachbuilders still were in demand, but were less appropriate in the ascetic world of postwar England, where most production was for export and delivery had to be quick.

The fact that few, if any, Bentleys were made for home consumption while their styling was slanted at the most subtly discriminating British taste, made the marque's struggle for overseas buyers more acute then most. *The Autocar* described the Mark VI's appearance as having "that unique effect of superb quality without a trace of bombast." The postwar Bentley's air of dignity and breeding, apparent to most Englishmen, was not enough to charm numbers of non-English buyers, who had come to expect more modern lines, more chrome, more gimmicks — in other words, more bombast — than the Bentley displayed.

Nevertheless, it was one of the most splendid cars made in the postwar world. The 1948 Mark VI was based on a modified version of the Rolls-Royce "Silver Wraith" chassis. Although engine size remained at 4¼ liters, the engine itself bore little resemblance to the I-head prewar Bentley. The new Bentley engine was an F-head, with exhaust valves in the block and intake valves placed in the aluminum head which was fitted with chrome-moly valve seats. This valve layout appropriately harked back to the engine designed by Sir Harry Ricardo for the 4-liter, the last of the "W. O. Bentleys." Its virtues were that it permitted the use of exceptionally large valves and ports as well as a very direct flow path for the combustible mixture. This engine design was revived in the postwar Rolls-Royce Wraith and it was the Wraith engine, equipped with dual carburetors and a hotter camshaft, that was chosen to power the 1948 Mark VI Bentley. Its all-out emphasis on quality

Early post-war Bentley chassis fitted with Gurney Nutting sedanca coupe body. Roof above front seats slides into top at rear.

was indicated by the fully chrome-plated cylinder bores which postponed the need for reboring well beyond the 100,000-mile mark.

The rest of the Mark VI chassis was largely the same as prewar, except for coil-spring independent front suspension which added to the car's already supreme comfort but reduced somewhat its precision handling qualities, particularly on wet pavement. The gear-shift lever occupied its traditional position against the extreme right-hand side of the car and ease of shifting was compared with drawing a knife through butter. The car's power brakes continued to wring rapturous praise from all critics but the performance of the heavy, steel-bodied car was not up to old standards. Zero to 60 m.p.h. in just under 20 seconds was about as good as one could hope for on the poor 72-octane "pool" gasoline of the period. Top speed was about 86 m.p.h.

The diminished performance of the Mark VI as compared with prewar Bentleys did not temper the ecstatic reactions of British experts who road-tested the car upon its introduction. All the superlative stops were pulled out for their songs of praise. "It has no single predominant features but gains its unique position from a combination of superbly matched qualities that raise it above the level of other cars," remarked The Autocar. "Such things are not to be measured by instruments; they are sensed and duly valued by the connoisseur who can afford the best."

It was the old story of Rolls-Royce perfection with better-than-R.R. speed and acceleration.

In 1952 the Mark VI was pepped up with an increase in bore of ⅛ inch, which added 19 cubic inches to the total displacement and boosted maximum horsepower from 132 to 150 at 3,750 r.p.m. The object of this change was to improve the Mark VI's general performance, which it did very successfully. Zero-to-60-m.p.h. time was reduced to 15 seconds and top speed leaped to an honest 100 m.p.h. English approval of the silent, powerful Bentley increased but the dent made in overseas markets was not noticeable.

Nineteen hundred fifty-two brought with it another innovation, one which really shattered the purists. The Rolls-Royce four-speed gearbox, shared by Bentley, had been worshipped as a masterpiece of automotive design and workmanship. Now, both Bentley and R.R. were made available with General Motors' Dual-Range Hydra-Matic transmission as optional equipment. Some reporters in the British press could not bring themselves to identify the Hydra-Matic by name, referring to it simply as the "Rolls-

Royce automatic transmission." The famous R.R. brake servo motor was added to the Hydra-Matic unit and it is not difficult to admit that, as a luxury automobile, the Bentley was much more distinguished with Hydra-Matic.

The biggest landmark in Bentley history since the 1933 introduction of the 3½-liter was the appearance of the Continental Sports Saloon, also in 1952. This ultra-high-speed luxury car was promptly subjected to exhaustive tests by members of the British automotive press and was unanimously voted "one of the world's great automobiles."

Although the name "Continental" suggested *autostrade* and *autobahnen* as its inspiration, American demand was credited with providing incentive for the creation of this latter-day classic. Such speed and luxury had not been offered in a single package since the days of the 540K Mercedes and the Rolls and Hispano 12's.

Mulliner's aluminum coachwork on the 4½-liter chassis gave the two-door sedan a ready-to-go-weight of about 3,900 pounds. With a 7.25-to-1 compression ratio the engine's horsepower output was pushed well over 160, giving the car a weight-to-power ratio in the low 20's. Zero-to-60 acceleration was in the 12-second area and top speed was between 116 and 120 m.p.h. The car's rapid acceleration was aided by a close-ratio gearbox which permitted a speed of 101 in third gear. Road-testers agreed that braking and handling were phenomenal.

Time may prove the Continental Bentley one of the most significant developments in the long history of its parent company. While Rolls-Royce had always been the price-and prestige-heavy member of the Rolls-Bentley duo, in 1952 the Continental Bentley carried a more stunning price tag than the most costly Rolls — $13,700 in England, before purchase tax. Perhaps this was a sign of the times. Rolls-Royce could never forsake its stateliness — was, in fact, stuck with it. But Bentley's heritage was one of high performance and it was high performance that the hard-currency world was buying. This seemed to indicate that the Bentley heritage of speed, purchased in 1931 by Rolls-Royce, might give R.R. a new lease on life more than two decades later.

THE BRISTOL AEROPLANE COMPANY WAS FOUNDED in 1910 and by the end of World War II was a gargantuan manufacturing empire producing jet- and piston-type engines and some of the most famous airplanes of the war. In anticipation of reduced peacetime demand for these products, the firm set a complex variety of new projects in motion as soon as hostilities ended. One of them dealt with prefabricated aluminum homes, schools and hospitals. Another dealt with cars.

The directors of Bristol's newly created Car Division decided to use an engine and transmission of proved design but with still-untapped development potentialities. They chose the B.M.W. 328, a product of another great aircraft-engine manufacturer. This choice naturally led them directly to the Aldington brothers of Frazer-Nash who knew more about B.M.W. products than anyone else in England and who had, in fact, been tooling to manufacture the 328 in 1939. The Aldingtons agreed to help Bristol develop the new car. They promptly contacted Dr. Fritz Fiedler, designer of the entire series of six-cylinder, overhead-valve B.M.W.'s, and proposed that he exchange the barren prospects that Munich offered at the time for a vital part in the development of a new, fine car along B.M.W.328 lines. Dr. Fiedler hastened to England and thus completed a rare combination of talent and facilities. Inevitably, the car produced was a good one.

The first prototype of the Bristol 400 ran under its own power in July, 1946, and the first production model appeared at the Geneva Show in March of the following year. The engine was an almost perfectly standard 328, with its top output somewhat reduced. The first engine Bristol had bench-tested developed 85.4 b.hp. at 4,750 r.p.m., with a compression ratio of 7.5-to-1 and a camshaft with 80-degree overlap. Low r.p.m. performance left something to be desired for touring use, and a 20-degree overlap shaft was therefore substituted. With this slight modification the engine, now developing between 75 and 80 b.hp. at 4,200 r.p.m., became the 85A, the trunk of the family tree from which the sports, touring and racing Bristol engines later branched.

The 400 car had the rack-and-pinion steering, the independent front suspension by means of transverse leaf and A-arms and the general body lines of prewar B.M.W. machines. Instead of having steel tubes for the chassis frame, however, this unit was of the rectangular-section box-girder type and was equally light and strong. Rear suspension, instead of being by semi-elliptics as in the B.M.W., hung the solid rear axle on longitudinal torsion bars.

About 650 of these first Bristols were manufactured but the largely hand-built bodies — two sedans and two convertibles — were costly to make and buy. The Car Division busied itself with a more rational body design for the 400's successor.

Meanwhile the fast, flat-riding 400 rapidly built a reputation for Bristol in Continental competition. It won its class in the then-important Polish International Rally of 1948. The following year Aldy Aldington and Count Lurani co-drove a well-tuned 400 with the original 80-degree "sports" camshaft and 8.5-to-1 compression ratio to an overall second place in the Targa Florio touring category, and to a third-place finish in the Mille Miglia. Then Lurani and Cortese won in the Tuscany Cup's touring class and Lurani took another third in the Stella Alpina. Treybal and Dobry, who had piloted the Bristol in the Polish Rally, entered the same car in the 1949 Monte Carlo Rally, finishing third overall. After the rally Treybal paused at Montlhery on his way to England. His odometer showed 15,000 miles and the rally seals were still on his engine, but the car easily averaged 92.08 m.p.h. for 100 kilometers on the speedway there. Bristol's original and ultimate goal was the development of an all-purpose vehicle for the connoisseur, one ideally fast, finished, controllable, safe and comfortable. By the end of 1949, the car's speed and handling had been adequately demonstrated. The Aldingtons revived the Frazer-Nash marque and their cars, fitted with Bristol-made engines, took over most of the research-through-racing tasks.

The Bristol 401 2-liter saloon.

While all this successful competition was going on, Dr. Fiedler pondered the body problem. He remembered that the 2-liter, 130-m.p.h. B.M.W. 328 that won the war time 1940 Mille Miglia had acquired much of its speed from the Carrozzeria Touring *Superleggera*, a super-light, aerodynamic body made especially for it. Now he called upon Touring again. Touring built a prototype for Bristol, and it was exhaustively worked over by Car Division engineers in the wind tunnel of Bristol University. The result was a Bristol with an entirely new body. It was called the 401 and was first shown in the fall of 1948.

The new Bristol body was a fascinating example of the pooling of the most advanced Italian streamlining and weight-saving techniques with those of a leading aircraft manufacturer. The rigid box-section frame remained unchanged but, except for two box-section steel pillars on each side of the car, the entire superstructure was made of welded steel tubes contoured to fit the body panels. These were all of aluminum alloy and were fixed to the skeleton by crimping their edges around lengths of angle-section light alloy which were riveted to the steel framework. Two new bodies based on this pattern were offered; the 401 two-door sedan and the 402 convertible coupe. In addition to providing more passenger and luggage space, the smoother, lighter new coachwork helped to achieve a top speed of about 98 m.p.h. as compared with the 400's 94, and fuel economy was similarly improved.

This was a big step forward for Bristol. And now, with the advanced body design firmly established, the Frazer-Nash organization proceeded with field development of the engine. The first Bristol power unit with the official F.N.S. (Frazer-Nash Series) coding appeared in March of 1949. It had intake ports 0.15 inch larger than standard, higher compression and an extreme-overlap cam — modifications which helped to boost peak output to 126 b.hp. at 4,750 r.p.m. A larger oil sump was provided and secondary balance of the crankshaft was obtained by means of bolt-on counterweights, in place of the normal integral type.

In October, 1951, two builders of Formula II (2-liter) racing cars, Cooper and E.R.A., approached Bristol's Car Division with requests for high-output engines. To meet this request, the B.S.1 engine, a new high-performance version then under development for F.-N. for sports-car use, was given further modifications. It was beefed up with a huskier crankshaft, rocker arms and pushrods were lightened, combustion chambers and ports were carefully hand finished and peak power was boosted to 132 b.hp. at 5,750 r.p.m. During 1952, the output of this engine series was raised by small detail refinements to 150 b.hp. The engines were used in four Formula II cars, which performed as follows during the 1952 season: the Cooper-Bristol won 10 firsts, five seconds, three thirds; the G-Type E.R.A. scored one second, one fourth, one fifth; the F.-N. single-seater made one third, one fourth, and one fifth; and a new car, the I.R.A., appeared at the season's end and took one fourth place. Mike Hawthorn's success in the Cooper-Bristol made national heroes of driver and car.

The Bristol Aeroplane Company took more than a sporting interest in these exploits. They were quickly translated into improvements in the Bristol car and a new model, the 403, appeared in the spring of 1953. Almost innumerable minute changes worked out for the B.S.1 and F.N.S. engines were made in production-engine details, including the larger main-bearing crankshaft with detachable counterweights, and a 30-degree-overlap camshaft. Along with a great increase in potential reliability, peak power was raised to 100 b.hp. at 5,250 r.p.m. Major chassis modifications were the adoption of bonded, finned-aluminum brake drums and an anti-roll bar; however, the two-door sedan body was almost identical to the 401.

The successes of the Formula II competition power units evidently spurred Bristol to take a more direct part in racing. A radically aerodynamic coupe was built for the 1953 Le Mans 24-Hour Race. It was powered by the 150-b.hp. engine and called the Type 450. Of the two cars entered, one went out after 70 laps, the other after 29, both with connecting-rod failures. But in the Rheims 12 Hour Race a few weeks later, the 2-liter-class winner and fifth finisher overall was one of the 450 coupes. In October, 1953 Jack Fairman drove the 450 at Montlhery to set six new international Class E records, the quickest being 200 miles at 125.87 m.p.h.

In the fall of 1953, Bristol's new offering for 1954 was announced. It was the Type 404, the most Italian-looking of all B.A.C.'s cars to date, a point the loyal British press meticulously avoided mentioning. It was also the handsomest by far. The entirely new body, on a drastically shortened chassis, was a close-coupled coupe bearing a close resemblance to the early, finned-fender Cisitalia. Unlike the previous bodies with steel-tube skeletons, the 404 was panelled in 18-gauge light alloy over a pitch-pine framework. The chassis remained basically unchanged, but was offered with a choice of engines giving 105 or 125 b.hp., the 80-

degree-overlap "sports" camshaft being used in the latter. With one horsepower for every 18½ pounds of car weight, the 404 was a revelation in fast luxurious motoring.

In 1954 this machine took first place in the Easter Handicap at Goodwood, and its hot aerodynamic brother, the 450, really hit its racing stride. It won its class 1-2-3, at Le Mans and placed 2-3-4 at Rheims. The same year saw a rash of Bristol-hybrid wins. Cooper Bristols, F.N. Bristols, Kieft Bristols, the Tojeiro Bristol, the Bristol-Warrior and the Lister-Bristol were all successful in G.P. and sports car racing. Still another hybrid appeared in 1954, the Arnolt Bristol. This consisted of a Bristol engine and chassis and a two-seater Bertone (Turin) body. It was made primarily for U.S. import and at about $4,500 it was a good sports car buy Several of these cars were raced in the U.S. during the '54 season with fair success.

Also in 1954 (by which time, incidentally, Bristol had taken to using the term *pur sang* with drawings of blooded horses in its ads, much to the indignation of the Bugatti addicts) the company introduced a new version of the 404 termed, rather logically, the 405. This was a long wheelbase version of the 404, a four-door sedan "town car" designed as much for elegance and comfort as for speed. Aside from using two three-branch manifolds instead of a single six-branch one, the power plant remained unchanged, and the 405's lines were, like the 404's, Italian. This most recent Bristol, like the other cars in the series it supplemented, represented a progressive and gifted organization's effort to combine an ultimate number of virtues in a single vehicle.

BUGATTI

THE WORLD OF ETTORE BUGATTI FELL APART PIECE by piece during the war years. On August 11, 1939 his son Jean was testing a car on a supposedly closed stretch of road at Molsheim and rounded a turn at high speed to find an inebriated local squarely in his path. Jean swerved, crashed and was killed. In March, 1940 Ettore's father, Carlo, died. The Germans occupied Alsace and bought the Bugatti factory and estate at their own price. Then Ettore's wife died.

When the occupation ended, Bugatti expected to have his raped property returned, but it was claimed by the state as a prize of war. Ettore sued and lost, then appealed to France's highest court. Finally in May, 1947 he witnessed in Strasbourg the judgment that returned his Molsheim holdings and granted him cash compensation for war damage. At least his factory was not lost. Exhausted, he drove back to Paris. He had to be carried into his home and he never left it again. He died August 21, 1947, aged 66.

Ettore Bugatti left five children: his son Roland and daughters Ebée and Lydia by his first wife, and two small children by the second Mme. Bugatti, whom he married during the war. Also left were a number of staunch friends, men who had worked with Bugatti for many years and had learned to live for the same creative goals. One of these was Pierre Marco, who had been with *le Patron* since 1919. His long experience had taught him the Bugatti approach to racing, engineering and production, and he was chosen by the family to direct the reconstruction of the Molsheim plant.

Marco returned there in August of 1947 to find what was left of the old factory-estate. The enemy had destroyed the factory as effectively as possible before retreating to the east. A great fortune in machine tools had been reduced to junk but some of it was reclaimable and the buildings, although dilapidated, still stood.

First post-war Bugatti was Type 101, powered by dohc engine essentially same as Type 57, pre-war power plant.

Vachon

There was almost no cash to work with and scarcely any trained personnel, but machinery was pieced together and a fast-moving apprentice system put to work. The plant contracted for any sort of appropriate work it could obtain and struggled back into activity building tools and jigs for the Citroën firm. Other contracts gradually materialized and, while Bugattists across the water pestered Molsheim with eager fan mail, Marco hewed to the task of keeping the company alive.

Ettore's last words are said to have been: "The factory must go on." The family — of which Marco may be considered a part — certainly felt that way, and felt also that the factory's real mission was to build automobiles in the Bugatti tradition. The first step was taken early in 1951, when this announcement was made: "Ettore Bugatti Automobiles have pleasure in informing their clientele that they have now opened a service department at Molsheim for repairs to Bugatti cars and the supply of spare parts for all (!) models."

The Paris Salon of the fall of 1951 was the setting for the next gambit; showing of the first postwar, production-model Bugatti cars. These were a convertible coupe and a close-coupled sedan on a chassis labelled Type 101, with bodies executed by Gangloff of Colmar. Chassis details differed little from those of the prewar Type 57, except for increased power output from improved manifolding and the provision of a five-speed transmission with overdrive on top or, optionally, a Cotal preselector gearbox.

M. René Bollore, a wealthy paper manufacturer who had married Ettore's widow, attended the Bugatti Owners Club's annual dinner in London in October, 1951. There he announced that the Type 101 was definitely in production and would soon be followed by a high-performance 1½-liter car equipped with independent front suspension. Cries of "Shame!" were uttered by the naively faithful.

Ettore had planned to produce a 1½-liter car immediately after the war but the engine he exhibited at the 1946 Paris Salon was a single-camshaft, three-valve throwback to the Type 37, differing mainly in having a closer stroke-bore ratio and having its supercharger mounted ahead of the engine instead of at the side. The newly projected 1½-liter, called the Type 102, was based on the 3.3-liter engine, with dual overhead camshafts, optional supercharging and an integral head for the four-cylinder block. The prototype chassis featured lavish use of light alloy throughout, as well as independent front suspension by transverse leaf springs and A-arms. The public was warned that it would take a few years to get the 1½-liter car into series production. The firm was regenerating itself without resort to outside financing and was having its hands full finding time to produce an occasional Type 101. As for the fabulous 350-c.c. (21.4 cu. in.), 16-valve, double-overhead-camshaft, supercharged engine Ettore also exhibited at the 1946 Paris show, no one could imagine a use for its 12,000 top r.p.m. Some felt that this project had been a trap set by Ettore to consume precious wartime man hours during the German occupation.

An encouraging sign of Bugatti recovery came in 1952, when Molsheim began answering its overseas mail for the first time since 1939. But the healthiest news of all broke in the winter of 1953. M. Bollore was again the guest of honor at the B.O.C.'s annual dinner. There he announced that Automobiles Bugatti had obtained the services of Ing. Colombo of Italian racing fame. Colombo's job: designing a 2½-liter, unsupercharged racing car for full Grand Prix competition. Bugatti was getting back into racing just as fast as the cars could be developed. As they say in Molsheim, *"Ettore Bugatti n'est plus, mais Bugatti continue."*

T HREE AMERICAN SPORTS CARS — CUNNINGHAM, Kurtis, Nash-Healey — have commendable competition records and thoroughly disappointing sales. They were built that way, crafted carefully and expensively to appeal to that small segment of the car-buying public that likes to race. Their impact on America's purchasing habits was small.

CHEVROLET

Not till General Motors came into the act was the pattern for domestic sports-touring machines finally laid down. The Chevrolet Corvette turned out to be the most influential sports-type automobile to be produced since the demise of the Stutz.

The nation's motoring press was thoroughly astounded when the Corvette actually went into production. It had been thought of as nothing more than another of General Motors' glittering show cars, an experiment in plastic and metal that wouldn't get beyond the show stage. Everyone had been sure that no manufacturer could afford to market a special-bodied automobile for less than $4,000; they were just as positive that none of the Big Three, least of all GM, would bother to spend the money to develop and promote a low-volume production unit like a sports roadster.

The doubts that preceded production were nothing compared to those voiced as the first Corvettes came into the nation's showrooms. Experts agreed that the Chevrolet sports car would be an impossible machine, one that couldn't begin to compete with foreign machinery in performance or handling qualities. Again they were wrong. The Corvette was powerful, agile, comfortable. On a performance-per-dollar basis of comparison it was the equal of any sports-touring machine made in the world. Only when engine displacement was used as the basis for comparison did the Corvette lag behind the imports. Engine displacement, however, is a subject which interests only the competition enthusiast. Chevrolet wasn't concerned with the crash-helmet set.

Road tests of the Corvette soon disclosed that it could be driven at high speeds for hours without tiring the dependable six-cylinder workhorse engine; that the Corvette could out-drag Jaguars from a stop light; that the Corvette could out-corner any stock American machine on the highway. Experts and amateurs agreed that it was lower, sleeker, smarter than anything the Michigan mills had ever ground out. And it was pleasant to be in. The spastic riding qualities of many of the foreign sports cars had been rejected in favor of an easy, yet firm, suspension, with coil-spring-and-wishbone independent front suspension and Hotchkiss rear drive.

Acceleration and top speed were in keeping with the sports-touring concept. The most conservative driver could find 108 mph in top and some Corvettes would pass 110. Acceleration was tremendous in the lower ranges, falling off a little in the higher speeds where the lack of a solid, four-speed transmission made impossible a proper gear selection. For some unexplained reason the Corvettes came equipped with an automatic transmission — the Chevrolet type of torque converter known as Powerglide — which not only cost the customer more money but hindered performance.

All this power and speed astonished the average American. He'd always considered the Chevrolet passenger car engine —

from which the Corvette engine was directly derived — as a model of conservatism and dependability, not as a fast engine. Chevrolet engineers proved the versatility of the pushrod engine by modifying it to produce 150 bhp at the high, for Chevrolet, peaking speed of 4,200 rmp. To do this, a three carburetor manifold was added; a special hot camshaft was installed; a dual exhaust system replaced the stock single exhaust; full pressure lubrication and aluminum pistons were adopted.

Best of all, the entire car was beautiful. Unlike Jaguar and the standard British designs, it had an Italian simplicity of line that appealed to many people who couldn't get excited over notched doors and long hoods. Its dimensions were in the best new sports car tradition — a short wheelbase of 102 inches, wide front and rear tracks of 57 and 59 inches respectively. Thanks to the plastic body it was light, weighing only 2,900 pounds ready for the road.

The handling qualities surprised everyone. The Corvette cornered fast and flat. There was more drift and sway than you could find in a competition car, but no more than was compatible with the riding comfort of a sports-touring machine. Most serious flaw was braking — after you'd stood on the brakes for an hour of swift in-and-out driving they just weren't there anymore. Lack of cooling facilities and inadequate lining area for the weight of the car had produced too much fade. Still the brakes were better than those of a stock U.S. passenger machine.

Under the initial sales program, the Corvette didn't cost too much for the average enthusiast, but an unwise dealer policy upped the cost to ridiculous heights. Chevrolet dealers, unused to dealing with sports car fans, insisted on heaping the Corvettes with every possible accessory in the book. Even though the factory advertised price was lower than that of a Jaguar, the final delivered price went above $4,000. Not many people can afford to pay a Cadillac price for a car to have fun with. There were others who could afford the tariff but didn't want to spend it for a Chevrolet of any type. Corvette sales were disappointing.

After Ford had broken the market wide open with the Thunderbird in 1954, Chevrolet came back fast with two important modifications in the Corvette. The V-8 engine was made optional and the price was lowered.

The new Corvette could out-accelerate the old one, could beat out such vast horsepower giants as the Chrysler C-300. Even with the handicap of powerglide, it could hold its own with the

Jaguar XK140 until the higher speeds when the double overhead cams of the Jag could operate with greater efficiency than the V-8's pushrods. The top speed of the V-8 Corvette was about 120 mph; its zero to 60 acceleration time was a fast eight seconds.

There remained one primary difference between the Corvette and the Thunderbird. Both had tremendous performance, so nearly equal that the debate as to which could outdrag the other is still going on. But the Corvette had clung to the classic sports-touring cliches of side-curtains and roadster top. To the true enthusiast this meant little, but to many not-so-ardent lovers of high winds and fast machinery it was an unnecessary test of loyalty.

CISITALIA

THE NAME OF PIERO DUSIO IS SCARCELY KNOWN to any but the best-informed enthusiasts. But few individuals have exerted such decisive influence in determining the course of the automobile's history. In a scant few years immediately after World War II he created a new Grand Prix racing category, a new type of sports car, a new coachwork ideal, and a Formula I Grand Prix car that might well have set entirely new standards of performance if his finances had held out. Having performed this wizardry he withdrew from the scene, temporarily at least.

During the war Dusio, a wealthy amateur racing driver who could afford to experiment, conceived the idea of building cheap but potent racing machines in series. His object was to get Italy's or the world's best drivers driving identical cars at the same time and — thus having eliminated mechanical variables — determining the best men. Naive as this project's beginning may have been it led very quickly to big things.

Dusio decided to power his little racing cars with the Fiat Tipo 1100, 1,090-c.c. (66.5 cu. in.), pushrod-overhead-valve engine. A gifted promoter, he had little difficulty in persuading the Fiat factory to lend one of its best designers, Ing. Giacosa, to assist in the good work. Engineer-driver Piero Taruffi was retained to contribute to the design of the new car and to manage Cisitalia's racing department. The first appearance of the little cars was in the summer of 1946, a few days after the Turin Grand Prix. Gordini was there with his Simcas, there were a few Maseratis and Fiat-based specials and a whole covey of Cisitalias driven by Nuvolari, Taruffi, Cortese, Chiron, Dusio and Biondetti. The new machines had the whole race their way and Dusio, the boss, was allowed to come home the winner. Cisitalia is widely credited with having touched off the creation of F.I.A. Formula II in 1948 and until Dusio's little *monoposti* became outclassed in that year by bigger Simcas, Cisitalia set a record for races won in such a short period. This was accomplished by means of fantastic weight reduction, an ultra-stiff frame, sublime suspension and an engine tuned within reliable limits. The cars weighed about 800 pounds, engines developed 65 b.hp. (nearly a horse for every inch, but they rarely burst), top speed was over 100 m.p.h., acceleration good and cornering perfect beyond description. Having demonstrated his ability to master this field, Dusio stepped out of it.

1947 Cisitalia convertible coupe, powered by modified Fiat 1100 engine. Body by Pinin Farina.   *Henry Ford Museum*

The lightning success of the *monoposto* suggested two things to Dusio: (1) if the hotted-up Fiat 1100 engine could work such wonders in a racing car, why not build a production sports car around it? and (2) why not build cars to race in the Big Time, in Grand Prix Formula I? He engaged the Porsche Studios to build for him the most advanced Grand Prix car ever attempted and, in Turin, went to work on sports cars.

Experience from the single-seater was carried over into the sports-car chassis. The steel tube, aircraft-type frame was an authentic masterpiece of lightweight construction. Independent front suspension was by transverse leaf springs and A-arms, and rear suspension retained the solid axle but used semi-elliptics in place of the single-seater's coil springs. Precise, non-reversible steering was by worm and sector and the Fiat 1100 engine was supplied in various stages of tune. Pinin Farina was called upon to create bodywork that would be in the spirit of what Dusio hoped would be a somewhat revolutionary automobile. The result was exceptionally beautiful and profoundly influential.

1949 Cisitalia.

Alexander Georges Photo
Museum of Modern Art,
New York

Under Dusio's inspired guidance, an automobile was created that set radically new standards of rigid lightweight construction and minimum wind resistance. The combination of low weight and low drag made possible performance undreamed-of from such a tiny power plant. The 50-b.hp. Special Sport could top 100 m.p.h. and the 60-b.hp. Mille Miglia model was good for well over 120 m.p.h. — all this from a mere 66.5 cubic inches and with superb ride and handling qualities thrown in.

The cars were as much a styling prophecy as they were pace-setters in the areas of performance and chassis design. In 1947, they had bodies with "portholes" and finned rear fenders that were imitated in later years on both sides of the Atlantic. The Cisitalia's portholes had the virtue of utility; they were the exhaust outlets on the competition coupe. The standard, Farina-bodied coupe, an early perfection of the *berlinetta* body style, will always remain a masterpiece of industrial design in which many complex shapes blended to form an ideally integrated whole.

F.O.B. Turin, this car sold for around $5,500, a price which made the Cisitalia attractive to the point of purchase only to wealthy connoisseurs of rare discrimination. While he produced sports cars for this small market, Dusio dropped nearly a million dollars into his Grand Prix challenger, the development of which was retarded by many external events. Finally, in December, 1948 Dusio's creditors were granted a lien on his factory and its contents. Dusio had engineered several major contributions to the art and science of the automobile and had also lost a large fortune in the process. He embarked for Argentina, his fertile brain teeming with schemes for the industrial development of that agrarian republic.

IN THE WORLD'S FEW FORMULA RACES, ALL CARS compete on an equal basis. The final calculations which decide the winner take into account not only the total distance covered and the average speed maintained, but the displacement as well.

CROSLEY

Such a race is Le Mans; another is the annual Sebring, Florida endurance contest which was won, in 1950, by a Crosley.

Borgeson

Pioneer post-war American sports car was Crosley, winner of first Sebring, Florida, endurance rac

The victory didn't exactly stun the sports-car world, but it refocussed attention on the little American sports cars which had been shoved far into the background by the M.G.'s and Jaguars. To quite a number of people it was a revelation to discover that Crosleys weren't all used for hauling light loads on city streets, but longtime car enthusiasts had known for four years that the Crosley's tiny, overhead-camshaft engine could be worked into a lightweight competition design.

Powell Crosley introduced this engine to the public in the frantic postwar year of 1946 when any kind of car could be sold. While the car shortage lasted Crosleys sold well — 25,000 in 1948 alone — but once the larger, more popular makes returned in greater numbers the company began to lose money quickly. In 1952 the last Crosley came out of the factory and the assets were sold to the General Tire and Rubber Company.

Crosley engines, however, will probably buzz on forever. They are still in demand as replacements for Crosleys yet on the road, they are used extensively in stationary installations and they have been adopted by a few drivers as sports-car engines. In California there is Nick Braje, a speed-equipment manufacturer for Crosley exclusively, who will sell you anything from a special valve spring to a full-race Crosley engine designed to burn alcohol. Braje has built a special Crosley dragster which will reach a clocked 100 m.p.h. in less than a quarter mile.

Only one thing keeps the Crosley from being the ideal American sports-car engine for the average enthusiast. It's too small. Forty-four cubic inches can't provide the performance the average driver wants for a combination touring-competition car. Even Braje admits that 80 m.p.h. is the very top speed obtainable from a 3/4 race Crosley in a super-light sports body, and at that speed the engine is wound up to a frightening whine. Within its displacement class — 500 to 750 c.c. (30.5 to 45.75 cu. in.) — it's a tough combination to beat, but few people are racing in that class in this country.

The last Crosley engines to appear were called Super Sports, and they could be purchased with a compression ratio that still sounds high today — 10-to-1. The standard Crosley engines had an 8-to-1 compression ratio, which produced 26.5 b.hp. at 5,400 r.p.m. and 32.5 lbs.-ft. of torque at 3,000 r.p.m. Piston speed was low despite the high engine speed because the stroke was only 2.25 inches. Bore was 2.50 inches, making the Crosley the first over-square production engine in the postwar era, as well as the only overhead-camshaft design on an American passenger car. The crankshaft had five main bearings, the maximum. In hopping up the engine, Braje increases the displacement. His 3/4 race engine has been bored out to 48.6 cubic inches and produces 40 b.hp. on standard gasoline. Price: $600. The full-race engine has been bored and stroked to 52.75 cubic inches and will turn out 60 b.hp. on alcohol. Price for this conversion: $680.

While the Crosley Hotshot's victory at Sebring is the best single public performance by a nearly stock Crosley, the engine has won honors of its own. At Vero Beach in 1952, in a 12-hour formula race similar to the Sebring affair, a Crosley-powered Siata won the handicap with the best index of performance. During the same meet a Bandini-Crosley was the formula winner of a one-hour event. In any race where displacement is not an advantage, the Crosley is a top contender. Pound for pound and inch for inch there isn't a tougher and more capable piece of machinery in the United States.

THE AMERICAN ENTRIES AT LE MANS IN 1950 WERE of a nature which raised the eyebrows of even the sophisticated French. From the nations of Europe had come more or less conventional sports machines, with the exception of the two slightly altered Grand Prix Talbots, but America's representatives were anything but ordinary. One was a stock-appearing Cadillac sedan, the other a Cadillac-powered, flat-sided, wedge-shaped creation styled like a Buck Rogers fantasy. The latter was promptly tagged "Le Monstre" by the working press, partly because of its tremendous bulk compared to the other cars at the race. Not at all disturbed by this evident disrespect was Le Monstre's owner, builder and co-driver, Briggs Cunningham.

Cunningham took the first driving shift at Le Mans, and on the second lap the streamliner lunged into a sand bank, partially destroying its left front. After digging himself out with his bare hands, Cunningham drove on. He finished 11th, one place behind the stock Cadillac sedan, which was driven by the Collier brothers and also sponsored by Cunningham.

The Americans had returned to Le Mans after more than a decade. All the credit for the attempt goes to Cunningham and his drivers and crew, particularly to Cunningham since he financed the operation. While the results were not all that might have been hoped for, the two cars with their largely freshman crews had beaten a lot of competition infinitely better suited to the course. Cunningham was determined to return with more and better equipment.

He set up a plant in West Palm Beach, Florida and proceeded to manufacture special cars on a commercial basis. In the next three years, four additional models appeared, each a little closer to the ideal of a Le Mans winner than the last. Besides these competition models, Cunningham turned out detuned versions to be sold as sports cars to wealthy buyers.

One of the first to appear was the C2, which was announced while preparations were underway for the 1951 Le Mans race. The buyer could have his choice of a stock or modified Cadillac or Chrysler engine, but the cars being readied for competition were getting highly modified Chryslers. There was little resemblance between C2 and Le Monstre. C2 had a short wheelbase (105 in.), independent coil-spring-and-wishbone front suspension and a De Dion rear end. Brakes were entirely special, with ample ventilation to prevent fade. The customer had his choice of a two-speed, quick-change rear axle or a standard rear end with overdrive. The ground clearance was only seven inches, and total curb weight was close to 4,000 pounds. In appearance, C2 was a conventional-bodied sports roadster for two.

At Le Mans, C2 started well but finished poorly, only one of the team of three actually completing the 24 hours. The other two were stacked up so badly they couldn't go on. However, the car that finished 18th held second place until the 20th hour before being forced to cut speed to pamper a failing engine. Burned valves and a collapsing rod bearing were the points of failure.

While the majority of the engine was stock Chrysler, the pistons and connecting rods had been taken from Cadillac, four carburetors and a special manifold had been added, the cam had been ground for speed, and a magneto had replaced the battery-and-coil high-voltage system. Bore and stroke were stock, but the use of the Cadillac pistons and rods had raised the compression ratio from 7.5-to-1 to 8.5-to-1. Horsepower output was 250 at 5,500 r.p.m., an increase of 70 over the normal 180 b.hp. of the Chrysler engine.

Critics of the Cunningham were quick to condemn the car

Hardtop Cunningham with coachwork by Vignale is powered by 270 b.hp. Chrysler engine, was clocked at 141.8 m.p.h.

Henry Ford Museum

for its large displacement and overall size. They pointed to the fact that the European cars which had now beat the Cunninghams twice were smaller in both respects. Cunningham, however, was grimly determined to win with an American car powered by an American engine, and short of building his own overhead-camshaft racing engine he had no choice but to adopt a semi-stock, pushrod engine. With the pushrod layout he needed the extra inches because he couldn't rev as high as the Jaguars and Aston Martins.

There was a lot of improvement necessary before the next Le Mans race, however. Cunningham went to work on a new car and simultaneously took his team of three C2 models barnstorming in American road races. Under the handling of John Fitch, Phil Walters, Cunningham and others, they dominated Eastern United States road racing for the rest of the year, winning first and third at Elkhart Lake and first, second and fourth at Watkins Glen. At the Watkins Glen race, the car in third spot was a Ferrari — Briggs Cunningham's Ferrari.

Next in numerical order in the Cunningham models was the C3, but it was not a competition car. C4 was finally introduced early in 1952, and made its racing debut at Bridgehampton in May of that year. A broken tail pipe took it out of the running in the early part of the race, but the railbirds noted that it performed better than the C2.

C4 showed that Cunningham was not averse to taking some of the advice of his foreign critics. The new Le Mans contender was five inches shorter and four inches narrower than C2, and this was only the external change — 1,000 pounds had been pared from the weight of the former car. At the same time the Chrysler engine had been hopped up to 300 b.hp., greatly improving the horsepower-to-weight ratio.

Cunningham again took a team of three to Le Mans — one hard-top coupe and two roadsters. In the early part of the race the coupe held a steady fourth behind the wild driving of the Ferraris and the Gordini, but nosed into a sand bank a little while later and lost two hours. Both it and one of the roadsters eventually retired completely with valve trouble. At the wheel of the other Cunningham was Briggs himself, and he played a conservative hand for the entire race, pushing himself home in fourth place behind the two Mercedes and a Nash-Healey. It developed into a contest of endurance not only for the car but for the driver as well, Briggs driving 20 of the 24 hours. This year, for the first time, the reports that came back from Europe recognized the seriousness of the Cunningham threat. The coupe was called by many the fastest car on the course and everyone noted the excellent preparation and teamwork of the Cunningham crew.

Back home, Cunningham again raced the United States circuits. At Elkhart Lake the big blue cars came in 1-2-3 in the main event; at Sebring, first; at McDill, first; leading at Watkins Glen before the race was called because of the fatal accident to a spectator; and a first at Convair. As far as most United States competition was concerned the Cunninghams were unbeatable. They only remained to be tested on the West Coast.

At West Palm Beach, the factory was busy preparing a new Cunningham for the next Le Mans. The C5, as it was called, represented a major departure in chassis designing. Cunningham scrapped the independent front suspension he had been using and shifted to a solid front axle. Torsion-bar springing replaced the previous front and rear springs. Brake drums were 17 inches in diameter, despite the fact that the wheels were only 16 inches in diameter. Weight had been cut even further, now totalling 2,590 pounds ready to drive. The Chrysler engine still had its stock bore and stroke, but output was now listed as 310 b.hp. at 5,200 r.p.m. and the torque peak, 344 pounds-feet, had been moved up to 4,400 r.p.m. The transmission was "modified Siata" with four speeds forward. Wheelbase and tread were the same as C4 — 100 inches and 55 inches respectively.

So back to Le Mans went Cunningham, again with a team of three. Only one, however, was a C5. The factory hadn't been able to prepare three of the new models in time, so a coupe and a C4 roadster accompanied the new car. This time the Cunninghams were pre-race favorites, along with Alfa Romeo and Ferrari. Jaguar, the eventual winner, was not given a chance because of slow speed trials and a poor performance the year before.

The race began with a stirring Jaguar-Ferrari duel for first place. When the race was only four hours old, one Jaguar and one Ferrari had lapped the new C5. The C4's were farther behind. At the six-hour point, the C5 held third behind two Jaguars, Villoresi's Ferrari having dropped back. And at the finish, the C5 came in third to the Jaguars. What was more important, all three Cunninghams finished in good order — the C4's coming in seventh and tenth. Only three teams finished intact — Jaguar, Cunningham and Austin-Healey. The C5 was in as good condition at the end of the race as it had been at the beginning, and during the race had consistently recorded top speed for the entire field on the long straightaway, though the Jaguar's superior braking had enabled them to post the higher lap speeds. There was nothing but praise for the Cunningham drivers and team organization, particularly for the pit crews' fast and efficient handling of their chores during pit stops.

In his Le Mans appearances Cunningham had improved his cars and teams remarkably, but by the time 1954 rolled around he found the idea of winning with an all-American product less enchanting. His C6R, introduced that year, was a marriage of the basic Cunningham chassis with a Ferrari engine measuring 4.5 liters. This was a lighter car than previous Cunninghams, thanks largely to the lesser weight of the racing-bred Ferrari engine, and it had one novel feature — liquid-cooled brakes, the coolant pressured by two pumps. Entered with the C6R at Le Mans were two C4R's, powered by the longtime Cunningham favorites, Chrysler V-8 engines.

Fitch drew the driving assignment for the C6R, but not even his talents could shake the Jaguar-Ferrari stranglehold on the event that year. The C6R was retired early with a broken valve spring, and it was left to the other Cunninghams to fill their usual roles. Spear and Johnson drove one to a solid third place, conservatively behind the first two cars, and Cunningham and Bennett brought the last C4R in fifth.

In American sports car events in 1954, Cunningham was somewhat less in evidence than in previous years. He further retrenched by closing the Florida plant and moving all his operations to New York. The most notable Cunningham success on the American circuits in 1954 was the Phil Walters victory at Watkins Glen, where once again one of the older models beat out the experimental C6R.

Cunningham is a very rich man in a fantastically expensive sport, trying to pit amateur enthusiasm and personal resources against the professional skills and factory funds of the European sports car makers. He is a sportsman in the great tradition, a modern counterpart of such early automotive enthusiasts as W. K. Vanderbilt and James Gordon Bennett. Men like this have long been prominent in automobile development. Almost every great racing marque of the past has had an angel behind it at the outset, someone who believed not only in the car itself but in racing.

Unfortunately, there is little room in modern sports car competition for the individual, unless he restricts his activities to the strictly-for-fun amateur events. At Le Mans, or any other sports car event on the international calendar, the entry lists are largely made up of factory cars and professional racing drivers. For them this is a serious business, not a sport. Because their economic welfare depends on winning, they usually do. Cunningham's position is just the opposite. He could make more money by quitting the sport entirely than he could by winning all the races in the world.

"The world's largest car" was an early Daimler description of its postwar Straight Eight Model, one of the few remaining cars which are almost indistinguishable in design and dimensions from the prewar classics. The Straight Eight's

| DAIMLER |

wheelbase of 147 inches was indeed greater than one can find on other luxury cars (the Russian Zis is the sole exception), but the overall length of 222 inches fell short of that particular dimension in American luxury cars, and other dimensions also failed to live up to the Daimler boast. This does not detract at all from the general excellence of the modern Daimlers, since 222 inches is long enough for almost any private passenger use. And there is little question that the company did make the largest convertible coupe in the world.

It was the Straight Eight convertible coupe which first awakened many Americans to the fact that England produced another luxury car besides the Rolls-Royce. In the early part of 1950, this coupe was the central point of interest at a gigantic foreign-car show in New York, and it was widely publicized. Aside from its tremendous size (the convertible coupe was a special body, 18 inches longer than the eight-passenger limousine), the Hooper body drew praise for the beauty of its finish, the matched vanity and cocktail compartments in the rear, and the generous use of highly polished woodwork. The automatic top, a rarity overseas, was completely concealed when down by a mechanically operated metal cover. The rear seats were so placed as to give the occupants an unobstructed view of the road ahead, between the heads of the driver and front-seat passenger.

Like prewar Daimlers, the Straight Eight was not a notable performer. Rated horsepower of 150 b.hp. at 3,600 r.p.m. gave a factory estimated top speed of 80 m.p.h. The engine was, as the name stated, a straight-eight. It had pushrod-operated overhead valves and a displacement of slightly less than the biggest Packard of the same year. Still Daimler features were the preselector transmission and the Fluid Flywheel. The final drive ratio in top gear was 4.09-to-1.

But even this mammoth coupe was driven into the background when Lady Docker, wife of Sir Bernard Docker, the executive chief of the entire B.S.A. combine, took delivery of her "Gold Star" Daimler. The Gold Star is distinguished not by its size, which is the same as the "ordinary" Daimler Straight Eights, but by frank and overpowering ostentation. The first estimate of the worth of the Gold Star was $26,000; since then there have been prices up to $100,000 mentioned.

"I believe," Lady Docker was quoted as saying, "people who

A custom-built 1950 Daimler 8-cylinder Straight Eight convertible.

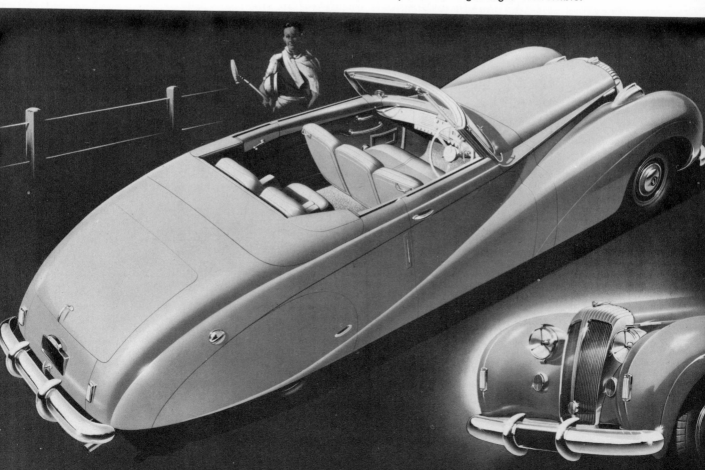

have money should have a good time and enjoy it." So she had the body painted midnight blue and dotted with gold stars to match a dress she admired greatly. Then, woman-like, she decided the other accessories on the car would have to match the gold stars. There was only one solution and she took it. Twenty ounces of pure gold were used to plate the grille and other interior and exterior hardware. The interior of the chauffeur's compartment was finished in conservative, rich leather, while the passenger section came in for the de luxe treatment. The floor mat was Persian Lamb, the woodwork was exceptionally beautiful, and there were four compartments holding teacups, cocktail glasses, a vanity and a tea table. This splendid body was built by Hooper, a B.S.A.-owned coachbuilding firm which stands in the same relationship to Daimler as Fleetwood does to Cadillac.

Besides the big Straight Eight series, the Daimler Company made a series of lighter cars designed especially for the man who wanted a small, quality car, or for someone who wanted Daimler prestige for a comparatively modest price. The price of the Straight Eight limousine was a little over $14,000 in 1953, so some price relief for the heavily taxed British aristocrat was definitely in order.

Foremost among the smaller cars was the Conquest 2½-liter series, which included an interesting semi-sports roadster. For this model the stock Conquest engine had been hopped up from 75 b.hp. at 4,000 r.p.m. to 100 b.hp. at 4,600 r.p.m. by upping the compression ratio to 7.75-to-1 and fitting dual carburetors, a high-lift camshaft and larger valves. To bring the top speed to over 100 m.p.h., the rear-axle ratio was raised to 3.73-to-1. Independent front suspension by laminated torsion bars was used, and the rear springs were the traditional Daimler semi-elliptics. The Fluid Flywheel and four-speed preselector transmission were retained on this, as well as all other Daimlers, and the engine was an in-line, pushrod-operated, overhead-valve six. In styling, the Conquest Roadster resembled a foreshortened Jaguar XK120 more than any other car, but it retained the Daimler grille.

Like Rolls-Royce, Daimler continued its prewar policies into the postwar era despite the general collapse of the luxury-car market. Both offered the equivalent of their old premium quality cars, the Daimler with its Straight Eight and the Rolls with the Phantom IV.

But just as Rolls has kept its Phantom IV straight eight out of the public's hands, Daimler has finally decided that their own straight eight was not the most sensible car to offer. It was chopped out of the line to be replaced by a six-cylinder chassis known as the Regency Mark II. No extreme reduction in price accompanied this move. You can still pay well over $12,000 before tax FOB England for a Daimler with a special Hooper body.

There is nothing about the Regency Mark II chassis to surprise the Daimler enthusiast. On hand are a big, well-made engine (its 281.5 cubic inches is considered large in England); the smooth, four-speed pre-selector gearbox; the classic grille. The car acts, handles and looks like the generations of Daimlers before it. Which is exactly the way Daimler and its customers want it to be.

FERRARI

In comparison to the factories of Mercedes, Jaguar and Alfa Romeo, the workshop at Maranello, Italy where the magnificent Ferraris are fabricated is of postage-stamp proportions. That it could have turned out one major sports car would have been a creditable achievement; that its products completely dominated Grand Prix racing in Europe for two years and sports-car racing all over the world for most of the postwar era was a miracle.

The man who worked this miracle was Enzo Ferrari, a racing professional in one capacity or another for more than three decades. Beginning as a driver, he became successively the owner of an Alfa Romeo racing stable, the chief of the factory Alfa Romeo team, and, in the postwar era, the builder of his own cars. These were chiefly a series of V-12's of highly volatile temperament and vast speed, almost sure winners in any event they entered if they held together. Around these cars he assembled the world's finest drivers; men like Ascari, Villoresi, Taruffi, Bracco, Hawthorne, Farina.

From the first, Ferrari's existence has been a precarious one despite his success. His small organization permits him to build and test one of Chief Engineer Lampredi's designs in three months, but that flexibility is gained at the expense of economy in the production of profitable passenger models. Each Ferrari sold to the public has 2,500 man-hours of time invested in it. Racing victories have brought Ferrari publicity and cash sales, but the investment in equipment, manpower and floor space required for victory have cut deeply into his ability to produce for customers. The lessons learned in competition have been applied to production cars with great benefit to their performance but at considerable expense to the factory. Ferrari can take justifiable pride in making the world's finest and fastest sports car. He has paid dearly for the distinction.

The story of the Ferraris begins in 1947 with a supercharged, 1½-liter (91.4 cu. in.) racing model and a 2-liter (122 cu. in.) sports model. Both were V-12's, both the work of one of Italy's most famous designers, Colombo, who was formerly an Alfa Romeo employee. The 2-liter chassis served as the basis for a Formula II racing car and five distinct sports models.

At the beginning it appeared as if Ferrari would have things his own way. After a few break-in appearances, the sports and racing models dominated the European tracks. In 1948 and 1949 there were sports-car victories in two Mille Miglias and one at Le Mans; a Formula II win at Florence; Formula I successes at Rheims, Monza, Silverstone, Luxemburg, Brussels, Rome and others. A factory statistician worked out figures proving that in a little over two years of competition Ferraris had traveled 218,000 kilometers racing in 93 events, had won 50 times, placed second 34 times and placed third 18 times.

It was too good to last. Alfa Romeo came along in 1950 with a rejuvenated Alfetta and a racing team headed by such stars as Fangio, Farina, Fagioli and Taruffi and proved beyond question that no blown 1.5-liter car in the world could match the Alfa. Alfa won all five of the *Grandes Epreuves*. Ferrari had two alternatives at the beginning of the 1950 season — he could try to refine his 1.5-engine to the point where it could outlast and outrun the Alfas or he could go to the other extreme of the formula and build a 4.5-liter (274 cu. in.) unsupercharged engine. He chose the latter.

By the Monza race in 1950 Ferrari had developed a 4.5-liter racing machine capable of frightening the Alfa team. Not until the Silverstone Grand Prix in England in 1951, however, did the new Ferrari design beat the Alfas, but that first victory led to more. Before Silverstone, Fangio had almost sewed up the 1951 world's championship with his Alfa; after Silverstone the race for the championship developed into such a tight contest that the

Ascari-Ferrari partnership came within a few points of stealing the award. In 1952 and 1953 the Alfas dropped out and Ascari won the championship both years.

This brief resumé of the Ferrari Formula I history is part of the background of the evolution of the sports cars Ferrari was building at the same time. The 2-liter unblown car was definitely lacking in the low-speed power needed for road racing. At first, before major competition appeared, extra power was not necessary, but with Jaguar, Aston Martin, Simca, Lancia and others making a strong bid for the wide-open sports-car market, new engines and chassis were continually being entered against the Ferraris. The first countermove was a 2.3-liter (140 cu. in.) version of the original sports model. It promptly won the 1950 Mille Miglia. Tested in the same race was a newer car with a 3.3-liter (201 cu. in.) engine, but the old transmission collapsed into rubble under the additional pressure.

The 3.3 marked a change in Ferrari designers. Colombo had rejoined Alfa Romeo, and his former assistant, Lampredi, succeeded to his position as chief designer at Ferrari. He had not thrown out the lessons learned from Colombo — the 3.3 being a logical continuation of the earlier sports cars — but he began to institute changes of his own. He had to. With Colombo at Alfa doing his best to drive the Ferraris off the tracks, Lampredi's designs had to be better than his teacher's.

The 3.3 became the foundation of the new Formula I car. It was first bored out to 4.1 liters (250 cu. in.), then the stroke was lengthened to increase displacement to the limit of Formula I — 4.5 liters. In that form, as has already been mentioned, it beat the Alfas. Meantime sports-car development had bloomed from the original 2-liter engine with 2.34-liter "Type 195" and 2.6-liter "Type 212" models being produced.

Almost on their heels came the most powerful to that date of the Ferrari sports models, the "America." In this car Ferrari finally managed to realize his ideal of a unified series of cars which could, with appropriate modifications, serve for Grand Prix racing, sports-car racing, and general passenger use. The America's engine was a special version of the racing 4.1-liter engine, and the America could be used for sports-car racing or for touring. Later, Ferrari made the expected modifications to the 4.5-liter Formula I engine so it could be turned to more peaceful uses. With the advent of these cars, the smaller sports models began to take a back seat, except for racing within their displacement classes or for use on courses where smallness and lightness were more desirable than power and speed.

The largest Ferrari, at least to this date, is the 4.9, winner at Le Mans and in Mexico during the 1954 sports car season. Most experts consider it the logical end-point of the development of the V-12 engine by Ferrari, and the appearance of the four-cylinder models, Mondial and Monza, in 1954 seems to bear out this theory. The four-cylinder, double-overhead-camshaft engine was derived from the two-liter Formula II car Ferrari introduced into European racing earlier. It had been a consistent winner and somewhat more dependable than the complex V-12's. In its 3-liter, Monza form, it proved to be a dependable sports car engine as well, winning the Monza race in Italy and placing first in average speed at the Irish TT in 1954.

To discuss each Ferrari in detail, as has been done with the products of some other firms, would require a small technical volume in itself. Since we are dedicated here to sports cars, a review of the basic types should suffice.

There are many points common to all the earlier sports models. The engines were V-12's, had a single overhead camshaft for each bank of cylinders and had a larger bore than stroke. Hairpin valve springs were used for their faster cooling and lesser tendency to surge (surge becomes a weighty problem in an engine which is revving up past 6,000 r.p.m. for peak horsepower and is capable of speeds as high as 8,000 r.p.m. in quick bursts). The combustion chambers were hemispherical, valves were laterally inclined. Each bank of cylinders had its own distributor and fuel pump. The connecting rods were fitted side by side on the crankshaft. Response to the accelerator was terrifically fast, and more than one competition driver has put an engine out of commission by over-revving while missing a shift. Originally the transmission was a straight crash box with five forward speeds, nice for experienced competition drivers but not for the casual tourist. To make matters more difficult, clutch action was decisive to the point of brutality. Operating a Ferrari required a sensitive throttle foot and precise coordination of clutch foot and right hand. In subsequent models, the transmission was revised, though never to the point where a novice could be happy with it. With the bigger engines of the 2.9, 4.1 and 4.5, the five speeds were no longer absolutely necessary, so a more orthodox four-speed box was substituted. The touring models had synchromesh on all gears, but this new convenience was partly offset by a heavier, multiple-disc clutch which proved to be even more violent than the single-disc type which had preceded it.

With the arrival of the Mondial, Ferrari began putting his transmissions in the rear, in unit with the rear axle. Typical of the custom nature of the Ferraris is the bewildering array of axle ratios and transmission ratios available on the competition models. In the Ferrari catalogue you can find proper gears for everything from wall-climbing to Bonneville speed runs. If it isn't right there they'll run it up in the factory on the spot.

Trying to sort out all the different Ferrari models is impossible within the scope of this chapter. In the table at the end of the book is a listing of the most important sports types produced since the first 2-liter car, but many variations within types have had to be omitted. There is no such thing as a "stock" Ferrari engine. Some have one, some two, some as many as four carburetors; some of the carburetors are two-throat, others are four-throat. There are many differences in cam design and many different compression ratios. A 1953 2-liter car will have a slightly different chassis than an earlier model with the same engine. The first 2-liter car was available in three forms, known as Type 166 Sports, Type 166 Inter and Type 166 Mille Miglia, each representing a different stage of tuning. The America is one version of the 4.1-liter engine; the Mexico is a hopped-up version of the same engine; if you don't like either and want the 4.1 engine, tell the factory and they'll modify it to suit your whims.

Two sports cars — the 2.7-liter and the 3.3-liter — have been omitted from the table because they did not survive competition testing as well as the others.

The chassis of most of the V-12 Ferraris is the same except for size and weight. There is independent front suspension employing a transverse leaf spring and two wishbones per wheel and a standard solid-axle rear end with two semi-elliptic springs, one above and the other below the axle. The frame itself is made of oval tubing. The recent 250 Europa, however, has coil springs in front and the Mondial and Monza both are equipped with De Dion rear ends.

Ferrari bodies, all custom built by the greatest names in Italian coachbuilding, are almost invariably extremely light. Two-seater roadster and coupe bodies predominate, but there are also a number of the peculiarly European three-seater sedan bodies. Catalogues describe them hopefully as four-seaters, but anyone who has been a back-seat passenger in one will testify to the accuracy of the three-seater designation.

Almost every Ferrari model has a list of competition successes behind it. After the 2- and 2.3-liter models had begun to take their lumps from sports cars with larger engines, the 2.6-liter Ferraris once again put Enzo back on top. Two of these cars won first and second places in the second Mexican Road Race. In America the 4.1-liter America driven by Bill Spear has been very successful, as has Phil Hill's 2.9 Ferrari. In fact, Ferrari's only bad-competition year in Europe was 1952, when Mercedes came out of Stuttgart with the 300SL coupes and roadsters. Ferraris in America have taken frequent beatings from the Cunninghams, but there is a vast difference in displacement between the two. Also, the Cunninghams have the advantage of being a factory team, while the Ferraris are privately owned, maintained and raced. In 1954, however, Jim Kimberly won the U. S. sports car championship with a 4.9 Ferrari.

The Ferraris usually sold to the private buyer for passenger use are more tractable machines than those intended for racing.

Ferrari competition two-seater at Pebble Beach road race.   *Borgeson*

Springs are milder, engines are detuned for the sake of easier low-speed operation and greater reliability. Despite these differences, the Ferrari you see on the streets is a remarkable piece of equipment. The factory claims a speed of approximately 170 m.p.h. for the Mexico, and road tests show that this figure is not too optimistic. Acceleration through the gears from a standing start to over 100 m.p.h. in under 20 seconds is just average for the small-engined passenger cars, and this time can be cut to under 15 seconds on the all-out road-racing modified jobs. Most testers have agreed that the performance of the Ferrari is so tremendous that any driver who attempts to handle one should give himself as well as the car a break-in period. This advice is not only for the health of the driver and others on the highway but for the car as well. When 280 horsepower is built into a machine weighing less than 2,000 pounds, there cannot be much allowance for overstress in the vital parts. In the hands of an incapable operator the car can literally commit suicide.

Ferrari followers were deeply disturbed late in 1953 when Enzo Ferrari announced his intention to retire from team competition of all kinds. Some reasoned that the rumored return of Bugatti, Alfa Romeo, Mercedes and others to active participation in the sport had made it almost impossible for the small shop at Maranello to compete successfully. Others rejected this theory on the grounds that Ferrari had never shunned a good fight, and offered the failing health of the master as the most logical reason. There was also the fact that Italy had not rewarded Ferrari with a subsidy, though he had carried his country's colors proudly and victoriously for many years. Undeniably, he had spent a lot of money and effort for comparatively little return, and the prospect of continuing to do so would be a powerful deterrent.

A later report from Maranello cancelled the decision to quit racing comfortably before the beginning of activity in 1954. Ferrari went on to one of the greatest years it had yet had in sports car racing, carrying Italy's colors to an undisputed world championship. In Grand Prix events, however, there was no Ferrari to challenge the Mercedes team successfully. But in the back rooms Enzo was rumored to be at work on one — some reports mentioned a two-cylinder car, others spoke of a V-6. It may be neither, but it's a cinch bet that something is being prepared to unseat the Germans. Signor Ferrari does not like to be second best in anything.

THE "ROMANCE" OF FORD'S FANTASTICALLY POPU-
lar Thunderbird does not spring from personalities or inspirations. The precedent of Edsel
Ford's single-handed creation of the old Lincoln
Continental was carefully avoided. Instead the

FORD

T-Bird was a product of design and engineering task forces, and
of a corporate, statistical kind of crystal-gazing. It was a calculated shot in the dark aimed so shrewdly that it not only found
the target but managed to skewer the bullseye.

The well-worn cry, "Why doesn't Detroit build a sports car?"
had not been coined back in 1949 when the men in Ford's
Market Research section noted the first spasms of the sports car
mania to come. They also observed a steady, substantial increase
in the number of two-car families in the U. S. If the sports car
trend and the second-car trend continued to build, they guessed,
a single product aimed at both markets could enjoy considerable
success. Market Research risked the forecast that both trends
would continue upward and recommended that Management put
the new kind of car in the works.

Management studied the analyses made by Market Research
and endorsed the project. Late in 1949 the ball was passed to
the Product Planning section, with instructions to run.

This group of professional seers went to work immediately
on the philosophy and general specifications for a car that they
hoped would be a hit five years in the future. They decided, first,
that the car's performance must at least equal anything the
owner is likely to encounter *on the highway*. Any car that hot
would have a good potential for racing, but that was merely a
by-product of the specified performance and not an objective.
Granted such performance, handling qualities would have to
be unlike standard Detroit issue. Quicker steering, better cornering ability, and a firmer, flatter ride would be demanded in the
interest of safety. Safe for the highway, that is. Not kidney-
busting safe for road racing.

In fact, there could be nothing harsh about the car. It must
be just as comfortable, convenient, and luxurious as any well-
accepted Detroit machine. Success could only lie in this direction. The car's appearance had to be acceptable to the conservative solid citizenry and to do this it must have the Made-in-U.S.A.
look. There must be nothing about it to suggest the hot rod or
"racer." On the contrary, the car's appearance should reflect the

owner's good taste. And it was crucially important that the unit's selling price should be highly competitive.

The car began taking form early in 1950, when its package size was determined. Because nothing contributes to nimble handling more than a short wheelbase, the design team selected a hub-to-hub dimension of 102 inches. Also to improve handling qualities they specified equal weight distribution on front and rear wheels. This meant that the V-8 engine had to be moved several inches aft, which intensified the packaging problem. With passengers seated and luggage stowed there would be no room in which to stack a conventional fabric top. So a new type of top was designed that could be stored vertically, behind the seat-back.

In every possible case the design team used standard or modified Ford components in the interest of economy and convenience for the owner as well as the manufacturer. The frame was basically the extra-stiff "X" frame that Ford put under its convertible bodies. But the new car's body panels were interchangeable with nothing else.

The crystal-gazing department devoted countless man-hours to study the desirability of making the new car's body out of the highly-publicised new material, Fiberglas. In spite of the virtues of this technique they decided against it. Part of their reasoning was that the public knew and accepted steel bodies; they confined their pioneering to areas where they were pretty sure it would do some good.

The project progressed from paper to wood to clay to metal. As extravagantly fanciful dream cars were tested on the public by many manufacturers and received with only lukewarm interest, the design team made the new car's form cleaner, simpler, and closer to the tried and true. The project progressed and actual prototypes were built. They were called the Fairlane, the gracious-sounding name of the elder Henry Ford's estate. But the strategists who were sighting-in on the target decided that while this was a name with appeal for the "show" buyer, it would leave the "go" buyer unmoved. By their computations, the cross-hairs lined up best on Thunderbird. The car was introduced under this name in October, 1954.

In the first two and one-half months of production more T-Birds were sold than the U. S. competition had been able to place in owners' hands in nearly a year. The rather surprising total of approximately 11,000 Thunderbirds was sold during the first year of production; the car hit its intended mark more squarely than anyone had hoped. With a production rate of 65 machines a day, the factory was still a couple of months behind on T-Bird deliveries in September, 1955.

The combination that stole the show from all domestic and foreign sports car manufacturers in 1955 was not even billed as a sports car. It was ambiguously and shrewdly termed a "personal car," a term that might mean anything to anyone — which was, of course, just the point.

It had a ride that was neither hard nor firm but definitely more solid than conventional U. S. practice. It had acceleration that really was hair-raising, based on a pounds per horsepower ratio of just over 14 to one. It was the most satisfying, exciting, and thoroughly enjoyable fast road machine that the U. S. public had ever been able to buy. In its very desirable basic form its factory-delivered price was a mere $2,695.

The T-Bird had everything that a second car should have, plus conveniences that no sports car has ever boasted. Transmission to taste: synchromesh, OD, or automatic. Power devices to taste: power windows, seats, steering, brakes. Top to taste:

Ford Thunderbird

hardtop or convertible. You could mix your own recipe and make it literally a personal car.

It could be an alarming car to drive, it was that hot. You had to stay on your toes or the fast steering and acceleration would catch you off guard. Its accelerating ability was, by Detroit standards, a revelation. Fitted with McCulloch supercharger it definitely was too much automobile for the driver of just average ability. There were few grades that the T-Bird would not fly up in top gear and at part throttle; its reserve power, under any reasonably normal road conditions was tremendous. Yet it was a luxuriously comfortable and convenient tool for the road.

For the road, not for road racing. The Thunderbird was an in-between car, a new type of car. But if Ford avoided calling it a sports car, the critics called it that without hesitation. They did not overlook its limitations. They pointed out that the T-Bird could hold its own with Jaguars and Ferraris on reasonably straight courses but that when extreme demands on cornering power and braking ability were made, Ford's fast road machine was not the equal of more uncompromising sports cars. But this was actually one of the T-Bird's assets.

Ford's new sort of automobile, with its concession to every popular prejudice and taste, made the sports-type car acceptable to a huge segment of the U. S. population. As a missionary instrument, as a brilliant piece of product planning and market analysis, and as a car, the Thunderbird was a memorable achievement.

| FRAZER-NASH |

IMMEDIATELY AFTER THE END OF WORLD WAR II the Frazer-Nash organization became associated with the Bristol Aeroplane Company, and played an important part in the development and production of the Bristol car. One of F.-N.'s prime contributions was the high-performance 2-liter engine, essentially the Type 328 B.M.W. that the Aldington brothers had tooled to produce in 1939 and which enabled Bristol to set a new 200-mile record of 125.87 m.p.h. in 1953. The Bristol association lasted until 1949, when the Aldingtons decided the time had come to revive the famous and virile Frazer-Nash marque. It was arranged that Bristol would manufacture the 328 engine to F.-N. requirements.

Multum in parvo, a favorite phrase of the British, applied perfectly to the cars they produced. Even in the plastic age the Aldington brothers held fast to their standards of building by hand small numbers of automobiles of extreme individuality and competition prowess. Right at the outset they announced, "While these new cars will fully justify the description of production models in the true sense of the word, they will be built in limited numbers only and so maintain the Frazer-Nash tradition between owner and manufacturer."

One of the very first of these personalized production machines was privately entered in the Le Mans 24 Hour Race in 1949 by ex-racing-motorcyclist Norman Culpan, with Aldy Aldington co-driving. It finished third overall and was the first British car home, with an average speed of 78 m.p.h. for 1,884.7 miles. The same year Culpan scored another overall third in the B.R.D.C.'s One Hour Production Car Race at Silverstone, and in spite of the F.-N.'s under-2-liter displacement took first in the 2500-c.c. class and was a serious threat to even larger cars.

Frazer-Nash Targa Florio two-seater, 1953 model. Dry weight is just 1,680 pounds. Car can be had in degrees of tune giving from 100 to 150 b.hp. from same B.M.W. Type 328-based engine.

The car which made this auspicious debut was first known as the High Speed Model, but was promptly rechristened the Le Mans Replica. The engine was not unnaturally the Type 328 B.M.W. with which the Aldingtons had had such outstanding success prewar and in the postwar Bristol. Bore, stroke, overhead-valve layout, light-alloy head, four-bearing fully counterweighted crankshaft — all such basic features were the same as in the production B.M.W. But the 1,971-c.c. (120.3 cu. in.) engine was given careful detail modifications that enabled it to produce 120 b.hp. at 5,500 r.p.m.

The chassis frame was made of four-inch-diameter steel tubes with three cross members and three main body hoops all integral with the frame. The structure was absolutely rigid and remarkably light. A solid rear axle was sprung on torsion bars and front suspension was independent by means of a transverse leaf spring and A-arms. The 2¼x11-inch brake drums had finned light alloy muffs and generous air scoops were provided in the backing plates. A somewhat torpedo-shaped aluminum body with cycle fenders and two external exhaust pipes hugged the chassis.

Few cars have received so much superlative praise from so many discriminating experts. Said *The Autocar*: "In performance, stability, steering and response to the controls this car is in the best half-dozen built anywhere today." *Autosport* observed: "For really fast driving, this car is a sheer joy. It is so well balanced that one can take tremendous liberties with it, in fact it puts the most advanced techniques within the reach of any normally competent driver." Everything that can be valued in a sports car was extravagantly praised in the postwar F.-N. Steering, braking, acceleration, hill-climbing, gear-changing, cornering — all were of the very best.

Proof that this honor was not undeserved came quickly in competition. Fraser-Nash cars finished third at Le Mans and in the T.T. in 1950. In 1951 they were first in their class in the Targa Florio (a tremendous achievement), in the Production Car Race at Silverstone and in the British Empire Trophy Race. In 1952 they were outright winners in the Sebring Twelve Hour Race, the Aix-Madrid-Aix Rally, the Rally Soleil, second in the Jersey road race and third in the Prix de Monte Carlo and the Empire Trophy.

Following a third-place finish in the 1949 Mille Miglia touring category by co-drivers Aldington and Lurani in a Bristol, a Mille Miglia model F.-N. was introduced in time for the Earls Court

Show in October. Unlike the starkly efficient torpedo-bodied Le Mans Replica, this was a luxurious, lovely to look at, Italianesque two-seater with a shape reminiscent of the Jaguar XK120C. It was the Le Mans chassis and was only 225 pounds heavier. A handsome, comfortable convertible coupe was also offered in 1949.

Cortese's 1951 Targa Florio victory in a 2-liter Frazer-Nash which outran and out-lasted 2.6- and 4.1-liter Ferraris inspired the introduction of the Targa Florio Grand Sport model in 1952. This car was available in degrees of tune giving from 132 to 150 b.hp. and had very smooth pontoon-type, two-seater coachwork. A touring version of this same car, identical in appearance but having smaller power output and with such racing touches deleted as oil radiator and bonded aluminum brake drums, was offered at the same time. Also in 1952, the Targa Florio Grand Sport chassis was fitted with the Le Mans'-style bullet body and renamed Le Mans Replica Mark II.

For the 1953 Le Mans 24 Hour Race a new, very Continental-looking hardtop two-place coupe was created, having a 150-b.hp.

Frazer-Nash Le Mans Fixed-head Coupe made first appearance at 1953 Le Mans race, was introduced as a production model in 1954. Dry weight is 1,875 pounds. 150 b.hp. engine is standard.

engine and De Dion rear axle. The one entry, driven by Ken Wharton, did no better than 13th. It was competing against much larger cars, many of which were special prototypes. The Aldingtons said of this racing effort, ". . . many Le Mans cars differ considerably in performance to those of the same make as sold. We guarantee the engine, chassis and body-work specification, even to seats and trimming, of the fixed-head coupe, as entirely standard and identical to every Frazer-Nash as sold." The car averaged 95.5 m.p.h. for the 24 hours. Of the 12 faster cars, 10 had engine displacements ranging from 3½ to 5½ liters. Frazer-Nash was not disturbed by having failed to place higher on the finishing list. The race was a satisfactory and completely encouraging test of a new production model.

The Le Mans Fixed-head Coupe was introduced as part of Frazer-Nash's 1954 selection at the October, 1953 Earls Court Show. The '54 line consisted of the Mark II, with De Dion rear end, the Targa Florio Grand Sport, Turismo and Le Mans Coupe, all with solid rear axle but with independent rear suspension optionally available.

Yet another business-like variation on the time-tested chassis appeared late in '54. This, called the Sebring, was a development of the Mark II competition model. It was a handsomer car, resembling the Maserati Sports 2000 and, although nearly 400 pounds heavier than its purely-for-racing forerunner, was far more comfortable. By mounting the engine lower and farther back a good plunging hood-line and lower overall height were achieved, making this the most aerodynamically correct of the F.-N.'s to date.

GORDINI

Most manufacturers who are active in racing can afford to be airily indifferent to prize money their cars may or may not win. They are frankly interested in good publicity and they're willing to pay for it with men, machines and entry fees. To Amadée Gordini, a designer and manufacturer with zest and stubbornness of impressive proportions, race prize money frequently meant the difference between survival and bankruptcy for his little factory. For him every race was a tense and crucial gamble — the prize money staked against the possibility of taking a total loss on cars he couldn't afford to insure.

Nevertheless the threadbare little Gordini *équipe* made a big mark in racing in the early Fifties, and gave French racing prestige an important boost. This was a fact that was clearly recognized by many French enthusiasts. In 1952 the magazines *l'Action Automobile et Touristique* and *l'Equipe* initiated a campaign by which the French people and the government could come to Gordini's financial aid. The campaign was not entirely successful. But if the five million or so francs (just over $14,000) collected for Gordini did not go too far in defraying his operating costs, the fact that the campaign was carried on in the interest of French prestige is some indication of the respect accorded the gaunt, gifted and tenacious Italian.

Gordini was always poor. Born in northern Italy, near Modena, he grew up in the kind of poverty that only a European can know. At 13 he went to work, first in a motorcycle shop in Bologna and then in a Fiat garage owned by Eduardo Weber, later the designer and manufacturer of what were among the world's very best carburetors. Gordini worked hard, studied hard at night school, and went through a period of apprenticeship at the vast Fiat factory in Turin. In 1925 he moved to Paris to work in the Simca factory, which was producing Fiat cars under license. Here he got his first real taste of racing, and by 1935 he was building competition cars for Simca in his own modest shop. In 1937 at the Paris Salon he exhibited a fine Simca 8CV chassis much modified for racing. It made its competition debut that year by finishing in the money in the Bol d'Or, Paris-Nice and the Le Mans 24 Hour Race and in 1939 it won the Index of Performance at Le Mans.

The war and the occupation naturally interrupted Gordini's steady rise. He served in the army of his adopted country, and his little shop was blasted to ruins. Characteristically undaunted, Gordini picked up the pieces and went to work. He rebuilt his shop and went back to work building racing cars for Simca. Then, in 1950, he took the first step toward striking out on his own. He began to acquire Simcas as a private contractor, designed and added dual-overhead-camshaft heads and two carburetors to the little four-cylinder, 1,100-c.c. (67.1 cu. in.) engines, and put the engines in lightweight tubular chassis. These reconstituted cars were raced with great success under the name Simca-Gordini, and had no difficulty beating Cisitalias and other contenders in their class. Later versions were increased to 1,500 c.c. (91.5 cu. in.);

these blown cars were fast but only moderately successful, for although they often placed well they could not take first money from the Formula I Alfas and Ferraris.

In 1952 Gordini took the final step of independence from his long association with Simca-Fiat engine design. Although his financial position was as poor and painful as always, he decided the time had come to build his own Grand Prix and sports cars from scratch. The Grand Prix Gordini was a 2-liter six, with twin overhead camshafts, three dual-throat Weber carburetors and really ultra-light construction throughout. This car raced in Formula II events throughout the 1952 season with notable success and won the Grand Prix at Rheims, Jean Behra driving, placed first and third in the Belgian Grand Prix des Frontieres, and 1-2-3 at Cadours. The sports-car range was one of prodigious variety for such a tiny firm. Gordini's approach consisted of tireless trial and occasional error; by early 1953 he had developed 1.5-liter, 2-liter, 2.3-liter and 3-liter sixes and a 3-liter eight. All had solid rear axles, rear as well as independent front suspension being by torsion bars.

Two of the 2.3-liter sixes were entered in 1952's Carrera Pan-americana, a daring and costly venture for such an undercapitalized firm. The little blue cars were patently underdogs in the race and won the immediate affection of the Mexicans, who called them the *cucarachas azules* — blue cockroaches. On the first and most difficult leg, from Tuxtla and Oaxaca, Behra's Gordini utterly astounded and delighted its new-found partisans by coming in first, way ahead of Mercedes and Ferrari, and setting a new record for the leg. Behra sustained this dazzling speed until, in the mountains between Puebla and Mexico City, he overshot a turn and crashed.

All this was quite enough to render the French enthusiasts white-hot with what one writer called "amity and fervor," and the subscription campaign was started. As has been noted, the results were morally encouraging but otherwise meager.

Gordini continued in 1953 with a pitiful lack of funds, but nevertheless entered several cars at Le Mans — a 2.3-liter six, a blown 1.5-liter, a 2.5-liter six, and a 3-liter eight. The latter was the most potent; it developed 220 b.hp. at 6,000 r.p.m. with only 1,500 pounds of dry weight to pull and consequently had a remarkably high power-to-weight ratio. The 2.5 developed 190 b.hp. at 6,000 r.p.m. All the cars had the same basic engine design, with twin overhead camshafts operating the valves through pivoted fingers, light alloy blocks with wet liners, and multiple carburetion. The varied entry was another indication of Gordini's search for just the right combination, and the results of the race seemed to demonstrate that his method had merit. The 3-liter never reached the starting line, the 1.5 got nowhere and retired early and the 2.3 dropped out after completing nine hours.

But the 2.5 ran magnificently, won the 3-liter class and finished sixth overall. The cars ahead of it were the winning XK120C Jaguars, a Cunningham and a 4.1-liter Ferrari. But the tiny Gordini was faster than the other Jags and Cunninghams in the race even though — in the case of Cunningham — its displacement was less than half. The second-best finisher in the Gordini's displacement class came in 12th.

This was a heartening victory for France and for Amadée Gordini. He could well afford to be proud, but he could afford little else. In two seasons his cars had won four firsts, two seconds, and 18 third and fourth places in major races, in addition to the Le Mans class win. But in spite of being France's "white hope" in international competition he was still operating on a shoestring, harassed by poverty although working with undiminished vigor.

The following year was a happier one. Gordini cars raced constantly, missing astonishingly few important events. They were not precisely a match for better-heeled Ferrari and Maserati competition but they pushed those marques uncomfortably hard. In '54 Gordini performed a *tour de force* of reliability as well as speed by winning outright the 3,775-mile Tour de France — a contest many times more gruelling than Italy's Mille Miglia. This was followed by further good fortune for *Le Sorcier,* as Gordini is called because of his ability to do so much with so little. A man of wealth, M. Garczynski of Le Mans, stepped forward with the funds to underwrite an aggressive Gordini campaign in sports and Formula 1 competition.

Note: Since it is Gordini's practice not to broadcast his cars' specifications — and almost every car of his is a distinct individual — there is no specification table for this make.

HEALEY

Cₒᵤₙₜ JOHNNY LURANI IS AN ITALIAN RACE driver, the veteran of more than two decades of deadly, furious competition in Europe and England. He does not restrict his talents to Italian cars. As long ago as 1933 he pushed an M.G. over the finish line to take first in his class in the Mille Miglia. In the 1948 running of the same race, he duplicated the feat with one of the three cars in the Healey team, winning first place in the touring category.

In the same race that year, Donald Healey and his son drove one of the Healey roadsters through to a ninth place in the general sports category, competing against Ferraris and other top-competition sports machines from England and the Continent. British writers considered the Healey showing as one of the most encouraging British efforts in many years of racing. And suddenly the rest of the world press discovered that the Healey cars were worth writing about.

Since that time the Healey name has been constantly in the news. After the original Healey there came the Nash-Healey, Alvis-Healey, and later the Austin-Healey, all high-performance sports cars built down to a price that could appeal to a middle-class purchaser. Donald Healey had cracked the tough British sports-car field and had succeeded.

Healey began his career as a garage operator, later becoming a competition driver in European rallies. By the time the war broke out he was the chief engineer for the Triumph Car Manufacturing Company. During the war he manufactured aircraft-engine parts and military engines, meeting one of the world's greatest engineers in the process. This was A. C. Sampietro, a former Alfa Romeo technician.

Healey and Sampietro celebrated VE Day by collaborating on the design of a sports-car chassis. It used independent front suspension of the trailing-link type, with coil springs. In the rear, the banjo-type rear axle was suspended by coil springs. Everything was sacrificed for lightness, the entire car having a dry weight of approximately 2,350 pounds. The engine used was of Riley manufacture, the famous four-cylinder plant that had made history for that old-line company. As used in the Healey it had a bore and stroke of 3.16×4.7 inches, a displacement of 149 cubic inches, just under the 2.5-liter mark. Pushrod-operated overhead valves were inclined at an angle of 90 degrees to each other. The combustion chamber was hemispherical. In stock trim this remarkable four developed over 100 b.hp. What was more remarkable was the absolute reliability of the engine, which was proved beyond doubt by its performance in the Mille Miglia.

This Healey was timed at 111.5 m.p.h. in July, 1947 in Belgium, and Count Lurani spoke of many sustained spells of over-100-m.p.h. driving during the running of the 1948 Mille Miglia. All in all, it seemed to be a solid design with years of utility ahead. But the price was high for the market — at a list of £1,500 for the roadsters the purchase tax in Britain was a whopping £834 16s 8d. Healey went to work to build a similar model which could be sold for under £1,000 in England. The result was the "Silverstone" Healey, introduced July 20, 1949, almost precisely the same as the first roadster but simpler, plainer and lighter. Price of this car, at the factory, was £975 plus a much lighter purchase tax.

Later, in December, 1949, talks began between Donald Healey and George W. Mason, president of Nash-Kelvinator Corporation, concerning the possibility of collaborating on a sports car. A prototype was entered at Le Mans in 1950, and succeeded in beating all American-engined competition there, including the Cunningham Cadillacs and a few Allards. The experimental Nash-Healey placed fourth overall, with an average speed of 87.6 m.p.h. for the 24 hours. This was solid evidence of the soundness of the Nash engine and Healey suspension. The car was introduced to the public for the first time at the London and Paris auto shows in the fall of 1950, and made its first American appearance at the Chicago show early in 1951. It received a tremendous publicity boost at the Le Mans race in 1951 by again beating all American-engined competition plus a field of Ferraris, a Lancia, several Jaguars and Aston Martins. In total distance covered it was sixth, with 2,142.58 miles in 24 hours.

Again at Le Mans the following year, one of the two team Nash-Healeys came home a solid third behind the two winning Mercedes, traveling 2,185.9 miles for an average of 91.1 m.p.h. The other Nash-Healey dropped out early. For the third consecutive year, the Nash engine had proved to be the best American engine in the race.

Healey dropped all his other projects to devote full time and plant space to the assembly of the Nash-Healeys. The frame and suspension were built at Healey; the body was designed by Healey but the panels were fabricated elsewhere and shipped to the

Healey plant; the engine, transmission, clutch, and rear axle came from Nash in America. All the finished cars were promptly shipped from England to America where they were distributed through Nash agencies.

Except for the large displacement of the engine, the Nash-Healey closely resembled a standard British sports car. Healey had taken his Silverstone chassis virtually intact as the basis for the Nash-Healey. The Nash engine was a long-stroke six of conventional pushrod-operated overhead-valve design, the same engine used to power the Nash Ambassadors. For use in the sports car a few modifications had been made — higher compression ratio, reworked intake manifolding, hotter cam, twin S.U. carburetors. At first the reported output was 125 b.hp. at 4,000 r.p.m., but later that figure was raised to 140 at the same crankshaft speed. The transmission was a standard three-speed device plus an automatic overdrive. One important change had been made in the operation of the overdrive to adapt it to competition. On most automatic-overdrive setups, engagement is effected by releasing the throttle momentarily so that engine vacuum can make the shift. When the driver wishes to return to direct drive for maximum acceleration, he floorboards the accelerator and a switch under the throttle pedal returns the transmission to the lower gear. On the Nash-Healey, the overdrive was engaged in the ordinary way, but the kickdown switch was moved up to the steering column so the driver did not have to use full throttle.

When Farina came into the Nash picture, the Nash-Healey became a three-country car as the body work was assigned to the Italian plant. A hard-top coupe was added to the line in 1953.

At Le Mans in 1953 the Nash-Healey showed up again for racing, but for the first time in years it was not the only member of the Healey stable at the starting line. A new car, the Austin-Healey, had been added. Once again Donald Healey had earned a cozy agreement with a major manufacturer, this one with Austin on the strength of the showing of the prototype Austin-Healey, then called the Healey Hundred, at Earls Court.

The Nash-Healey finished 11th in the 24-hour race, but the Austin-Healey team was not far behind. Gatsonides and Lockett pushed their car into 12th place, and the duo of Beckquart and Wilkins were 14th. This showing, coupled with the announcement that the makers intended to market the Austin-Healey for under $3,000, intrigued fans on both sides of the Atlantic.

At the heart of the new car was the old Austin A-90 engine, a substantial long-stroke four of 162.2 cubic inches displacement that develops 90 b.hp. at 4,000 r.p.m. and 144 foot-pounds torque at 2,000. Such high torque at low engine speed is one of the competition assets of the Austin-Healey. Another proven asset of the Austin-Healey's engine is its durability — in 1949 a stock Austin A-90 trudged for seven consecutive days to set a mark of 11,850 miles at an average of 70.54 m.p.h.

Use of the Laycock de Normanville overdrive has permitted the installation of a three-speed gearbox rather than the customary British four-speed transmission. With the overdrive, which can be kicked in and out manually at the driver's discretion, the car has five useful forward speeds. In high overdrive — 3.38-to-1 — top speed is estimated at 110 m.p.h. At the safe piston speed of 2,500 feet per minute, the road speed in this same gear is 81.4 m.p.h.

Healey developed a special chassis for the new car. The frame consists of two box-section rails running down the center of the car 17 inches apart. In the rear it passes under the rear axle, in the front it is below the lower wishbones of the front suspensions. The body is carried by brackets extending out from the two rails, and is further supported by two braces which extend downward from the cowl and pass through the engine compartment. Sus-

Austin-Healey set 170 new speed records on the Bonneville Salt Beds in September, 1953. Best speed obtained by one of these modified production sports cars was 142.6 m.p.h. for the flying mile.

son

pension is independent in front, with coil springs and wishbones, and semi-elliptic in the rear.

The Austin-Healey went on a junket to the Bonneville Salt Beds in 1953 and set a number of new records. In stock form, it toured the distances from five miles to 30 hours, averaging 109.243 for the first five miles and 104.000 for the entire 30 hours. A hopped-up Austin-Healey clocked 142.636 for the flying mile, 122.93 for a 12-hour average, during the same series of attempts. Clearly, this was a car of amazing potentialities.

American buyers took to the Austin-Healey immediately. It became the first car to challenge the supremacy of the Jaguar in the medium price class, a situation that led to a minor performance race between the two makes. Jaguar's announcement of the XK140 in 1954 was paralleled by the introduction of a hopped-up Austin-Healey, the 100S.

This was no superficial hop-up job. Weight had been cut by making the body of a light alloy rather than steel; aerodynamic efficiency had been improved by restyling the front end. The engine underwent extensive re-working. The lower-end bearings were toughened to withstand the higher compression ratio; valves were enlarged; a cylinder head of light alloy replaced the old cast iron part and in the process the siamesed ports were abandoned in favor of separate ports for each cylinder. In addition, a hotter cam with longer duration and higher lift was designed. Result: a horsepower increase of almost 50 percent without sacrifice of reliability.

There were other changes, too, but the most important concerned brakes. Healey decided to go all the way and switch to disk brakes, an improvement long indicated by competition experience.

As a matter of fact, this A-H made its bow as a competition model, a surprising development in view of the fact that Donald Healey had dramatically withdrawn from major competition the same year. In a note to the press, he criticized the current practice of allowing prototypes to race and put in a strong pitch for a return to the stricter limitations of the past, at least to the point where the hottest cars permitted to enter a sports car race would be modified *production* cars. Since this statement was released shortly before Le Mans, the French press reacted in a manner something less than friendly. Healey issued a second statement, pointing out that he had spent a not inconsiderable sum of money in the famous French endurance race in years past and could see little reason for spending more in what would necessarily be a

futile attempt to transform the humble, four-cylinder Austin engine into something to challenge the Ferraris and Jaguar D's.

And then in the late summer at Bonneville, Healey proceeded
to set a two-way average speed of 192.62 with his new Austin-
Healey streamliner, a special-bodied, supercharged version of the
basic design. During the same week, he trotted out the 100S and
clocked a one-way top speed of 143.12 m.p.h., a 24-hour mark of
132.2 m.p.h., the latter a new record for Class D (two to three
liters, 122 to 183 cubic inches). In November, Healey entered two
cars in the Mexican Road Race, but neither managed to put up a
good showing.

The 100S is a natural development of Healey's work to date,
another in the series of highly-salable, cross-bred cars he's produced since the end of World War II.

AT THE CONCLUSION OF WORLD WAR II IN 1945,
William Lyons changed the name of his plant to
Jaguar Cars Ltd., and slammed it back into automobile production at such speed that airplanes
were still being produced to complete govern-

| JAGUAR |

ment contracts on one side of the plant, while new cars were
assembled on the other.

Like most concerns, he went back into business with pre-war
tooling, and the 1946 Jaguar Mark IV can hardly be distinguished
mechanically from the 1939 SS Jaguar. To the car-hungry world
of the post-war years, though, anything new was welcome. The
Mark IV performed well, was finished with a degree of luxury
that was not equalled in American post-war production, and had
a decidedly "classic" look about it that appealed to a surprisingly
large group of enthusiasts.

Realizing that the world would not long be content with 1939
models, Lyons accelerated development of those radically new
cars that he had been planning before the war. Characteristically,
he refused to be rushed into offering a new product until it could
be thoroughly tested and he could feel confident of its performance
and reliability. With the utmost secrecy, the X engine went
through revision after revision — the XA, XB, XC, until the XK

finally reached the prototype stage as a 3,442-c.c. (210 cu. in.) six cylinder model, and a 1970-c.c. (120 cu. in.) four cylinder model of the same design. Carefully disguised cars with the new engines installed were threshed mercilessly over English back roads as weaknesses in the new power plants were sought.

To gain time for this exacting developmental work, Lyons introduced the Jaguar Mark V. It was powered by the same type of 2½ or 3½ liter pushrod-operated ohv engine as previous models, but it was restyled considerably and a few new features appeared to hint at things to come. Torsion bar independent front suspension appeared for the first time to replace the old semi-elliptic springing; full-hydraulic two-leading-shoe brakes improved the stopping power; and, although the car followed neither vintage nor modern lines exactly, its appointments were luxurious and the overall appearance was aristocratic and graceful.

When the now-famous XK120 was unveiled at the London International Motor Show of 1948, the Mark V was forgotten immediately. From its sleek two-seater body to its clean-looking double overhead camshaft engine, it was entirely new. Great sections of the sports-car fraternity were swept off their feet, and other groups that reasoned that no $4,000 car could possibly be effective in competition were embarrassed somewhat when a stock but faultlessly-tuned XK120, running on pump gas, attained an all-time speed record for production cars by covering a publicly observed and officially timed run at 132.6 m.p.h.

Private enthusiasts rushed their Jaguars into competition and found that the new design (though the engine had been planned originally as a reliable power plant for sedans) was a winner. The stock XK's speed was all that was required at that time, the torsion-bar independent front suspension with semi-elliptics to the rear provided good stability at competition speeds, but at the same time the car rode comparatively smoothly, and proved completely docile and maneuverable in traffic. Along with the joy of watching much, much larger American production cars dwindle abruptly in the rear view mirror, the slinky appearance and a very low price made the XK120 an immediate smash hit throughout America. Only the M.G. — which presented classic sports car styling at a minimum price — could claim more credit for developing the American interest in sports cars.

Further and conclusive proof of the new engine's reliability came when, in 1950, a Jaguar ran for 24 hours at Montlhery with an average speed of 107.46 m.p.h. In 1952, again at Montlhery, another XK120 ran continuously for 168 hours (one solid week) to cover 16,851 miles at an average speed of 100.3 m.p.h. At the end of three days of continuous running the average speed was 105.55 m.p.h.

The engine was an in-line six, with two overhead camshafts which acted directly on the cam followers and were driven by two-stage duplex roller chains. The valves were set at a 70 degree angle in hemispherical combustion chambers. The head and pistons were of aluminum alloy, the connecting rods of steel. Much of the high-speed reliability of the engine could be traced to the massive crankshaft with its seven unusually large main bearings. In stock form, the engine produced 160 b.hp. at 5,000 r.p.m.

Responding to the surprising competition success of the new model, and to demands of private owners all over the world, the Jaguar company issued a special booklet on high-speed tuning and offered pistons which gave compression ratios of 7, 8, and 9 to 1; high lift cams; a lightweight flywheel; a dual exhaust system; larger diameter torsion bars; and racing wire wheels. Finally the factory released a more powerful model named the XK120M (Modified) which was fitted with the same speed equipment at the factory and produced 190 b.hp. as delivered.

After the introduction of XK120, Jaguar sales continued to soar until Lyons again found his factory of over 600,000 square feet and a staff of 3,000 people inadequate. A deal was closed with the British government to acquire a million-square-foot factory in Coventry which had been a war-time arsenal. One department at a time, the equipment was moved until the changeover was complete in December of 1952.

In 1950 Lyons considered that the XK120 design had been adequately tested both by factory-sponsored endurance trials, and by private enthusiasts in competition throughout the world; so a surprise entry in the London Motor Show of that year was the new Jaguar Mark VII sedan. It was powered with the XK120 engine, and based on the Mark V chassis, slightly modified so that the longer power plant could be moved five inches forward to allow more passenger space. The all-steel body, though breaking completely with former Jaguar styling, was pleasing in appearance and allowed ample space for five passengers and luggage. Generally speaking, the car could be considered a sound, 100 m.p.h. family sedan which retained many characteristics of sports-car handling.

Since the Mark VII was frankly designed for the dollar market (as contemporary British automotive publications stiffly pointed out), it should not have been such a nasty shock when a model was released in 1953 which offered a convenient and efficient Borg-Warner automatic transmission in place of the cherished, centrally-mounted shift lever. The Mark VII Jaguar, in spite of its rather bulbous saloon body, was based on a sports car chassis in the midst of which a self-shifting gearbox seemed utterly out of place to the knowledgeable British critic. However, the Mark VII had been designed primarily to meet the needs of a certain discriminating class of American motorist and the optional Borg-Warner box, closely similar to the Merc-o-Matic transmission, was a distinct success overseas.

The English were quietly pleased with the startling accomplishments of the production XK120 in competition, but when the new competition model, the XK120C, appeared as a surprise entry at the Le Mans 24 Hour Race of 1951, the British reputation for dignity and reserve suffered a frightful setback among the spectators. The English section of the stands dissolved into a happy, turbulent pandemonium as a C model driven by Moss and Fairman moved out in the fourth lap to take the lead from the highly imposing modified 4½ liter Grand Prix Talbot.

Moss set such a blistering pace that he successfully broke up much of the competition. He steadily increased his lead, breaking records in the 18th, 20th, and 31st lap — the last at 105.85 m.p.h. When he retired in the 92nd lap with a rod through the side of the crankcase, another XK120C driven by Walker and Whitehead was in second place and automatically took over the lead. So from the fourth lap on, Jaguar led the race and was never seriously threatened. By the time 23 hours had elapsed, it was announced that Jaguar had broken the previous distance record, and when the C crossed the finish line it had covered 2,244 miles at an average speed of 93.50 m.p.h. For the first time in 16 years, an English car had won the greatest distance race of them all.

Long before a comprehensive description of the new XK120C filtered down through the ecstatic British press, it became apparent that Lyons had reversed the standing policy of his company and was entering competition with a vengeance. The competition model was placed in extremely limited production at a remarkably low price. But money alone couldn't buy one. The cars were for distribution only to drivers known as consistent competition entries.

The power plant of the XK120C was the regular XK120 engine, factory tuned and with the speed equipment listed in the tuning manual, although naturally the engine received such tender care at the factory that it could never seriously be compared with a "kit hop up" version. It developed 210 b.hp. at 5,800 r.p.m. and reportedly had been clocked in competition at something over 150 m.p.h.

The greatest modifications were made in the chassis and suspension system. The chassis framework was constructed of tubular steel, triangulated for strength, and with additional rigidity given in the horizontal plane by a much-drilled series of light-gauge channel members. The business-like, streamlined body was sectioned: the hood was hinged forward of the front axle and lifted up, while the rear section was quickly removable.

Front suspension was the same as on the stock Jaguar — wishbones and individual torsion bars — but in the rear the semi-elliptic springs were replaced by a single, center-mounted torsion bar. The central mounting gave the effect of two short torsion bars while economically solving the problem of transverse location at the same time. Each end of the torsion bar was connected to the rear axle by means of a trailing link. The system was refined further by a single torque-reaction damper which was coupled

Jaguar XK120 fixed-head coupe appeared in 1951.

to the axle near the right rear wheel in such a way that it also controlled the tendency of that wheel to lift under severe acceleration, as well as to check twisting effects in the axle housing due to acceleration and braking. The entire rear suspension system (patented) was said to provide wheel adhesion "similar to the De Dion axle" and was largely responsible for the superb road-holding qualities which the car has demonstrated.

In 1953 the XK120C Jaguars again repeated their surprise upset at the Le Mans race. In addition to improved top speed, suspension and cooling, the cars were equipped with new disc brakes that gave them a tremendous advantage. Phil Walters, who drove a Cunningham into third place in the same event said, "It was strange to accelerate past the Jaguars in the long straight, outrun them in top speed and then shut off for the turn at the end — only to see the Jaguars go 100 yards or so further into the turn before braking." Previous Jaguar brakes definitely had not been equal to the XK's speed on road circuits; that the defect had surely been eliminated was proved at Le Mans.

Jaguar set a terrific pace from the start, drove steadily, and finished first, second and fourth, with the lead car able to boast an average speed of 106 m.p.h. That was the first time any car had averaged over 100 m.p.h. throughout the entire 24 hours of the Le Mans classic. To prove that the victory was no fluke, the XK120C models went on to finish a close second in the 1953 world's sports car championship, with a total of 27 points to Ferrari's 30. In addition to finishing 1, 2, 4 at Le Mans, Jaguars came in 3, 4 at Sebring, 2, 3 in the Belgian 24-hour race, 2, 6 in the Nurburgring Thousand Kilometer Race, and fourth in the Tourist Trophy — an excellent season's activity.

Jaguar's final *coup* of the season took place late in 1953 on the long straightaway near Jabbeke, Belgium, where the XK's first, famous record of 132.6 m.p.h. was made. This time Jaguar was galled by the recent Austin-Healey record of 142.636 m.p.h. set in Utah and was determined not to let the title of "world's fastest production car" slip away so easily. A standard XK120, *not* a C, was fitted with catalog speed equipment and a modicum of streamlining and under the scrutiny of the Automobile Club of Belgium turned the appalling speed of 172.412 m.p.h. During the same session a Jaguar competition prototype blistered the road at a clocked 178.381 m.p.h., a dramatic gesture to let the world know that Jaguar was not about to rest on the XK's laurels, that even better things were in store.

First to arrive on the scene was the new competition car, labelled simply "D." Three came to Le Mans for the 1954 running of the event. There they met and were defeated by the new 4.9 Ferrari, but if there can be such a thing as a moral victory in a race, it went to Jaguar. The margin of victory Ferrari managed to preserve was 89 seconds — less than a minute and a half in 24 hours.

During the race the new Jag clocked 172.76 m.p.h. for the highest straightaway speed of the day, remarkably close to the 178 m.p.h. posted in Belgium by the prototype the preceding year. And at the end of the race when the index of performance was computed, Jaguar had actually beaten the Ferrari because of the 40 percent greater displacement of the Italian car.

In making the D, Jaguar engineers had built a smaller, lighter, more powerful car. The basic engine was unchanged, but it now produced 250 b.hp. In keeping with its competition, the new Jaguar body was lower, more streamlined than the old XK120C competition model. It even sported a large rear fin as a stabilizer.

Second new Jaguar arrival of the year was the smaller version of the "D" — a 2½-liter (152 cubic inches) competition car. At the Irish Tourist Trophy race two of these cars were entered with the larger "D" and pushed the winning 3-liter Ferrari hard. The fastest Jaguar in the race turned out to be Whitehead and Wharton's 2½-liter.

There were other new Jaguars yet to come. At the Earls Court show in London in 1954, the XK140 made its first appearance. The greatest single improvement over the XK120 was in engine output — the 140 had a higher, fatter torque curve, as well as 30 more horsepower. Also available was a C-type cylinder head for the stock engine, a modification that brought total engine output up to 210 horsepower. These increases were largely brought about by improving the breathing. The valve lift of the stock engine had been raised, and the XKC-type head had larger intake and exhaust ports and a larger exhaust valve.

Changes were also evident in chassis and body. The engine had been moved forward, providing more room for the passengers. Front torsion bars were larger, giving a firmer suspension. Steering was changed to rack and pinion.

During the year 1954, Jaguar's greatest single success as a marque was in the commercial field. The good showing at Le Mans and a subsequent victory at Rheims where the D models placed first and second, plus victory at Le Mans in 1955, showed that William Lyons hadn't deserted competition on the track, but as in the past he turned most of his efforts to business. In the United States the Jaguar continued to be highly popular. Lyons' taste in body design, his ability to mass-produce high performance were unmatched. The prewar SS Jaguars were among the world's most brilliantly conceived cars; the XK120 was easily the most influential postwar sports car; the XK140 represented more performance per dollar than any other car manufactured anywhere in the world.

JENSEN

JENSEN BEGAN ITS LONG CAREER IN THE AUTOMO-bile industry as a bodybuilder for the British trade, eventually branching out into the manufacture of its own chassis and bodies. Up through the postwar era this duality was continued, Jensen having been the firm which manufactured both the Austin A-40 sports and the Austin-Healey bodies.

In the prewar era there were two famous Jensens, the most

1953 Jensen Interceptor is powered by 244 cubic inch, 130 b.hp. ohv Austin engine.

popular of which was the Jensen-Ford combination that began in 1936. These cars are probably best described as stylish hot rods, since they utilized the favorite hot-rod engine and cloaked it in a low, handsome British body with a definite sporting flavor. The famous V-8 had been modified by replacing the stock distributor with a Scintilla Vertex magneto, twin S.U. downdraft carburetors, and a higher compression ratio. A two-speed rear axle was fitted, giving the driver six speeds to use. In high ratio, second gear was good for 75 m.p.h. Top speed was a surprisingly low 83 m.p.h.

Just before the war Jensen changed engines, dropping the Ford in favor of the Nash overhead-valve six-cylinder plant. Performance improved. Top speed was now in the neighborhood of 100 m.p.h., and at 90 m.p.h. in overdrive high the engine was turning over at only 3,000 r.p.m.

After the war the firm began to use a straight-eight engine designed and built by Henry Meadows, Ltd., but shortly changed to what was undoubtedly a less expensive source of power, the big Austin engine. American buyers see little of this power plant since the models it powers, Princess and Sheerline, have never been popular in this country. It is a six-cylinder, pushrod-overhead-valve engine, which produces modest horsepower but quite a lot of torque (See Table), of conventional, long-stroke design. The car matches the engine — it is a conventional, high-speed tourer rather than a sports-competition model. Independent front suspension and a standard semi-elliptic rear suspension have been designed to take care of comfort first and roadability second. Maximum speed is in the neighborhood of 100 m.p.h., depending on the rear-end ratio chosen. In appearance it looks like the Austin A-40 sports and the Austin-Healey, though it is more luxurious than either. As with the Ford and Nash Jensens, the Austin Jensen is intended to be a luxury vehicle. Upholstery is the finest leather obtainable, and the body panels are fitted with a skill that has been lost in most parts of America.

The "Interceptor," as this Jensen has been called, ranks with a number of other European and British automobiles as a skillful compromise between the sports car and the touring car. Its newer running-mate, the 541, is similar but places greater emphasis on performance and less on luxury. Lighter, lower, smaller, more powerful, it has received excellent notices in the British press as one of the most desirable of the closed high-speed cars available. The construction is unusual in that the frame and body supports are welded into one unit. The frame, actually, is the floor of the car with extra support gained from two five-inch tubes running the length of the chassis and a centrally-located cross-member. The body itself is made of fiberglas-reinforced plastic, doubly reinforced at some points by steel.

The engine's higher output is derived largely from the use of three sidedraft S.U. carburetors in place of the Interceptor's single downdraft carburetor, a modification that is simple to make and well worth its price. According to the factory 10 b.hp. is gained. This, coupled with the increased aerodynamic efficiency of the body, provides a top speed that is right around 120 m.p.h. — sufficient to challenge the world-famous Bentley Continental.

But the greatest single appeal of the Jensen 541 is its styling. Where the Bentley Continental is conservative, the Jensen is radical. It doesn't look like the latest in a long line of traditional cars — rather, it resembles the first of a new line.

By de-emphasizing luxury in the 541, Jensen was able to produce it for $1,162 less than the Interceptor. It's still expensive — $3,598 at the factory in England is not a small price for a non-competition car — but probably the cheapest four-passenger, high-performance car in Europe.

Americans have not seen many Jensens since the war, and there are not yet any firm plans for bringing them here in quantity. Just why is not clear. That 541 looks like a solid contender in the U. S. market.

JOWETT

INNOVATION IS SOMETHING ONE DOES NOT ORDINARILY associate with the British, particularly in the manufacture of sports cars. So many of the popular makes are little changed from the prewar designs — M.G. being the foremost example. Quite a few of the postwar sports cars are newly developed, but their engines and chassis follow such traditional lines that they seem like something from the past. One of the few exceptions is the Jowett Jupiter.

Jowett has been in the business since 1901, but the idea of

producing a serious sports car did not take hold there until after the war. In 1948 the first rumors in the British press told of a compact between E.R.A., the famous racing concern, and Jowett to produce a lightweight competition car, and at the London Show in 1949 the car appeared. From E.R.A. came the frame, a highly unusual unit designed by Eberan von Eberhorst, who was formerly with the German Auto Union. It consisted of two straight steel tubes running the length of the car, braced with an X-shaped tubular member in the rear. In front, further support came from a built-up section of tubes which carried the radiator (located in the rear of the engine), the footboard, and the wishbones for the independent front suspension. Springing all the way around was by torsion bars, longitudinal in front, transverse in rear.

The engine of the new Jowett sports car was taken directly from the already successful Jowett Javelin. It was a flat-opposed four of proven reliability and potentially one of the finest small British engines for competition. Displacement was 90.6 cubic inches, barely under the top limit of the 1,100-1,500-c.c. racing class. Bore and stroke were 2.85x3.54 inches; overhead valves were pushrod-operated; compression ratio was originally scheduled to be 7.2-to-1, but by 1953 had worked its way up to 8-to-1.

Top speed of the Jowett Jupiter, as it was named, was about 85 m.p.h. with the 8-to-1 compression ratio, not a surprising figure but one that proved to be good enough to give the marque three consecutive class wins at Le Mans from 1950 through 1952. Acceleration compared favorably with the M.G. and Singer.

In 1953 the Mark 1A Jupiter appeared, but it was little more than a slightly more comfortable version of the original. Not till 1954 did the firm make a more important change, succeeding the Jupiter 1A with the R4 model. On this car the rear torsion bars were replaced by semi-elliptics; the conservative body of the 1A had been thrown out for an entirely new design, highly streamlined, made of laminated plastics. The engine remained the same but top compression ratio had been boosted to 8.5-to-1 with an optional 7.5-to-1 head available. With 8.5-to-1, the engine produced 64 b.hp. at 5,000 r.p.m., and at 6,000 r.p.m. the factory claimed 100 m.p.h. in top gear, more in overdrive, if fitted. Curb weight was very low, 1,568 pounds. This, coupled with the low wind resistance of the body, made the high top speed and excellent acceleration possible. For a firm which had no history of high-performance sports cars, Jowett was unusually successful in the first few years of production of the Jupiter and R4, design-wise, but not commercially. In 1954 the company ceased production.

KURTIS

Until 1953 most sports-car fans considered the American track-racing machine as functionally limited as a merry-go-round mustang. "Stand on it and turn left" was supposed to be the championship drivers' single driving rule, and their machines were good for no other operation. So thought devotees of rack-and-pinion steering and De Dion rear ends. Anyone foolish enough to suggest converting an A.A.A. sprint-car chassis to F.I.A.

Bill Stroppe at the wheel of his Kurtis sports car, rarely beaten in U.S. West Coast competition in 1953. Power unit was side-valve Mercury engine. Front and rear axles are solid, suspension by torsion bars.

sports-car regulations received a heavy-lidded stare of pity and contempt.

After building some 850 track-racing chassis over a 30-year period — probably a world's record — Frank Kurtis of Glendale, California did not agree. The problems he lived with — lived, in fact, to solve — were the fundamental problems of the sports-car designer; stability, handling qualities, tire wear, frontal area, wind drag. His ability to control and improve these factors grew through the years until he built the first Kurtis chassis of the 500 Series in 1952. It was made for Indianapolis but to Kurtis it looked like the prototype of a sports car he would someday build.

When Bill Vukovich drove the Offy-powered roadster at the Speedway that year, it was a revelation. At 180 m.p.h. it was as smooth as a Buick and it handled so beautifully that Vuky could pass other cars in the turns almost as easily as on the straightaways. The new Kurtis led for 375 miles of the 500-mile race, won 75 per cent of the lap prizes and would have been the easy winner, as it was in 1953 and 1954, if steering failure hadn't forced Vukovich to retire with only four laps to go. As Frank Kurtis watched its smooth flight around the 2½-mile oval he knew he had his sports-car prototype.

Early in 1953 the first Kurtis 500 sports car, with the same basic body and chassis, was sold to speed mechanic Bill Stroppe, a former driver of racing midgets. It had been designed to take any current production-car engine but Stroppe ignored the big-displacement power units and installed a hotted-up Mercury engine with a swept volume of 257 cubic inches. Of his first nine West Coast races, Stroppe won seven and lost two! One was lost when the engine's magneto failed, the other when Stroppe deliberately drove off the course to avoid hitting another car. In the 1953 Palm Springs race, the three-speed transmission's second gear became useless early in the main event. Nevertheless, Stroppe crossed the finish line 2½ miles ahead of the second-place finisher! The best European sports cars were unable to catch the new Kurtis.

Although none of the several other Kurtis sports jobs sold during the year approached Stroppe's degree of competition success, the formidable inherent potentialities of these machines had been impressed deeply upon American followers of the sport.

It was a fabulous car to drive. It literally defied the most desperate efforts to break it loose in turns. Whether taking a gentle curve in top gear at 120 m.p.h. or a sharp one in low at 40, the tires bit into the pavement without giving a lateral inch. On patches of sand or gravel they slid sideways until they touched clean pavement; then the car instantaneously resumed its rocketing forward course.

The enormous, conflicting forces of a car cornering at speed are scarcely apparent to the driver of a Kurtis. The camera may record a very slight heeling of the chassis during violent cornering but as far as the driver can tell his mount remains perfectly flat.

This is the all-important virtue of the Kurtis 500 sports car. Such stability is supposed to be an exclusive specialty of the four-wheel independent-suspension system. But Frank Kurtis had built many racing chassis with independent suspension all around, had watched them run in competition and had become convinced that it was not necessarily the answer. His experience was that independent suspension introduced variations in track and camber, and thus in steering geometry, which destroyed an otherwise perfect chassis balance. Furthermore they added weight, parts, joints, and clearances and the less of all these the better.

Because of its flat-riding qualities Stroppe used stock Mercury wheels on his Kurtis. Extra-strong racing wheels just aren't necessary when side-loading on the hubs is so slight. This relatively negligible side-loading had an important effect upon Stroppe's tire wear, just as it had upon the Indianapolis Kurtis 500's, which used less rubber than any of the other cars.

The Kurtis' superb chassis had a disarmingly, almost absurdly simple appearance. The tubular steel frame was as light as it could be made but also had the extreme rigidity essential to control under high stress. Front and rear suspension was by torsion bars which blended so well with the tubular frame structure that it could take a good moment's searching to discover the suspension at all. The torsion bars ran from side to side, wider than the frame itself. Between the axles and the live ends of the torsion bars were "torsion arms" which completed the suspension linkage. By mounting the front bars as far to the front as possible and the rear bars well behind the rear axle, the distance between critical pivot points was made about two feet longer than the wheelbase and a few inches wider than the frame. And by causing these critical points of the suspension to form the largest possible rectangle, a considerable "bracing" effect with good stability was achieved. Solid axles eliminated variations which could affect steering and added to overall chassis rigidity.

The sports-car body derived from the Vukovich body which, in turn, was based on the world's-record-holding Cummins Diesel racing car which Kurtis had completed in 1952. The contours of this body were developed at great cost in the full-scale wind tunnel at the University of Wichita to achieve the smallest possible frontal area and wind drag.

The authors have road-tested a Kurtis-Cadillac owned by Frank McGurk of Inglewood, California, with the following results:

ACCELERATION

Speed	Seconds
0-30	1.5
0-45	2.5
0-60	4.7
0-100	11.1
80-125	12.4
Standing ¼-mile	13.6

Approximate top speed — 150 m.p.h.

Kurtis 500 M sports model, introduced November, 1954.

But the 500K, as the first Kurtis sports car was called, was not enough to satisfy the customers. The greatest single drawback was appearance. Most people don't like to drive something that looks so frankly like a competition machine. This brought another design out of the Kurtis workshops — the 500M, introduced late in 1954. Like the 500K, the M was obtainable with any engine the customer wanted. If you asked Kurtis to install the engine of his choice, you received a Cadillac V-8 complete with Hydra-Matic transmission. This was strictly a road car, and the factory believed that the Hydra-Matic was the ideal compromise between performance and ease.

As a running mate, there was another new model, the 500X. Made solely for racing in the under-1500-cubic-centimeter class of sports car events, it was designed around a special Offenhauser engine. Meyer and Drake had taken the 105-cubic-inch Offy, reduced the bore sufficiently to bring displacement down to the required 91 cubic inches. Coupled with the 1948 M.G. four-speed transmission, this engine was capable of performance with the best of the OSCA's and Porsches.

Though Kurtis' efforts are still necessarily scaled small, there are many who believe that he is the logical man to build *the* American sports car. His methods are reminiscent of the old Ettore Bugatti formula: "Build the best racing chassis you can, then make it your regular stock in trade."

LAGONDA

THE VENERABLE LAGONDA MAKE WAS DUE FOR many postwar changes. First the luxurious and powerful Bentley-designed V-12 was abandoned in favor of a lighter car and a smaller, high-performance engine. A superb six-cylinder double-overhead-cam power plant of 2,580 c.c. (157.4 cu. in.) displacement was designed by W. O. Bentley and three cars were built. Then the new design, a stock of parts and the respected Lagonda name were bought by David Brown, the aggressive and dynamic new owner of Aston Martin.

Brown did not acquire the Lagonda works, and therefore production of the new cars proceeded slowly. In 1949 the Lagonda engine was used to power the Le Mans Aston Martins which became the basis of the DB2 models, and by 1950 a healthy number of DB2 Aston Martins and Brown-built Lagondas had been manufactured. Both used the same power unit (described in detail in the Aston Martin chapter), and what the DB2 was to sports cars Lagonda was in the area of fast and aristocratic tourers.

In addition to the 105-b.hp. engine, Lagonda had such progressive features as all-around independent suspension; by coil springs and A-arms at the front and at the rear by a highly original variant of the De Dion system, with double-jointed half shafts and springing by torsion bars. It had rack-and-pinion steering. And it had a light, stiff, true-cruciform frame, with brake drums mounted inboard on the differential housing, an arrangement which reduced unsprung weight by one-third.

Until 1953 Lagonda coachwork provided a good-looking if not inspired example of the traditional British approach. In 1954 it changed entirely, capitulating finally to the postwar epidemic of pontoon-type contours. The sweeping front fenders were replaced by smooth slabs, but Lagonda's designers were apparently unable to make a clean and total break with the past. The car retained vestigial rear-fender bulges and an uncurved windshield which looked oddly anachronistic in its "jello-mold" surroundings. The engine in this car was basically unchanged but its displacement was increased to 2,922 c.c. (178.3 cu. in.) by enlargement of the bore, *à la* Aston Martin DB3S. Compression ratio went up

1955 3-liter Lagonda 4-door sedan, Tickford body.

from the 6.5-to-1 of the earlier models to 8.16-to-1, and output was increased to a claimed 140 b.hp. Price went up too, from about $5,500 to about $6,300. Since the additional purchase tax brought the total cost in England to the rarified $9,000 stratum, it seemed likely that this new Americanized Lagonda was intended primarily for export sale.

Three Lagonda body styles were offered to the public in 1954 — two-door and four-door sedans and a convertible coupe. But the highlight of the year as far as this marque was concerned was David Brown's stillborn effort to match big-displacement Ferrari and Cunningham might with a new competition car.

The body, frame and running gear were simply modifications of the Aston Martin DB3S. The engine was the car's really arresting feature, being a V-12 with dual overhead camshafts for each bank of cylinders. Its 4,487 c.c. (273.8 cu. in.) displacement was accomplished by the fantastically over-square bore and stroke of 82.6 by 69.9 mm. (3.25 x 2.75 in.). Three big four-throat Weber carburetors gave the massive engine a startling steam-calliope look.

It was a formidable contender as it screamed around the Le Mans course. But a crash in the early hours of the 24-hour race caused its early retirement, and nothing further was heard of this exciting car.

LANCIA

BIG, BLACK-HAIRED GIANNI (PRONOUNCED Johnny) Lancia was the image of his father in more ways than the physical. He was scarcely more than a baby when Vincenzo Lancia died in 1937, but already he knew his heritage. He studied engineering after the war and then took over the duties of managing the factory his father founded. He completed his studies in on-the-job training that other young men might well envy — working with the great engineer Vittorio Jano on a car that revived the Lancia name and fame with unforgettable impact.

The new car was designed by Jano to replace Vincenzo's famous and long-lived Aprilia, which after 14 years of production was, not surprisingly, obsolescent. Thus in May of 1950 visitors to the Turin Automobile Show discovered that symphony in mechanical engineering called the Lancia Aurelia. It was immediately compared to the sensational and far-more-costly Spanish Pegaso and the comparison did credit to both. The Aurelia was as impressive for the quality finish of each component as it was for daringly advanced engineering. First sight of the sectioned display chassis shown at Turin was enough to thoroughly enslave the *cognoscenti*. And when unostentatious little Aurelias began beating big Ferraris in important races, the uninitiated public was given undeniable evidence that here was vastly more automobile than met the eye.

The Aurelia's V-6 engine was an exciting and revolutionary innovation. Its displacement was 1,754 c.c. (107 cu. in.) and it produced 56 b.hp. at 4,000 r.p.m. which, in terms of piston speed (about 2,000 feet per minute), was loafing. For racing purposes output was ultimately pushed beyond 100 b.hp. Earlier V-4 Lancias had always utilized an ultra-narrow angle of vee with a single head for both banks of cylinders, but the V-6 had two distinct banks opened out to form a 60-degree angle. Both banks and the upper half of the crankcase formed a single light-alloy casting in which replaceable wet liners were fitted. This casting carried a six-throw crankshaft with four large main journals providing a generous amount of overlap and, therefore, stiffness in the shaft. Both main and rod bearings had fine anti-friction alloy centrifugally cast in bronze shells. Like the earliest Lambdas, the Aurelia had pistons which used three compression rings and two oil rings.

Each bank of three cylinders had its own cast-aluminum head, with bronze valve seats and cast-iron valve guides. The combustion chambers were hemispherical and contained vee-inclined valves which, with startling originality, were slanted longitudinally instead of laterally. The valves were operated by rocker arms, concentric springs, and hollow aluminum pushrods from a 12-lobe, chain-driven camshaft situated just above the crankshaft.

Carburetion was by a two-throat Solex mounted between the banks and feeding two water-jacketed, three-port manifolds. Each cylinder had its own exhaust port, each bank its own three-branch "header" and separate exhaust system. Water jacketing around plugs, ports and valves left nothing to be desired and thermostatically controlled shutters were provided in front of the radiator core. There was a thermostatic valve in the water-circulating system.

The Aurelia had no clutch, no bell housing at the rear of its engine, but only a small flywheel carrying the starter ring gear and a cast light-alloy universal-joint spider. The spider was coupled to a two-piece small-diameter drive shaft running at engine speed. Potentially detrimental vibrations were absorbed by self-aligning rubber couplings at the front, middle and rear of the shaft.

In place of the normal differential housing was a light-alloy casting incorporating, front to rear, single-plate clutch, four-speed gearbox, and final drive assembly. All transmission gears were indirect ratios and top gear was an overdrive. A touch to titillate the connoisseur was a separate oil pump in the gearbox which lubricated all cogs and bearings under pressure. The rear brakes

Lancia competition sports car. Body is by Pinin Farina.   *Publifoto*

were carried inboard, on each side of the differential housing.

This entire, compact rear-end unit was mounted on the chassis by means of rubber-insulated connections, and it constituted sprung weight. In the interest of long universal-joint life, angular movement of the joints was kept as small as possible by using the longest possible rear-axle half-shafts. The outboard universal joints were actually located outside of the wheels. This unorthodox detail was one of many adopted in the interest of genuine reliability. Springing of the independent rear wheels was by coils and trailing A-arms.

The Aurelia's front suspension dated back to the Lambda of 1922, but was still modern and supremely adequate. Worm-and-wheel steering, in the best racing-car tradition, eliminated all traces of backlash and three quick turns brought the front wheels from lock to lock.

Thanks to the arrangement of the Aurelia's drive train, no foot-room was sacrificed to a transmission tunnel and scarcely any to the driveshaft tunnel. Seating completely adequate for six passengers was provided by the unit-construction body. The front-seat backs were adjustable for rake and could be laid flat to form a bed.

Lancia Aurelia transmission and rear-axle assembly.

All critics agreed that the V-6 engine was very satisfactorily smooth throughout its entire speed range and that the car could be driven flat out indefinitely — it had been specifically designed for that type of service. Its roadworthiness, even on wet Alpine roads, was remarkable.

The car deserved to be an immediate market success, and it was. Soon it was offered with alternative displacements and outputs, ranging up to 2,457 c.c. (149.9 cu. in.) and 118 b.hp. at 5,000 r.p.m. Lancia, for the first time in over four decades, had a car that was a real threat in competition. An Aurelia won its class in the 1951 Mille Miglia, ahead of all the two-liter Ferraris and finished second overall, behind a 4.1 Ferrari. In the Italian Dolomite race Aurelias placed first, second, and fourth, winning outright, in competition against Ferraris ranging from two to 4.1 liters. *Road and Track* brought two Aurelias over for the 1951 Carrera Panamericana, but sheer bad luck kept them from making a good showing.

In 1952 an Aurelia won the two-liter class at Le Mans and finished third in the Mille Miglia, ahead of Caracciola's 300SL Mercedes and behind Bracco's 4.1 Ferrari and Kling's 300SL. Aurelias took the first three places in the Targa Florio and Maglioli finished fourth in the Panamericana, behind two Mercedes 300SL's and Chinetti's 4.1 Ferrari.

Up to this time the competition Lancias had been standard Aurelia touring models tuned for racing and fitted with stock bodies. For the 1953 season a new competition chassis was made, powered by an approximately three-liter version of the V-6 engine. Aerodynamic open and closed two-place bodies were built for these cars. Retained from the Aurelia were the V-6 engine and independent rear suspension with transmission built into the rear center-section. Abandoned were unit-body-frame construction and Lambda-derived front springing. The new independent front suspension was by transverse leaf spring and trailing links. Huge inboard-mounted front-brake assemblies were secured to the frame and were connected to the wheels by short universal-jointed shafts. Thus, front-end unsprung weight was greatly reduced and a solution was found to the problem of combining big brakes with small wheels.

These cars were highly experimental and ran in different form in six races during the 1953 season. Four of them, with closed bodies and 2.6-liter (159 cu. in.) supercharged engines, were tried at Le Mans with discouraging results, due primarily to blower-drive failure. In the Mille Miglia Lancias ran with open bodies and three-liter (183 cu. in.) unblown engines and finished third and eighth. This seemed the most promising combination and it was retained for the Targa Florio. Lancia won. For the Panamericana, at the end of the season, the open bodies were used again and displacement was increased slightly to 3.1 liters (189 cu. in.). Against some of the world's toughest competition the Lancias ran in a pack for the entire 1,934 miles and finished first, second and third. With this remarkable demonstration of reliable and consistent performance Lancia was firmly established as a major force in international sports-car competition. The next year's results bore out the make's '53 promise. In '54 the 3.1 engine was enlarged to 3.3 liters, a size which had been tried in the previous year's G.P. at Monza with the result that Lancia took second place. In this form it set new records and swept to absolute wins in some of Europe's most classic and important races, the Mille Miglia and the Targa Florio, to name two. In the same year the Aurelia took first overall in the Monte Carlo Rally and a nearly-endless string of other races.

The second postwar model of the marque was introduced at the April, 1953 Turin show. It replaced the vintage-of-1939 Ardea and was named Appia, for the most ancient and famous of the Roman roads. Vittorio Jano and Gianni Lancia were credited jointly for the Appia's design. In appearance and detail it was largely a scaled-down Aurelia and every bit as much a quality car. Like the venerable Lambda, it featured unit-body-chassis construction, typical Lancia independent front suspension, and a V-4 power unit. But for sheer compactness the Appia engine put the Lambda to shame.

From the front of the fan pulley to the rear of the flywheel its length was just 13¾ inches, and the cylinder block itself was 9½ inches long. Displacement was 1,090 c.c. (66.5 cu. in.) and 38 b.hp. was produced at 4,800 r.p.m., giving a moderate .57 b.hp. per cubic inch. An even narrower than before 10-degree vee angle was used in the cast-iron cylinder block which was assembled to a separate light-alloy crankcase which, of course, carried a separate sump, also cast in deeply-finned light alloy. The tiny four-throw crankshaft was counterweighted and electronically balanced. Being very short, it required only two main bearings which, like the rod journals, ran in indium-coated bronze shells.

The single head for all four cylinders was a light-alloy casting retained by ten studs and fitted with bronze valve seats and cast-iron guides. Two camshafts located on each side of the crankcase operated laterally (unlike the Aurelia) vee-inclined valves in approximately hemispherical combustion chambers. Two siamesed intake ports on the right-hand side of the engine were fed by a single-throat carburetor and four exhaust ports on the opposite side discharged to a single-pipe, twin-muffler exhaust system.

The Appia's clutch, transmission and rear suspension were all quite orthodox, the solid rear axle riding on semi-elliptic springs. Steering was by worm-and-sector gears, for practical purposes as desirable as the Aurelia's more costly worm-and-wheel.

The foundation of the body was the floor, which included the box-section "frame rails." This, the firewall, engine-compartment side walls' wheel arches and roof were all steel stampings and made up the stressed portion of the body-chassis unit. To save weight, hood, fenders and trunk lid were of aluminum.

This little car had a top speed of about 75 m.p.h., and it was geared to sustain that speed all day. It did not have the "geared to the road" handling qualities of the considerably more expensive Aurelia but in its size and price it was one of the world's best. Like all products that carried the blue-flag-on-a-lance trademark, the Appia seemed to prove that the policies of Italy's second-largest automobile-manufacturing firm were still determined by engineers, not by cost accountants and stylists.

LEA-FRANCIS

Anyone who remembers how United States midget-auto racing mushroomed into really big business for a few years after the war can readily understand what an attractive market it must have seemed to overseas builders of small, high-output engines.

The management of Lea-Francis Cars, Ltd., knew that no car could crack the market unless it could compete successfully against the Meyer and Drake Offenhausers that were winning the lush purses at the midget tracks. But R. H. Rose, L.-F.'s enthusiastic and enterprising technical director, felt certain that their current

1½-liter racing engine, enlarged to 1,674 c.c. (102 cu. in.), would have a reasonable chance aginst the Offy's potent 102.4 inches. On paper it looked pretty good. The Lea-Francis engine was basically the same rational design that had been developed late in the Thirties — twin camshafts high up on each side of the block operating 90-degree-inclined overhead valves in polished hemispherical combustion chambers. The engine developed 125 b.hp. at 6,000 r.p.m. on a methanol-benzol-castor oil mixture with 14-to-1 compression ratio, and it was possible to modify to 8-to-1 for normal fuel. The Offenhauser reached 127 b.hp. at 6,200 r.p.m. — close enough for L.-F. to be in the running.

Consequently, a Lea-Francis crew sailed for America in May, 1948 bearing with them a racing engine, a two-seater sports model bulging with spare parts and a sturdy determination to give the engine any quick, race-bred modifications it might require to make it a hot export item to United States midget-car owners. The engine was installed in a midget chassis as soon as possible after arrival, and during the next six weeks the *équipe* travelled 7,000 miles over the Eastern racing circuits in a gallant attempt to learn

1951 Lea-Francis sports model was this open, two-four seater powered by 152 cubic inch, ohv, 100-b.hp. engine.

as much as possible as quickly as possible about what was a virtually unknown sport in England.

It is to Lea-Francis' credit that they actually won a few heat races — nothing spectacular, but enough to whet their appetites for more. In the middle of June they returned home, having attended 15 meetings, run the car in 26 races, and worked feverishly for the solid six weeks. At the end of the year there was an announcement that the firm was producing a special version of the 1½-liter engine for midget competition, but little was heard after that, and it is assumed that the project died a natural, painless death.

Why did the Grand Experiment fail? There were a number of reasons. First was the fact that the Offenhausers, descendants of Harry Miller's thoroughbred engines, had the enormous initial advantage of constant development under extremely specialized racing conditions over a period of decades. The engine specifications were all on the Offy's side. No exact weight figures are available, but it is known that the L.-F. engine was pounds heavier than the Offenhauser. More important, probably, was the bore-stroke relationship of the L.-F. engine — 2.88×3.94 — a proportion somewhat obsolete for racing purposes, compared to the Offy's closer-to-square 3.00×3.63 bore and stroke. The Offy's dual overhead camshafts were another factor; the traditional Lea-Francis valve gear, which was quite efficient and rugged enough for ordinary hard use, simply could not function as nimbly. It all boiled down to the fact that midget racing was just too tough, too specialized, and too effectively monopolized by Offenhauser because of that make's supreme adaptation to the job.

This admirable but quixotic episode was an unhappy chapter in the generally successful Lea-Francis history. After the war the make renewed its popularity with English consumers with touring models that were almost indistinguishable from prewar except for stressed-skin aluminum bodies that were a bit more streamlined. Two four-cylinder engines were offered, one 1,496 c.c. (91.2 cu. in.), the other 1,767 c.c. (107.8 cu. in.), developing 50 and 56 b.hp. at 4,700 r.p.m. with 7.25-to-1 compression ratio. The 111-inch wheelbase chassis specifications were the same as for the 1939 model.

The first postwar sports model was introduced in 1948. Wheelbase had been shortened to 99 inches and a good-looking convertible four-seater sports-body fitted. The 1½ liter engine, modified by dual carburetion and higher-lift camshafts, developed 64

1953 Lea-Francis four-door, four-light saloon is powered by 109 cubic inch, ohv engine. Wheelbase is 111 inches.

b.hp. at 5,300 r.p.m. with top speed in the neighborhood of 80 m.p.h. Further development was apparent in the 1950 models. The 1½-liter engine was dropped, the same chassis now carrying a 1,767-c.c. engine developing 65 b.hp. The biggest change was the addition of independent front suspension by torsion bars to this chassis and the introduction of a brand-new 2½-liter engine in a slightly heavier chassis. Both had 111-inch wheelbases and independent front suspension.

The new engine was identical to the old except for displacement and a few minor details. Valves were inclined 80 degrees instead of 90, rockers were grouped in pairs under four detachable boxes, and the twin, high camshafts were driven by a single duplex chain, thereby eliminating the helical gears from the drive. With 6.8-to-1 compression the engine developed 95 b.hp. at 4,000 r.p.m. in the standard sedan model. The new power plant was fitted to the sports model and with dual carburetion, hotter cams and 7.63-to-1 compression was capable of 120 to 125 b.hp. at 5,200 r.p.m. This engine became the power unit of two British Formula II "Grand Prix" competition cars, the Connaught and the supercharged Turner, thus achieving prominence in a form of racing far more suited to it than the American midget variety.

MASERATI

AFTER THE WAR THE THREE MASERATI BROTHERS continued to work at the Alfieri Maserati plant and in 1947 produced a new car, the A6G, for the Geneva Show. It was an effort at a popularly-priced Maserati sports car and, although the chassis was in the Grand Prix tradition, the six-cylinder engine was a departure in that it used a chain- rather than gear-driven single overhead camshaft. The 1.5 liter engine was set up to run on alcohol, a fact which limited its suitability for road use. The chassis had a tubular frame, i.f.s. by coil springs and A-arms, and half-elliptic springs at the rear. The engine in later versions was increased in displacement to two liters, and three carburetors re-

1953 Maserati Type A6GCS has a dry weight of 1,540 pounds. 1,988 cc, (121.3 cubic inch) engine develops 160 b.hp. at 7,000 r.p.m.

placed the original single Weber. This engine developed 130 b.hp. at 6,000 r.p.m. and gave the car a speed of better than 125 m.p.h. The A6G was raced widely in sports events and stripped of road equipment was an effective Formula II contender.

At the same time a much detuned 65 b.hp. sports touring version with the old 1.5 liter displacement and single carburetor was marketed. Its suspension was modified by substitution of coil springs for the rear half-elliptics. The coachwork was by Pinin Farina in smooth coupe and convertible coupe form, and the cars' interiors were handsomely finished, usually in striking and beautiful corduroy.

In 1948 a new Maserati car, the 4CLT, was introduced for racing in Argentina. It was powered by a four-cylinder two-stage-blown double overhead camshaft 1.5 liter engine with equal bore and stroke and in eight-branch exhaust manifold. It won almost everything that South America had to offer, and in 1951, enlarged to 1,730 c.c. (105.6 cu. in.) its engine was used by Piero Taruffi to power his twin-boom speed projectile "Italcorsa," in which he set a new flying mile record for the two-liter class at 185.49 m.p.h.

The 4CLT was the last of the "Maserati-made" Maseratis. Soon after its introduction the Maserati brothers left the firm and went home to Bologna to build their OSCA cars. The Alfieri Maserati firm was left with their name, their assets and their achievements — and a competition record that only a few makes could better: 106 firsts, 112 seconds and 104 thirds in major Grand Prix, Sports and other events from 1927 to 1949.

The new management of Alfieri Maserati lost little time in picking up the gauntlet. A new six-cylinder engine was designed, and in 1952 the famous Italian engineer Colombo, who was responsible for some of the best Alfas and Ferraris, was hired to develop it both for Formula II and sports car use.

Colombo raised top speed of the G. P. engine from 6,500 r.p.m. to 8,600 r.p.m., and output was increased to 200 b.hp. at 8,000 r.p.m. with a 15 to one compression ratio. He redesigned the combustion chambers, in a unique manner. Each chamber had two valves, inclined in a 90-degree vee, and a hemispherical transverse cross-section but an inverted U-shape in longitudinal section. The extremities of the U were bevelled, as though the U were about to form a Y, and in each bevelled side of each chamber a spark plug was provided, the dual ignition accounting for a 5 percent rise in power output over the original single-plug version of the engine. This arrangement was adapted to the sports Maserati, and gave 160 b.hp. on 80 octane fuel; in 1954 trim, power output was raised another ten b.hp. Suspension on both versions was by A-arms with torsion bars at the front, quarter-elliptic springs at the rear, and radius arms and anti-roll bars front and rear. Both had front brake drums with transverse cooling fins, and rear drums with normal fins. The sports body was wide and low with smooth flaring integral fenders, and was strongly reminiscent of Colombo's Alfa "Flying Saucer."

The factory's revived interest in racing began to show immediate dividends. In late 1952 a 12-plug six took an unexpected second place at the G.P. at Monza for Formula II cars, a bare 70 seconds behind Ascari's winning Ferrari, and the next year won the same race against the same competition after a 312-mile neck-and-neck duel.

Its prowess in sports trim was affirmed mercilessly in 1954. The two-liter Maserati won its class in no less than 24 important European events, including the Targa Florio in which Luigi Musso's Maserati had the second-fastest time of all, regardless of engine size. The marque's rise in Formula I competition — beyond the scope of this book — was equally meteoric and confirmed the already ample evidence that a renaissance had taken place at the Modenese factory that wears the Bolognese arms.

MERCEDES-BENZ

A YEAR AFTER THE END OF WORLD WAR II, Mercedes-Benz was back in production. All the once-mighty firm could turn out in its bombed-out, looted factories was a dressed-up version of the prewar 170V, but this was enough to keep the name alive and bring in money for the long expensive process of rebuilding. The first signs of new creativeness came in 1949 when the 170V was split into two types and redesigned — the 170S and the 170 Diesel. As before, the 170 series was a low-displacement, economy passenger car with no pretensions toward being a sports machine or a classic.

The Mercedes 300 introduced in 1951 was something else entirely, a luxury car with the quality, if not the classic lines, of

Rolls-Royce and Daimler. However, its performance disappointed those who remembered the great days of the SS and 540K. Then, in 1952, Mercedes proved it was ready to do business in its time-honored way. That year both the 300S and 300SL were introduced.

Nothing could have been more dramatic than the manner in which the 300SL rocketed to international fame. Running in the rain in the 19th Mille Miglia, three Mercedes coupes challenged the Ferrari domination of the sports-car world. Drivers of the Mercedes were Lang, Kling and the aging genius of Mercedes' days of glory, Rudolph Caracciola. Ferrari's top driver, Ascari, was at Indianapolis and Villoresi was out with injuries, but the remainder of the Ferrari aces were present — Taruffi, Bracco and others. Bracco was driving the new 2.9-liter Ferrari.

Mercedes made the first error when Lang cracked his rear wheel against a milepost after 136.7 miles and was retired for the day. At the next check point, Bracco led in a Ferrari and Kling was second. Caracciola trundled along well in the rear, biding his time as ordered. By Aquila, however, Kling was ahead by eight minutes. In Rome, Kling was still ahead. Shortly after that Taruffi went out and Bracco was the only Ferrari within striking distance. By a tremendous feat of driving he managed to pass the Mercedes and win, but by only 4½ minutes. Caracciola finished fourth, slightly over eight minutes behind the third-place Lancia and 34 minutes behind Kling. For a first appearance, the silver Mercedes had shown up extremely well — one car out due to accident, which can happen to any team, and the other two finishing near the top without mechanical difficulty.

During the post-mortems, Italian and British drivers were sorely concerned. It wasn't so much the speed and road-holding abilities of the 300SL's that bothered them as it was the demonstration that the Mercedes team organization was still as good as it had been in the days before the war. There could be no doubt of the seriousness of Mercedes' intentions, no question that the ability of Neubauer — Mercedes' team director — to weld his mechanics, service personnel and drivers into a cohesive, winning unit was as great as it had ever been. It required no extra-normal powers to predict that Mercedes would be the car to beat that season.

At Berne, where the 300SL team appeared next, this proved true. Mercedes took the first three places, with Lang recording the fastest lap of the field. Shortly after that, at Le Mans, Mercedes won first and second places, Lang and Reiss setting new distance records with their car. Le Mans showed again the cool teamwork of Neubauer's crew. Both of the winning cars held a steady, unhurried pace throughout most of the race, deliberately running behind the Gordini and the Ferraris and the Cunningham, waiting for them to blow up. They obligingly did, and the German cars were not challenged thereafter.

At Nurburgring, Mercedes surpassed its own previous records by winning the first four places, this time with roadster-bodied 300SL's rather than hard-top coupes. Fastest lap went to Karl Kling. To finish the season properly, the Mercedes team journeyed across the Atlantic to Mexico and once again walked away with top honors, the first two places in the sports category being won by Kling and Lang in coupes. John Fitch, the American sports-car driver, was well on his way to third place in one of the 300SL roadsters when he was disqualified for turning back after the start of one of the legs of the race. In Mexico, again, it was nerveless, consistent driving and superb preparation that won over cars which were recording faster times for shorter distances.

At this point Mercedes withdrew from active competition in the sports-car category. Withdrew completely, even ignoring the defiant challenge of the Ferrari team to meet for the 1953 season or, lacking that, just one more race anywhere, anytime. As far as the Stuttgart works was concerned, the superiority of Mercedes was proved beyond question.

Not once during this successful 1952 season, nor in the season following, were the Mercedes sports cars made available to the public. On this point there was considerable unhappy discussion in other countries, since sports cars are customarily production chassis and engines and, however expensive to buy or difficult to produce, are offered for sale. Mercedes, however, disregarded the grumbling and kept the competition cars to itself, releasing only the 300 and 300S for the market in those years.

The engine of the three cars is the same, an in-line six with overhead valves operated by a single overhead camshaft. Bore and stroke are 3.35×3.46, a displacement of 183 cubic inches. There is a seven-main-bearing crankshaft and an oil cooler. Combustion-chamber construction is unusual in that there is no opening in the cylinder head. The top of the block is cut at a 30-degree angle to the horizontal, and the face of the cylinder head is cut at the same angle to fit. The top of the piston is also cut at the same angle, and follows the 30-degree slant for slightly over half the width of the bore, then drops abruptly to make a pocket. This pocket forms the larger part of the combustion chamber, the rest is in the cylinder wall. The spark plug enters the combustion chamber through the side of the block rather than through the head.

Valves are positioned in the head, vertical to the face of the head. Rather than being in a line, they are staggered, the intake valve being located closest to the intake port, the exhaust valve away from the exhaust port. Intake and exhaust system are on the same side of the engine.

Compression ratios vary with the use of the engine. On the 300, the ratio is 6.4-to-1; the 300S has a ratio of 7.5-to-1; the 300SL is rated at 8-to-1, though what it actually uses undoubtedly has varied from race to race. Valve timing on the three models is also different. The various outputs are rated at: 300, 115 b.hp. at 4,600 r.p.m.; 300S, 150 b.hp. at 5,100 r.p.m.; 300SL, 175 b.hp. at 5,200 r.p.m., though this last figure is again open to question. Certainly it is conservative, and estimates of the actual output have varied from the factory's figure up to 200 b.hp.

Of the two passenger models, the 300S is the most interesting. Virtually the same as the 300, it has been hopped-up, lightened, and fitted with semi-sports bodies. The factory claims an honest 108 m.p.h., which is again conservative. A comparison between this car and the 540K of prewar days shows that Mercedes has kept pace with the industry. The 540K had a supercharged engine of almost 50 per cent more displacement, yet could find no more top speed and actually had slower acceleration.

The suspension system of the 300 series has been derived from the marque's racing experience. Independent front suspension is employed, with a coil spring and two wishbones per wheel. The inner bearings of the wishbones are pivoted about a post bolted to the frame, leaving the front wheels free to rotate. This rotation is controlled to a small movement either way, but the little freedom that is permitted is enough to absorb road shocks that would otherwise be transmitted to the passenger or the steering system. In the rear, independent suspension is also employed. Two coil springs per wheel and swinging axles are used. These axles permit the wheels a slight forward and backward movement, as well as motion through an arc about the points where the swinging axles join the differential.

There are four forward speeds in the transmission, with the last three being silent synchromesh. The gear-shift lever is on the steering column in the 300 and 300S, on the floor in the 300SL.

Different frames are used on the competition version and the two touring types. The 300 and 300S have an X-shaped frame, constructed of oval tubing, with five cross members, three of which are also used as body hangers. The 300SL has an extremely light skeleton of tubing, so engineered that no single member is required to assume a bending stress. On the 300SL closed cars, which are only 50 inches high, the doors are hinged in the roof and open upwards. No part of the body carries any of the load.

Top speed for the 300SL has been announced by the factory as 168 m.p.h. for the production model, finally offered to the public in 1954. The roadability of all the cars is superb, such respected publications as *The Autocar, Road and Track* and *The Motor* agreeing that the 300 has no superior among transportation automobiles of its size. Drivers who have competed against the SL report that it passes them smoothly and quietly at fantastic speed.

A companion car to the 300SL, the four-cylinder 190SL, appeared in 1954. This is a convertible with similar but not identical styling, equipped with rather less luxury features and designed to sell in the more modest price ranges. The single-overhead-cam engine delivers 125 horsepower from 115.75 cubic inches, can provide a top speed of 118 m.p.h. according to the factory figures.

Mercedes-Benz 300SL production model, 1954.

Strangely, once Mercedes had announced these cars they seemed to be relegated to the dead past. Deliveries from the factory were painfully slow, so slow that by the end of 1954 there were few Mercedes sports cars in U.S. showrooms and fewer on the highways. You could get a demonstration ride but little more.

Meanwhile, Mercedes avoided sports car competition to concentrate on Grand Prix racing. While this book does not attempt to give a well-rounded picture of the Grand Prix events or even the cars in them, the Mercedes entry was so startling that it is worth more than passing mention.

For 1954 the Formula I Grand Prix cars were limited to 2.5 liters unsupercharged and 0.75 liters supercharged. (That's 152.5 cubic inches and 45.75 cubic inches, respectively.) Mercedes came up with a straight eight engine of 2.5 liters, an engine divided actually into two four-cylinder engines. Power was taken off the crankshaft in the center. In building the engine, the Mercedes staff headed by Dr. Fritz Nallinger dispensed with two traditional parts — the carburetors and the valve springs. Fuel was supplied to the cylinders by direct injection, pumped in by a Bosch-developed variation of the familiar diesel-engine injection pump. Biggest difference is the use of plastic parts instead of metal parts, a substitution made necessary because gasoline lacks the lubricating qualities of diesel oil. Use of fuel injection provided greater fuel economy, a vital element in modern Grand Prix racing where a pit stop for fuel is out of the question for a winning car.

In place of valve springs the Mercedes Grand Prix car has what Dr. Nallinger describes as "a mechanical forced timing device (for) opening and closing the valves quickly by a guided motion."

Nallinger pointed to two chassis improvements, the inboard-mounted front and rear brake drums and the use of a "genuine swing axle." The joint center of motion of the swing axle arms lies in the middle of the vehicle below the rear axle housing. Thus the swing arms are both longer and lower than on the more familiar Mercedes swing-axle set-ups.

Perhaps the greatest single improvement on the new Grand Prix car was the streamlined body, something evidently derived from experience in sports-car racing. For the first time since the day long past when racing cars eliminated fenders, the four wheels were covered. Unfortunately the racing drivers had become accustomed to seeing the wheels when driving, so the streamlined cars were not as successful during 1954 as they undoubtedly will be in the future. Mercedes had to make open-wheel versions of the cars to finish out the '54 season.

With these cars Mercedes proceeded to win four of the six Grand Prix races entered. The brilliant driver, Juan Manuel Fangio, star of the Mercedes team, won the world's championship by the runaway margin of 17 points.

Nothing could have been more typical of Mercedes than its competition performance during the two seasons — 1952 and 1954 — of competition. Neubauer and his cohorts simply picked up from where they had left off in 1939, acting for all the world as if the '52 season were just one year removed from that pre-war period. There was the same team discipline, the same thoroughness of preparation, the same technical excellence of both cars and drivers. As before, they were not completely invincible but there seemed to be no other team in Europe that could sustain the kind of performance required to beat the Germans over the season.

M.G.

M.G. SPORTS CARS WERE IMPORTED BY A FEW enthusiastic American automobile dealers in 1947. They sold the little TC's in pathetically small numbers that year and the next. Then an M.G. dealer in California hired a press agent who planted a feature story on sports cars (M.G.'s) in a magazine with a weekly circulation of better than five million copies. That seemed to light the fuse.

The dealer had been trying to get rid of 20-odd M.G.'s for months. Within a week after the magazine article hit the newsstands he wished he had hundreds and so did the few other dealers scattered across the country. Oddly enough, the article was on the sarcastic side. It emphasized snobbishness among sports-car owners, implied they were a self-styled élite. But it also implied that you, too, could be the gay, madcap owner of an "expensive foreign car" and a member of this élite — and it would cost you less than $2,000.

Snob appeal is a determining factor in auto sales in Topeka or Timbuktu and it sold M.G.'s. Monday-through-Friday welders donned trick hats and accents and hit the roads on weekends in their natty two-seaters, complete with "GB" plates and British flag decals. This group, bolstered by a minute core of non-conformists who were convinced that Detroit had lost the ball in the early Thirties, bought M.G.'s and got them in the public eye. Soon the demand for these cars was staggering, and thousands of Americans who were devoid of pretensions became M.G. owners because they liked the car's appearance, operating economy and ease of handling in traffic. The M.G. had romantic, dynamic lines that had not existed on the native scene since the days of the Stutz Bearcat, Mercer Raceabout, and Kissel Gold Bug. Its design was as functional as the Jeep's and was esthetically satisfying to boot. Although it rode with a merciless disregard for passengers' spines it cornered like no American car had since the Thirties. Its approximate 75-m.p.h. top speed was not very fast by American standards but it was still a genuine, spartan sports car.

The Nuffield Organization (as Morris Motors Ltd. had come to be called) found itself blessed with a "hit" and geared for greatly increased production to supply the American demand. Sports-car clubs, M.G.-owners' clubs, and four-cylinder-car clubs mushroomed throughout the United States. Sports-car racing, which had been the hobby of an infinitesimal few, became a big American spectator sport, and until a better car came along, TC M.G.'s either dominated or monopolized the 1,500-c.c.-competition class from Long Island to Palm Springs.

Although the T-type Midgets had never been racing favorites in England, the factory hastily published a booklet in 1949 which explained six stages of M.G. tuning, ending with supercharging and a 97.5-b.hp. output.

The upshot of this phenomenal situation was that during England's most critical postwar years Nuffield's M.G. division came to the rescue of the national economy as heroically as any other British automotive manufacturer. Lord Nuffield, who as William Richard Morris had started out in business at the age of 16 with £4 capital and had guided M.G. to its present success, was one of Great Britain's most honored citizens. Of course he was a very lucky man; he could not have known when he created the T-type M.G. in 1936 that it would spread the sports-car gospel around the postwar world.

The M.G. TC was only slightly different from the 1936 TA and practically identical to the immediately prewar TB. Bore, stroke, power output and gearing were all the same. The TC's suspension was remarkable in that the rear half-elliptic springs were mounted on "outriggers," as far from the frame and as close to the hubs as possible. This gave the chassis much of its flatness of ride, and the front half-elliptics, mounted inboard and quite close together, gave it the extreme steering lock that makes for best maneuverability. The engine was impressive above all for its performance characteristics: .72 horsepower per cubic inch of displacement and 2.5 horsepower per square inch of piston area. In spite of this high specific output, careful camshaft and port design maintained excellent torque characteristics throughout the r.p.m. range, and fuel economy was excellent. When the TC was introduced late in 1945 it caused a controversy by retaining an "obsolete" prewar wheel and tire size. Actually, the big 4.50×19 tires, on wire wheels with knock-off hubs, made an important contribution to the well-balanced and sporting appearance of this high-performance small car.

Then, early in 1950, the M.G. TD was announced and the situation immediately became tangled. The new version of the T-series was an improvement but it definitely lacked the visual

Arnholt MG-TD has closed Italian body by Bertone, weighs only 40 pounds more than stock TD. 1953.

Henry Ford Mu

elan of the TC and warfare broke out, the camps being divided into supporters of the new and the old.

There were few mechanical differences between the two cars. The engines were the same, but the TD had a new frame and offered left-hand drive and independent front suspension for the first time. The 19-inch Rudge-type wheels were retired in favor of much less colorful 15-inch pressed-steel bolt-ons. Rack and pinion steering was added, along with an up-to-date hypoid rear axle and wider tread. Although most objections to the TD were based solely on its "shockingly modern" appearance, all the seriously voiced objections were given a technical ring. A typical protest was that the TD's softer springing ruined its roadability, that it had been designed to appeal to the American housewife. Another was that the economy move which deprived the M.G. of wire wheels also robbed its brakes of their reliability. Neither of these objections was true.

The TD, although it did not pretend to have the TC's purity of "vintage" line, was the better car. It steered more easily, was generally more comfortable, and had a more friendly, softer ride. These conveniences were decisive but, in addition to them and given even odds, the new M.G. would beat the old one in a road race every time.

The Mark II TD was introduced a few months after the TD. For an extra price the enthusiast got stronger (150-lb.) valve springs, 1½-inch carburetors in place of the stock 1¼-inch SU's, oversized valves and an extra set of shock absorbers all around. The Mark II was roughly a TD raised to the factory-recommended Stage One tune, giving about 62 b.hp. and having a beefed-up suspension system. The TD in standard and Mark II form carried on the marque's role as backbone of American amateur racing in the 1,500-c.c. class — this in spite of the fact that M.G. gives away 250 c.c. of precious displacement because the engine cannot be bored safely to a full 1500 c.c. without resorting to cylinder sleeves.

Innumerable "specials" have been based on the M.G. chassis and many of them have been formidable contenders in competition. Notable cars were the Lester M.G.'s, produced in small series in England, and John Edgar's and John von Neumann's race-winning modifieds, produced in this country. In 1952, Porsches and OSCA's costing from two to three times the price of an M.G. began running away from the Abingdon product in American races. In 1953 things changed, when the Ken Miles M.G. began running in West Coast events and besting competition in its class. It had a special tubular frame and modified Morris Minor suspension, plus a souped-up TD engine with big, 72-mm. (2.84 in.) bore and 1,466-c.c. (89.5 cu. in.) displacement. Rumor spread that the Miles car was actually a prototype of a new M.G. competition car. Miles quickly squelched the suggestion: his special, like all the others, was privately developed.

The only factory-sponsored M.G. of note since the war has been old EX 135 in which Lieutenant-Colonel Goldie Gardner continued his record-breaking career. Using the 750-c.c. (45.8 cu. in.) six-cylinder oh.c. engine which had been developed in 1939, Gardner ran the streamliner at Jabbeke, Belgium to set new Class H records at 159 m.p.h. In 1947 he used the same power plant with pistons and rods removed from numbers two and five cylinders and crankshaft balance compensated by counterweights to take 500 c.c. (30.5 cu. in.) records at 118 m.p.h.

In 1948 Piero Taruffi pushed a Guzzi-powered car through international record traps at 129 m.p.h., and engineer Sid Enever of the M.G. plant was assigned to rectify the situation. Enever's method was to use half of an MG K3 1,100-c.c. engine. With a specially designed crankshaft which carried only three throws at 120 degrees and a bore and stroke of 57×64.5 mm. (2.25×2.54 in.) the displacement came out at 493.8 c.c. This amazing power unit made Taruffi's best speeds seem halting and took the records at 154 m.p.h.

Pulling a leaf from the same book, Enever subtracted one more cylinder, leaving only two in operation, and took the under-350-c.c. (21.4 cu. in.) records. When Gardner came to America, he and the streamliner had already broken some 80 international records in classes E, F, G, H, I and J — from under-350 to 2,000-c.c.

Running at Bonneville Salt Beds in 1951 with a factory-prepared Shorrock-blown M.G. Mark II engine, Gardner broke six international records including the standing-start international hour record at 137.47 m.p.h., and ten international records. Only a broken oil line kept him from continuing on to take records up to two hours.

Gardner's plan had been to attempt the short, sprint records with a second TD Mark II engine, but a combination of circumstances — mainly vicious weather conditions — postponed the run and the crew had to return to Europe to meet other commitments.

Since the special sprint engine produced 210 b.hp. at a little over 6,000 r.p.m., there is little doubt that an attempt would have set some awesome records. In a practice run the car turned 160 m.p.h. easily and speeds in excess of 200 m.p.h. were confidently expected.

In August of 1952 Gardner was back on the Salt for another try. This time he topped 202 m.p.h., using a 1,245-c.c. M.G. engine. He set 21 new records, bringing the record harvest of his Reid Railton-designed car up to 101, and proving beyond doubt that the performance potential of the 1¼-liter M.G. engine is, for practical purposes, almost limitless.

The M.G. TF announced at the end of 1953 followed the evolutionary line that began with the TA. The body was a little longer and lower; the radiator pleased the TD advocates but caused more snarls from TC diehards who, while grudgingly approving the return to wire wheels even at extra cost, were horrified by the more streamlined appearance and the headlights, which were blended with the fender line. They waxed especially vitriolic over the dummy radiator cap.

It did them no good. The next M.G. to make its appearance in America was defiantly TF in styling. One major concession had, however, been made to American taste. The engine, at long last, was enlarged to a displacement of 1,466 cubic centimeters (89.4 cubic inches). With the additional inches the M.G. was still no bomb, but it did have more satisfactory hill-climbing ability, better acceleration and top speed. And it retained the flat, hard ride so dear to the hearts of all M.G. enthusiasts — not quite as solid as the old TC but noticeably better than most other imports.

M.G. was clearly heading for a showdown in the sales lists with Triumph and Austin-Healey. Much to everyone's surprise, a full-fledged horsepower race was shaping up. It had previously been thought that sports car manufacturers were superior to this vulgar sort of competition.

But M.G. continued to disappoint that segment of the British public which felt that the firm should enter international major league sports car competition. Nothing would suit the British public better than to see a small-displacement, professionally designed and prepared companion to the big Jag competition cars, but if it was to be built, M.G. did not seem ready to build it. Instead the Morris descendant blossomed out with another streamlined record car — the EX-179. At Bonneville, in the late summer of 1954, it clocked 153.69 m.p.h. in Class F (from 1.1 to 1.5 liters) for ten miles, then went on in a slightly different version to run for 12 hours at 120.74 m.p.h.

With no intention of disrespect, it can safely be said that the M.G. continues to be the Model T of the sports car field. Today it's the cheapest ($1,995 delivered in America), most trouble-free, most conservative sporting machine available in the world.

| MORGAN |

THE GREAT DAYS OF THE THREE-WHEELER MORGAN were largely over when the company went back into production after the war. The car continued to be sold for several years, but the Matchless engine of prewar days was no longer available and was replaced by a Ford Ten engine of 1,172-c.c. (72.8 cu. in.) displacement which was discreetly tucked in under the hood. The disappearance of the naked engine tempered the aggressively virile appearance of the old three-wheelers, but the car still had a good power-to-weight ratio and fine performance. The 4/4 four-wheeler reappeared after the war too, still with the 1,267-c.c. (77.3 cu. in.) Standard pushrod-operated-overhead-valve engine. It was frequently entered in competition and performed nicely in rallies, often with the ageless H. F. S. Morgan himself at the wheel.

All this was not, however, quite in the tradition of the potent Morgans, and in 1951 an important change took place in the line. The three-wheeler was discontinued entirely, and the 4/4 was replaced by the much more powerful Plus Four. Few modifications were made in the basic chassis design of the new model, and weight was increased by less than 100 pounds. But the Plus Four's Standard overhead-valve engine was of 2,088 c.c. (127.4 cu. in.) displacement, a good 70 per cent bigger than the old engine, and the power-to-weight ratio was profoundly improved from 41 to 25 pounds per horsepower.

The Plus Four's chassis frame, with its Z-section side members, was traditionally rugged and compact, and was considerably beefed up to withstand the higher loads imposed by the more powerful engine. The four-speed synchromesh gearbox was mounted on a sturdy steel frame well back from the engine and clutch, almost at the center of the car, an arrangement which permitted a short, direct-acting gear lever to be placed ideally for brisk gear changing. The front wheels were independently but firmly sprung by a modernized version of the 40-year-old Morgan method, with long, small-diameter, vertical coil springs and sliding axles. The front suspension was provided with a simple one-shot oiling system.

The Plus Four had an honest top speed of over 85 m.p.h., could maintain a comfortable cruising speed of 75 m.p.h. indefinitely and accelerated from zero to 50 m.p.h. in under 10 seconds. The car was sold in two-seater, four-seater and two-seater convertible (with roll-down windows) versions, all with good-looking bodies of the traditional English sports-car type. Finish and interior appointments were on the stark side, but Morgan's advertising slogan was "the fastest of its price," and the Plus Four could be bought for $1,580 before taxes, a small price for lively performance in England.

Nevertheless, the makers of Morgan did not lose interest in giving the rugged little Plus Four even more steam. For 1954 the engine of the "two seater tourer" was replaced by the 1,991 c.c. (121.5 cu. in.) Triumph TR2 power unit which in spite of its slightly smaller displacement produced a beefy 90 b.hp. compared to the Vanguard's 68, an increase in maximum power of 32 per cent. With the new engine, acceleration and hill-climbing ability were among the best that English small cars could offer, and top speed was comfortably over 100 m.p.h. The price was increased only $112, and this fact, added to the Morgan's racy good looks, fine handling qualities and now impressive power-to-weight ratio, made it one of the better buys in its class. Some critics were heard to murmur, however, that it would be nice to have more potent brakes to cope with the TR Plus Four's new speed potential.

THEIR ASSOCIATION WITH ALFIERI MASERATI GAVE the Maserati brothers little but incomparable experience. They left the Modena plant impoverished by inflation and went home to Bologna to start from scratch in an old barn a few hundred

OSCA

yards from the one in which they had once manufactured cars bearing the red trident. They immediately fell into their old functional relationship: Bindo, wiry and tireless, ran the office and made policy; placid Ettore directed the mechanical work; and robust Ernesto, the youngest, was the designer. No longer owning the family name, they called their enterprise OSCA. Officially, the initials stood for Officine Specializzate Costruzione Automobili but OSCA also happened to be the name of an ancient Italian people and their language.

What the brothers wanted to build more than anything else was a 4.5-liter car for Formula I racing but this, they knew, would be a big and costly project. They built a 1,100-c.c. (68.4 cu. in.) sports car instead. This little machine had a chain-driven, d.oh.c., four-cylinder engine which developed 85 b.hp. at 6,600 r.p.m. and gave the sleek, squat, 1,000-pound two-seater a speed of around 110 m.p.h. Its every detail — aerodynamic body, stiff tubular chassis, faultless handling and potent little engine — all testified that the Maseratis' talents were still razor-sharp. The 1,100 became absolute ruler of its displacement class in the 1951 racing season and won great respect on both sides of the Atlantic.

But astute Bindo knew that 1,100-c.c. races were not the most direct route to recapturing his clan's past glories and the market mirrored this state of affairs. In an effort to increase the car's sales appeal its displacement was enlarged to 1,342 c.c. (81.9 cu. in.), its output increased to 98 b.hp. at 6,300 r.p.m. and then to 1,452 c.c. (88.6 cu. in.) and 110 b.hp. The technical press and the enthusiasts were as impressed as before, but their esteem did not pay the bills and the Maseratis continued to be greatly respected but poor.

They did not forget, however, their expensive but urgent desire to build the name in top-prestige racing. With the sporadic help of friends they created in 1950 a new, unblown 4.5-liter car for Formula I competition, a beautiful V-12, gear-driven d.oh.c. engine mounted in a 4CLT Maserati chassis. Four were made, one of them for Prince Bira, who took it to England and promptly won the first major race of the 1951 British season.

But it generally takes financial backing to be a winner and OSCA's successes in Formula I were more than rare. Another line of attack was tried, this time the two-liter Formula II, an under-square six with gear-driven d.oh.c. and a car which also had excellent sports-competition potentialities. Its best performance in '52 was a second in the Monte Carlo G.P. and in '53 it could do no better than second in the G.P. of Syracuse. But Bindo, Ettore and Ernesto were glad to be working again among the towers of Bologna; they had cracked the combination there once and they were determined to do it again.

The 1,452 c.c. OSCA's tiny displacement class is not a spectacular one — as a rule. But in the 1954 running of "the American Le Mans," as the Sebring 12-hour race often is called, OSCA scored an historic upset. 60 cars, including Europe's and America's biggest and best, left the starting line at 10 A.M. March 7. At 10 P.M. that night only 25 machines were still in the race. Against Lancias, Ferraris, big Allards and all, the little Italian car driven by Stirling Moss and Bill Lloyd won the event three different ways: in distance covered, in its class, and on handicap. OSCA enjoyed a good season of racing but this performance, in one of the first big races of the season, will take many seasons to match.

1953 O.S.C.A. with Vignale *berlinetta* coachwork. This is on the 1,100 cc chassis which was a major sensation of the 1951 racing season. Engine has four cylinders, 66.6 cubic inches displacement. Car's top speed is about 112 m.p.h., engine develops 85 b.hp. at 6,600 r.p.m.

Walter Breveglieri

PEGASO

THE PEGASO 102 WAS THE MOST ASTONISHING *tour de force* to appear in the early postwar era. It embodied more advanced engineering than almost any car of its time, more traditional high-performance features, more of the superbly finished hand-craftsmanship that identifies the really fine car. Its performance was stunning; the top speed was high enough to be quick suicide on msot roads and for most drivers. The Pegaso had, in short, all the elements necessary to make the sports-car addict twitch restlessly in his sleep.

But what was most unexpected was the fact that this lavish and potent package was produced in Franco's backward Spain. The story of its development provides a fascinating glimpse of the problems of creating a complex and advanced industry in a poverty-wracked dictatorship pitifully retarded in technological know-how and thoroughly resigned to failure.

This was the environment in which the Pegaso miraculously blossomed, and many Spaniards even today can scarcely imagine how it happened. Spain had, in the first place, never been able to develop and produce a successful car. The Hispano-Suiza, while of Spanish origin, was developed largely in France, and the lesser-known Nacional Pescara had a swift, short history. Even more important, the idea of an industrial setup which actually

Miarnau photo   1955 Pegaso convertible coupe.

functioned, and functioned efficiently, was almost unheard of in Spain.

It was not surprising, then, that the first rumor, in 1946, of a new Spanish automotive factory was greeted by Spaniards with reactions ranging from indifferent scepticism to out-and-out derision. Many such rumors had been heard; none had led to anything you could sit in and drive. But the next news was more specific. The brave and foolhardy firm was E.N.A.S.A. (Empresa Nacional de Autocamiones, S.A.), a semi-private enterprise controlled by Franco's National Industrial Institute (I.N.I.). Arrangements had been made to start production in the old Barcelona shops of Hispano-Suiza. Spaniards were now willing to believe that the project existed but they were morosely certain that it would fail. The Hisso works were obsolete and dilapidated. E.N.A.S.A.'s financial position was known to be precarious, and with the hot bureaucratic breath of I.N.I. on its neck its prospects seemed even dimmer.

The first products to trickle from the works were gasoline-engine trucks, and they were met in Spain with the usual fatalistic pessimism. They were deficient, said the critics, they used too much fuel, and an ambitious manufacturing enterprise like Pegaso had no business trying to operate in Spain anyhow.

But visitors to the plant around this time began to get a dif-

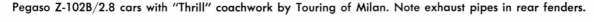

Pegaso Z-102B/2.8 cars with "Thrill" coachwork by Touring of Milan. Note exhaust pipes in rear fenders.

ferent feeling. The directors of E.N.A.S.A. had faith in their own efforts even if nobody else did, and they had pledged their personal holdings to the last *centimo*. Technical chief of the organization was Wilfredo P. Ricart, formerly of Alfa Romeo and Nacional Pescara.   He was a skilled and dynamic organizer and a shrewd student of economic affairs, and under his whirlwind supervision the factory was beginning to take impressive shape. Old buildings were going down, new ones were going up, and through the gates was passing a constant flow of fine machine tools and precision engineering equipment. In 1949 a new Pegaso diesel-engined bus was designed and tested, in 1950 it appeared in production, and in October of that year it was taken to the Paris Salon where, to the shock of the Spanish populace, it was unanimously acclaimed by the international press.

The impossible had happened. A Spanish automotive product had not only been built, but it was *good,* good enough so that Pegaso buses became eagerly sought after by foreign buyers. Spain may have reeled, but its more astute citizens recovered quickly enough to buy up two years of Pegaso production in advance.

Now the company was ready to introduce its second bombshell, the gorgeous, the fast, the magnificent Pegaso 102 automobile. Why, in the midst of poverty, did Pegaso choose to produce this millionaire's delight? Ricart had the answer, succinctly. "We are a poor country," he said, "and therefore we must make jewels for the rich. In jewels, in exceptional products like the Pegaso 102, destined for a limited élite and made with great mechanical refinement, handwork is the most important factor, and only a low standard of living and low labor cost can provide handwork economically." Furthermore, E.N.A.S.A.'s government parent, I.N.I., had recently combined with the major Spanish banks and Fiat to build a factory for the mass production of inexpensive cars, and Pegaso prudently did not attempt to compete with this colossus.

Thus the 102, and it was indeed a jewel. The first cars were of 2.5-liter displacement but the company soon began to concentrate on a larger-engined car of the same design in two versions, the B/2.8 and the supercharged BS/2.8. Both had a V8 2,816 c.c. (171.5 cu. in.) engine with two gear-driven overhead camshafts for each cylinder bank. The bore and stroke carried the postwar trend toward a square ratio farther than most — it was oversquare, 3.14×2.76. There were two inclined valves for each cylinder, each pair seating in polished hemispherical combustion chambers. All possible components — engine block and crankcase, heads, sump, clutch housing and drive-shaft housing — were cast of light alloy. The unblown engine developed over 170 b.hp. at 6,200 r.p.m., the supercharged version over 250 b.hp. at 6,800 r.p.m. As if this might not be enough in 1954 Pegaso introduced another model, the 102 BS/3.2, which had its engine bored to a total displacement of 3,178 c.c. (194 cu. in.)

Power transmission was unique. Drive was taken from a single-plate clutch and carried through an open drive shaft to two spur gears located at the back of the rear-axle center section in the manner of an American-track-racing-type quick-change rear end. From here the torque was unleashed upon the contents of a five-speed transmission (synchromesh on all but low gear) which was neatly contained in this same light-alloy center-section housing. Spiral bevel gears, a Z-F limited-slip differential, and big, finned, light-alloy inboard brake drums completed this busy little package. A De Dion tube was arched around the forward side of the assembly in order to join the hubs, from which tubular radius arms extended to converge at the chassis center line's rear extremity. Torsion bars were used for both front and rear springing, conventional A-arms being used for the independent front suspension but rendered unusual by having bars extending both fore and aft of the lower arm.

The car was extremely rugged structurally, having a low platform-type frame well-reinforced with sheet-steel box members. The firewall, front body pillars and wheel arches were also parts of this structure which was further strengthened when the body was installed; coachwork was designed to form a structural unit with the chassis assembly. The Pegaso was one of the quickest-steering cars in the world, requiring just under two turns of the steering wheel to bring the front wheels from lock to lock.

The chassis could be had without coachwork for about $6,000 f.o.b. Barcelona, but the standard body was an aerodynamic dream built for Pegaso by Touring and it added another $3,000 to the price. The closed two-seater body was smooth and Italian, with rear fenders prolonged from the back of the car to blend harmoniously with the roof and form a body section which carefully coped with air-layer turbulence. With this body the unblown car had a conservative top speed of 115 m.p.h., the blown car 145 m.p.h. Pegaso gave an unconditional three-year guarantee for all the parts of its own manufacture — and what more could the connoisseur want?

In spite of bad luck in a few important races like the '54 Pan-americana, in which a Pegaso looked terrific until it crashed and burned, the make still looked potentially good for competition. It won many Spanish hill-climbs and rallys, and in stock form set class records at 151.0 m.p.h. for the flying kilometer, 85.6 m.p.h. for the standing kilometer, 149 m.p.h. for the flying mile and 98.7 m.p.h. for the standing mile. And, of course, it took innumerable and unanimous first places in concours d'élégance all over Europe.

The demand for the marvelous Pegaso soon far exceeded the supply, which by early '55 was a scant 60 in all. If ever a manufacturer was vindicated, E.N.A.S.A. was the one. The daring Pegaso venture affirmed to the world and to sceptical Spain that Spanish technology could develop and produce one of the best cars built anywhere.

PORSCHE

IF THE OWNER OF A DETROIT AUTOMOBILE HAS A difficult time understanding why anyone wants to own an M.G. or a Jaguar, he is completely baffled by the man who buys a Porsche. Here is a toylike car, powered by a tiny engine and selling for the Cadillac-size price of $4,200. Outwardly it looks like a pretty toy, but a glance over the competition records shows how wrong that superficial impression can be.

In the under-1500-c.c. class in United States road racing, top honors have gone successively to a series of marques. At first the M.G.'s had the field almost to themselves, then came the amazing little Simca specials of Roger Barlow, which were in turn displaced by the Porsches. Until the advent of the OSCAs, nothing in this country could give a good Porsche a close contest. Besides being fast and roadable, the streamlined coupes and roadsters were utterly reliable.

The Porsche had three birthdays: first, when the late Dr. Porsche began his long and noteworthy career in the automobile industry; second, when Hitler created that memorable peoples' myth, the Volkswagen; third, the production of the Porsche itself. In his design of the Volkswagen, Dr. Porsche incorporated many of the principles he had learned during his years as chief engineer of Auto-Union's racing stable; in the later design of the Porsche, the Doctor took the Volkswagen and rebuilt it for maximum performance. A Porsche is really little more than a hot-rodded Volkswagen.

Volkswagen owners had long contended that their cars were embryo sports cars, and could prove it on a tight, twisting mountain highway by keeping up with M.G.'s until horsepower ran out. The laminated-torsion-bar suspension of the VW would keep the car rock-steady on corners, rutty roads and in the rain, yet afforded sufficient springiness to make the ride comfortable. In its displacement class (1131 c.c. or 69 cu. in.) the rear-mounted, air-cooled engine could keep up with any European family car on the highway, though it wasn't made to cruise at over 65 m.p.h. In all its essentials the Volkswagen was an automobile that a modern American factory could turn out for less than $1,000 in big lots, but the added expenses of small production quantities, transportation and relatively high dealer-mark-ups kept the price well above that in the United States.

Like the VW, the first Porsche had a flat-opposed, four-cylinder, air-cooled engine mounted in the rear. In fact, it was the same engine as the VW, but with a slightly smaller bore to bring displacement under 1100 c.c. and squeeze the car into that class in sports-car competition. This was the small Porsche, and it was the first offered to the public. Later, a larger engine of 90.7-cubic-inches displacement was made for the next larger sports car class — 1100- to 1500-c.c. It is this second car that has been most seen in America. A third model with a 78.4-cubic-inch engine is not as popular as the other two. All three cars are the same, varying only in engine displacement. Within the larger displacement class, there are also varying degrees of hop-up available, the maximum rated at 100 b.hp., which is a lot of power to drag from less than 91 cubic inches on pump gasoline.

Most of the engine was made of aluminum, including the crankshaft bearings. In the high-performance models, the connecting rods had roller bearings. The cylinders, cast individually and finned for cooling, were of aluminum. Inclined overhead valves were operated by pushrods. Bore was 3.14 inches, stroke 2.91 inches in the large, 90.7-cubic-inch engine, and all the engines were oversquare (i.e., larger bore than stroke). Compression ratios varied, according to the degree of hop-up the engine had been put through, but the 75-horsepower model had a ratio of 8.2-to-1. The horsepower peak, in this same model, was at 5,200 r.p.m., at which point the piston speed was just a shade over 2,500 feet per minute, considered the safe cruising maximum. In that factor lies much of the secret of the Porsche's engine reliability.

The Porsche frame was an economical unit made of pressed steel. Since both engine and transmission were in the rear there was no equipment to hang under the driver's compartment, and no drive shaft to run between the frame rails. This permitted the use of a bellypan which was also the floor of the car.

Suspension was independent all the way around, as in the Volkswagen. Laminated torsion bars took the place of springs, as might be expected since Porsche was the inventor of the laminated torsion bar. In the front, two trailing arms attached each wheel to the torsion bars, and in the rear, swing axles and a single trailing arm were used.

The bodies were efficiently and handsomely streamlined, the originators of a new decade of styling if Studebaker's '53 models are to be regarded as a reliable indication. Even if they lose favor stylewise, they have demonstrated that good streamlining can pay off in additional speed and increased fuel economy. Despite the small displacement of the engine, the Porsche could be cruised comfortably at highway speeds between 70 and 80 m.p.h. Fuel consumption in the city, where high-revving competition engines do not usually do so well, was in excess of 25 m.p.g. Top speed was substantially more than 100 m.p.h., probably in the neighborhood of 110 — a remarkable achievement for an engine of only 75 b.hp. pushing a body and chassis weighing over 2100 pounds.

Proof of that performance has been in racing. On the day that John von Neumann's Porsche established its superiority over Barlow's Simca specials, he had complete control coming out of the corners and on the straights. John von Neumann was only one of a group of United States drivers who toured the sports-car events in Porsches, winning stock and modified events in the under-1500-c.c. class with maddening regularity. In Europe, the Porsche took home a class win in the Grand Touring Class in the 1952 Mille Miglia; a 1100-c.c. Porsche won its class in the 1952 Le Mans event, duplicating the feat accomplished the previous year; at the Eifel races on the Nurburgring course in 1952, one 1500-c.c. Porsche won its class and two 1100-c.c. Porsches placed first and second in theirs. These are only a few of the notable Continental successes, and they came after the OSCA's were developed and racing. In Europe the smaller classes are hotly contested, and some of the cars the Porsche has beaten are seldom seen in the United States. The team Simca-Gordinis of a few years back, the OSCA's, Maseratis and many others fight it out in the 1100 and 1500-c.c. classes.

Some idea of the intensity of this competition can be inferred from the efforts the manufacturers make to win. Porsche plunged into the task of redesigning and rebuilding the competition models in 1953, paying particular attention to body and engine. Before the season of 1954 these cars had been tested and rebuilt some five times.

What finally emerged was the Model 550-5. It came out fighting, completely dominating its class in European events in 1954. The body was an open roadster, beautifully streamlined, with two small, fat fins in the rear for better control at high speed. The engine was a double-overhead-camshaft version of the horizontally-opposed four-cylinder engine that powers the street and pleasure cars built by Porsche, but it had been modified by decreasing the stroke and increasing the bore. With four camshafts, it wasn't cheap, but its probable top speed was about 140 m.p.h. That is a lot to drag from 91 cubic inches.

1953 Porsche Le Mans prototype. Car is 30 inches high, has engine ahead of and transmission behind rear-wheel centers. Car won its class with an average of 86.24 m.p.h.

For the man on the street, the factory had another surprise in 1954 — an economy roadster. Mechanically, it was made with the same incredible precision and care as the more expensive sedans. Performance-wise, it had as much top speed and perhaps more acceleration. Basic price with the America engine — $2,995, delivered in America. For an extra $500 the customer could get the same body and chassis with the more potent "Super" engine.

In many ways the Porsche was the most satisfactorily developed sports car of the postwar era. No other small-displacement car was obtainable in such a wide price range; no other manufacturer had so well combined beauty, utility and performance in a small car. Even more than Mercedes, the Porsche was the Jaguar of Germany.

RILEY

THE EFFICIENT TWIN-CAMSHAFT, OVERHEAD VALVE engine that Percy Riley designed for the Riley Nine in 1926 was not rendered obsolete by decades of technological progress. With some detail modifications but no basic changes it became the power unit of the two postwar Riley cars introduced right after the war by the Nuffield Organization, which eventually merged with the Austin Motor Company to become the massive British Motor Corporation.

Riley 2½-liter three-seater.

Under this management the new Riley represented the respectable middle-aged version of the car which in its flaming youth had gone roaring around the Brooklands track with such outstanding success. There was, however, life in the old boy yet. It had what was still, in spite of its hoary origins, one of the world's most advanced and powerful — for its size — passenger-car engines. Although it was marketed with sedan and coupe bodies that seemed altogether too big and heavy for its four-cylinder, 1,496-c.c. (91.3 cu. in.) and 2,443-c.c. (149 cu. in.) power plants, the Riley, particularly in its larger version, was still a fast car with good all-around performance. The 2½-liter developed a sturdy 100 b.hp. at 4,400 r.p.m., had an honest top speed of around 94 m.p.h. and good acceleration — it took just 12 seconds to get from zero to 50 m.p.h. The less-adequately powered 1½-liter model developed just 54 b.hp. at 4,500 r.p.m., and its best speed was 75 m.p.h. To give this model a little more snap, the makers in 1954 designed an optional twin-carburetor conversion kit for it, giving the engine an additional ten b.hp. Both Riley forms were equipped with precise rack-and-pinion steering, and had independent front suspension by means of torsion bars. Both were eminently road-worthy, with good handling qualities and stability and a firm, solid ride.

The coachwork, like the chassis, was almost identical for both sizes, an attractive but not dazzling combination of traditional lines — somewhat smoothed and rounded for modern tastes — and the usual careful British finish.

Thus the postwar Riley became a compromise car, with near-sports performance that made it excellent for high-speed touring, plus the comfort and good manners that the general public had come to demand.

THE POSTWAR ROLLS-ROYCE WAS AN ANACHRONISM in anachronistic clothing, valuable primarily as a symbol of the greatness that was, and possibly could be again, Britain's. Rolls-Royce Limited produced the car almost as a hobby, only 10 per cent of its output going into this section of the business. Whether

ROLLS-ROYCE

the automobile division made a profit on the car is not known and probably is not at all important. What did count was that once again England was producing the "Best Car in the World," despite war damages and austerity and in the face of the incontestable fact that there was virtually no market for such a car. Little of comparable quality in the luxury-car field was being manufactured in any of the other nations of Europe or in America.

For the most part, postwar Rolls-Royces were a continuation of the prewar small cars. Two models — the Silver Wraith and the Silver Dawn — were all that were available to the general buying public. They were sold for a new low price and one of them, the Silver Dawn, was offered with a factory body, something Rolls-Royce had never done before. The closest they came to this practice in the prewar era was when they bought the Brewster body factory in New York and turned out what can best be called semi-custom bodies for Rolls' Springfield chassis. But postwar economics called for postwar solutions, and Rolls did not hesitate to take the necessary step.

Dawn and Wraith were the same under the skin except for the dimensions of the chassis. Both used the 4½-liter (275 cu. in.), F-head, six-cylinder engine developed during World War II in the laboratories of the company; both had coil-spring independent front suspension and semi-elliptic rear springs. The ride control had been retained on the rear shock absorbers. With its small

Two-door Rolls-Royce Silver Wraith sedan. Chassis descends directly from first "Wraith" of 1939.

engine and rather heavy weight (4,000 pounds for the Silver Dawn, the smaller of the two) Rolls performance was less brisk than it was before but quite adequate for normal needs.

Phil Hill, one of America's outstanding competition-sports-car pilots, drove a Silver Dawn from New York to Los Angeles. Like most of the United States road testers who had taken a shakedown cruise in the Rolls-Royce, he was impressed by the feel of the car — its solidness and seemingly effortless high-speed cruising, its sureness on the road. Hill, and the others who have reported to the public on the Rolls, are men who have driven every United States car on the market and many of the best importations. They are unanimous in saying that driving a Rolls is an experience that can't be duplicated.

To the classics enthusiast, the Dawn and the Wraith seem small and underpowered after the big engines and bigger bodies of the prewar cars. Another source of disappointment has been Rolls' recent liberal attitude toward modernization. The Dawn, which was exclusively an export car, came fitted with Hydra-Matic and a body which deviated noticeably from the square lines of yesteryear. Outraged Britishers saw in this the deliberate destruction of one of Britain's grandest institutions for the sake of American dollars. They need not have worried — Hydra-Matic, curves and all, the Rolls was still solidly British. The flat, uncompromising radiator and shell were almost precisely the same as before. Most important of all, so was the workmanship. As long as the company felt secure in giving a solid, three-year guarantee on each car and regarded it as a solemn duty to send a factory representative to call on each owner every six months, no one could possibly confuse the Rolls-Royce with an American car.

After the Dawn and the Wraith had been solidly established, the postwar Phantom appeared. The first model was made especially for Queen Elizabeth (then a Princess) and the Duke of Edinburgh, and the few that came from the factory at Crewes since were cut from the same pattern. This was a car of true classic dimensions, with its 145-inch wheelbase and 346-cubic inch engine, a fitting successor to the three prewar Phantoms. The design of this car made no compromise with American styling or gadgetry.

Essentially the P-IV was an expanded Wraith. Its straight-eight engine was the Wraith plus two cylinders, the pistons, rods, valves, and other components being interchangeable with the Wraith. Like the Wraith it used an F-head, a valve arrangement that was little seen in postwar cars yet one that lends itself admirably to an engine which is not required to wind up to racing r.p.m. On the Phantom there was a dual exhaust system, complete with dual twin mufflers, the two systems joining at the rear of the chassis and leading into a single tail pipe. There were also two fuel systems, each operated by two fuel pumps mounted under the body on the frame. One tank was the regular 23-gallon supply; the other was a four-gallon reserve.

Like the prewar Phantom, the P-IV offered little in the way of innovations, the manufacturers preferring to use a tested, dependable design. The P-IV transmission was a standard four-speed box and the bodies so far delivered featured razor-edge styling unrelieved by curves.

By far the most important recognition accorded Rolls-Royce since the war was the selection of the P-IV by Queen Elizabeth as the royal method of transportation, an honor heretofore reserved for Daimler. It comes as a surprise to many people that the Rolls has not always been the royal car. Of the two makes, Daimler's fame is largely confined to Britain, while the Rolls has been an international star. Her Majesty's recent move will not change this situation, but it will give Rolls added strength in its drive to establish a postwar tradition of craftsmanship and quality.

SIATA

AMERICANS BECAME INTRODUCED TO SIATA WHEN New York dealer Antonio Pompeo conceived the idea of marketing a popular sports car composed of a light Italian two-seater powered by the American Crosley engine. He had Siata build a small number of cars with bell housings to fit the Crosley, imported them and installed Crosley engines in them. As excellent as the power plant was, its name was not one to intrigue class-conscious sports car buyers and the reception of the Siatas by American consumers was cool.

Furthermore, the Siata name itself was unknown to Americans, although the initials of the Societa Italiana Auto Transformazioni Accessori had been familiar to Italians since 1926, when its founder, Ambrosini, had been building manifolds, camshafts, and other articles of speed equipment for Fiat cars. His two sons became partners in the business as they came of age and small-scale expansion took place; Siata began building transmissions for racing cars, then complete racing cars. The nearby Fiat factory took an increasingly sympathetic attitude toward the Ambrosinis, and they eventually found themselves functioning as the unofficial experimental and racing department of the immense Fiat organization, which for years made it a point to have no formal connection with speed events. It was rumored that when the Ambrosinis had only a bombed ruin to return to after the war, helpful Fiat put up the money for reconstruction of the little plant.

By "specialist" standards it eventually grew fairly large. In 1953 its 35-man personnel dwarfed the OSCA and Nardi plants. This tight little staff, not unlike its American counterparts, found the work a source of pleasure, even adventure, and morale was always at peak level. The craftsman who stood all day hammering beautifully-formed aluminum bucket seats out on a tree stump may have been doing it the hard way but he was more than a faceless cog in a great, impersonal machine. He knew he was a key man essential to the manufacture of a product of rare quality.

Siata built a bevy of different car types in the early Fifties. There were the Daina and Gran Sport Series powered by modified Fiat 1400 engines and the Cad or Chrysler powered 200 Series, masterpieces of chassis engineering which aimed at but again failed to inflame American buyers. In 1953 the 208-S series was begun; it was Siata's finest car to date.

With their direct pipeline into Fiat it is not surprising that the Ambrosinis were able to obtain small numbers of the new and rare 1,996 c.c. (121.8 cu. in.) Fiat V-8 engine, designed, built, and developed in secret in Fiat's aircraft engine plant. It was first revealed in a Fiat sports car at the Geneva show in March, 1952. About ten of these experimental Fiats were built and, for the first time in recent years, raced by the factory in Italian events, with fair success. The 110 b.hp. engine was the outstanding feature of the car. Heads, block, and sump were light alloy castings, spigoted liners being used for the cylinders. The in-line valves seated in wedge-shaped combustion chambers and were operated by pushrods and rocker arms. A radically short stroke gave a peak piston speed of just over 2,400 feet per minute and graceful four-branch manifolds led the exhaust gases away from each head. Two Weber dual-throat carburetors fed mixture to two siamesed ports in each head.

Siata's first shipment of these engines — about 15 of them — arrived in June, 1953; at their then-normal rate of production of about six handbuilt cars per month, this was a good ten weeks' supply. The Ambrosinis designed a chassis worthy of the Fiat V-8. For their *spider* open two-seater with full weather equipment, they used a robust box-section frame and four-speed gearbox. For the *berlinetta,* the closed bodywork of which added structural strength and streamlining to the car as a whole, they supplied a lighter tubular frame and five-speed transmissions. Excellent independent suspension was provided for all four wheels, using Fiat Jeep-based suspension components built to Siata specifications. The final drive unit was a light-alloy casting fitted with half-shafts U-jointed at each end. A light-alloy casting containing vertical coil spring with concentric tubular shock absorber provided completely independent suspension for each of the four wheels, and was connected to them by an A-arm at the

Model 208-S Siata *spider,* Fiat V-8 engine.

Model 208-S Siata coupe, Fiat V-8 engine.

bottom and a single rocker at the top which acted upon spring and shock absorber. All of these parts were interchangeable for all wheels.

Carrozzeria Bertone, located about a mile from the Siata plant, made most of Siata's bodies. They were roughed out at Bertone, taken on a pickup truck to Siata where they were fitted to the hand-built chassis, hauled back to Bertone for finishing, then back to Siata for final installation.

The Siata 208S was one of the best-handling cars made in its day. West Coast dealer Ernie McAfee entered one of the *spiders* in the 1953 Carrera Panamericana. He had made up special cylinder liners and pistons to bring his engine's displacement within the 1,600 c.c. (97.6 cu. in.) small sports class displacement limit. He swore that on the tortuous Tuxtla-Oaxaca leg he never had to take his foot off the throttle in a turn. When he reached Oaxaca on the heels of factory-prepared Borgwards and Porsches the tire engineers wanted to know how far back he had stopped for new rubber. He hadn't, and his tires were good enough for a repeat performance. The Siata's chances were good in the Panam until McAfee crashed at the same mountain turn that had stopped Behra's Gordini the year before.

By the end of 1953 about 40 Fiat V-8 engines had been made and ten of them found their way to the U.S. installed in Siata 208S cars. They were optionally available with Siata camshafts which raised power output to 120 b.hp. and made these lighter cars a full match for the two-liter Ferrari. Just announced was a four-intake-port head which boosted the Fiat engine to 140 b.hp. and put the car on an obviously competitive level with both Ferrari and Maserati, while costing far less.

FOR A YEAR AND A HALF THE BRIGHT BLUE SIMCAS of Roger Barlow dominated their class in the California road-racing circuit, the second most important series of sports-car events in the United States. Barlow's cars served for most fans as an introduction to the marque, since few Simcas had been seen in this country and none had shown up in competition.

SIMCA

What Barlow was racing was no stock machine. He and his crew of mechanics had started with a Simca Huit (for "Eight" taxable horsepower) chassis, widened and lightened it as much as possible, stripped a few leaves out of the rear springs and installed lighter coils in front, added lowering blocks and changed the stock wheels for Borrani-Rudge equipment. On the engine they had raised the compression ratio to 9.25-to-1, installed an Abarth dual manifold and twin carburetors, attached two S.U. fuel pumps, chopped the flywheel, moved the engine back six inches and moved the radiator forward six inches. On top of all this went a brand new extra-light racing body.

Beginning at Pebble Beach in 1951, Barlow strung together a series of successes, including one victory at Elkhart Lake where he bested Eastern competition. Not till the Porsches and OSCA's arrived in America was the little Simca outclassed.

What Barlow did for the Simca in America, Amadée Gordini had accomplished earlier in Europe.

Gordini began running teams of special Simcas in European races in 1938 and had worked up a consistent class winner before the war stopped not only racing but Simca production as well. Victories included the 1939 Monte Carlo rally and the Le Mans race the same year. In the postwar era, the Simcas were successful in Grand Prix racing as well. One of the drivers for the Simca team was the Argentine ace, Fangio, who later was to win championships with Alfa Romeo and Mercedes-Benz.

Originally the Simca was a French-bodied version of the Italian Fiat, produced in a suburb of Paris by an organization with the impressive title of Société Industrielle de Mécanique et Carrosserie Automobile (S.I.M.C.A.). The first product was a copy of the 500 c.c. (31 cu. in.) Fiat "Topolino," the second was the Huit, with the popular four-cylinder, 67-cubic inch engine developed by Fiat for its Balilla model some years before. In Italy this engine was already popular with the local hot rodders, and it became just as popular in France. Gordini was only one of a number of accessory manufacturers who made racing versions of the stock engines.

After the war, Simca made the Huit on the same pattern as before for one year, then switched to a new one. Engine displacement was upped to 74.5 cubic inches, which raised the horsepower output to 40. Later, the Simca Nine was rated at 45 b.hp. at 4,400 r.p.m. and the Simca Sports at 50 b.hp. at 4,800 r.p.m. Bore and stroke were 2.83×2.95 inches, remarkably close to square.

Simca Huit sports model of 1950, though costly, was one of France's most popular middle-sized cars.

In general performance, the 50-b.hp. model was capable of nearly 85 m.p.h., although the 2,000-pound road weight made acceleration slow — zero to 60 in 23 seconds. Gasoline consumption was extremely low, and at cruising speeds 30-35 m.p.g. was the norm.

The chief appeal of the Huit, aside from its economy, was the excellent body styling.

Farina is given credit for the Huit bodies which were exported to America, and they made the Simca look like an expensive, Italian custom car. The Nines, however, were patterned after American styling, and were actually made from dies bought in this country. Thus, they lacked the sleek, swift look of the Huits. Only the Nine Sports retained the lines of the Huit.

Like Sunbeam-Talbot and Jensen and a few others in this volume, the Simca is not primarily a sports car. Most of the company's money is made on the ordinary passenger models. Rather the Simca is a solid base upon which a sports car *can* be built, and on which several admirable competition machines have actually been constructed.

SINGER

SINGER WENT BACK INTO POSTWAR PRODUCTION with a well-established reputation for moderately lively performance at a low price. The days of the hairy old Le Mans Singers were long gone, and the company's first postwar offerings were the two family sedans and the open four-seater "semi-sports" Nine Roadster that comprised the prewar line. Unique among cars of its price class, Singer still had the chain-driven-overhead-camshaft engine, a vivid reminder of the old high-performance days.

The Nine Roadster was designed for economical fun with a sports flavor, rather than for actual sports performance. Its 1,094-c.c. (66.8 cu. in.) engine developed 36 b.hp. at 5,000 r.p.m. gave the car a top speed in the high 60's and with its consumption of one gallon of fuel in about 33 miles kept operating costs at a minimum. The straightforward semi-elliptic springing gave a stable ride with a sports-car feel, and the car retained its chunky but clean prewar lines.

The Nine continued almost without change until 1951, although a four-speed gearbox replaced the three-speed unit in 1950. In 1951 Singer introduced a new sports model, the SM Roadster, which was powered by the 1,497-c.c. (91.4 cu. in.), overhead-camshaft engine previously reserved for the heavier sedans. It developed 48 b.hp. at 4,200 r.p.m. and gave the Roadster a top speed of around 75 m.p.h. The new model was equipped with independent front suspension by coil springs and A-arms. For 1953 Singers were given a little extra urge by a dual-Solex-carburetor version of the engine which was made optionally available for both sedan and Roadster, increasing output to 58 b.hp. at 4,600 r.p.m. and top speed to about 80 m.p.h.

This was a big increase in power and speed over the first postwar models, but did not significantly change Singer's latter-day emphasis on sports-like performance that was mild and pleasant rather than hackle-raising.

S UNBEAM, THE HISTORIC BRITISH RACING MARQUE, and Talbot (related to the French Talbot) came together under Rootes group pressure in 1938. The first car produced under the hyphenated name set the pattern for all future models; it was a sports touring car, developed from one of the Hillmans of the period, rather than a competition sports design. There was nothing unusual about the small (72 cu. in.; bore and stroke, 2.48 ×3.74 in.), L-head engine, but it was well made and completely reliable. Shortly there appeared a larger Sunbeam-Talbot, the 184 cu. in., 2.95×4.72, six-cylinder model, also an L-head.

SUNBEAM

In the postwar era, Sunbeam-Talbot production has followed the original plan. As compared to the Jaguars and Ferraris, these modern cars are prosaic, but satisfying. The original engine has been modified to use pushrod-operated overhead valves, and a larger four-cylinder engine has replaced the prewar sixes. It is this larger four that is the basis of the very commendable Sunbeam-Alpine, introduced in March, 1953 and named for a memorable showing in the Alpine Rally, where a factory team won four Coupes des Alpes plus the Coupe des Dames.

The Alpine was derived from the Sunbeam-Talbot "90" which was an orthodox passenger model. A sporty roadster body was designed for the Alpine, and the engine received special attention from the engineers, who hopped it up for better performance yet retained the durability for which the marque has been famous. By upping the compression ratio to 7.5-to-1 and re-designing the intake manifold, horsepower was increased to 80 at 4,400 r.p.m. The springs were stiffened considerably both front and rear, providing firmer control and detracting slightly from the easy riding qualities of the passenger car, and the wishbones-and-coil-spring independent front suspension of the front wheels was bolstered by a heavier anti-roll bar.

A "Super-Tuning Kit" was also available to buyers who wished to get yet more performance from their Alpines. With this, compression ratio shot up to 8.5-to-1, raising output to 105 b.hp. at 4,500 r.p.m. One of these cars, further modified by the addition of a belly pan, a metal cockpit cover and the Laycock de Normanville overdrive, clocked a high speed of 120.459 m.p.h. at Jabbeke, Belgium, then went on to Montlhery to average 111.2 m.p.h. for one hour.

Despite its high-speed potential, the Alpine is intended as a dependable pleasure car for highway use rather than a sports racing machine. The relatively long wheelbase and heavy weight tag it as an endurance car, which is precisely why the factory specializes in affairs like the Alpine and Monte Carlo rallies. In body and engine design it appeals to that special class of driver the British have always been so successful with, the man who likes high-speed, responsive cars, yet does not care to fuss with them interminably. It is primarily a masculine car.

TALBOT LAGO

THE AUTOMOBILE WAS BORN IN GERMANY BUT ITS cradle was liberal, tolerant France. From the earliest days engineers who sought information, inspiration or a sympathetic atmosphere in which to work on things automotive chose to go to France, usually to the manufacturing centers of Suresnes or Levallois near Paris. Some looked, learned, and when home. Others, like Bugatti, Gordini, and Lago, stayed. France's early interest paid big dividends later. If it had not been for these talented Italian expatriates her record in international racing would have been barren from the late Twenties on.

Antonio Lago saved from senile mediocrity one of France's — and the world's — oldest car-manufacturing plants. It was founded in Suresnes in 1893 by Messrs. Darracq, Serpollet, and Clement, and during the next decade became the Société Darracq et Cie. which established an English branch under the name of S. A. Darracq (1905) Ltd. In 1922 the English entity absorbed Sunbeam in Wolverhampton and the merged result was renamed Sunbeam Talbot Darracq Motors Ltd., usually abbreviated as

S.T.D. At the same time the parent organization in France was christened Automobiles Talbot S.A. and this was the firm eventually taken over by Tony Lago.

His start was with Sunbeam at Wolverhampton as an ordinary mechanic. He had a great native mechanical gift and a rudimentary formal education which he supplemented by constant study. He advanced rapidly with the firm, became a member of the British Society of Aircraft Engineers, left Sunbeam to work for the Wilson gearbox firm, then for Pratt and Whitney in the United States, and finally returned to Sunbeam, where he soon achieved the position of assistant director. In 1933 Lago's superiors decided he was the man to send to France to whip some new vitality into the doddering Automobiles Talbot.

Talbot's personnel and the French car-buying public shared an immense feeling of apathy for the marque. Lago's remedy was as effective as it was obvious. He determined to build cars that would win races. He was convinced that racing was not only the industry's greatest laboratory but also the greatest promotional device of all. At the same time he found little to emulate in the noisy, fuel-devouring, supercharged Grand Prix and sports cars of the day, which in most cases bore little resemblance to production models. Lago wanted to build Talbots that would be winners and still use as many production-car parts as possible.

He had an excellent foundation to work with in the form of the Talbot-Darracq Four-Liter Type H78. This had a seven main-bearing, six cylinder engine with in-line, pushrod-operated overhead valves and a displacement of 3,820 c.c. (233.1 cu. in.). During 1934 Lago designed and perfected a high-performance head for this engine, using vee-inclined valves in hemispherical combustion chambers. The single camshaft remained in its normal position in the crankcase and long rocker arms were used to span the valves' vee. The 1935 sports models fitted with this soon-famous Lago head were available in two- or three-carburetor form. Important chassis details of both standard and sports versions were solid rear axle and independent front suspension by transverse leaf and A-arms, with radius arms transmitting torque to the frame.

Lago became so encouraged by this project and so thoroughly engrossed in it that he formally resigned the high position he still held at Wolverhampton in order to devote his full time to the new, and to him utterly fascinating, work. In 1936 he unleashed his competition sports machines, which were simply souped-up versions of the cars sold to the public. They ran with complete reliability and what they may have lacked in speed was made up for in fuel economy that permitted long runs between pit stops. They were consistent finishers in the top money in important national and international competition and overnight the old apathy was replaced by interest, pride — and sales appeal.

The 3.9-liter production sports Talbot became one of the few fabulous cars of the late Thirties. Figoni and Falaschi were inspired to create some of their most radically beautiful coachwork for this powerful, supremely roadable chassis and a Figoni teardrop coupe in good tune had a top speed of 115 to 120 m.p.h. Since the bare sports chassis sold for around $5,000, the number produced was small.

Next to Lago's assumption of control and introduction of the vee-valve head, the most important event in recent Talbot history was the appearance of the 4.5-liter (273.5 cu. in.) unsupercharged full Grand Prix Talbot in 1938. (This car, somewhat modified, reappeared in sports production form in postwar years.) The G.P. engine, with block and Lago head in light alloy, produced 240 b.hp. Almost every part in the engine and chassis was taken from production-parts stock, including the Wilson preselector gearbox. There was the same solid rear axle and the major changes in chassis layout were independent front suspension by A-arms without radius arms and offset mounting of the engine to provide a low seating position. Like its immediate sports-competition forebears, the G.P. Talbot Lago had reliability and a relatively ascetic appetite for fuel. After many years of enforced exile in foreign-made mounts, France's best racing drivers had good French cars to race again. They were, of course, no real threat to the Teutonic masters of Grand Prix racing in the late Thirties. But while the German victories demonstrated what could be accomplished by the most radically advanced engineering, Lago showed what could be done within the limits of practical, everyday design. He entered the same machines in both sports and Grand Prix events, adding and deleting fenders and other road equipment to meet the requirements.

Soon after the end of the war Lago adapted the big 4.5-liter power plant to his production cars. Further improvements were made to this engine in both standard and racing versions. The single camshaft was replaced by two located high in the block, in the long-lived Riley and Lea-Francis manner. Thus the action of the vee-inclined valves was speeded up and made more efficient.

In three-carburetor, high-compression, 190-b.hp. *Grand Sport* form these engines were mounted in a longer and heavier chassis than the prewar sports model but still were claimed capable of reaching 125 m.p.h. pulling normal coachwork. The catalog bodies were moderately exciting, but for this chassis Saoutchik and Figoni et Falaschi were moved to build some of their most famous and fantastic bodies. Their custom creations were, of course, for the very few. They were bought by people like King Michael of Rumania, the Bey of Tunis, King Ibn Saud, and even a few commoners like American hotel-man Louis Ritter. The Ritter car cost over $17,000, with most of the cost in the coachwork. The chassis sold in Paris for just $3,980 and could be had in 1953 with an extremely attractive Italian-type *berlinetta* body for the reasonable price of $5,980.

Improvements continued to be made in the engine, and by 1953 the *Grand Sport's* output had been increased to 210 b.hp. at 4,200 r.p.m. The one important chassis change occurred in 1951, when the transverse leaf of the independent front suspension

Talbot Lago Grand Sport, circa 1950.

was replaced by coil springs. During these years 170- and 210-b.hp. versions of the same engine were made available in the less sensational-looking Lago Record, and the line was rounded out by the Lago Baby, a popular-price car of average quality and performance. All of these cars bore the Lago nameplate except in France and the countries on its borders, where the Talbot name was officially retained.

Meanwhile, Lago's big, never-say-die 4.5-liter racing cars were still hammering away in international competition. In 1953 Rosier finished fifth in the Carrera Panamericana behind three Lancias and a Ferrari. In their most successful years, from 1936 through 1950, Talbot-Lagos scored 21 first, 21 second, and 28 third places in major international events. And displaced Italian Tony Lago said, "When one of my cars wins a race I feel that I am paying a moral debt to the country which has permitted me to realize my life's dream."

Prior to 1952 the firm's output was around 1,000 cars per year. With the dropping of the Lago Baby from the line at that time, production was deliberately limited to 100 machines annually. This rate continued throughout 1954 while a new 2.5-liter sports model was undergoing design and development. The plan was to increase production when the new sports car should be ready. But Tony Lago stated that he had no desire ever to build more than 1,000 good cars each year!

| TRIUMPH |

ALMOST NOTHING COULD BEAT THE AUSTIN SEVEN during the days of its glory, but Triumph made a valiant attempt with its Supercharged Seven Sports, the first of that firm's true sports cars. Though the four-cylinder, L-head engine had a displacement of only 50.7 cubic inches, the car was so light (1,350 lb.) and small (81-in. wheelbase) that top speed was close to 70 m.p.h. Surprisingly, it carried a transmission with only three speeds. Whether that was the reason or not, the Triumph could not match the amazing little Austin so it was discontinued.

Triumph's next notable venture into the sports-car field occurred in 1932. Coventry-Climax now was the engine supplier, and it was the C-C, 62-cubic-inch four that formed the basis for the Southern Cross model. Other engine sizes are also mentioned in connection with this model name, all with the same 3.54-inch stroke and with bores varying from 2.32 to 2.60 inches. The Coventry-Climax engine was one of England's few F-head designs, with the intake valve located in the head and operated by a pushrod, and the exhaust valve in the block, the same arrangement employed by Rolls-Royce today. There was also a six-cylinder Coventry-Climax F-head engine employed in a few models beginning in 1932.

By far the most notable single Triumph of the prewar period arrived after Donald Healey had taken over as experimental manager of Triumph. This was the first of the Dolomite specials, a straight-eight with two overhead camshafts, hemispherical combustion chambers, valves at 90 degrees to each other, center-located spark plugs. The cams were gear-driven, with the gears located between the two blocks of four into which the engine was divided. The crankshaft ran on ten main bearings, the extra one introduced because of the split between the blocks. The blocks were made of aluminum alloy, and the cast-iron cylinder liners were shrunk into the blocks. The removable heads were cast of the same material as the blocks, and the steel valve seats were pressed into place.

In addition to all this, the engine was supercharged with a Roots-type blower which put out a maximum of 10 pounds pressure. The power rating was 140 b.hp. at 5,500 r.p.m., a seemingly small output from the 110 blown cubic inches. The Wilson preselector transmission had very close ratios for the top three gears, and the customer had his choice of either a 4.5-to-1 or 4.1-to-1 rear end. Semi-elliptic springs front and rear, augmented by special shock absorbers, were designed to handle the guaranteed 100-plus m.p.h.

The first Dolomite was an astonishing car, considering the rather conservative character of the rest of the Triumph models. Its design was almost exactly the same as the 2.3-liter Alfa Romeo introduced in 1932, even to the splitting of the engine into two blocks and the central cam drive. Not more than a few of the straight-eight Dolomites were made, but the name passed down to models introduced in 1937 and continued until the beginning of the war. Only one of these later Dolomites, the roadster, qualifies as a semi-sports car. The others were primarily transportation vehicles.

The Standard Motor Company acquired Triumph in 1945, and until 1952 production was limited to passenger cars of little sports interest. When the Triumph sports car was finally unveiled at the London Show in 1952, it still was a long way from actual production. Between show time and delivery time, the design was extensively reworked for higher speed, until 124.889 m.p.h. had been recorded on the Belgian Jabbeke highway. While that figure was made with the car in special form (without bumpers or windshield; with bellypan, racing windshield, metal cockpit cover, rear-fender skirts), the same car in stock condition except for the presence of a bellypan registered a speed of 114.890 in overdrive, 108.959 in standard top gear.

Since the Triumph Sports (TR2) had to be built for a moderate price, most of the chassis and body components were either stock or modified Triumph or Standard parts. The engine was the Standard Vanguard pushrod-overhead-valve four. To bring displacement down to under two liters, the bore was decreased 0.08 inch by adding to the wall thickness of the wet cylinder liners. To raise the output to the advertised 90 b.hp. at 4,800 r.p.m., dual carburetors were fitted, compression ratio raised to 8.5-to-1 and a high-lift, long-duration cam installed.

Front suspension was independent, by coil springs and wishbones. Rear suspension was semi-elliptic. Total weight was 2,125 pounds, including fuel, oil and water. The Triumph was another in the growing list of low-cost, high-speed cars the British had managed to put together out of components which had been around for several years.

What distinguished the Triumph TR2 from others of its type was something its makers could not have predicted — popularity. For the American buyer, the TR2 proved to be the logical successor to the M.G. With its comfortably larger engine the Triumph could do far more than the Morris product. It was faster, quicker, more responsive in traffic, less finicky about gears on hills. It was the perfect "fun" car.

Road tests, both British and American, have emphasized this fun factor. The car required neither pampering nor skill, but instead responded readily to the touch of the novice. In performance it was a perfect compromise. It combined the agility of the M.G. with the acceleration and top speed of the big American cars. Along with that, incidentally, it showed exceptional fuel economy. Even under rough and spirited handling, it delivered 30 or more miles per gallon.

Owners were not able to resist taking the Triumphs into competition. Unfortunately American races are not set up for a car of 1,991 cubic centimeters, so Triumph owners had to be content with class wins within races that included cars of much larger displacement. When the chips were down in a big race, however, the Triumph showed its true road colors. It could go forever, as it did the day it finished 15th at Le Mans after 1792.14 continuous miles of operation, but it couldn't compete with the race-bred cars like Bristol and Frazer-Nash. It shouldn't, really. It cost about one-fourth as much — you could buy a TR2 in America for $2,450 — as the thoroughbreds.

With the sudden and lasting commercial success of the Triumph TR2 came, inevitably, well-planned attempts to market similar products. The basic Standard engine was utilized in the Morgan chassis (see Morgan chapter) and also in a special, Italian-looking car, the Doretti. The Doretti was not simply a deluxe TR2, but rather the combination of a new frame and body with the TR2 working components. For his extra $500 the buyer got more luxury, better handling.

Having established a sound design, British practice is to leave it alone. This is precisely what Triumph did. After the first year of heavy sales, the only modifications made to the TR2 were larger rear brakes (increased from nine to 10 inches in diameter; from 1¾ to 2½ inches in width); redesigned body sides with higher door sills and more road clearance at the bottom; a larger rear window. In addition, a Fiberglas hard top was added to the line of optional equipment. Britain's newest version of the poor man's sports car was ready for another year.

INTRODUCTION TO TABLES

Here are the brief specifications of the cars covered in the three sections of this book. Trying to get some of these figures has been a tremendous job, and we haven't succeeded in all cases. We believe, however, that no automobile book has ever presented such a comprehensive list of facts and figures on the great and historic marques.

Some explanation of symbols and terms will help you use the tables.

Under the heading, "Cylinders," all are assumed to be in-line arrangements unless otherwise specified.

"Valve Arrangement" is indicated by the standard abbreviations in use today. "L" means the valves are both on the same side of the cylinder in the block; "I" means the valves are located in the head and are operated by pushrods; "V-pushrod" describes pushrod-operated overhead valves which are set at an angle to each other rather than being in a straight line (the Chrysler V8 with the hemispherical combustion chambers is a modern example); "F" indicates that the intake valve is in the head and the exhaust valve is in the block; "T" means that both valves are in the block but are located on opposite sides of the cylinder; SOHC and DOHC mean Single Overhead Camshaft and Double Overhead Camshaft, respectively. In each case the number refers to the number of camshafts per bank of cylinders. If the cylinders are arranged in line, a DOHC valve arrangement means there are two overhead camshafts on the engine; if the cylinders are arranged in a V or are opposed, a DOHC valve arrangement means there are two overhead camshafts per bank of cylinders, or a total of four on the engine. "Sleeve" means, of course, that the familiar poppet-valve set-up has been abandoned in favor of sleeve valves. For further explanation, see the Daimler chapter in the Classics section.

Most of the rest of the headings are self-explanatory, but there is bound to be a lot of confusion in the tire size department. We've adhered to a policy of using the sizes given in primary references.

Under "Price" are listed factory prices. Obviously we couldn't list the entire catalogue of such manufacturers as Packard. In those cases we have selected the minimum price.

The Authors

SPORTS—SPECIFICATIONS

Year	Model	Cylinders	Bore & Stroke	Displacement, Cu. In.	Valve Arrangement	Comp. Ratio -to 1	Max. Brake Horsepower at RPM	Max. Torque Lb. Ft. at RPM	No. Forward Speeds	Transmission Ratios -to 1				Rear Axle Ratio -to 1	Wheelbase, Inches	Tire Size	Car Wt., Lbs.	Price
										1st	2nd	3rd	4th or OD					
A. C.																		
1920	1.5 liter	4	2.72 x 3.94	91	L				3					4.5	106	700 x 80, 710 x 90	1,100 Chassis	$1,335
1920	2 liter	6	2.56 x 3.94	122	SOHC		40 to 82		3, 4					4.0 4.33 4.50 4.66	106, 111, 117, etc.	700 x 80, 710 x 90, 500 x 19	1,350 to 1,820 Chassis	$1,700
1939	2 liter S/C	6	2.56 x 3.94	122	SOHC		90 at 4,250		4					4.0 4.33 4.50 4.66	112	500 x 19	1,600 Chassis	$2,410
ALFA ROMEO																		
1925	22/90 RLSS	6	2.99 x 4.32	173	I		90		4						123	31 x 525		
1926	12/50 1.5 liter sports	6	2.44 x 3.22	91	SOHC		50		4					4.0	114	29 x 500		$2,670 Chassis $3,640 to $4,120
1928	15/85	6	2.44 x	91	DOHC	5.3	85		4					5.25	114	27	1,76	

SPORTS (Continued)

Year	Model	Cylinders	Bore & Stroke	Displacement, Cu. In.	Valve Arrangement	Comp. Ratio -to 1	Max. Brake Horsepower at RPM	Max. Torque Lb. Ft. at RPM	No. Forward Speeds	Transmission Ratios -to 1				Rear Axle Ratio -to 1	Wheelbase, Inches	Tire Size	Car Wt., Lbs.	Price
										1st	2nd	3rd	4th or OD					
ALFA ROMEO (Cont'd.)																		
1929	17/75 and 17/85	6	2.55 × 3.46	107	DOHC		75 and 85 at 4,400		4						108, 114	27 × 475		$2,670 to $3,150 Chassis $3,640 to $4,120
1929	17/95 S/C Spyder	6	2.55 × 3.46	107	DOHC	5.8	95		4					3.75 4.08	108	27 × 475	1,900	$6,180
1931	20/220, 21/220 Monza	8	2.55 × 3.46	143	DOHC	5.8	160		4					4.50	108, 124	550 × 19	2,460	$9,580
1934	19/68 and 19/76	6	2.75 × 3.93	141	DOHC				4					4.35, 4.56		550 × 18		$4,050 to $7,520
1936	23/180 S/C	8	2.67 × 3.93	177	DOHC	5.8, 6.7	180 to 200 at 5,000		4					4.16, 4.54	106, 110		2,650	$9,440 to $13,200
ALVIS																		
1923	12/50	4	2.67 × 4.05	91	I				4					4.30	112.6	29 × 4.4	1,850 Chassis	$1,940 Chassis
1923	12/50 Touring	4	2.67 × 4.32	100	I				4					4.50	112.5	29 × 495	1,900 Chassis	$1,940 Chassis
1927	Eagle (later Silver Eagle)	6	2.48 × 3.93	114	I				4	3.88	2.31	1.53	1.00	5.22	112.5, 118	29 × 475	2,750	$2,500
1928	Front Wheel Drive S/C	4	2.67 × 4.01	90	SOHC		50 (1928) 75 (1929)		4					4.70	102, 120	29 × 475		$3,060
1929	8/15	8	2.16 × 3.09	91	DOHC				4									$4,760
1931	12/60	4	2.67 × 4.32	100	I				4	3.24	2.13	1.42	1.00	4.77	112		2,350	$2,000

SPORTS (Continued)

Year	Model	Cylinders	Bore & Stroke	Displacement, Cu. In.	Valve Arrangement	Comp. Ratio -to 1	Max. Brake Horsepower at RPM	Max. Torque Lb. Ft. at RPM	No. Forward Speeds	Transmission Ratios -to 1				Rear Axle Ratio -to 1	Wheelbase, Inches	Tire Size	Car Wt., Lbs.	Price
										1st	2nd	3rd	4th or OD					
ALVIS (Cont'd.)																		
1932	Firefly	4	2.71 × 3.93	91	I				4	3.15	2.04	1.41	1.00	5.20	118.5	30 × 500		$2,400
1932	Speed Twenty	6	2.87 × 4.32	169	I	6.5	98 at 4,250		4	3.15	2.04	1.41	1.00	4.55	123	30 × 525	3,000	$3,350
1935	Firebird 12/70	4	2.87 × 4.32	112	I	5.9	61 at 4,300		4					5.22	118.5	500 × 20	2,121	$2,400
1936	Speed Twenty Five	6	3.26 × 4.32	218	I	6.4	110 at 3,800		4	3.15	2.03	1.43	1.00	4.11, 4.33	124	600 × 19	2,576 Chassis	$3,400
1936	4.3 liter	6	3.67 × 4.32	268	I	6.3	123 at 3,600		4	3.15	2.03	1.43	1.00	3.82	124	550 × 19	3,800	$4,800
AMILCAR																		
1921	C4	4	2.16 × 3.73	57	L				3					4.28	91	700 × 80		$1,250
1922	Grand Sport Surbaisse	4	2.36 × 3.73	66	L				3	2.84	1.60	1.00		4.50	91	27 × 4	1,290	$1,400
1926	Super C Sports S/C	6	2.20 × 2.91	67	DOHC				4	2.61	1.82	1.38	1.00	4.50	74, 84	27 × 420		$3,300
ASTON MARTIN																		
1922		4	2.62 × 4.21	91	L				4					4.1	96, 105	7.10 × 90		$3,030 Chassis
1927	T-Type International	4	2.73 × 3.95	91	SOHC	6.0			4	3.77, 2.56	2.19, 1.60	1.38, 1.17	1.00, 1.00	4.75	103	4.50 × 21	2,125	$2,790
1932	Standard	4	2.73 × 3.95	91	SOHC	6.0			4	3.50	2.42	1.38	1.00	5.11	120	4.50 × 21, 5.25 × 19	2,350	$2,900

ASTON MARTIN (Cont'd.)

Year	Model	Cylinders	Bore & Stroke	Displacement Cu. In.	Valve Arrangement	Comp. Ratio -to 1	Max. Brake Horsepower at RPM	Max. Torque Lb. Ft. at RPM	No. Forward Speeds	Transmission Ratios -to 1				Rear Axle Ratio -to 1	Wheelbase, Inches	Tire Size	Car Wt., Lbs.	Price
										1st	2nd	3rd	4th or OD					
1933	Le Mans	4	2.73 x 3.95	91	SOHC	7.5			4	3.01	1.88	1.27	1.00	4.66	103, 120	5.25 x 18	2,570	$2,900
1934	Mark II	4	2.73 x 3.95	91	SOHC	7.5	73 at 5,200		4	2.78	1.74	1.27	1.00	4.66	103, 120	5.25 x 18	2,570	$2,950
1935	Ulster	4	2.73 x 3.95	91	SOHC	9.7			4	2.78	1.74	1.27	1.00	4.25	103	5.25 x 18	2,240	$3,637
1937	15/98	4	3.07 x 4.02	119	SOHC		95 at 5,000		4					4.66	116	5.25 x 18	2,470	1937: $2,900 '38, '39: $2,310
1937	Speed Model	4	3.07 x 4.02	119	SOHC	7.8	95 at 5,000		4						102			$3,760
1939	Speed Model Type C	4	3.07 x 4.02	119	SOHC		110 at 5,000		4								2,580	$3,760

BALLOT

Year	Model	Cylinders	Bore & Stroke	Displacement Cu. In.	Valve Arrangement	Comp. Ratio -to 1	Max. Brake Horsepower at RPM	Max. Torque Lb. Ft. at RPM	No. Forward Speeds	Transmission Ratios -to 1				Rear Axle Ratio -to 1	Wheelbase, Inches	Tire Size	Car Wt., Lbs.	Price
										1st	2nd	3rd	4th or OD					
1922	2 liter	4	2.75 x 5.10	122	DOHC				4					3.75	110	820 x 120		$9,000
1923	2 liter	4	2.75 x 5.10	122	SOHC				4					5.00	122.5	820 x 120		$4,000
1927	RH	8	2.67 x 4.13	186	SOHC				4					5.00	134	577 x 30		$4,875

BENTLEY

Year	Model	Cylinders	Bore & Stroke	Displacement Cu. In.	Valve Arrangement	Comp. Ratio -to 1	Max. Brake Horsepower at RPM	Max. Torque Lb. Ft. at RPM	No. Forward Speeds	Transmission Ratios -to 1				Rear Axle Ratio -to 1	Wheelbase, Inches	Tire Size	Car Wt., Lbs.	Price
										1st	2nd	3rd	4th or OD					
1921	3 liter	4	3.14 x 5.85	181	SOHC	4.3	69 at 3,500		4	2.64	1.63	1.33	1.00	3.53	112	820 x 120		$5,090 Chassis
1922	3 liter Standard	4	3.14 x 5.85	181	SOHC		71 at 3,500		4					3.92, 4.23	117, 130	820 x 120		

SPORTS (Continued)

Year	Model	Cylinders	Bore & Stroke	Displacement, Cu. In.	Valve Arrangement	Comp. Ratio -to 1	Max. Brake Horsepower at RPM	Max. Torque Lb. Ft. at RPM	No. Forward Speeds	1st	2nd	3rd	4th or OD	Rear Axle Ratio -to 1	Wheelbase, Inches	Tire Size	Car Wt., Lbs.	Price
BENTLEY (Cont'd.)																		
1924	Speed Model	4	3.14 x 5.85	181	SOHC	5.3	81 at 3,500		4	3.83	2.07	1.45	1.00	3.78	117 130	820 x 120		
1926	Le Mans	4	3.14 x 5.85	181	SOHC	6.5	87 at 3,500		4	3.36	1.82	1.36	1.00	3.78	117 130	525 x 21		
1925	6-1/2 liter	6	3.93 x 5.50	402	SOHC	4.4			4	3.36	1.82	1.36	1.00	3.84	117 130	525 x 21		$7,015 Chassis
1927	4-1/2 liter	4	3.93 x 5.50	269	SOHC	4.8			4	2.64	1.63	1.33	1.00	3.53	130	600 x 21		$5,100 Chassis
1930	8 liter Speed Six	6	4.33 x 5.50	487	SOHC				4	3.37	1.83	1.36	1.00	3.53	144 156	525 x 21		$8,960 Chassis
1930	4-1/2 liter S/C	4	3.93 x 5.50	269	SOHC				4						130	33 x 600		$8,320
1931	4 liter	6	3.35 x 4.45	239	F	5.5	120 at 4,000		4	3.24	1.79	1.35	1.00	4.58	134 140			$5,920 Chassis
B. M. W.																		
1935	321	6	2.56 x 3.77	117	I	6.0	45 at 3,750		4	3.64	2.05	1.49	1.00	3.9	96	525 x 16	2,180	$1,700 to $2,180
1936	328	6	2.59 x 3.77	119	V-pushrod	7.5	80 at 4,500		4	3.67	2.08	1.39	1.00	3.9	96	525 x 16	1,850	$3,370
BUGATTI																		
1910	Type 13	4	2.55 x 3.93	83	2/cyl SOHC		25		4					3.21, 3.46	94.5, 100.5	710 x 90	1,230- 1,570	$1,335 to $1,700

In the case of Bugatti, as in rare instances elsewhere, an extra description has been added to the column headed "Valve Arrangement." This means, in each case: 2/cyl—two valves per cylinder, the orthodox arrangement; 3/cyl—three valves per cylinder, two intake and one exhaust; 4/cyl—four valves per cylinder, two intake and two exhaust.

BUGATTI (Cont'd.)

Year	Model	Cylinders	Bore & Stroke	Displacement, Cu. In.	Valve Arrangement	Comp. Ratio -to 1	Horsepower at RPM	Torque Lb. Ft. at RPM	Forward Speeds	1st	2nd	3rd	TH or OD	Axle Ratio -to 1	Wheelbase, Inches	Tire Size	Car Wt., Lbs.	Price
1908	5 liter	4	3.93 x 6.28	307	3/cyl SOHC		100		4					1.8	100	710 x 90	2,800	
1914	Type 22	4	2.67 x 3.93	89	4/cyl SOHC		30		4	2.93	1.85	1.30	1.00	3.0 3.46	100.5	710 x 90		$1,700 Chassis
1921	Type 23 Full Brescia	4	2.71 x 3.93	91	4/cyl SOHC				4	2.93	1.85	1.30	1.00	3.46 3.75 4.00	78 93	710 x 90		$1,720 to $2,300 Chassis
1923	Type 23 Brescia Modified	4	2.71 x 3.93	91	4/cyl SOHC		48 at 3,800		4	2.93	1.85	1.30	1.00	3.46 3.75 4.00	93	710 x 90		$1,580 Chassis
1923	Type 30	8	2.36 x 3.46	119	3/cyl SOHC		90		4	2.93	1.85	1.30	1.00	4.16 4.50	112	765 x 105		$2,475 Chassis
1924	Type 35 2 liter G. P.	8	2.36 x 3.46	119	3/cyl SOHC		90		4	2.42	1.85	1.30	1.00	3.37 3.60 3.85 4.15 4.50	94	29 x 500	2,000	$5,100 Chassis
1924	Type 35A 2 liter Modified G. P.	8	2.36 x 3.46	119	3/cyl SOHC		80		4	2.42	1.85	1.30	1.00	3.37 3.60 3.85 4.15 4.50	94	29 x 500	2,000	$2,550 Chassis
1927	Type 35C 2 liter G. P. S/C	8	2.36 x 3.46	119	3/cyl SOHC		130		4	2.42	1.85	1.30	1.00	3.37 3.60 3.85 4.15 4.50	94	29 x 500	2,070	
1926	Type 35T 2.3 liter G. P.	8	2.36 x 3.93	138	3/cyl SOHC				4	2.42	1.85	1.30	1.00	3.37 3.60 3.85 4.15 4.50	94	29 x 500	2,040	

SPORTS (Continued)

BUGATTI (Cont'd.)

Year	Model	Cylinders	Displacement, Cu. In.	Bore & Stroke	Valve Arrangement	Comp. Ratio -to 1	Max. Brake Horsepower at RPM	Max. Torque Lb. Ft. at RPM	No. Forward Speeds	Transmission Ratios -to 1				Rear Axle Ratio -to 1	Wheelbase, Inches	Tire Size	Car Wt., Lbs.	Price
										1st	2nd	3rd	4th or OD					
1926	Type 35B 2.3 liter G. P. S/C	8	138	2.36 × 3.93	3/cyl SOHC		140 at 5,300		4	2.42	1.85	1.30	1.00	3.37 3.60 3.85 4.15 4.50	94	29 × 500	2,070	
1925	Type 37 4-cyl. G. P.	4	91	2.71 × 3.93	3/cyl SOHC		60		4	2.42	1.85	1.30	1.00	3.37 3.60 3.85 4.15 4.50	94	28 × 350	1,735	$2,300 Chassis
1927	Type 37A 4-cyl. G. P. S/C	4	91	2.71 × 3.93	3/cyl SOHC		90		4	2.42	1.85	1.30	1.00	3.37 3.60 3.85 4.15 4.50	94	28 × 350	1,750	
1926	Type 38 2 liter Touring	8	119	2.36 × 3.46	3/cyl SOHC		70		4	2.78	1.80	1.29	1.00	4.66	123	28 × 350		
1927	Type 38A 2 liter Touring S/C Grand Sport	8	119	2.36 × 3.46	3/cyl SOHC		90		4	2.78	1.80	1.29	1.00	4.66	123	28 × 350		$2,250 Chassis
1926	Type 39 1.5 liter G. P.	8	91	2.36 × 2.59	3/cyl SOHC		80		4	2.42	1.85	1.30	1.00	3.37 3.60 3.85 4.15 4.50	94	29 × 500		
1927	Type 39A 1.5 liter G. P. S/C	8	91	2.36 × 2.59	3/cyl SOHC		120		4	2.42	1.85	1.30	1.00	3.37 3.60 3.85 4.15 4.50	94	29 × 500		

BUGATTI (Cont'd.)

Year	Model	Cylinders	Bore & Stroke	Displacement, Cu. In.	Valve Arrangement	Comp. Ratio -to 1	Max. Brake Horsepower at RPM	Max. Torque Lb. Ft. at RPM	No. Forward Speeds	1st	2nd	3rd	4th or OD	Rear Axle Ratio -to 1	Wheelbase, Inches	Tire Size	Car Wt., Lbs.	Price
1926	Type 40 1.5 liter Tourer	4	2.71 x 3.93	91	3/cyl SOHC		45		4	2.78	1.80	1.29	1.00	4.50 4.66	107	28 x 350, 27 x 440	2,200	$1,575 Chassis
1931	Type 40A 4-cyl. Tourer	4	2.83 x 3.93	99	3/cyl SOHC		50		4	2.78	1.80	1.29	1.00	4.50 4.66	107	27 x 440		$1,575 Chassis
1927	Type 41 La Royale	8	4.91 x 5.10	779	3/cyl SOHC		300 at 2,000		3						170	24 x 750	3,580 Chassis	$25,500 Chassis
1927	Type 43 2.3 liter Grand Sport	8	2.36 x 3.93	138	3/cyl SOHC		115		4	2.78	1.80	1.29	1.00	3.60 3.85 4.15 4.50	117	29 x 500		$6,620 Chassis
1930	Type 43A 2.3 liter Roadster	8	2.36 x 3.93	138	3/cyl SOHC		100		4	2.78	1.80	1.29	1.00	3.60 3.85 4.15 4.50	117	29 x 500		
1927	Type 44 3 liter Tourer	8	2.71 x 3.93	183	3/cyl SOHC		80		4	2.78	1.80	1.29	1.00	4.17	123	29 x 500		$2,670 Chassis
1929	Type 46 5 liter Tourer	8	3.18 x 5.10	327	3/cyl SOHC		120		3	2.50	1.40	1.00		3.91		32 x 600		$4,760 Chassis
1931	Type 46S 5 liter Tourer S/C	8	3.18 x 5.10	327	3/cyl SOHC		130		3	2.50	1.40	1.00		3.91		32 x 600		
1930	Type 47 16-cyl. Racing S/C	16	2.36 x 2.59	182	3/cyl SOHC		300		4									
1930	Type 49 3.3 liter Tourer	8	2.83 x 3.93	199	3/cyl SOHC		85		4	2.78	1.80	1.29	1.00	4.17		28 x 525	2,880	$3,030 Chassis
1930	Type 50 4.9 liter Sports S/C	8	3.38 x 4.20	295	2/cyl DOHC		200 at 4,000		3	2.49	1.39	1.00		3.46	122	32 x 600	2,570 Chassis	$8,360 Chassis

SPORTS (Continued)

Year	Model	Cylinders	Bore & Stroke	Displacement, Cu. In.	Valve Arrangement	Comp. Ratio -to 1	Max. Brake Horsepower at RPM	Max. Torque Lb. Ft. at RPM	No. Forward Speeds	Transmission Ratios -to 1				Rear Axle Ratio -to 1	Wheelbase, Inches	Tire Size	Car Wt., Lbs.	Price
										1st	2nd	3rd	4th or OD					
BUGATTI (Cont'd.)																		
1932	Type 50T 4.9 liter Tourer	8	3.38 × 4.20	295	2/cyl DOHC		150		3	2.49	1.39	1.00		3.91	138	32 × 600		$6,900 Chassis
1931	Type 51 2.3 liter G. P. S/C	8	2.36 × 3.93	139	2/cyl DOHC		180		4	2.42	1.85	1.30	1.00	3.37 3.60 3.85 4.15 4.50	94	29 × 500		
1931	Type 51A 1.5 liter G. P. S/C	8	2.36 × 2.59	91	2/cyl DOHC		130		4	2.42	1.85	1.30	1.00	3.37 3.60 3.85 4.15 4.50	94	29 × 500		
1931	Type 54 4.9 liter G. P. S/C	8	3.38 × 4.20	295	2/cyl DOHC				3	2.49	1.39	1.00		3.46	108	32 × 600		
1931	Type 55 2.3 liter Super Sport Roadster	8	2.36 × 3.93	139	2/cyl DOHC		135		4	2.73	1.81	1.29	1.00	3.38 4.15	108	29 × 500		
1934	Type 57 3.3 liter Tourer	8	2.83 × 3.93	199	2/cyl DOHC	6.2	135		4	2.78	1.80	1.29	1.00	4.17	130	18 × 550		$2,660 to $3,760 Chassis
1935	Type 57T 3.3 liter T. T. Model	8	2.83 × 3.93	199	2/cyl DOHC		140		4	2.69	1.80	1.29	1.00	3.85	130	18 × 550		
1935	Type 57S 3.3 liter Sports	8	2.83 × 3.93	199	2/cyl DOHC	8.3	185 at 5,500		4	2.69	1.80	1.29	1.00	3.85	117.5	18 × 550 Front, 18 × 600 Rear		$4,170 to $4,820 Chassis
1937	Type 57SC 3.3 liter Sports S/C	8	2.83 × 3.93	199	2/cyl DOHC	6.2	220 at 5,500		4	2.69	1.80	1.29	1.00	3.85	117.5	18 × 550 Front, 18 × 600 Rear		

| Year | Model | Cylinders | Bore & Stroke | Displacement Cu. In. | Valve Arrangement | Comp. Ratio -to 1 | Max. Brake Horsepower at RPM | Max. Torque Lb. Ft. at RPM | No. Forward Speeds | Transmission Ratios -to 1 | | | | Rear Axle Ratio -to 1 | Wheelbase, Inches | Tire Size | Car Wt., Lbs. | Price |
										1st	2nd	3rd	4th or OD					
BUGATTI (Cont'd.)																		
1938	Type 57C 3.3 liter Tourer S/C	8	2.83 × 3.93	199	2/cyl DOHC		160		4	2.69	1.80	1.29	1.00	3.85		18 × 550 Front, 18 × 600 Rear		$3,610 Chassis
CHENARD-WALCKER																		
1922	3 liter	4	3.12 × 5.90	182	DOHC				4						122, 132	895 × 135		
1923	2 liter	4	2.73 × 5.10	120	DOHC				4						120	820 × 120		
DELAGE																		
1922		6	3.15 × 5.91	276	—		88 at 2,380		4					3.1	135			
1927		6	3.74 × 5.51	363	—				4					3.8	151			
1938	D6-70	6	3.19 × 3.56	171	—	6.9	83 at 4,000		4	3.03	2.17	1.33	1.00	4.18	124	5.50 × 17	2,094 Chassis	$3,500 In England
1938	D8-120	8	3.30 × 4.21	292	—	7.3	143 at 4,000		4	3.03	2.17	1.33	1.00	3.91	130	6.50 × 18	4,225	$6,650 In England
DUESENBERG																		
1917	4-cyl. Touring	4	3.98 × 6.00	299	4/cyl horiz.		90 at 2,600		3									
1920	4-cyl. "Rochester" Touring	4	4.24 × 6.00	340	2/cyl horiz.		81 at 2,600		3									
1920	"A"	8	2.89 × 5.00	260	V-SOHC 2/cyl	5.0	92 at 3,800		3	3.17	1.65	1.00		4.60	134	33 × 5	3,300	$6,500

SPORTS (Continued)

Year / Model	Cylinders	Bore & Stroke	Displacement Cu. In.	Valve Arrangement	Comp. Ratio -to 1	Max. Brake Horsepower at RPM	Max. Torque Lb. Ft. at RPM	No. Forward Speeds	Transmission Ratios -to 1				Rear Axle Ratio -to 1	Wheelbase, Inches	Tire Size	Car Wt., Lbs.	Price
									1st	2nd	3rd	4th or OD					
DU PONT																	
1928 E and F	6	3.38 × 5.00	268	I		75 at 3,000		E: 3 / F: 4					E: 4.70 / F: 4.45	125, 136	620 × 32	3,850	$2,800
1929 G (Le Mans)	8	3.38 × 4.50	322	L		75 at 3,000		3 or 4					3.75 to 4.70	125, 136		4,550	$4,410
FRAZER-NASH																	
1928 S/C	4	2.71 × 3.93	91	L	5.3	85		3					3.8	99	19 × 350	1,710	$2,330 Chassis
1933 T. T. 1.5 liter	6	2.24 × 3.85	91	DOHC	6.9	80 at 4,500		4	3.09	1.84	1.26	1.00	3.8, 4.1	102, 108		1,575 Chassis	$2,890
1937 F-N B. M. W. Type 328	6	2.59 × 3.77	120	V-pushrod	7.5	80 at 4,500		4	3.64	2.05	1.49	1.00	3.90	95	525 × 16	1,565 dry	$3,370
H C S																	
1923 4	4	3.75 × 5.50	243	I		52 at 2,950		3	3.33	1.68	1.0			120	32 × 4.50	3,560	$2,475
INVICTA																	
1926 3 liter	6	2.85 × 4.71	181	I				4	2.89	1.95	1.36	1.00	3.6	120	28 × 495	2,800	$4,560 Chassis
1928 4.5 liter	6	3.48 × 4.74	273	I		110 at 3,200		4	2.89	1.92	1.33	1.00	3.9	118, 120, 126	30 × 525	2,900 to 3,450	$7,000
1931 Small	6	2.04 × 3.93	78	SOHC		50 at 5,000		4	3.75	1.97	1.33	1.00	6.1			2,500	$1,900
1932 Small S/C	6	2.24 × 3.85	91	SOHC		90 at 5,000		4									$1,900
1947 Black Prince	6	3.18 × 3.81	183	DOHC				4	Torque converter								$16,000

Year	Model	Cylinders	Bore & Stroke	Displacement, Cu. In.	Valve Arrangement	Comp. Ratio -to 1	Max. Brake Horsepower at RPM	Max. Torque Lb. Ft. at RPM	No. Forward Speeds	1st	2nd	3rd	4th or OD	Rear Axle Ratio -to 1	Wheelbase, Inches	Tire Size	Car Wt., Lbs.	Price
KISSEL																		
1923	6-45	6	3.31 × 5.50	284	L		61 at 2,300		3					3.92	124	32 × 4.50	4,010	$3,075
LAGONDA																		
1926	2 liter (some supercharged)	4	2.83 × 4.72	119	DOHC				4	3.14	1.95	1.20	1.00	4.40	120	21 × 4	3,360	$3,200
1934	Rapier	4	2.46 × 3.54	67	DOHC				4	3.40	2.00	1.36	1.00	5.28	100		1,900	$1,300 Chassis
1934	Rapide 4-1/2 liter	6	3.48 × 4.74	273	I	6.7	140 at 4,000		4	3.13	2.01	1.28	1.00	3.31	123, 129	550 × 19	4,000	$4,000 to $4,300 Chassis
1937	Vee Twelve	V12	2.95 × 3.32	273	SOHC	7.0	175 at 5,500		4					4.27, 4.45	124	650 × 18	3,020	$5,760 Chassis
LANCIA																		
1922	Lambda 1st through 6th Series Type 67 engine	13° V4	2.95 × 4.71	129	SOHC	4.5 to 5.1	49 at 3,250		3 1st through 4th Series / 4 5th and 6th Series					4.10, 4.16	122, 135	765 × 105		$3,275 to $4,000
1927	Lambda 7th Series Type 78 engine	14° V4	3.12 × 4.71	145	SOHC	5.2	59 at 3,250		4					4.10	122, 135	765 × 105		$3,615 to $4,340
1928	Lambda 8th, 9th Series Type 79 engine	13° 40' V4	3.24 × 4.71	157	SOHC	5.2	69 at 3,500		4					4.16, 4.45	122, 135	14 × 50		$3,130
1928	Dilambda	24° V8	3.12 × 4.71	242	SOHC		100 at 3,800											$4,240
1931	Artena	17° V4	3.25 × 3.54	117	I	5.3	54 at 4,000		4					4.70	124	450 × 140	1,890	$2,400

SPORTS (Continued)

Year	Model	Cylinders	Bore & Stroke	Displacement Cu. In.	Valve Arrangement	Comp. Ratio -to 1	Max. Brake Horsepower at RPM	Max. Torque Lb. Ft. at RPM	No. Forward Speeds	Transmission Ratios -to 1				Rear Axle Ratio -to 1	Wheelbase, Inches	Tire Size	Car Wt., Lbs.	Price
										1st	2nd	3rd	4th or OD					
LANCIA (Cont'd.)																		
1931	1st, 2nd Series Astura	19° V8	2.75 x 3.34	159	I	5.5	73 at 4,000		4					4.27	131	450 x 140	2,110	$3,370
1933	Augusta	18° 15' V4	2.75 x 3.07	73	I	5.4	35 at 4,000		4					4.78	104.5	400 x 140	1,300	$1,895
1936	Aprilia 1st Series	18° 7' V4	2.83 x 3.26	83	V-pushrod	5.7	48 at 4,300		4					4.10	108.3	400 x 140	1,280	$1,190
LEA-FRANCIS																		
1927	Hyper Sports S/C	4	2.71 x 3.93	91	I				4	3.33	1.99	1.30	1.00	3.75, 4.27	111	27 x 4.4		$2,550
1931	Ace of Spaces	6	2.56 x 3.93	122	I				4	3.19	2.0	1.37	1.00	4.70	114			$2,400
1939	Twelve	4	2.72 x 3.93	91	V-pushrod	7.5	50 at 4,800		4	3.94	2.42	1.45	1.00	5.10, 5.25	111	525 x 17	1,792 Chassis	$1,915
1939	Fourteen	4	2.83 x 3.93	99	V-pushrod	7.5	56 at 4,800		4	3.94	2.42	1.45	1.00	5.10, 5.25	111	525 x 17	1,792 Chassis	$1,915
LORRAINE-DIETRICH																		
1924	Silken Six (Le Mans)	6	2.95 x 5.10	209	I				3					3.5	114	820 x 120	1,435 Chassis	$4,000 to $5,300
MASERATI																		
1936	4CM-1100	4	2.56 x 3.23	67	DOHC	5.0	105 at 6,500		4						94.5	550 x 16	1,435 Chassis	
1936	4CM-2400	4	3.31 x 4.41	151	DOHC		160 at 5,300		4						96.5			

MERCEDES-BENZ

Year	Model	Cylinders	Bore & Stroke	Displacement Cu. In.	Valve Arrangement	Comp. Ratio -to 1	Max. Brake Horsepower at RPM	Max. Torque Lb. Ft. at RPM	No. Forward Speeds	Transmission Ratios -to 1				Rear Axle Ratio -to 1	Wheelbase, Inches	Tire Size	Car Wt., Lbs.	Price
										1st	2nd	3rd	4th or OD					
1914	28/95 Sports, Tourer	6	4.12 × 5.50	432	SCHC		95 at 1,800		4					3.8	132.5, 120.5	895 × 135	2,770 Chassis	
1924	15/70/100 4 liter tourer S/C	6	3.15 × 5.10	239	SOHC		70 100 s/c		4					4.30	144	895 × 135		$5,820 to $6,540 Chassis
1924	24/100/140 6 liter tourer S/C	6	3.69 × 5.91	381	SOHC		100 140 s/c		4					3.09 3.28 3.50 4.30	134 148	895 × 135	3,300 Chassis	$8,000 to $8,720 Chassis
1927	24/110/160 6.2 liter sports S/C (33/180)	6	3.69 × 5.91	381	SOHC		110 160 s/c at 3,000		4					3.09 3.28 3.50 4.30	134 148		2,800 Chassis	$7,520 to $8,000 Chassis
1927	26/120/180 Model S sports S/C (36/220)	6	3.85 × 5.91	415	SOHC		120 180 s/c at 3,000		4					2.50 2.76 3.09	134		2,800 Chassis	$9,700 Chassis
1928	26/170/225 Model SS sports S/C (38/250)	6	3.94 × 5.91	428	SOHC		170 225 s/c at 3,200		4					2.50 2.76 3.09	134	700 × 20, 650 × 20	2,690 Chassis	$10,800 to $12,100 Chassis
1928	26/170/225 Model SSK sports S/C	6	3.94 × 5.91	428	SOHC		250 s/c		4					2.50 2.76 3.09	116	700 × 20, 650 × 20	2,690 Chassis	$13,550 Chassis
1931	Model SSKL S/C	6	3.94 × 5.91	428	SOHC		290 to 300 s/c		4					2.50 2.76 3.09	116	700 × 20, 650 × 20		

SPORTS (Continued)

Year	Model	Cylinders	Bore & Stroke	Displacement, Cu. In.	Valve Arrangement	Comp. Ratio -to 1	Max. Brake Horsepower at RPM	Max. Torque Lb. Ft. at RPM	No. Forward Speeds	Transmission Ratios -to 1				Rear Axle Ratio -to 1	Wheelbase, Inches	Tire Size	Car Wt., Lbs.	Price
										1st	2nd	3rd	4th or OD					
MERCER																		
1920	Series 5 Raceabout	4	3.75 x 6.75	298	L	75 at	75 at 2,980		4	3.70	2.14	1.47	1.00	3.22	115, 132	32 x 4.50	3,200	$3,950
1922	Series 6 Runabout	6	3.75 x 5.00	331	I			84 at 2,550	3					3.77	132	32 x 4.50	3,750	$3,750
M. G.																		
1927	M	4	2.24 x 3.26	52	SOHC		20 at 4,000		3	3.5	1.83	1.00		4.89	78	19 x 4		$850
1930	M 12/12	4	2.24 x 3.26	52	SOHC		27 at 4,500		3	3.5	1.83	1.00		4.89	78	19 x 4		$850
1930	Mark III Tigresse	6	2.71 x 4.32	151	SOHC				4	3.42	1.84	1.31	1.00	4.28	114	19 x 5		$4,340
1931	C Montlhery Midget	4	2.24 x 2.87	46	SOHC		37 at 6,000		4	2.69	1.86	1.36	1.00	5.37 5.50	81	27 x 4		$2,790
1932	J2	4	2.24 x 3.26	52	SOHC		36 at 5,500		4	3.58	2.14	1.36	1.00	5.37 5.88	86	19 x 4		$1,450
1933	K2 (KB Magnette)	6	2.24 x 2.79	66	SOHC		41 at 5,500		4	3.58	2.14	1.36	1.00	5.78	94	19 x 475		$1,750
1934	QA S/C	4	2.24 x 2.87	46	SOHC		113 at 7,200		4	3.4	2.0	1.36	1.00	4.13 4.5 4.88	94	18 x 475		$2,670
1939	TB	4	2.61 x 3.54	76	SOHC		54 at 5,200		4	3.38	1.95	1.35	1.00	5.12	94	19 x 450		$1,080
MORGAN																		
1910-1924	Grand Prix	V2	Various L-head and OHV engines, made by J. A. P., Precision, M. A. G., and Anzani. Typical bore and stroke 3.34 x 3.34, typical displacement 66 cu. in.						2					4.5	84	700 x 80	500	$620 (in 1923)

Year	Model	Cylinders	Bore & Stroke	Displacement, Cu. In.	Valve Arrangement	Comp. Ratio -to 1	Max. Brake Horsepower at RPM	Max. Torque Lb. Ft. at RPM	No. Forward Speeds	1st	2nd	3rd	4th or OD	Rear Axle Ratio -to 1	Wheelbase, Inches	Tire Size	Car Wt., Lbs.	Price
MORGAN (Cont'd.)																		
1924	Aero	V2	Various J. A. P., Blackburne, Anzani engines, displacements from 60 to 67 cu. in., mostly OHV.						2						72	700 x 80	600 to 900	$560
1931	M and F Series (Matchless engine)	V2	3.37 x 3.37	60	V-pushrod		41 at 4,200		3									$435
1935	4/4 Coventry-Climax engine	4	2.43 x 3.54	69	F		35 at 4,500		4					5.0	92	500 x 16	1,400	$940
1939	4/4 (Standard engine)	4		77	I		40		4					5.0	96	525 x 16	1,625	$970
O. M.																		
1924	2 liter	6	2.56 x 3.93	122	L or I										110, 122			$3,030
RILEY																		
1919	Eleven (Redwing)	4	2.59 x 4.32	91	L				4					4.7	108	27 x 4.4		$1,450 Chassis
1926	Nine, Brooklands Nine	4	2.37 x 3.74	67	V-pushrod		34 at 4,000 / 55 at 5,500		4	3.90	2.52	1.46	1.00	4.75, 5.2	107.5, 91.5	27 x 4.4	1,950	$2,000
1933	Brooklands 1-1/2 liter	6	2.26 x 3.74	91	V-pushrod				4	2.47	1.50	1.25	1.00	4.77	108	29 x 5		$2,885
1936	Sprite	4	2.71 x 3.93	91	V-pushrod		55 at 4,500		4	3.60	2.09	1.42	1.00	5.22	107.5	475 x 18	2,200	$2,000 to $2,200
SALMSON																		
1919	1100	4		67	I				3							700 x 85		

SPORTS (Continued)

Year	Model	Cylinders	Bore & Stroke	Displacement Cu. In.	Valve Arrangement	Comp. Ratio -to 1	Max. Brake Horsepower at RPM	Max. Torque Lb. Ft. at RPM	No. Forward Speeds	Transmission Ratios -to 1			4th or OD	Rear Axle Ratio -to 1	Wheelbase, Inches	Tire Size	Car Wt., Lbs.	Price
										1st	2nd	3rd						
SALMSON (Cont'd.)																		
1922	Grand Prix	4	2.44 x 3.54	66	DOHC	4.8			3, 4					4.1, 4.5	98, 102	710 x 90		From $770
1928	1100 S/C	8	1.96 x 2.75	67	DOHC		100 at 5,800		4								905	
1936	1-1/2 liter (British)	4	2.72 x 3.86	90	DOHC	6.0	55 at 4,500		4					5.2	110.5	500 x 18	1,568 Chassis	From $2,160
1936	2.6 liter (British)	6	2.95 x 3.86	158	DOHC	6.4	95 at 4,500		4					4.1	112	625 x 16	1,792 Chassis	From $3,370
SINGER																		
1927	Junior, Porlock	4	2.20 x 3.38	52	SOHC				3					5.00	69	27 x 4	1,760	$725
1933	Nine (Le Mans)	4	2.36 x 3.39	59	SOHC	7.4	38 at 5,000		4					5.57	92	450 x 18	1,735	$785
1934	1-1/2 liter	6	2.32 x 3.58	91	SOHC	6.5	63 at 4,800		4					4.44	92	475 x 18	2,240	$1,575
1939	Nine Roadster	4	2.36 x 3.54	66	SOHC		30 at 5,000		3					5.40	91	500 x 16	1,820	$820
SQUIRE																		
1935	1-1/2 liter	4	2.72 x 3.94	91	DOHC	6.6	120 at 5,000		4					3.60, 4.25	102, 123	500 x 18	1,600, 1,725	$6,400 short $6,500 long
S. S.																		
1931	SSI	6	2.55 x 3.98	125	L		43 at 3,400		4					4.66	109			$1,580
1936	SS100	6	3.22 x 4.32	213	I	7.2	120 at 4,500		4	3.17	1.86	1.21	1.00	3.8	104	550 x 18		$2,160

Year	Model	Cylinders	Bore & Stroke	Displacement, Cu. In.	Valve Arrangement	Comp. Ratio -to 1	Max. Brake Horsepower at RPM	Max. Torque Lb. Ft. at RPM	No. Forward Speeds	Transmission Ratios -to 1				Rear Axle Ratio -to 1	Wheelbase, Inches	Tire Size	Car Wt., Lbs.	Price
										1st	2nd	3rd	4th or OD					
S. S. (Cont'd.)																		
1936	SS Jaguar 3-1/2 liter	6	3.22 x 4.32	213	I	7.2	120 at 4,500		4	3.17	1.86	1.21	1.00	4.25	120	550 x 18		$2,160
STUTZ																		
1923	K L D H	4	4.38 x 6.00	361	T	5.0	88 at 2,400								130	32 x 4.50		
1924	Speedway Six	6	3.50 x 5.00	289	I	4.5	80 at 3,000		3	3.04	1.81	1.00		4.90 or 4.45	130	32 x 4.50	3,800	$3,550
1928	B B Black Hawk	8	3.25 x 4.50	299	SOHC		95 at 3,200		3					3.60 or 5.50	131	32 x 6.75	4,466	$4,945
1931	D V 3 2	8	3.37 x 4.50	322	DOHC		156–161 at 3,900		4					4.75 or 4.50 or 4.25	134.5	7.00 x 18	4,895	$4,995
SUNBEAM																		
1925	3 liter (S/C optional)	6	2.95 x 4.32	178	DOHC		105 at 3,800 138 s/c		4	3.02	2.02	1.22	1.00	3.90, 4.50	130.5	525 x 21		$6,500
1934	Dawn	4	2.83 x 3.93	98	I		49 at 4,200		4	4.00	2.27	1.46	1.00	5.77	110	475 x 18		$2,350
VAUXHALL																		
1919	E 30/98	4	3.86 x 5.90	276	L		90-2,800		4					3.0	114	820 x 120		$5,750 to $8,002
1922	OE 30/98	4	3.86 x 5.51	272	I	5.2	112-3,500		4	3.69	2.36	1.57	1.00	3.3	118	32 x 4.25	2,460	$6,062

CLASSICS—SPECIFICATIONS

Year	Model	Cylinders	Bore & Stroke	Displacement, Cu. In.	Valve Arrangement	Comp. Ratio -to 1	Max. Brake Horsepower at RPM	Max. Torque Lb. Ft. at RPM	No. Forward Speeds	Transmission Ratios -to 1				Rear Axle Ratio -to 1	Wheelbase, Inches	Tire Size	Car Wt., Lbs.	Price
										1st	2nd	3rd	4th or OD					
AUBURN																		
1930	125	8	3.25 x 4.50	299	L	5.3	125 at 3,600		3					4.45	130	30 x 6.50	3,995	$1,595
1933	8-101A Custom Eight	8	3.00 x 4.75	269	L	5.3	100 at 3,400		3					3.40 5.10	127 136	6.00 or 6.50 x 17	3,815	$995
1933	12-165 Salon Dual Ratio Twelve	V12	3.13 x 4.25	391	Modified OHV	5.7	160 at 3,500		3					3.04-4.55	133	6.50 or 7.00 x 17	4,870	$1,745
1935	SC 851	8	3.06 x 4.75	280	L	6.5 or 7.0	150 at 4,000		3					3.23-4.30	127	6.50 x 16	3,729	$1,545
BENTLEY																		
1934	3-1/2 liter	6	3.25 x 4.50	224	I		104 at 3,800		4	2.75	1.73	1.24	1.00	4.1	126		3,300	$5,340 Chassis
1937	4-1/4 liter	6	3.50 x 4.50	260	I		125 at 3,800		4	2.75	1.73	1.24	1.00	4.1	126			$5,580 Chassis
CADILLAC																		
1933	355C	V8	3.38 x 4.94	353	L	5.4	115 at 3,000		3					4.40 4.60	140	7.00 x 17	5,000	$2,895

Year	Model	Cylinders	Bore & Stroke	Displacement, Cu. In.	Valve Arrangement	Comp. Ratio -to 1	Max. Brake Horsepower at RPM	Max. Torque Lb. Ft. at RPM	No. Forward Speeds	Transmission Ratios -to 1				Rear Axle Ratio -to 1	Wheelbase, Inches	Tire Size	Car Wt., Lbs.	Price
										1st	2nd	3rd	4th or OD					
CADILLAC (Cont'd.)																		
1937	3775	V8	3.50 × 4.50	346	L		135 at 3,400		3					4.60	138	7.50 × 16	4,745	$2,815
1937	3785	V12	3.13 × 4.00	368	I		150 at 3,600		3					4.60	138	7.50 × 16	5,050	$3,535
1933	452 C	V16	3.00 × 4.00	453	I	5.7	185 at 3,400		3					4.64 4.31	149	7.50 × 17	6,070	$6,250
1938	38-90	V16	3.25 × 3.25	431	L		185 at 3,600		3					4.31	141	7.50 × 16	5,105	$5,135
CHRYSLER																		
1927	E-80	6	3.50 × 5.00	289	L	4.7	92 at 3,000		3						120 127 133	30 × 6.75	4,105	$3,095
1929	L-80	6	3.63 × 5.00	310	L	4.7(2) 5.8(1)	100(2) at 3,200 112(1) at 3,200	197 at 1,000	4	3.38	2.19	1.40	1.00	3.77 4.08	136	700 × 18	4,125	$2,945
1931	CL	8	3.50 × 5.00	385	L	5.2(2) 5.8(1)	125(2) at 3,200 135(1) at 3,200	260(2) at 1,200 280(1) at 1,200	4					4.1	146	700 × 18 (1931) 17 × 7.50	5,045	$2,895
1934	CW	8	3.50 × 5.00	385	L	6.5	150 at 3,000	300 at 1,600	3 + OD	2.67	1.50	1.00	.70 OD	4.42 OD	146	17 × 7.50	5,780	$5,000

(1) Red Head engine; (2) Silver Dome engine

CLASSICS (Continued)

Year	Model	Cylinders	Bore & Stroke	Displacement, Cu. In.	Valve Arrangement	Comp. Ratio -to 1	Max. Brake Horsepower at RPM	Max. Torque Lb. Ft. at RPM	No. Forward Speeds	Transmission Ratios -to 1			4th or OD	Rear Axle Ratio -to 1	Wheelbase, Inches	Tire Size	Car Wt., Lbs.	Price
										1st	2nd	3rd						
CORD																		
1930	L 29	8	3.25 x 4.50	299	L	5.3	125 at 3,400		3	3.11	1.69	1.00		4.08 4.4 4.8	137.5	18 x 7.00	4,560	$2,395
1936	810 and 812	V8	3.50 x 3.75	289	L	6.5	125 at 3,500 (170 at 4,000 S/C)		4	2.34	1.51	1.00	.71	3.88	125	16 x 6.50	3,500	$1,995
CUNNINGHAM																		
1933	V-9	V8	3.88 x 5.00	471	L	5.0	140 at 2,800		3					4.25	132 or 142	7.00 x 20	4,900	$9,100
DAIMLER																		
1926	N45	6	4.62 x 5.12	516	Sleeve				4						162	35 x 6.75		$11,000
1928	Double Six 40/50 HP	V12	3.21 x 4.48	435	Sleeve				4	3.23	2.08	1.57	1.00	4.86	163		4,000 Chassis	$14,000
1928	Double Six 30 HP	V12	2.56 x 3.70	228	Sleeve				4						145.5	32 x 6.00		$11,000
1937	Straight 8	8	3.15 x 4.53	282	I	6.0	103 at 3,600		4					4.38	142	7.00 x 18	3,585 Chassis	$7,000
DOBLE																		
1924	E	4	2.62 x 5.00(1) 4.50 x 5.00(2)	213	Piston-type									1.52	142	6.50 x 20	4,325- 3,000 Chassis	$11,800

(1) High pressure; (2) Low pressure

Year / Model	Cylinders	Bore & Stroke	Displacement, Cu. In.	Valve Arrangement	Comp. Ratio -to 1	Max. Brake Horsepower at RPM	Max. Torque Lb. Ft. at RPM	No. Forward Speeds	Transmission Ratios -to 1				Rear Axle Ratio -to 1	Wheelbase, Inches	Tire Size	Car Wt., Lbs.	Price
									1st	2nd	3rd	4th or OD					
DUESENBERG																	
1929 to 1937 J, SJ (S/C)	8	3.75 × 4.75	420	DOHC	5.2	J: 265 at 4,200 SJ: 320 at 4,750		3	2.49	1.40	1.00		4.0, 4.3	142.5, 153.5	7.00 × 19 7.00 × 18 7.50 × 17		$8,500 Chassis
FRANKLIN																	
1933 S/C Airman Six	6	3.50 × 4.75	274	I	5.1	100 at 3,100		3					4.73	132	6.50 × 19	4,420	$1,935
1933 S/C Twelve	V12	3.25 × 4.00	398	I	5.1	150 at 3,100		3					4.45	144	7.50 × 17	5,600	$2,885
HISPANO-SUIZA																	
1928 37.2 HP	6	3.94 × 5.51	402	SOHC		135 at 2,400		3	2.81	1.78	1.00		3.33	145	33 × 5	4,250	$7,200 Chassis
1928 45 HP	6	4.33 × 5.51	486	SOHC	4.5, 6.0			3					3.17	145	33 × 5		$9,400 Chassis
1937 T12	V12	3.94 × 3.94	575	I	5.0	200 at 3,000		3	2.00	1.50	1.00		2.72 2.88 3.40 3.64	135 146 150 158		4,500	$13,350 Chassis
1937 K-G	6	3.94 × 4.33	299	I	5.0	120 at 3,200		3	2.00	1.50	1.00		3.64 3.40	134.6 146.5	16 × 45	3,920	$8,000 Chassis
ISOTTA-FRASCHINI																	
1925 8	8	3.35 × 5.11	350	I				3					3.75	145	895 × 135		$6,062 to $6,700 Chassis
1925 to 1938 8A, B	8	3.74 × 5.11	449	I	5.0	110 at 2,400		3					3.75	145	32 × 6.75	3,700 Chassis	$5,092 to $9,500 Chassis

CLASSICS (Continued)

Year	Model	Cylinders	Bore & Stroke	Displacement, Cu. In.	Valve Arrangement	Comp. Ratio -to 1	Max. Brake Horsepower at RPM	Max. Torque Lb. Ft. at RPM	No. Forward Speeds	1st	2nd	3rd	4th or OD	Rear Axle Ratio -to 1	Wheelbase, Inches	Tire Size	Car Wt., Lbs.	Price
LINCOLN																		
1932	KA	V8	3.50 × 5.00	384	L	5.3	120 at 2,900		3					4.58	136	7.50 × 18	5,430	$3,200
1933	KB	V12	3.50 × 4.50	448	L	5.3	150 at 3,400		3					4.58	145	7.50 × 18	5,750	$4,600
1933	KA	V12	3.00 × 4.50	382	L	5.5	125 at 3,400		3					4.58	136	7.00 × 18	5,270	$3,200
1937	K	V12	3.13 × 4.50	414	L	6.4	150 at 3,400		3					4.58	136	7.50 × 17	5,690	$4,546
1941	Continental (Zephyr engine)	V12	2.88 × 3.75	292	L	7.0	120 at 3,500		3					4.44	125	7.00 × 16	3,890	$2,727
MARMON																		
1928	75	6	3.75 × 5.13	340	I		84 at 2,700		3					4.10	136	32 × 6.75	4,498	$3,565
1931	88	8	3.25 × 4.75	315	L	5.5	125 at 3,400		3					4.90	130 136	6.50 × 19	4,375	$2,220
1933	Sixteen	V16	3.13 × 4.00	491	I	5.8	200 at 3,400		3					3.78	145	7.00 × 18	5,360	$4,825
MAYBACH–ZEPPELIN																		
1930	Twelve	V12	3.62 × 3.94	487	I		200 at 3,200		5	3.00	2.00	1.50	1.00*	3.58	147	7.50 × 20	4,200 Chassis	
MERCEDES–BENZ																		
1930	150/200 7.7 liter Grosser Mercedes	8	3.75 × 5.31	464	SOHC		150, 200 s/c at 2,800		3 + OD						147.6	700 × 20	4,080 Chassis	$14,750 Chassis

*Fifth speed, a compound low: 4.50 to 1.

Year	Model	Cylinders	Bore & Stroke	Displacement Cu. In.	Valve Arrangement	Comp. Ratio -to 1	Max. Brake Horsepower at RPM	Max. Torque Lb. Ft. at RPM	No. Forward Speeds	1st	2nd	3rd	4th or OD	Rear Axle Ratio -to 1	Wheelbase Inches	Tire Size	Car Wt., Lbs.	Price
MERCEDES-BENZ (Cont'd.)																		
1932	100/160 5 liter 500K	8	3.38 × 4.24	306	I		100, 160 s/c		4									$6,760 Chassis
1937	115/180 5.4 liter 540K	8	3.46 × 4.36	330	I		115, 180 s/c		4					2.8	129, 132	700 × 17	3,960 Chassis	$6,760 Chassis
1937	155/230 7.7 liter Grosser Mercedes	8	3.73 × 5.30	467	I		155, 180 s/c		4					2.96	152.5	825 × 17	4,830 Chassis	$16,750 Chassis
PACKARD																		
1932	903 DeLuxe Eight	8	3.50 × 5.00	385	L	6.0	135 at 3,200		4					4.69	142	7.00 × 19	5,045	$3,795
1933	1005 Twelve	V12	3.44 × 4.00	446	Modified L	6.0	160 at 3,200		3					4.69 4.41	142	7.50 × 17	5,385	$3,860
1937	150 Twelve	V12	3.44 × 4.25	473	Modified L	6.4	175 at 3,200		3					4.41	139	8.25 × 16	5,525	$3,740
1941	160 and 180 Series 1903, 4, 5, 6, 7, 8	8	3.50 × 4.63	356	L	6.5 6.9	160 at 3,600		3					3.92 4.09 4.36	138	7.00 × 16	4,350	$2,632
PEERLESS																		
1932	Sixteen	V16	3.25 × 3.50	464	I		173 at 3,300		3						145		4,050	
PIERCE-ARROW																		
1928	36	6	4.00 × 5.50	415	T		100 at 3,600		3					4.3	138	33 × 6.75	4,830	$6,375

CLASSICS (Continued)

Year	Model	Cylinders	Bore & Stroke	Displacement, Cu. In.	Valve Arrangement	Comp. Ratio -to 1	Max. Brake Horsepower at RPM	Max. Torque Lb. Ft. at RPM	No. Forward Speeds	Transmission Ratios -to 1				Rear Axle Ratio -to 1	Wheelbase, Inches	Tire Size	Car Wt., Lbs.	Price
										1st	2nd	3rd	4th or OD					
PIERCE-ARROW (Cont'd.)																		
1931	42	8	3.50 x 5.00	385	L	5.1	132 at 3,000		4					4.42	142	7.00 x 18	4,982	$3,695
1933	1236	V12	3.38 x 4.00	429	L	6.0	160 at 3,400		3					4.42 4.57	136 139	7.00 x 17	4,892	$2,975
1933	1242	V12	3.50 x 4.00	462	L	6.0	175 at 3,400		3					4.42 4.57	137 142	7.50 x 17	5,288	$3,785
ROLLS-ROYCE																		
1922	Silver Ghost	6	4.25 x 4.75	453	L				4						144		3,360 Chassis	$12,900 In U. S.
1928	Phantom I	6	4.25 x 5.50	470	I				4					3.50	144	33 x 6.75	4,310 Chassis	$13,325 In U. S.
1932	Phantom II	6	4.25 x 5.50	470	I	5.3			4					3.72	150	7.00 x 19	4,150 Chassis	$13,325 In U. S.
1936	Phantom III	V12	3.25 x 4.50	448	I	6.0			4					4.25	142	7.00 x 18	3,920 Chassis	$9,100 Chassis
1928	20 HP	6	3.00 x 4.50	190	I				4					4.50	129	32 x 5.25	2,660 Chassis	$5,275 Chassis
1936	20/25 HP	6	3.25 x 4.50	224	I	5.7			4					4.50	132	6.00 x 19	2,900 Chassis	$5,050 Chassis
1939	25/30 HP Wraith	6	3.50 x 4.50	260	I	6.0			4	3.31	2.10	1.37	1.00	4.50	132	6.00 x 19	4,425 Chassis	$5,275 Chassis

WILLS SAINTE CLAIRE

Year	Model	Cylinders	Bore & Stroke	Displacement, Cu. In.	Valve Arrangement	Comp. Ratio -to 1	Max. Brake Horsepower at RPM	Max. Torque Lb. Ft. at RPM	No. Forward Speeds	Transmission Ratios -to 1				Rear Axle Ratio -to 1	Wheelbase, Inches	Tire Size	Car Wt., Lbs.	Price
										1st	2nd	3rd	4th or OD					
1921	A-68	V8	3.25 x 4.00	265	SOHC	4.1	67 at 2,700		3	3.02	1.70	1.00		4.45, 4.90	121, 127	32 x 4.50	3,115	$3,375
1925	W6	6	3.25 x 5.50	274	SOHC		66 at 3,000		3					4.45	127		3,630	$3,185

POSTWAR—SPECIFICATIONS

Year	Model	Cylinders	Bore & Stroke	Displacement, Cu. In.	Valve Arrangement	Comp. Ratio -to 1	Max. Brake Horsepower at RPM	Max. Torque Lb. Ft. at RPM	No. Forward Speeds	1st	2nd	3rd	4th or OD	Rear Axle Ratio -to 1	Wheelbase, Inches	Tire Size	Car Wt., Lbs.	Price
A. C.																		
1947	2 liter	6	2.56 × 3.94	121	SOHC	6.5	76 at 4,500	105 at 2,750	4	3.39	1.98	1.37	1.00	4.55	117	670 x 16	2,912	$3,340
1953	Ace	6	2.56 × 3.94	121	SOHC	7.5	85 at 4,500		4	3.39	1.98	1.37	1.00	3.64	90	550 x 16	1,680	$2,515
ALFA ROMEO																		
1947	6C 2500 Sports	6	2.83 × 3.93	149	DOHC	7.0	90 at 4,600		4						118	600 x 18	2,370	
1947	6C 2500 Super Sports	6	2.83 × 3.93	149	DOHC	7.5	105 at 4,800		4						106, 118	600 x 18	2,200	$7,420 up
1950	1900, 1900 L	4	3.25 × 3.46	115	DOHC	7.5	80 at 4,800		4						93	600 x 16	2,470	$3,600 up
1951	1900C	4	3.25 × 3.46	115	DOHC	7.8	100 at 5,500		4						98	600 x 16	2,310	$3,830 up
1952	2 liter sports Disco Volante Spider, Coupe	4	3.34 × 3.46	122	DOHC	8.0	130		4						87	600 x 16	1,450	
1952	3 liter sports Disco Volante Spider	6	3.24 × 3.61	183	DOHC	8.0	200 at 5,500		4						95	600 x 16	1,680	

Year	Model	Cylinders	Bore & Stroke	Displacement, Cu. In.	Valve Arrangement	Comp. Ratio -to 1	Max. Brake Horsepower at RPM	Max. Torque Lb. Ft. at RPM	No. Forward Speeds	Transmission Ratios -to 1				Rear Axle Ratio -to 1	Wheelbase, Inches	Tire Size	Car Wt., Lbs.	Price
										1st	2nd	3rd	4th or OD					
ALFA ROMEO (Cont'd.)																		
1953	3.5 liter sports Spider, Coupe	6	3.42 × 3.85	213	DOHC	8.0	230		5						95	650 × 16	1,980, 2,090	
1954	Giulietta	4	2.93 × 2.95	79	DOHC		65 at 6,000		4					4.55	94	155 × 380	1,765	
ALLARD																		
1949	J 2	Cadillac V8	3.81 × 3.63	331	I	7.5	160 at 4,000	312 at 1,800	3	1.80	1.36	1.00		3.20	100	6.00 × 16	2,350	$3,360 without engine
1954	Palm Beach	Ford Zephyr 6	3.13 × 3.00	138	I	6.8	68 at 4,000	112 at 2,000	3	3.26	1.70	1.00		4.11	96	6.40 × 13	1,900	$2,995 complete, U. S. Port of Entry
1954	K 3	Ford V8	3.06 × 3.75	221	L	6.1	85 at 3,500		3	2.88	1.77	1.00		3.78	100	6.25 × 16	3,190	$4,995 with Cadillac engine, U. S. Port of Entry
1954	J R	Cadillac V8	3.81 × 3.63	331	I	8.3	210 at 4,150	165 at 3,600	3	2.4	1.5	1.00		3.29 3.50 3.78 4.10	96	6.00 × 16	2,200	$5,800 without engine U. S. Port of Entry
1954	Monte Carlo Sedan	Ford V8	3.06 × 3.75	221	L	6.1	85 at 3,500		3	3.11	1.77	1.00		3.78	112	6.25 × 16	3,190	$5,603 without engine U. S. Port of Entry
ALVIS																		
1946	Fourteen Sports	4	2.91 × 4.32	116	I				4	2.97	1.93	1.33	1.00	4.33	108	600 × 16		$2,790
1950	3 liter	6	3.30 × 3.54	183	I	8.0	104 at 4,000	163 at 2,500	4	2.97	1.93	1.33	1.00	4.09	111.5	600 × 15	3,164 dry	$3,500

POSTWAR (Continued)

Year	Model	Cylinders	Bore & Stroke	Displacement, Cu. In.	Valve Arrangement	Comp. Ratio -to 1	Max. Brake Horsepower at RPM	Max. Torque Lb. Ft. at RPM	No. Forward Speeds	Transmission Ratios -to 1 1st	2nd	3rd	4th or OD	Rear Axle Ratio -to 1	Wheelbase, Inches	Tire Size	Car Wt., Lbs.	Price
ASTON MARTIN																		
1948	2 liter sports	4	3.25 × 3.62	120	I	7.3	90 at 4,750		4	2.92	1.87	1.26	1.00	4.10	108	575 × 16	2,520	$7,260
1950	DB2	6	3.07 × 3.54	157	DOHC	6.5	107 at 5,000	130 at 3,000	4	2.92 2.92	1.98 1.87	1.33 1.26	1.00 1.00	3.50 3.67 3.77 4.10	99	600 × 16	2,460	$8,480
1950 1953	DB2 "Vantage" DB2-4	6	3.07 × 3.54	157	DOHC	8.2	123 at 5,000	144 at 2,400	4	2.92 2.92	1.98 1.87	1.33 1.26	1.00 1.00	3.50 3.67 3.77 4.10	99	600 × 16	2,460	$8,980 (DB2-4)
1953	DB3S	6	3.27 × 3.54	178	DOHC	8.5	180 at 5,500		4	2.92	1.87	1.26	1.00	3.73 to 4.50	87	600 × 16		$7,280
BENTLEY																		
1947	Mark VI 4-1/4 liter	6	3.50 × 4.50	260	F	6.4	132	214 at 2,250	4	2.98	2.01	1.34	1.00	3.73	120	650 × 16	4,075	$7,130
1951	Mark VI 4-1/2 liter	6	3.63 × 4.50	279	F	6.4	150 at 3,750		4	2.98 HydraMatic optional	2.01	1.34	1.00	3.73	120	650 × 16	4,080	$8,050
1953	Continental Sports	6	3.63 × 4.50	279	F	7.3	160 plus		4	2.67	1.54	1.22	1.00	3.08	120	650 × 16	3,750	$13,700
BRISTOL																		
1947	400 (85A engine)	6	2.59 × 3.77	119	V-pushrod	7.5	75–80 at 4,200	105 at 3,000	4	4.30	2.17	1.30	1.00	3.9	114	550 × 16	2,600	$7,050
1948	401, 402 (85C engine)	6	2.59 × 3.77	119	V-pushrod	7.5	85 at 4,500	113 at 3,000	4	4.30	2.17	1.30	1.00	3.9	114	550 × 16	2,800	$8,380
1953	403, 404 (100A, 100B, 100C engines)	6	2.59 × 3.77	119	V-pushrod	7.5 to 8.5	100 at 5,250 to 125 at 5,500	117 at 3,500 to 128 at 4,200	4	3.61	1.83	1.29	1.00	3.9	114(403) 96(404)		2,690 (403) dry 2,294 (404) wet	$7,000

Year	Model	Cylinders	Bore & Stroke	Displacement Cu. In.	Valve Arrangement	Comp. Ratio -to 1	Max. Brake Horsepower at RPM	Max. Torque Lb. Ft. at RPM	No. Forward Speeds	1st	2nd	3rd	4th or OD	Rear Axle Ratio -to 1	Wheelbase Inches	Tire Size	Car Wt., Lbs.	Price
BRISTOL (Cont'd.)																		
1954	405	6	2.59 × 3.77	119	V-pushrod	8.5	105 at 5,000		4 with OD	3.61	1.83	1.29	1.00	4.22	114	575 × 16	2,660	$6,300
BUGATTI																		
1951	Type 101 (Supercharger optional)	8	2.83 × 3.93	199	DOHC		135 at 5,500 190 s/c		5	Cotal preselector gearbox optional					130	600 × 17	3,250	On request
CHEVROLET																		
1954	Corvette	6	3.56 × 3.94	235.5	I	8.0	150 at 4,200	223 at 2,400			Powerglide			3.55	102	6.70 × 15	2,880	$3,295
1955	Corvette	V8	3.75 × 3.00	265	I	8.0	195 at 4,600	260 at 2,800			Powerglide			3.55	102	6.70 × 15	2,880	$2,595
CISITALIA																		
1947	Special Sport	4	2.67 × 2.95	67	I	7.2	50 at 5,500		4	3.90	2.72	1.18	1.00	3.67	93.6	500 × 15	1,540 dry	$5,500
1947	Mille Miglia	4	2.67 × 2.95	67	I	9.5	60 at 5,500		4	3.40	1.86	1.22	1.00	3.25	93.6	500 × 15	1,540 dry	
CROSLEY																		
1952	CD	4	2.50 × 2.25	44	SOHC	8.0	27 at 5,400	33 at 3,000	3					5.17	80	4.50 × 12	1,340	$915
CUNNINGHAM																		
1952	C4	V8	3.81 × 3.62	331	I	7.5	210 at 4,000		3(1)	2.43	1.51	1.00		3.36	105	8.00 × 15	3,400	$9,500

(1) Also available with Siata 4-speed transmission

POSTWAR (Continued)

Year	Model	Cylinders	Bore & Stroke	Displacement, Cu. In.	Valve Arrangement	Comp. Ratio -to 1	Max. Brake Horsepower at RPM	Max. Torque Lb. Ft. at RPM	No. Forward Speeds	Transmission Ratios -to 1				Rear Axle Ratio -to 1	Wheelbase, Inches	Tire Size	Car Wt., Lbs.	Price
										1st	2nd	3rd	4th or OD					
DAIMLER																		
1954	Straight 8	8	3.35 × 4.73	333	I	6.3	150 at 3,600		4	4.17	2.36	1.53	1.00	4.09	147	8.00 × 17	6,000	$14,000
1954	Conquest	6	3.00 × 3.50	148	I	7.8	100 at 4,600	122 at 1,750	4	3.84	2.21	1.47	1.00	3.73	104	6.00 × 15	2,700	$3,300
1955	Regina	6	3.77 × 4.24	282	I	6.5			4	4.17	2.36	1.53	1.00	4.27	132	7.50 × 16		$12,000
DELAHAYE																		
1936	Type 135 Coupe des Alpes	6	3.15 × 4.21	197	I	6.4	95 at 3,600		4	3.46	2.22	1.64	1.00	3.42	116	5.50 × 17	2,950	$4,350 In England
1949	Type 175	6	3.70 × 4.21	274	I		160 at 3,600		4						116	6.50 × 18	2,310 Chassis	
FERRARI																		
1947	2 liter "Type 166, Mille Miglia"	V12	2.36 × 2.31	122	SOHC	8.0	130 at 7,000		5	3.08	1.90	1.38	1.00 5th .93	5.00	88.6	5.50 × 15	1,760	Prices begin at about $8,500 at the factory and vary according to type of car, technical specs, body style, etc.
1950	2.3 liter "Type 195, Inter"	V12	2.56 × 2.31	143	SOHC	7.5	130 at 6,000		5	3.08	1.90	1.38	1.00 5th .93	5.00		5.90 × 15	2,016	
1951	2.6 liter "Type 212 Export"	V12	2.68 × 2.31	156	SOHC	8.0	150 at 6,000		5	3.08	1.90	1.38	1.00 5th .93	5.00 4.67	92.4	5.90 × 15	1,980	

FERRARI (Cont'd.)

Year	Model	Cylinders	Bore & Stroke	Displacement, Cu. In.	Valve Arrangement	Comp. Ratio -to 1	Max. Brake Horsepower at RPM	Max. Torque Lb. Ft. at RPM	No. Forward Speeds	Transmission Ratios -to 1				Rear Axle Ratio -to 1	Wheelbase, Inches	Tire Size	Car Wt., Lbs.	Price
										1st	2nd	3rd	4th or OD					
1952	2.9 liter "Type Mille Miglia"	V12	2.87 × 2.31	180	SOHC	9.0	240 at 7,000		4	2.54	1.70	1.26	1.00	4.44 4.00 3.64	94.5	6.40 × 15	1,980	Prices begin at about $8,500 at the factory and vary according to type of car, technical specs, body style, etc.
1951	4.1 liter "Type 342 America"	V12	3.15 × 2.68	250	SOHC	8.0	220 at 6,500		4	2.54	1.70	1.26	1.00	4.00 3.50	104.3	5.90 × 16	2,002	
1954	4.5 liter	V12	3.15 × 2.93	274	SOHC				4	2.54	1.70	1.26	1.00	3.50	104.3	5.90 × 16	2,000	
1954	4.9 liter	V12	3.31 × 2.93	302	SOHC		360		4					3.0 3.26 3.57				
1954	500 Mondial	4	3.54 × 3.07	121	DOHC	9.2	170 at 7,000		5					3.92 4.12 4.34	88.6	6.00 × 16	1,588	
1955	750 Monza	4	4.06 × 3.54	183	DOHC	9.2	250 at 6,000		5					4.55 5.06	88.6	6.00 × 16	1,675	
1955	250 Europa	V12	2.87 × 2.31	180	SOHC	8.5	220 at 7,000		4					and	102.4	6.00 × 16	2,315	
1955	(Not yet named)	6	3.70 × 3.54	229	DOHC	9.2	330 at 6,300		5					others			1,855	

FORD THUNDERBIRD

Year	Model	Cylinders	Bore & Stroke	Displacement, Cu. In.	Valve Arrangement	Comp. Ratio -to 1	Max. Brake Horsepower at RPM	Max. Torque Lb. Ft. at RPM	No. Forward Speeds	Transmission Ratios -to 1				Rear Axle Ratio -to 1	Wheelbase, Inches	Tire Size	Car Wt., Lbs.	Price
										1st	2nd	3rd	4th or OD					
1955	40A, 40B Std. Trans. and OD	V8	3.75 × 3.30	292	—	8.1	193 at 4,400	280 at 2,600	3	2.32	1.48	1.0		3.73 3.92—OD	102	6.70 × 15	2,986 (dry)	$2,695
	Automatic Trans.					8.5	198 at 4,400	286 at 2,600	3	2.40	1.47	1.0		3.31			3,085 (dry)	

POSTWAR (Continued)

Year Model	Cylinders	Bore & Stroke	Displacement, Cu. In.	Valve Arrangement	Comp. Ratio -to 1	Max. Brake Horsepower at RPM	Max. Torque Lb. Ft. at RPM	No. Forward Speeds	Transmission Ratios -to 1				Rear Axle Ratio -to 1	Wheelbase, Inches	Tire Size	Car Wt., Lbs.	Price
									1st	2nd	3rd	4th or OD					
FRAZER-NASH																	
1948 Le Mans Replica (High Speed)	6	2.59 × 3.77	119	V-pushrod	9.5	120 at 5,500	125 at 4,000	4	2.92	1.83	1.29	1.00	3.54	96	525 or 550 × 16	1,530 dry	$5,520
1952 Targa Florio Turismo	6	2.59 × 3.77	119	V-pushrod	7.5	100 at 5,000	118 at 3,750	4	2.97	1.92	1.31	1.00	3.60 to 6.10	96	525 or 550 × 16	1,845 dry	$5,460
1952 Le Mans Replica Mark II	6	2.59 × 3.77	119	V-pushrod	8.5 to 10.0	132 to 150 at 5,750		4	2.97	1.92	1.31	1.00	3.60 to 6.10	96	525 or 550 × 16	1,372 dry	$6,300
HEALEY																	
1948 2.4 liter	4	3.20 × 4.70	140	V-pushrod	6.9	104 at 4,500		4	3.65	2.15	1.42	1.00	3.50	102	6.00 × 15	2,575	$4,200
1950 Silverstone	4	3.20 × 4.70	140	V-pushrod	6.9	104 at 4,500		4	3.65	2.15	1.42	1.00	3.50 3.25 3.10	102	5.50 × 15		$2,730
1954 Nash-Healey	6	3.50 × 4.38	253	—	8.0	140 at 4,000	230 at 2,000	3	2.57	1.55	1.00	.70 OD	4.10	102	6.40 × 15	2,820	$6,200 U.S. Port of Entry
1954 Austin-Healey	4	3.44 × 4.38	162	—	7.5	90 at 4,000	144 at 2,000	3	2.25	1.42	1.00	.82 OD	4.10	90	5.90 × 15	2,150	$3,000 U.S. Port of Entry
1955 100 S	4	3.44 × 4.38	162	—	8.3	132 at 4,700		4	3.08	1.90	1.33	1.00	3.66 4.13 2.92 2.60	90	5.90 × 15	1,888	$4,995 U.S. Port of Entry
JAGUAR																	
1946 Mark V 3-1/2 liter	6	3.22 × 4.32	213	—	7.8	125 at 4,250		4	3.38	1.98	1.37	1.00	4.3	120	670 × 16	3,580	$2,770

Year / Model	Cylinders	Bore & Stroke	Displacement, Cu. In.	Valve Arrangement	Comp. Ratio -to 1	Max. Brake Horsepower at RPM	Max. Torque Lb. Ft. at RPM	No. Forward Speeds	1st	2nd	3rd	4th or OD	Rear Axle Ratio -to 1	Wheelbase, Inches	Tire Size	Car Wt., Lbs.	Price
JAGUAR (Cont'd.)																	
1951 XK-120	6	3.26 × 4.17	210	DOHC	7.0, 8.0	160 at 5,400		4	3.38	1.98	1.37	1.00	3.64 3.27	102	600 × 16	2,850	$3,050
1951 Mark VII	6	3.26 × 4.17	210	DOHC	7.0, 8.0	160 at 5,400		4	3.38	1.98	1.37	1.00	4.27	120	670 × 16	3,698	$3,050
1952 XK-120C	6	3.26 × 4.17	210	DOHC	8.0	200 at 5,800		4	2.98	1.75	1.21	1.00	3.31	96		2,240	$4,190
1955 Mark VII	6	3.26 × 4.17	210	DOHC	8.0	190 at 5,500	210 at 2,500	4	2.98	1.75	1.21	1.00	4.30	120	6.70 × 16	3,780	$4,450 U. S. Port of Entry
1955 XK-140	6	3.26 × 4.17	210	DOHC	8.0	190 at 5,500	210 at 2,500	4	2.98	1.75	1.21	1.00	3.54	102	6.00 × 16	2,770	$3,450 U. S. Port of Entry
1955 D	6	3.26 × 4.17	210	DOHC	9.0	250 at 6,000	242 at 4,000	4	2.14	1.64	1.29	1.00	2.79	90	6.50 × 16		$7,500 U. S. Port of Entry
JENSEN																	
1953 Interceptor	6	3.40 × 4.40	230	—	6.8	130 at 4,000	212 at 2,200	4 + OD	3.37	2.33	1.43	1.00 .76 OD	4.09	112	6.00 × 16	3,350	$4,760
1955 541	6	3.40 × 4.40	230	—	6.8	140 at 4,000		4	3.37	2.33	1.43	1.00	2.93	105	5.50 × 16	2,912	$3,598
JOWETT																	
1950 Jupiter	Opposed 4	2.86 × 3.55	91	—	8.0	60 at 4,500	82 at 3,100	4	3.56	2.17	1.37	1.00	4.56	93	5.50 × 16	2,107	$2,380
1954 R 4	Opposed 4	2.86 × 3.55	91	—	8.5	64 at 5,000	81 at 3,250	4	3.88	2.38	1.5	1.00	4.44	84	5.90 × 15	1,568	$2,600 U. S. Port of Entry

POSTWAR (Continued)

Year	Model	Cylinders	Bore & Stroke	Displacement, Cu. In.	Valve Arrangement	Comp. Ratio -to 1	Max. Brake Horsepower at RPM	Max. Torque Lb. Ft. at RPM	No. Forward Speeds	Transmission Ratios -to 1				Rear Axle Ratio -to 1	Wheelbase, Inches	Tire Size	Car Wt., Lbs.	Price
										1st	2nd	3rd	4th or OD					
KURTIS																		
1953	500 (with modified Cadillac engine)	V8	3.94 × 3.63	354	I	8.3	325 at 5,000		Dual range HydraMatic					3.64	92	6.50 × 16	2,280	$5,000
1955	500 M	Engine to be selected by customer													99 or 90	6.70 × 15	2,506	$6,200 complete if Cadillac engine and HydraMatic are used
1955	500 X	4	2.88 × 3.50	91	DOHC	9.5	100 at 6,000	112 at 6,000	4	3.38	1.95	1.35	1.00	Choice of many	86		1,600	$9,000 with Offenhauser engine
LAGONDA																		
1947	2-1/2 liter	6	3.07 × 3.54	157	DOHC	6.5	105 at 5,000	133 at 3,00	4	2.98	2.01	1.36	1.00	4.56	113.5	600 × 16	3,475	$5,500
1953	3 liter	6	3.26 × 3.54	178	DOHC	8.2	140 at 5,000	166 at 2,500	4	2.92	1.98	1.33	1.00	4.56	113.5	600 × 16	3,600	$6,300
LANCIA																		
1950	Aurelia B10	60° V6	2.76 × 2.99	107	V-pushrod	6.9	56 at 4,000	78 at 3,000	4	3.32	2.14	1.44	1.00	4.05	113	550 × 16	2,380	$3,010 to $4,430
1951	Aurelia Gran Turismo	60° V6	3.06 × 3.36	150	V-pushrod	8.0	118 at 5,000		4						105	550 × 16	2,325	
1953	Appia	10° 14' V4	2.67 × 2.95	67	V-pushrod	7.4	38 at 4,800	52 at 3,000	4	3.90	2.17	1.42	1.00	4.56	97.5	155 × 15	1,790	$2,180
1954	Aurelia Second series	60° V6	2.95 × 3.36	138	V-pushrod	7.4	87 at 4,300		4	3.32	2.14	1.44	1.00	3.67	113	165 × 400	2,630 dry	

Year	Model	Cylinders	Bore & Stroke	Displacement, Cu. In.	Valve Arrangement	Comp. Ratio -to 1	Max. Brake Horsepower at RPM	Max. Torque Lb. Ft. at RPM	No. Forward Speeds	Transmission Ratios -to 1 1st	2nd	3rd	4th or OD	Rear Axle Ratio -to 1	Wheelbase, Inches	Tire Size	Car Wt., Lbs.	Price
LEA-FRANCIS																		
1946	Fourteen	4	2.95 × 3.93	108	V-pushrod		56 at 4,700		4					4.87	111	550 × 17		$4,020
1946	Competition engine	4	2.87 × 3.93	102	V-pushrod	14.0	125 at 6,000											
1948	Sports Twelve	4	2.72 × 3.93	91	V-pushrod	7.3	64 at 5,300		4	3.32	2.16	1.38	1.00	4.87	99	525 × 17		$3,990
1950	Fourteen	4	2.95 × 3.93	108	V-pushrod	7.3	65 at 4,700		4	3.53	2.13	1.42	1.00	4.87	111	550 × 17	2,910	$3,160
1950	2-1/2 liter Sports	4	3.34 × 4.32	152	V-pushrod	7.1	100 at 4,000		4	3.53	2.13	1.42	1.00	3.64	99	600 × 16	2,575	$3,420
MASERATI																		
1948	A6GC5	6	2.83 × 3.14	121	SOHC		130 at 6,000		4	3.68	1.78	1.35	1.00		90.4	550 × 16	1,410 dry	On request
1948	A6 Turismo	6	2.59 × 2.85	91	SOHC		65 at 5,000		4	3.68	1.78	1.35	1.00	4.4	100	550 × 16	2,160 curb	On request
1952	A6GCS (Colombo)	6	3.05 × 2.83	121	DOHC	8.3, 8.8	160 at 7,000		4	2.67	1.62	1.27	1.00		91	600 × 16	1,540 dry	On request
1954	Sport 2000	6	3.05 × 2.83	121	DOHC	8.5	170 at 7,300		4	2.67	1.62	1.27	1.00	4.52	91	600 × 16	1,630 curb	On request
MERCEDES-BENZ																		
1951	300	6	3.35 × 3.46	183	SOHC	6.4	115 at 4,600	144 at 2,500	4	3.33	2.12	1.45	1.00	4.44	120	7.10 × 15	4,002	$6,980 In U. S.
1952	300S	6	3.35 × 3.46	183	SOHC	7.5	150 at 5,100	166 at 3,500	4	3.33	2.12	1.45	1.00	4.44	114	6.70 × 15	3,568	$12,500 In U. S.
1954	300 SL	6	3.35 × 3.46	183	SOHC	8.6	240 at 6,000		4	3.14	1.85	1.31	1.00	3.42	94.4	6.70 × 15	2,493	$7,463 U. S. Port of Entry

POSTWAR (Continued)

Year	Model	Cylinders	Bore & Stroke	Displacement, Cu. In.	Valve Arrangement	Comp. Ratio -to 1	Max. Brake Horsepower at RPM	Max. Torque Lb. Ft. at RPM	No. Forward Speeds	1st	2nd	3rd	4th or OD	Rear Axle Ratio -to 1	Wheelbase, Inches	Tire Size	Car Wt., Lbs.	Price
MERCEDES-BENZ (Cont'd.)																		
1954	190 SL	4	3.35 × 3.27	116	SOHC	8.0	125 at 5,500		4	4.05	2.38	1.53	1.00	3.70	94.4	6.40 × 13	2,314	$3,988 U. S. Port of Entry
M. G.																		
1945	TC	4	2.61 × 3.54	76	I	7.3, 7.5	54 at 5,200	64 at 2,700	4	3.38	1.95	1.35	1.00	5.13	94	450 × 19	1,735	$1,155
1950	TD	4	2.61 × 3.54	76	I	7.3, 9.3	54 at 5,200	64 at 2,700	4	3.49	2.07	1.38	1.00	5.13 4.88 4.55	94	550 × 15	1,995	$1,485
1954	TF	4	2.61 × 3.54	76	I	8.0	57 at 5,200		4	3.49	2.07	1.38	1.00	4.88 etc.	94	550 × 15	1,995	$1,551
1955	TF 1500	4	2.84 × 3.54	89	I	8.0	65 at 5,500	76 at 3,000	4	3.49	2.07	1.38	1.00	4.88	94	5.50 × 16	2,015	$1,995 U. S. Port of Entry
MORGAN																		
1946	F4 Three Wheeler	4	2.50 × 3.64	73	L	6.2	33 at 3,500		3	2.75	1.66	1.00		4.58	95, 99	18 × 3	900	$966
1946	4/4	4	2.25 × 3.93	77	I		40		4	3.42	2.42	1.42	1.00	5.0			1,625	$1,220
1951	Plus Four	4	3.34 × 3.62	127	I	6.7	68 at 4,200	112 at 2,300	4	3.29	1.95	1.31	1.00	4.1	96	525 × 16	1,680	$1,580
1954	Plus Four TR engine	4	3.27 × 3.62	122	I	8.5	90 at 4,800		4	3.44	1.98	1.42	1.00	3.73	96	525 × 16	1,792	$1,665
OSCA																		
1951	Mt4 1100/2AD	4	2.75 × 2.79	67	DOHC	9.0	85 at 6,600		4	3.37	2.02	1.36	1.00	4.20 to 5.13	86.6	500 × 15	1,165 dry, 1,610 curb	On request

Year	Model	Cylinders	Bore & Stroke	Displacement, Cu. In.	Valve Arrangement	Comp. Ratio -to 1	Max. Brake Horsepower at RPM	Max. Torque Lb. Ft. at RPM	No. Forward Speeds	1st	2nd	3rd	4th or OD	Rear Axle Ratio -to 1	Wheelbase, Inches	Tire Size	Car Wt., Lbs.	Price
OSCA (Cont'd.)																		
1951	Mt4 1400/2AD	4	3.06 × 2.99	89	DOHC	8.8	110 at 6,200		4	3.37	2.02	1.36	1.00	3.88 to 5.00	86.6	590, 500 × 15	1,210 dry, 1,650 curb	On request
1951	F2	6	2.99 × 2.87	121	DOHC	12.0	170 at 6,500		4						87.4	650, 525 × 16	1,255 dry, 1,740 curb	On request
PEGASO																		
1951	102 B/2.5	V8	2.95 × 2.75	151	DOHC	8.9	167 at 6,500	138 at 3,900	5	3.0	1.84	1.33	1.00 5th .75	4.36, etc.	92	550 × 16	2,120	$9,000
1951	102 B/2.8 102 BS/2.8	V8	3.14 × 2.76	172	DOHC	8.8	170 at 6,200, 250 at 6,800		5	3.0	1.84	1.33	1.00 5th .75	4.18, etc.	92	600 × 16	2,180	$9,000
1954	102 BS/3.2 Supercharged	V8	3.35 × 2.76	194	DOHC	6.0		311 at 3,800	5	3.00	1.80	1.21	1.00 5th .87	3.75	92	650 or 700 × 16	2,350	
PORSCHE																		
1953	1500 Super	Opposed 4	3.14 × 2.91	91	V-pushrod	8.2	70 at 5,000	79 at 3,500	4	3.18	1.76	1.13	1.00	4.4	83	500 × 16	1,684	$4,200
1953	1100	Opposed 4	2.89 × 2.52	66	V-pushrod	7.0	40 at 4,200		4	3.18	1.76	1.13	1.00	4.4	83	500 × 16	1,684	
1953	1300	Opposed 4	3.14 × 2.52	79	V-pushrod	6.5	44 at 4,200		4	3.18	1.76	1.13	1.00	4.4	83	500 × 16	1,684	
1954	Super Roadster	Opposed 4	3.15 × 2.91	91	V-pushrod	8.2	70 at 5,000		4	3.18	1.76	1.13	.82	4.38	83	5.25 × 16	1,698	$3,495 U.S. Port of Entry

POSTWAR (Continued)

Year	Model	Cylinders	Bore & Stroke	Displacement, Cu. In.	Valve Arrangement	Comp. Ratio -to 1	Max. Brake Horsepower at RPM	Max. Torque Lb. Ft. at RPM	No. Forward Speeds	Transmission Ratios -to 1				Rear Axle Ratio -to 1	Wheelbase, Inches	Tire Size	Car Wt., Lbs.	Price
										1st	2nd	3rd	4th or OD					
PORSCHE (Cont'd.)																		
1954	550	Opposed 4	3.35 x 2.60	91	DOHC	9.0	110 at 7,000	88 at 5,000	4	3.18	1.76	1.13	.82	4.38	83	5.25 x 16	1,210	$7,000 U. S. Port of Entry
RILEY																		
1946	1-1/2 liter	4	2.71 x 3.93	91	V-pushrod	6.8	55 at 4,500	76 at 2,500	4	3.98	2.29	1.48	1.00	5.12	112.5	575 x 16	2,860	$2,500
1946	2-1/2 liter	4	3.16 x 4.72	149	V-pushrod	6.8	100 at 4,400	134 at 3,000	4	3.65	2.16	1.42	1.00	4.11	119	600 x 16	3,000 to 3,300	$3,000
ROLLS-ROYCE																		
1949	Silver Wraith	6	3.50 x 4.50	260	F	6.4			4	3.06	2.01	1.34	1.00	3.73	127	6.50 x 17	4,000	$11,300
1954	Phantom IV	8	3.50 x 4.50	346	F	6.4			4	2.99	2.02	1.34	1.00	4.25	145	7.00 x 17	5,040	
SIATA																		
1953	208S Berlinetta (Fiat engine)	V8	2.83 x 2.41	122	I	8.5	110 at 6,000		5	2.69	1.77	1.26	1.00 5th .87	4.10	94.5	650 x 16	1,960	$8,400 U. S. Port of Entry
1953	208S Spider (Fiat engine)	V8	2.83 x 2.41	122	I	8.5	110 at 6,000		4	2.93	1.92	1.37	1.00	4.10	90.5	650 x 16	1,720	$5,600 U. S. Port of Entry
SIMCA																		
1951	Huit	4	2.83 x 2.95	74	I	7.8	50 at 4,800		4						95	5.25 x 15	1,984	$2,800 U. S. Port of Entry
1953	Nine Sport	4	2.83 x 2.95	74	I	7.8	51 at 4,800		4	3.70	2.38	1.61	1.00	4.78	96	5.50 x 15	2,050	$2,050 U. S. Port of Entry

Year	Model	Cylinders	Bore & Stroke	Displacement, Cu. In.	Valve Arrangement	Comp. Ratio -to 1	Max. Brake Horsepower at RPM	Max. Torque Lb. Ft. at RPM	No. Forward Speeds	Transmission Ratios -to 1				Rear Axle Ratio -to 1	Wheelbase, Inches	Tire Size	Car Wt., Lbs.	Price
										1st	2nd	3rd	4th or OD					
SINGER																		
1945	Nine Roadster	4	2.36 x 3.54	66	SOHC		30 at 5,000		3						91	500 x 16	1,820	$1,260
1951	SM-4AD Roadster	4	2.87 x 3.51	91	SOHC	7.0	48 at 4,200		4	2.98	1.94	1.26	1.00	4.87	91	500 x 16	1,820	$1,750
1953	SMX Roadster	4	2.87 x 3.51	91	SOHC	7.4	58 at 4,600		4	2.92	1.90	1.23	1.00	4.44	91	500 x 16	1,820	
SUNBEAM-TALBOT																		
1953	Alpine	4	3.19 x 4.33	138	I	7.4	80 at 4,200	124 at 1,800	4	2.83	2.19	1.33	1.00	3.90	97.5	5.50 x 16	2,968	$3,000 In U.S.
TALBOT LAGO																		
1948	Record	6	3.65 x 4.32	274	V-pushrod	7.0	170 at 4,200		4					3.33, 3.57	114	600 x 18		$5,120
1948	Grand Sport	6	3.65 x 4.32	274	V-pushrod	7.9	190 at 4,200 to 210 at 4,200		4					3.33, 3.57	114	600 x 18		$5,980
1954	Grand Sport Record Sport	6	3.65 x 4.32	274	V-pushrod	8.0	210 at 4,300		4					3.36	114 124	600 x 18		
TRIUMPH																		
1930	Supercharged Seven Sports	4	2.22 x 3.27	51	L				3	2.86	1.60	1.00		5.25	81	27 x 4.00	1,350	$1,250
1934	Dolomite	8	2.36 x 3.15	110	DOHC	6.5	140 at 5,500		4	3.10	1.85	1.23	1.00	4.50 4.10	104		2,128	$5,000 Chassis
1935	2 liter Southern Cross	6	2.36 x 3.94	121	F				4	3.90	2.34	1.53	1.00	4.75	104		2,360	$1,675
1954	T R 2	4	3.27 x 3.62	121	I	8.5	90 at 4,800		4	3.38	2.01	1.33	1.00	3.70	88	5.50 x 15	1,960	$2,495 U. S. Port of Entry

Index

461